THE
STEPS
TO WAR AN EMPIRICAL STUDY

PAUL D. SENESE AND JOHN A. VASQUEZ

PRINCETON UNIVERSITY PRESS

Princeton and Oxford

Published by Princeton University Press, 41 William Street, Princeton, New Jersey 08540

In the United Kingdom: Princeton University Press, 6 Oxford Street, Woodstock, Oxfordshire OX20 1TW

Library of Congress Cataloging-in-Publication Data

Senese, Paul Domenic.
    The steps to war : an empirical study / Paul D. Senese and John A. Vasquez.
        p. cm.
    Includes bibliographical references and index.
    ISBN 978-0-691-13421-5 (hardcover : alk. paper)—ISBN 978-0-691-13892-3 (pbk. : alk. paper)
1. War—Causes—Research.   2. Conflict management—Research.   3. International
relations—Research.   I. Vasquez, John A., 1945–   II. Title.
    JZ6385.S46 2008
    355.02′7—dc22

                                                                    2008003922

British Library Cataloging-in-Publication Data is available

This book has been composed in Minion

Printed on acid-free paper. ∞

press.princeton.edu

Printed in the United States of America

10 9 8 7 6 5 4 3 2 1

To the two most important
women in my life—
My Mother and Tracy
for life, love, and laughter
—Paul

and

To Marie
for friendship, loyalty, and love
—John

Contents

List of Figures and Tables

Preface

This is a book about patterns. A common pattern in books is that the preface is read first, but often written last, or in this case, among the last things written. Because prefaces are among the last things and they deal with beginnings and endings, they have a certain metaphysical quality to them. They are short pieces of reflection about a body of work that is being born and a peek at the intellectual lives that produce them. This is especially the case with this preface. It begins a book, which has, in one way or another, occupied our intellectual lives for nine years, and it comes at the end of the life of Paul Senese, who died a few days before the completion of the draft submitted to Princeton University Press.

I write from Buffalo, Paul's home, the morning after his funeral, trying to complete what will be the capstone of our collaboration together. This is a book about war, and the factors that make human beings, all too frequently, collectively kill each other in large numbers. Paul and I were drawn together by a mutual scientific interest in this question—in terms of explaining it and perhaps providing some knowledge that might some day aid in reducing the probability of war—but not so much by a mutual political interest in the question. We did not really know much about each other's politics when we began the book, and I think it came as a pleasant surprise to each of us, the extent to which our concern with the subject stemmed from the normative position of nonviolence, although the book itself does not deal with that normative position.

Both of us have felt that an alternative to collective killing is possible, and that getting at the causes of war is a first step in trying to eliminate them. Paul was to teach a summer course in Buffalo on nonviolence a few weeks before his untimely death. He had a keen interest in Eastern religion's and philosophy's dealing with nonviolence and worked in his own local Catholic church on nonviolence initiatives. Like Lewis Richardson, one of the founders of peace science, his commitment to the truth and the use of the scientific method superseded any commitment to a specific political position or claim. Paul had an open mind about the causes of war, and there is little indication of his, or my, political views discernible in the main body of this book, and that is as it should be in a scientific work. The motivation in searching for truth and the utility of empirical truth is separate from the nature (or content) of that truth.

Nevertheless, Paul thought that the empirical study of war was so important in bringing about peace that he chose to spend most of his professional life devoted to it. As it became more apparent that his time to work on the book might be limited by his illness, instead of doing other things—and there were many things he enjoyed, from being outside and communing with nature, to sports, to being with friends—he chose to work on this book and its larger project. Weekends and late nights became increasingly devoted to the book, and this continued until the day in May when he collapsed at home.

By that time, all but the concluding chapter, part of chapter 7, and my own chapter 5 were completed. From the beginning, we had agreed that we would each write one chapter on our own. Paul is primarily responsible for chapter 4 and I for chapter 5. Other than these, we coauthored the introduction and all of the chapters, except the concluding chapter 8, which we had outlined. Paul and I coauthored about half of chapter 7, and he and I conducted all the data analyses in this chapter, except for the last part on the post–Cold War period. I completed these, and here I missed his skill and subtlety, especially when I ran into collinearity problems.

The end result is a book with several interrelated but independent data studies that build on each other. Anyone familiar with data analysis need not be forewarned that this is not the sort of book one can read in a couple of sittings. There are at least five separate empirical studies herein and, although they are interrelated, it will take as much work to read them as it would to read five journal articles. We believe that the work will be worth the effort and that the whole is much greater than the parts. With the exception of chapter 4 (which is based on a 2005 analysis using updated data), all the data analyses are new.

We enjoyed working on this project, and I will miss Paul's contributions as will the field as a whole. Paul liked to emphasize happy thoughts, and I will end with one of the happiest we had while working on this book. It was in October 2004. Paul's wife, Tracy, tells the story of how the morning after the Red Sox had lost all the games in the playoffs and were now one game short of elimination, Paul woke up and said, "I have only four words to say, 'four in a row.'" It actually turned out to be eight in a row, and for the first time in eighty-six years the Boston Red Sox were world champions once again.

This was a happy moment while working on the project, and there were many others. But we also had rough spots, and throughout the conception, data analyses, and writing we were supported by two people: Tracy "the love of my life" (Paul) and Marie, "lover, partner, wife" (John).

June 25, 2006–June 8, 2007
Block Island, Rhode Island

Acknowledgments

Any book incurs debts to others who are generous with their time, insights, and knowledge. A scientific work, in particular, builds on the work and especially the data of others. Without the larger peace science community, we could not have written this book. We build upon the data of the Correlates of War project founded by J. David Singer and continued by his many students and other colleagues for well over forty years. We have reaped the benefit of his vision and in turn we hope our effort has helped the field to get closer to actualizing his. This book relies in particular on the Militarized Interstate Dispute (MID) data of the project. These data, which in many ways have transformed the scientific study of peace and war, were collected by numerous scholars, but the formal release and cleaning of the data set was supervised by Stuart Bremer to whom we, and all peace scientists, are indebted, not only for his scientific rigor but his intellectual insight.

The extension and update of the MID data to 2001 was made possible by an NSF grant to Paul Diehl and colleagues, and these data have been of immense use to us, as have been the efforts of the Correlates of War 2 project at Penn State under the direction of Scott Bennett and Glenn Palmer. We also appreciate the efforts of two of our former students who collected relevant data: Susan G. Sample, who collected data on arms races for minor states (and generously shared them with us), and Douglas M. Gibler, who (along with our Correlates of War colleague, Meredith Reid Sarkees) collected formal alliance data through 2000. Both Sample and Gibler have also given us sound advice over the years. Our thanks also to Paul K. Huth and Todd Allee for unselfishly sharing their data on territorial disputes.

Our own data analyses have been greatly aided by an NSF grant (#SES-9818557), although the views expressed here should not be attributed to NSF. Studies like this require time, made possible to us by the following: Paul Senese was granted a sabbatical to write this book in fall 2005, and he was thankful to the University at Buffalo, SUNY, for this leave. He was also thankful to the

Baldy Center for Law and Social Policy, University at Buffalo, SUNY, for financial support. He was thankful to the graduate students for their close reading of the manuscript, and his colleagues at Buffalo, especially Frank Zagare, for their intellectual stimulation and support throughout his years there and especially during the spring 2006 semester. Grants to John Vasquez from the Helsinki Collegium for Advanced Studies (at the University of Helsinki) and from the Academy of Finland provided him with a semester leave in fall 2005 during which much of this book was coauthored. He wishes to thank Juha Sihvola, director of the Collegium; Maria Soukkio; and Terhi Elomaa for making his stay productive, and Tuomas Tammilehto for research assistance. He also wishes to thank Raimo Vayrynen of the Academy of Finland for his encouragement and support and to thank Colgate University and the University of Illinois at Urbana-Champaign, which provided research support, respectively, through the Harvey Picker Chair and the Thomas B. Mackie Scholar in International Relations research funds. He would like to thank his colleagues at both these universities for an intellectually congenial and stimulating environment conducive to serious research and thought.

Three research assistants did considerable data cleaning, merging, and measurement construction for us, and we greatly appreciate their work. Using NSF funds, Chris Leskiw collected data and constructed our measure of issue dominance and politically relevant alliances for the MID 2.1 data in an efficient and professional manner. Choong-Nam Kang updated these measures for the MID 3.02 data and worked tirelessly getting the data into shape for this book. Karen Petersen helped in a pinch in 2005 (even though by then she was an assistant professor) by comparing and cleaning our territorial dispute MID 2.1 and MID 3.02 data sets. Our deepest thanks go to each of them. In addition, we benefited from the advice of Brandon Valeriano on several papers related to the book, especially with regard to the role of interstate rivalry. Andy Owsiak and Toby Rider completed important research tasks in the last stages of the book. Delinda Swanson helped with formatting some intractable footnotes and tables, and she prepared the references on short notice, which was a great aid.

Over the years, various scholars have given generously of their time to comment on papers related to the steps-to-war project. The list is too long to acknowledge their individual contribution, but we have benefited greatly from both formal and informal conversations with them, even though many did not read specific parts of this book: John Agnew, Michelle Benson, Sean Bolks, Bear Braumoeller, Mark Brawley, Michael Brecher, Bruce Bueno de Mesquita, Claudio Cioffi-Revilla, Dave Clark, Michael Colaresi, Vesna Danilovic, Paul Diehl, Tom Doleys, Daniel Geller, Nils Petter Gleditsch, Gary Goertz, Gang Guo, Jude Hays, Marie Henehan, Paul Hensel, Paul Huth, Pat James,

Tracy Jarvis, Zeev Maoz, Manus Midlarsky, Sara McLaughlin Mitchell, Cliff Morgan, Glenn Palmer, Brad Palmquist, T.V. Paul, Stephen Quackenbush, James Lee Ray, Bill Reed, Jean-Sebastien Rioux, Curtis Signorino, J. David Singer, William Thompson, Jim Vreeland, Peter Wallensteen, Frank Wayman, Frank Zagare, and Chris Zorn. The two anonymous readers for Princeton, who turned out to be Doug Lemke and Jack Levy, both provided detailed reviews and comments on the manuscript from which we have benefited greatly and for which we are deeply appreciative. We also wish to acknowledge important methodological advice on collinearity problems from Michael Mousseau, Mark Souva, and Richard Tucker, all of whom were especially helpful during the period after Paul's death.

Although we have learned from the advice and suggestions of all of the above, we have not always followed it, so we are solely responsible for any errors that remain. Many have commented on our work on this project for a number of years, so our apologies to those who have been inadvertently omitted. Lastly, our thanks to Chuck Myers, with whom it has been a real pleasure to work from beginning to end, the staff at Princeton University Press, Marsha A. Kunin, our copy editor, and Carolyn Sherayko for preparing the index. Paul always wanted to go with Princeton, and we are glad we had the opportunity to do so.

We also acknowledge and are indebted to Sage Publications, and Taylor and Francis Inc., respectively, for granting us permission to reprint two tables in chapter 2, and to Blackwell Publishers for permitting us to reprint the tables and draw upon the text of Paul D. Senese, "Territory, Contiguity, and International Conflict: Assessing a New Joint Explanation." (*American Journal of Political Science* 49 [2005]: 770–80) in chapter 4 herein.

THE
STEPS
TO WAR

Introduction

The wrath of war has long been with humanity and even more so in the twentieth century. This book is an attempt to understand its causes by using the scientific method to delineate those factors that increase the probability of war. It does this by testing one of the major contemporary explanations of war—the steps to war. The explanation provides an analysis of why interstate wars occur in the modern global system and how a knowledge of these factors can help uncover the conditions of peace.

Today, war is still a pressing social scourge and an intractable intellectual problem. To explain it will require the best method available and this, we believe, is the scientific method. A variety of approaches and methods have their place in the analysis of war and greatly enrich each other, but we focus here on the use of statistical analyses of long-term interactions to delineate patterns. We do this in the context of an historical understanding of how different eras can have different patterns of behavior and in the context of insights we have derived from the numerous case studies of interstate wars and international crises that have been conducted in the last two decades. Nevertheless, we think that the systematic and rigorous analysis of replicable data that have been painstakingly collected provides a body of evidence, separate from historical and case-study analysis, that needs to be more fully incorporated into our theories and discussions of why war occurs. In addition, scientific analysis provides a way of thinking, a *perspective*, about social problems and the historical record that can be a source of new insights. It also provides a self-correcting mechanism—statistical testing—that allows the analyst to see whether theoretical explanations are empirically inaccurate and where they might be reformulated. Thus statistical analysis is a way of learning from evidence and building theory through a process of conjectures and refutations (Popper, 1963).

Because we adopt a scientific approach, the logic underlying the book is fairly straightforward. We begin with an explanation. We review some of the previous tests that have been conducted on it, and on the basis of these we construct a research design to test aspects of the explanation. We then present the various tests we have conducted and their implications for the explanation. We conclude with an overall assessment of the explanation's empirical accuracy and the implications for the future study of the steps to war and for the prospects of peace.

Part I lays out the foundation on which the rest of the book is built. It presents the underlying theory of the analysis and the research design of the study. Chapter 1 presents the explanation and its logic. In brief, the explanation sees war as arising from a series of steps actors take to deal with the issues and grievances that separate them. Territorial issues, if handled in a certain way, are posited as the most war prone. Territorial issues are intrinsically salient and attract hard-line domestic constituencies, which makes compromise difficult. As disagreement persists, states resort to the threat or use of force. If militarized disputes repeat, this leads to a sense of rivalry between the contending parties. In the modern global system, realist diplomatic culture suggests that in the presence of security threats, states should increase their power by making alliances and/or building up their military. Because of the security dilemma, the making of alliances often leads to counter-alliances, and military buildups can produce arms races. These actions, instead of preventing war by peace through strength, as some realists claim, actually constitute a series of steps to war. The repetition of crises increases the number and influence of hard-liners in each side, which in turn tends to increase the level of conflict across crises and a sense of rivalry between disputants. Eventually a crisis comes along that escalates to war. While territorial issues are the most prone to this syndrome of power-politics behavior, any issue subject to it has an increased probability of going to war. All of these propositions hold, ceteris paribus. The details, as well as the logic connecting the steps, are discussed in the chapter.

Chapter 2 reviews the previous studies on the steps to war and how the research program has evolved in light of criticisms and in light of competing explanations. This chapter also sets out the research design and how the empirical tests conducted in the remainder of the book build on one another. It presents an overview of the data and measures used in the analysis.

Part II deals with the relationship between territory and war; in particular it deals with some of the main criticisms of previous research that shows that territory are highly war prone. Chapter 3 investigates the role of territorial disputes in increasing the probability of a militarized dispute escalating to war. A variety of tests (including a two-stage analysis that looks at possible selection bias) will be conducted. The chapter examines whether it is the mere presence of territorial disagreement or how territorial issues are handled that is more significant for bringing about war. The chapter addresses the issue of selection bias by seeing whether it is territorial disputes that give rise to war or the factors that produce territorial disputes in the first place that are responsible for war breaking out.

Chapter 4 looks at the joint role of contiguity and territory for increasing the probability of conflict and war. It also employs a two-stage analysis, that tests the counter-proposition that it is not territorial disputes that increase the probability of war, but the contiguity of states that accounts for war; that it is really the proximity of states and not territory per se that explains the onset of war. It also tests for other possible general selection effects that might be operating.

Part III examines the relationship between power politics and war. Chapters 5 and 6 examine the role of outside alliances, repeated disputes (including rivalry), and arms races as factors increasing the likelihood of both territorial and nonterritorial disputes escalating to war. Chapter 5 conducts this investigation by examining the long-term relations of pairs of states (e.g., Britain and Germany) during three historical eras (1816–1945, 1946–89, 1990–2001) to see whether the probability of a pair of states having at least one war increases as those states make outside alliances, have repeated disputes, engage in arms racing and are contending primarily over territorial questions. Chapter 6 tests the same set of hypotheses during the same historical eras, but by looking at specific militarized disputes and their characteristics rather than the long-term relations of two states. Here we identify the risk factors that increase the probability that a militarized dispute will escalate to war. This design permits us to get at timing (e.g., which comes first, territorial disputes or outside alliances). Chapter 7 is the most technical chapter; it looks at statistical interaction effects for the propositions examined in the previous chapter. It also looks at why the post-1945 period is different from the classic 1816–1945 international politics period, and whether the current era (post-1990) will more likely resemble the classic earlier period or the Cold War nuclear period.

Chapter 8 brings together the major results to see what we have learned about the probability of war and how well the steps-to-war explanation has captured the major patterns of interstate warfare from 1816 through 2001. It then looks at the implications of the study for future research in general, as well as within the steps-to-war research program. It closes by looking at some of the policy implications of the analysis for promoting peace in the future.

This book is the product of many years of collaboration. Its origins go back to 1998 when we were both at the same university. We applied for and received an NSF grant (SES-9818557) to test aspects of the steps-to-war explanation. We spent the next five years doing so, publishing a number of peer-reviewed studies. These studies, along with those we have published with others and those of our former students, constitute the larger research program on the steps to war. This book is the capstone of our NSF grant. It supersedes the earlier studies in that it is based on data going from 1816 through 2001, whereas the earlier studies went only through 1992. This enables us to look at three distinct historical periods, 1816–1945 (the classic international politics period), 1946–89 (the Cold War period), and 1990–2001 (the post–Cold War period). These three eras permit us to make historical comparisons we could not do before. This book also extends the analysis into new areas, specifically an examination of interaction effects inherent in the steps to war.

One of the distinctive qualities of science is that it is a collective enterprise that has many scholars and students studying the same problem often using shared data and common conceptualizations. If the puzzle of war is ever to be solved, it will most likely be by such a community of scholars and not by a single individual working alone in a study. Today, there are more scholars working on the problem of war than at any other time in history. We have been fortunate to be working within a larger peace science community. This community of scholars, centered around the Peace Science Society (International), has been in the forefront of collecting data, developing new measures, debating concepts and methods, and encouraging the publication of rigorous research, all with the purpose of understanding war in hopes of promoting peace. We offer this book as our contribution to this larger effort.

I

Foundations

1

The Steps to War

*Step by step decision makers are led down
the road to war having the possibility of exiting,
but failing to do so.*

The study of international relations, at least in the West, has been coterminous with the study of war. It was the Peloponnesian War that led Thucydides to reflect on the origins, causes, and consequences of war. Similarly, the modern founders of a scientific approach to the study of peace and war, Quincy Wright (1942, 1965) and Lewis F. Richardson (1960a, 1960b), each reacted to the horrors of World War I and were motivated to delineate the causes of war in the hopes that this would lead to knowledge that would facilitate the building of peace. The leading scholars of the early post–World War II era who studied war and violence—Harold Guetzkow (1950, 1968), Robert North (Holsti, North, and Brody, 1968), and J. David Singer (1979)—all shared this motivation.

Studying the causes of war scientifically involves identifying patterns common to the onset of war. In other words, what is it—about the relations among states, the crises in which they are engaged, or other conditions—that is associated with the outbreak of war? The earliest scientific studies, like those of Singer (1979, 1980), involved a search for the conditions that give rise to interstate war. These were referred to as correlates of war because of the difficulty of inferring that a specific correlate might be an actual cause. At the time Singer (see Singer and Small, 1972) began his work, there was not even a definitive list of wars, let alone replicable data sets that could be used to study the causes of war in a scientific manner. By the end of the 1980s, a number of statistical studies, mostly on interstate war, had been conducted. These aided in the identification of some patterns, but still cried out for some coherent explanation that would tie these together (see Geller and Singer, 1998; Geller, 2000). The steps-to-war explanation is an attempt to do that (Vasquez, 1987,

7

1993). It was originally synthesized by reviewing about thirty years of statistical research in the field of peace science, as well as theoretical analyses of international conflict.[1] The explanation was later expanded by Senese and Vasquez (2003) into a more general explanation of conflict. As with the early work on war, it is confined to explaining interstate conflict, although it has strong implications for why war and conflict occur in general.

In our time, there has been a shift from studying the correlates of war to studying the probability of war. Since the work of Bremer (1992), it is now common to study war in terms of looking at what factors increase the probability of war rather than searching for sufficient conditions for the outbreak of war. The steps-to-war explanation also takes this approach. It seeks to identify those actions that states take toward one another that increase the probability that war will break out between them.

These factors increase the probability of war in that when they are present it is more likely that war will occur than when they are absent. They should not be confused with necessary conditions of war. In other words, the steps to war outlined here do not precede every war, but reflect one path to war. It is believed that the steps to war delineated in this chapter constitute the most common path to war followed by the strongest states in the system, but that other paths also exist. The analysis assumes that war is multicausal and seeks to identify one important path to war in the modern global system since 1495—what might be called the realist road to war (see Vasquez, 1993: ch. 5).

Overview

Through a good deal of the post–World War II twentieth century, most international relations scholars thought about the causes of war in terms of struggles for power, the anarchic system, and/or differences or shifts in capability (see Morgenthau, 1948; Waltz, 1959, 1979; Organski and Kugler, 1980; Doran and Parsons, 1980; Geller, 1992; Gilpin, 1981; Bueno de Mesquita, 1981 [cf. Bueno de Mesquita and Lalman, 1992]; Thompson, 1988; Van Evera, 1999; Copeland, 2000; cf. Midlarsky, 1975; see Levy, 1989a and Midlarsky, 1989, for overviews). One concern with such approaches is that they tend to ignore how the foreign policy of one state affects that of another and can lead each to war. Out of a foreign policy perspective comes the idea that certain policy practices

---

[1] Among the theoretical analyses that were especially influential were those of Rummel (1979), Choucri and North (1975), Guetzkow and Valdez (1981), Singer (1979), Wallace (1972), and Midlarsky (1986, 1988).

have the effect of increasing hostility and threat perception. This has both external effects (in terms of a state's relations with an opponent) and internal effects (in terms of the number of foreign policy hard-liners and accommodationists). The end result is that certain foreign policy actions can be seen as a series of steps to war in that each step increases the probability of war. The goal of theory construction is to identify those steps and foreign policy practices and to explain how they increase the probability of war.

Whereas realists assume that foreign policy is a struggle for power, and war a natural consequence of that struggle, the steps-to-war explanation looks at international relations from more of an issue politics paradigm that sees politics in terms of the raising and resolving of issues and David Easton's (1965: 50) definition of politics as "the authoritative allocation of valued things" (Mansbach and Vasquez, 1981: 28–29). This perspective asks whether there are some issues that are fundamentally more war prone than others. For realists, the answer is that all important issues can be reduced to the issue of power because power is what counts in the end (see Morgenthau, 1960: 27). In this book, when we refer to realists, we always mean the classical realism of Morgenthau (1948, 1960, 1978), unless otherwise stated.[2]

From an issue perspective, some issues are much more prone to violence than others. In the steps-to-war explanation, territorial issues are posited as more war prone than other types of issues, ceteris paribus. Why this is the case is not obvious, but it is the case that neighbors account for most interstate wars, and it is assumed that their wars grow out of territorial disputes. While this is an assumption that must be checked empirically, it provides some insights as to why states fight, and over which issues they are willing to expend the lives of their people. If in fact most wars are between neighbors, this would suggest that at some point most neighbors have fought. This implies that human collectivities have learned in history that the institution of war is a way of handling territorial disputes, and it may have been selected out as a practice for dealing with certain kinds of territorial conflict. All of this would be consistent with an assumption that war is a human institution that has been learned and passed on (see Vasquez, 1993: ch. 1).

How did territorial issues become so important? Clearly, if humans were not territorial, wars over territory would not be so prevalent. Since territoriality is a characteristic we share with other vertebrates (Valzelli, 1981: 81), this trait can be seen as part of our biological or genetic inheritance. Also, like other mammals, humans use aggressive displays to keep and gain territory

---

[2] For a discussion of the various types of realism, including defensive realism, neorealism, and offensive realism, among others, see Vasquez and Elman (2003).

(Wilson, 1975: 256; Goodall, 1990: 100–101, 104), but unlike most animals, humans resort to collective violence in defending territory.[3]

We define human territoriality as the tendency for humans to occupy and, if necessary, defend territory (Vasquez, 1993: 124). The nature of human territoriality, its connection to territoriality in other species, and how it is related to the formation of modern nation-states must be treated as exogenous to this analysis, but certain things can be said about how we do and *do not* conceive of human territoriality. We maintain that the reason territory looms so large in everyday life and in the history of international relations cannot be properly understood without looking at studies in the life sciences, including ethology, biology, and neuroscience.[4] At the same time, we do not want our position to be conflated with earlier simplistic views that have drawn on biology to posit territoriality and war as an instinct or a drive that makes war inevitable and ends up giving a very deterministic view of the causes of war (as in the work of Ardrey [1966], for example). Our view agrees more with that of Somit (1990: 569) who sees humans as not hard-wired, but soft-wired, which means that they are predisposed to learn certain behaviors easily and others only with much more difficulty.[5]

Learning to occupy territory and then to defend it with aggressive displays is something we believe humans learn fairly easily. Based on what is known about the origin of war as a human institution (e.g., Mead, 1940; Wright, 1965: ch. 4; Kelly, 2000), we also think that at some point, perhaps at the time of the development of agriculture, or even earlier, humans learned to handle sharp disputes over territory by inventing the institution of war and making it available as a tool in their culture. The apparent success of this invention led it to be replicated and passed down through history.[6]

What is it about territory that makes humans push these issues to the forefront and be more willing to die for them than other types of issues? This answer must ultimately come from the life sciences, but early applications of neuroscience to decision making about war suggest that different parts of the brain, including evolutionary older parts, like the limbic system, may be involved in decisions about war (see Rosen, 2005: ch. 2). What we do know is that emotion (and the hormonal and chemical states that generate those emo-

---

[3] Most animal species do not engage in collective violence; some exceptions in addition to humans are ants, rats, and chimps (Goodall, 1990; see also Wrangham, 2006). On the rarity of war among animals, see Huntingford (1989).

[4] See Masters (1989) for a general argument on the importance of the life sciences for political science; see also Falger (1997).

[5] More detailed treatment of this issue can be found in Vasquez (1993: ch. 4) from which this and the related sections on territoriality have been drawn. On the question of aggression and instinct, see Bateson (1989).

[6] On the concept of learning in international relations and its difficulties, see Levy (1994).

tions) plays an important part in focusing the brain, cutting down long (if not endless) synoptic searches, and giving preferential status to certain strategies or options (see Damasio, 1995). Damasio's (1995) somatic marker hypothesis suggests that traumatic experiences (of which war would be one) sear important lessons into our memory and make certain strategies more likely to be followed in the future when facing a similar situation. Such neuroscience hypotheses are fruitful lines of inquiry to pursue in terms of determining why territory is so salient to humans and why humans are prone to learn that collective violence is a way to handle territorial disputes.

These factors, while fundamental, are outside the scope of political science and our own expertise. What is important for political science is to establish that territorial issues (when handled in certain ways) are in fact more war prone than other types of issues and then to delimit the political factors responsible for this and the consequences of this for international history.

If we use the principle of human territoriality as an axiom, we can derive from it several theoretical expectations about international politics and the course of war in international history (Vasquez, 1993: 140–41). An emphasis on human territoriality would suggest that the division of the world into territorial units is not an accident, but has a biological basis, no doubt connected to the use of territory for food and shelter. It would also be expected that collectivities would pay a great deal of attention to their borders, which seems to be the case. What is less obvious, and a key prediction, is that where there is contact, the boundaries between two contiguous countries will be established through a struggle involving the threat or use of force, and often war. From this, it also follows that new states must make a space for themselves, and their emergence, unless handled carefully (see Maoz, 1989), will increase the probability of territorial disputes and hence war. The typical war in the system can be seen as originating from a territorial dispute between neighbors.[7]

According to this perspective, war is an inherent part of history. If war between neighbors were constant, then a more deterministic view of human territoriality might be in order, but in fact most neighbors do not persistently fight over their borders; they settle them. Territoriality and war are not inevitably linked; there are other ways of maintaining and even establishing boundaries. Not all territorial issues need be handled by the threat and use of force. Primates, it must be remembered, not only use aggressive displays but

[7] The source of human territoriality, whether it be biological, as assumed here, or purely a social construct as assumed by Sack (1986), does not affect the theoretical expectations that we derive from it, but only their persistence. For constructivists, human territoriality could be unlearned and disappear (see Ruggie [1993] for a recent version of this interpretation); whereas for those who take a more evolutionary perspective, getting rid of territoriality (or territorial behavior) would be much more difficult and unlikely.

also engage in peacekeeping, which must also be seen as part of our biological inheritance (see de Waal, 1989). Therefore, it would be a misunderstanding to say that human territoriality is a direct cause of war or a cause of constant warfare. Rather what is being said here is that of all the issues humans can disagree on, territorial issues seem to be sensitive ones, and if they are handled in certain ways, they increase the probability of war, but if they are handled in other ways or settled, they need not be associated with war.

Territorial issues that are handled by the threat or use of force, we define as *territorial disputes*. *Territorial issues* is a broader category and refers to disagreement about territory—what belongs to whom, where a boundary should be drawn, what rights each actor has regarding its own and others' territory, and so forth. A territorial issue becomes, by definition, a territorial dispute, when one side resorts to the threat or use of force to get its position on the issue implemented. Territorial disputes increase the probability of war because they involve handling territorial issues in a certain way.

From this analysis, we conclude that territorial issues are an underlying cause of war. They are an underlying cause in two senses—(1) in that they do not directly give rise to war, but rather, under certain conditions (namely, threatening or using force to settle the issue), they set off a train of events that result in war, and (2) in that if neighbors can resolve their territorial issues, they can have very long periods of peace, even as other salient issues might arise. The latter proposition is one of the major testable differences between the steps-to-war explanation and realism. It also makes the steps-to-war explanation much more optimistic about the possibility of peace. It not only says that peace is possible; it identifies the key factor in bringing it about.

Assuming that human territoriality shapes the broad contours of international history in the above fashion, what kinds of political models can be specified that would identify the process by which specific territorial disputes go to war? How do these processes occur politically? Why territorial disputes are prone to war can be explained by two political processes to which these disputes are prone. First, territorial disputes tend to recur. Once territorial claims are militarized by resorting to the threat or use of force, this reflects a certain level of commitment on the part of actors that they are not willing to give in on their claims, and that other possible paths to resolving the dispute (such as negotiation) do not appear fruitful. When the territorial issue is of equal salience to each side, neither is going to accede to the demands of the other, nor is simply threatening to use force likely to be successful on the first try. This means that such disputes, especially between relative equals, are apt to produce repeated confrontations. As disputes recur, they give rise to stalemates that fester and then escalate as states try to prevail by being more coercive.

Second, the territorial disputes that are most war prone generate domestic constituencies that pressure leaders to pursue hard-line policies. These two processes are linked in that recurring disputes tend to generate hard-line constituencies. Both of these processes result from how territorial issues are handled in the first place and as such will be elaborated upon later in the chapter. Both processes are critical in making territorial disputes intractable and in making leaders and followers frame territorial issues in a manner that makes compromise and peaceful resolution difficult.

Territorial issues that are handled by resorting to force succumb to these two political processes and are at greater risk of going to war than territorial issues that are handled in other ways. It is expected that because of human territoriality, territorial issues are slightly more likely to give rise to the threat or use of force than nonterritorial issues, but by themselves they are not sufficient conditions for the outbreak of war.

The foreign policy practices of a state, how it handles issues between itself and those that contend with it, are posited as the proximate cause of war. These practices, including the institution of war, should not be seen as given. On the basis of Mead (1940), as well as constructivist insights (e.g., Berger and Luckmann, 1966; Foucault, 1980), it is argued that war is a social invention that is learned in history and changes in history. It is also argued that leaders, diplomats, and others create folklores or diplomatic cultures that guide states and inform their leaders when it is appropriate to handle a situation with the use of force (Vasquez, 1993: ch. 1). In the West, one of the most important roles of realist thinking, beginning with Thucydides and going down to Morgenthau (1948) and beyond, is that it has provided a folklore that tells leaders how they should act when faced with security issues. It is assumed in the steps-to-war explanation that, among equals, these realist foreign policy practices become a series of steps to war, rather than a way of avoiding war.

Realist folklore or culture (see Johnston, 1996) informs leaders that, in the face of security issues, they should increase their power. For realism, the two main ways of doing that are to either make alliances and/or build up one's military. The problem, however, as realists recognize, is that this gives rise to a security dilemma, in that taking these actions makes one's opponent insecure and encourages them to do the same thing.[8] The end result can often be that alliance making leads to counter-alliances, and military buildups lead to arms racing. One of the ironies of realism is that, among relative equals, each of

---

[8] On the concept of the security dilemma, see Herz (1950) who is the main originator of the concept. Realists also recognize how a security dilemma arises out of realist prescriptions; see Jervis (1978) and Van Evera (1999: 117n), but on the whole they are more sanguine about the pacifying effects of power and resolve.

these steps increases insecurity, threat perception, and hostility. In this sense, they can be seen as steps that bring each party closer to war.

Realist folklore recommends these practices, and states take them to increase their security and to press their claims or defend their positions. Alliance making and military buildups not only signal resolve, but also provide a means of attaining foreign policy objectives. To attain an objective, however, a state must do more than make alliances or build up its military; it must take action, and in the face of action, a target must defend itself. Realism sees the threat and use of force (and a host of realpolitik tactics) as one of the main ways (and of course it is the only unilateral way) of bringing about changes (or redistributions) in the existing allocation of valued things in the international system. Since territory is so salient, resorting to the threat or use of force is not apt to produce many concessions, especially among equals. It is more likely to lead to a stalemate or simply to no resolution at all. Nevertheless, because the issue is salient to leaders (and to hard-liners within the polity), territorial disputes tend to recur. The steps-to-war explanation posits that crises and militarized interstate disputes that recur tend to become more escalatory and increase the number and influence of hard-liners domestically. Eventually, a crisis emerges that escalates to war.

Power politics can be seen as a set of proximate causes of war in that it tells leaders how to handle security issues, including territorial issues. It is a *proximate* cause in that it is closer to the outbreak of war. It is a *cause* in that if issues could be handled in other ways, then war could be avoided, or at least have a higher probability of being avoided. Power politics, because it involves a way of handling issues that increases the probability of war, will increase the probability of any issue going to war and not just territorial issues.

Power politics behavior increases the probability of war because it leads each state to feel more threatened and more hostile toward the other side and to take actions against its opponent. This means that if states with a territorial dispute handle it by resorting to the practices of power politics, then the probability of war goes up. Thus, if one state makes an alliance with an outside party that can be used to aid it in its territorial dispute, this will increase the probability of war. If, in addition, states become mired in the repeated use of military force (or the threat to do so), then this can be seen as further increasing the probability of war. Lastly, if states engage in this syndrome of behavior and also build up their militaries to the extent of becoming involved in an arms race, then the probability of war goes up yet again. In this sense, having a territorial dispute can be considered a first step to war, and engaging in other power politics practices can be seen as additional steps to war. Not too much emphasis should be placed on the order of these steps, for the time being. The major claim on which to focus is that each practice increases threat perception and therefore the probability of war. As these threatening practices accumulate, they make it more likely that eventually a crisis or militarized dispute will occur that escalates to war. Realism, then, provides a way of identifying and even predicting what leaders will do in situations of high security threat. It is the resultant realist road to war that the steps-to-war seeks to explain.

The steps-to-war explanation deviates from realism in that it sees the adoption of realist prescriptions among equals leading to a series of steps that increase the probability of war rather than to capitulation or encouraging peace through strength. The security dilemma generates a vicious cycle of threat perception and hostility reinforced both by the interactions of states and by the indirect effect these interactions have on the domestic political environment of each nation-state. Threatening interactions tend to produce at least reciprocal responses, so a state can compensate for the advantages a particular action gave the first state. Thus, an alliance made by actor (x) will leave actor (z) vulnerable unless it can match whatever advantage the alliance provided to actor (x). Of course actor (z) may, if it can, seek a greater advantage (by having more powerful allies) and therefore can be seen as escalating and not just reciprocating. With military buildups, this means that increased spending, adoption of conscription, extending times of enlistment, or technological breakthroughs in weaponry must be matched or bettered. This can easily lead to an arms race, as exemplified by the Anglo-German naval race preceding World War I. Domestically, such interaction tends to reinforce the positions of hard-liners that the opponent is indeed a threat, and that such a threat must be met by taking a hard line. Escalatory interactions tend to increase both the number and influence of hard-liners and push decision makers toward more realpolitik strategies.

While realists emphasize the objective nature of external threats, it must also be recognized that there is a domestic component to such interactions. Hard-liners are more sensitive to external threats and more apt to respond to them in a firm and often escalatory fashion. Accommodationists are just the opposite.[9] How decision makers in a state will react therefore will depend on the relative influence of hard-liners and accommodationists in the decision-making elite and the larger set of policy influencers. It is assumed that success in the most recent war gives a significant edge to hard-liners (Vasquez, 1993:

[9] Hard-liners and accommodationists are defined in terms of belief systems and not personality characteristics. Hard-liners believe in the efficacy and legitimacy of the use of threats, force, and violence for attaining goals. Accommodationists, by contrast, reject this belief and tend to find the use of violence, especially collective violence, repugnant, and advocate the use of negotiation and compromise in its place, as well as the creation of norms and rules as a way of settling disputes. See Vasquez (1993: 202) for formal definitions and further details.

207–10; see also Nevin, 1996; Singer and Small, 1974: tables 2 and 3), which can be reinforced by the conflictive actions of an opponent. Persistent conflict, the use or threat of force, and the adoption of power politics to handle issues tend to increase the number and influence of hard-liners while simultaneously reducing that of accommodationists.

Alliance making and arms races give rise to the above patterns by posing an external shock to the interstate relationship (see Diehl and Goertz, 2000: ch. 7); that is, the impact of an opponent making an alliance or engaging in a rapid military buildup gives rise quickly and sharply to hard-line attitudes in the other side. This is particularly the case since these tend to be one-shot or at the most two-shot affairs. Crisis initiation and involvement give rise to this pattern through a more complicated process, since they tend to be repeated affairs. The first major crisis between two states can, in the absence of a long-term hostile relationship, act as a kind of baptism of fire (see Vasquez, 1985), and thus serve as an external shock to the system that locks in hostile attitudes. However, after this initial shock, the repeated crises follow a more evolutionary model in their impact (see Hensel, 1999), giving rise to hard-line sentiments more slowly but persistently and reducing the ability of accommodationist options to compete, eventually leading to a crisis that escalates to war. Major states are more prone to this evolutionary process, since they tend to have longer fuses than minor states.[10]

These domestic processes feed back into the way a state interacts with its opponent. The increase in hard-liners tends to encourage disagreement and the use of coercive (or negative) acts if these disagreements cannot be resolved through discussion and persuasion. The use of negative acts (sticks as opposed to carrots) to change the position of the other side gives rise to hostile attitudes in both sides. This conflict spiral makes leaders and followers infuse the concrete stakes at hand with symbolic and, in extreme cases, transcendent qualities. This promotes framing the issue in zero sum terms, which reduces the chances that compromise proposals will receive serious attention. As these processes repeat, a vicious circle sets in, and the leaders in each side see their competition less as one over specific stakes and more as a "we-they" competition. The emergence of this "actor orientation" replacing a "stake orientation" is the hallmark of a sense of rivalry (Vasquez, 1993: 80–82).[11]

---

[10] However, it may be the case that minor states may also have a long fuse, if (1) there are a large number of accommodationists or (2) the leadership is very risk averse. For a discussion and theory of risk propensity in foreign-policy decision making, see Levy (1992, 1996, 1997).

[11] The conceptual framework used in this paragraph dealing with conflict and actor orientation was originally laid out in Mansbach and Vasquez (1981: ch. 7).

The impact of these conflict spirals on perceptions helps explain why territory, which in its material form should be seen as a divisible stake, becomes so intractable. It should be the case that a divisible concrete stake could be parceled out in some form of negotiated settlement. Concrete and tangible stakes that become embroiled in conflict spirals, however, become transformed, through framing, into intangible stakes that are not divisible. We know from a variety of studies that intangible stakes are difficult to divide (see Pruitt and Rubin, 1986; Rosenau, 1966; Vasquez, 1983; Brams and Taylor, 1996). The way otherwise concrete and tangible stakes become intangible is that they are infused with first symbolic and later transcendent qualities. Concrete stakes become symbolic when they begin to represent stakes other than themselves. When this occurs, contending parties are reluctant to give them up because in doing so they: (1) set a precedent for giving up other stakes that are similar and/or (2) signal that their resolve to stand fast on these other stakes is not firm. Symbolic stakes by definition involve reputational effects and costs beyond the intrinsic value of the concrete stake under question, and therefore give rise to a commitment by the defending party to expend more costs than would seem warranted by a superficial examination of the concrete stake itself.

Infusing a concrete stake with symbolic qualities becomes more prevalent as actors become (psychologically) hostile in their attitudes toward one another. This hostility, which is a product of repeated conflictive interactions, is also related to the generation of an "actor orientation" that links the various concrete stakes under contention. As the contending parties begin to see each other as the main problem in settling disagreements, they link a variety of disagreements they have with each other into a single overarching grand issue (Mansbach and Vasquez, 1981: 59–61, 240–55). Linking the stakes in this manner automatically makes each symbolic of the other. An example in the Cold War is West Berlin, standing for West Germany, and then West Germany standing for Western Europe, and the latter standing for the entire Free World.

Conflict that persists can also result in concrete stakes also becoming infused with transcendent qualities. Fights then become not only ones of fundamental conflicts of interests, but of values and ways of life, and eventually good and evil (see the cases in White, 2000). Such frames go beyond reputational effects and make the conflict even more salient, as well as expanding the domestic constituency (audience) upon which hard-liners can draw and leaders must satisfy. Such a conceptual analysis helps explain why territorial issues, which seem like they could just be divided, become infused with symbolic and transcendent qualities that make them difficult to divide and intractable (on this question, see Walter, 2003; Newman, 2006).

For all of the above reasons crisis involvement acts as the engine fueling threat perception and hostility with each escalating as crises repeat.[12] The steps-to-war explanation posits that crises between relatively equal states tend to stalemate and recur, and as they do, they are more apt to escalate to war.[13] As they repeat, one or both sides can be expected to escalate their use of force in order to coerce or intimidate the other side into agreeing with its issue position. Such bargaining tends to give rise to hard-liners in each side, which makes the issue more intractable, reduces the prospects of compromise, and encourages more escalation. As both sides climb this ladder of escalation, the external bargaining situation and internal political climate increase the chance that a crisis will emerge that ends in war.

Since the original publication of the steps-to-war explanation, work on interstate rivalry has come to the forefront. This literature assumes that a pair of states that has a history of repeated militarized disputes is engaged in a rivalry. An enduring rivalry is conventionally operationalized as six disputes within a twenty-year period (Diehl and Goertz, 2000: 45) with the rivalry terminating when no MID has occurred for ten years. Thompson (1995), however, maintains that perceiving another state as one's principal enemy is the key to rivalry and that recurring disputes proceed from that (see also Thompson, 2001). Bennett (1996) makes the key point that what fuels recurring disputes and hostility is the issue at stake, and he uses the resolution of the issue to determine when a rivalry terminates. If rivalry and the repetition of disputes increase the probability of war, it is important in looking at dyadic conflict to have an idea of whether the current dispute is the first, second, or nth dispute between the same pair of states. The literature on rivalry, regardless of the particular definition of rivalry employed, assumes that once a threshold of repeated disputes or level of hostility is crossed, the probability of war increases.[14] Put another way, war tends to increase in probability as disputes between the same states recur. All of this suggests that rivalry and recurring disputes are a step to war.

However, not all enduring rivalries may be the same. We believe that pairs that have a very high number of previous disputes can come to learn how to manage their relations and even to a certain extent ritualize their militarized disputes so that they are not as dangerous as those they had earlier. In effect, at a certain stage, interstate interactions become regularized, generating expectations within the contenders that result in ritualized interaction. Such a

---

[12] For evidence supporting this proposition, see Leng (1983): 379–419); Vasquez (1993: ch. 5); Brecher and Wilkenfeld (1997: 826–28, 837–38); for an analysis of how the spiral works within a single crisis, see Holsti, North, and Brody (1968).

[13] Vasquez (1993: 184–90, 316–18); see also Wallensteen (1981).

[14] See Diehl and Goertz (2000); Wayman (1996, 2000); Thompson (1995, 2001).

depiction is in line with an earlier assertion by Mansbach and Vasquez (1981: 117) that a ritualized stage of relations ". . . involves the continuation of competition and repetitive probing, but within mutually understood limits, and governed by tacit rules in accordance with standard operating procedures that actors develop to prevent surprise and uncertainties. . . . Hostile moves are undertaken by adversaries, but such moves are expected and so can be parried."[15] The Cold War relations of the United States and Soviet Union provide an illustration of this process (see George et al., 1988).

A ritualization process implies that there should be a diminution in the probability of war for dyads that have experienced a very large number of prior militarized disputes. Put another way, the relationship between recurring disputes and war may not be linear but curvilinear, something that the idea of crossing a "rivalry" threshold misses. We expect the probability of war to increase as disputes repeat, but once the disputes exceed the average number of disputes between pairs of states in the system, we would expect their probability of war to decrease.

Up to this point, we have analyzed the processes increasing the probability of war in terms of two levels of analysis—the external interactions of states (what is often treated in the literature as dyadic or two-party analysis; see Bremer [1992]) and the impact of the domestic political environment. To this must be added a third level of analysis—the international system and its structure (Singer, 1961). Neorealists treat the international system as anarchic, with Waltz (1979: 114–15) insisting that anarchy must be treated as a strict dichotomy—a structure is either anarchic or hierarchical. Along with many others, we think that the presumption of anarchy is incorrect (Alker, 1996). We think that anarchy-order is the proper concept and that it is best seen as a continuum, which implies that some historical systems have been more ordered than others. This means that rules, norms, and institutions, particularly as they relate to the management of relations among major states and the raising and resolving of territorial issues, are key variables, because they make a system less anarchic and more ordered. We therefore look at the global institutional context as a third level of analysis that affects the probability of war breaking out.

---

[15] For additional discussion on how dyadic interaction becomes patterned, see Azar (1972), who recognizes a similar process in his normal relations range, where he maintains that it is not so much the level of hostility that makes for a crisis between two states, but how much that level deviates from the average or typical level of hostility. Thus, a typical negative act between the United States and Soviet Union would not have as much impact as the same act would if it transpired between the United States and the United Kingdom. Azar's concept implies that states in long-term rivalries learn to manage their crises so as to make them less dangerous.

It was stated earlier that a key component in the probability of war is how territorial issues are handled. The extent to which leaders resort to power politics to handle such issues is directly related to the presence of norms, rules, and institutions in the system (Vasquez, 1993: ch 8). When there are no norms for transferring territory, predation and power rule. Norms and rules channel short-term interest and regulate the use of brute force, but when norms are ambiguous or two norms are in conflict, loopholes are provided and force rather than principle can become the arbiter (Vasquez, 1993: 148–49).

Despite claims about anarchy, norms are often present in the global political system, although they change through history. Since the end of the nineteenth century, the combined principles of nationalism and self-determination have been the prevalent norms for transferring territory; dynastic succession was the previous norm in Europe for transferring territory. Today there is also a fairly substantial body of international law dealing with borders, their demarcation, territorial seas, fishing zones, and so forth as well as an important norm protecting the territorial integrity of states (Luard, 1986; Zacher, 2001). There are also certain institutions that can aid states in managing territorial disputes.

The presence of such norms and institutions gives actors a set of mechanisms for resolving an issue without resorting to war. The key point to keep in mind is that if war is a way of making binding decisions and if norms come to be accepted as a procedure for making binding decisions, then norms can become a functional equivalent to war. Two states disputing a piece of territory could then settle their dispute by compulsory arbitration (if there is such a mechanism in place), by a war, or by flipping a coin. A rich global institutional context, regardless of how restrictive or permissive its norms, is posited as reducing the probability of war. The reason for this is that merely providing alternative ways of making political decisions reduces the need to resort to force and moving states down a road that leads to the use of power politics and taking the various steps to war. Historical eras or regions that have a rich institutional context can be expected to make fewer attempts to handle territorial issues through the threat or use of force and therefore have fewer wars.

The crucial question is whether actors will accept the outcome of such a mechanism as a binding decision. A normative order is defined as more restrictive the less latitude parties have in either having to use a procedure before resorting to war and/or accepting the outcome as a binding decision. The element of compulsion can include not only force, but a feeling of having to conform to the social ethos of the group. Of course, there are reasons why states may voluntarily seek to resolve an issue by selecting one of the mechanisms or procedures in the normative order, including the lower costs, the avoidance of war, the increased likelihood of winning, or the deflection of domestic criticism (on the latter, see Simmons, 1999). The reasons why actors use the procedures embodied in an order is an exogenous question, but once they do, this should reduce the number of wars in the system. Raymond (2000) and Kegley and Raymond (1990) argue and provide some evidence to show that restrictive normative orders have fewer militarized disputes and wars than permissive normative orders.

A global institutional context, however, involves more than just norms and rules about decision principles for the transfer of territory. It also involves establishing certain rules of the game for managing relations among states, especially the major states in the system or region. Such rules can act as a system of inchoate governance. Institutions like the Concert of Europe can use conference diplomacy to try to resolve differences on the basis of the collective interests of the major states (see Schroeder, 1994: preface). There is also some empirical evidence that even when major states attempt to establish such rules of the game, the frequency of war between them goes down (Wallensteen, 1984). Be that as it may, it is posited that a global institutional context that has attempted to establish such rules is richer than one that has not, and is therefore less likely to have major states resorting to power politics and to war among themselves.

Of course, such a system may also have rules about the ease with which territorial issues can be put on the agenda. If the steps-to-war explanation is correct, then when major states or other actors attempt to keep territorial issues from even getting on the agenda, the probability of war will go down. Such rules are especially pertinent to minor states. When major states cooperate, it is often to restrict the freedom of minor states, especially their right to go to war. Major states often seek to establish some system of governance of minor states and to restrict certain kinds of behavior or demands. For this reason, sometimes the territorial issues dividing minor states are kept off the agenda by major states, which should reduce the likelihood of war. Even if these issue are not kept off the agenda when major states attempt to establish a system of governance, minor states have many obstacles placed in front of them when they try to go to war. While a rich global institutional context can be expected to also reduce the probability of minor states going to war with each other, it may not reduce the probability of major-minor wars, since the system rules may reflect a cabal among major states not to come to the aid of a minor state attacked by a fellow major state. Again, there is some limited evidence supporting this proposition (Wallensteen, 1984). Peace is not the same as justice.

This overview of the explanation should make it clear that the focus of our analysis is on the probability of war breaking out between two or more actors. We assume that the war arises out of a crisis that escalates to war, although that assumption is more a function of the configuration of current data sets used in the field and need not be treated as fixed. What is a more serious assumption is our dyadic approach. We assume that the leadership of each state makes a conscious decision about going to war with another state, and that in multiparty wars, a decision to go to war is made with regard to each belligerent, if only it be recognizing the impossibility of avoiding war with the state given the nature of wartime coalitions, geography, and so forth. The explanation therefore is couched in terms of the dynamics between two states. Nevertheless, we recognize that there are differences between dyadic or two-party wars and those that are multilateral or, what we refer to as, complex wars (see Vasquez, 1993: ch. 2).

We also recognize that there is a difference between explaining the onset of a war (whether it be between two or more parties) and the expansion or spread of war later on. Bremer (1995) was among the first within the Correlates of War project to emphasize this distinction, pointing out that an explanation of the behavior of the originators of the war would not be the same as an explanation regarding joiners that enter the war at a later date. The latter, if nothing else, would have to take cognizance of factors like contagion and diffusion processes. The explanation presented in this chapter is limited to the onset of war.[16]

The independent variables in the explanation—territorial disputes, alliance making, arms racing, repeated crises, and rivalry—can be seen as a set of risk factors for war that operate in a dynamic and nonlinear fashion. In this study, we are interested in seeing whether the presence of these risk factors, singly or in combination, at the beginning of a crisis will increase the likelihood that the crisis will escalate to war. Before proceeding further, we turn to some important elaborations about the dynamics of the steps to war and address some common criticisms associated with the explanation's analysis of those dynamics.

The Dynamics of the Steps to War: Elaborations and Criticisms

The Sequence of Steps

Using the language of "steps to war" is meant to convey that pursuing certain objectives by adopting realist practices—such as the making of alliances, buildups of the military, and resorting to the threat and use of force—in-

---

[16] For an analysis of why wars spread, see Vasquez (1993: ch. 7), (1996b); Vasquez and Gibler (2001).

creases the risk that two states will go to war. The language of steps implies a sequence of actions or even transitions across phases (see Cioffi-Revilla 1998: 140–50, 158–63; see also Bremer [1995]. What is important to keep in mind during the early stages of research is that the presence of more than one step, regardless of its order, results in an increase in the probability of war. What is crucial is not the sequence of the steps, but that they are mutually reinforcing. Alliances may precede or follow military buildups, and militarized disputes are likely to punctuate the entire relationship, thereby occurring before and after certain practices are adopted; however each increases the risk of war.

This does not mean that a sequence pattern cannot be theoretically derived or inductively established. The original explanation, based on a rational deductive analysis, suggested that first there is an issue, then one or more crises stemming from disagreements on the issue, then attempts to augment power by making alliances and/or military buildups. These encourage further crises and reinforce a sense of rivalry. Perceptions of rivalry would be expected to flow from all three of these processes, but precisely when it would emerge was not specified. Nor was the sequencing between alliance making and military buildups specified, although it is clear from the logic of the explanation that as steps are taken, contending parties can be expected both to make alliances and to build up their military against each other.[17]

Realist logic gives us some hint as to why states might overcompensate and whether alliance making or arms races would come first. Generally, if allies are available, they will be sought before costly arms races. This is because the domestic costs of military buildups typically are greater than the perceived external costs of making an alliance (see, for instance, Barnett and Levy, 1991). The major problem is availability and what must be traded to gain an ally. One would expect from realist logic that alliance would be the first perimeter of defense. A realist might even hope that such alliances would be sufficiently intimidating to prevent an attack by an opponent. What is more likely, however, is that the opponent will make a counter-alliance and that the next line of defense will be to build up their military. Such actions are most likely if crises continue to erupt between the two parties.

Serious and more immediate threats of war, however, must be handled by a military buildup. This is because finding an ally may take too long and/or is never as reliable as one's own efforts. Whether such military buildups lead to a mathematical arms race is often difficult to discern with current data re-

---

[17] In other words, states in a rivalry or in the process of becoming rivals tend not to substitute these two practices (contrary to most explanations, see Most and Starr, 1984; Most and Siverson, 1987; Palmer et al., 2002; Palmer and Morgan, 2006; see also Morrow, 1993; Clark and Reed, 2005). The dynamics of the rivalry make them less willing to rely on one practice and they overcompensate.

sources, but suffice it to say that given the budgetary process in the modern state, building up arms and having the other side respond takes a long time. Thus, even if a military buildup occurs because war seems imminent, this is unlikely to instantly become an arms race in the technical sense, simply because there will not be enough time. For these technical reasons, arms racing, at least in current data sets, is usually going to follow alliance making rather than precede it.

The steps-to-war explanation also assumes that the road to war between equals is a somewhat drawn-out process, which implies that it is only after a period of time that there is an immediate threat of war; this again implies that arms racing would follow alliance making rather than vice versa, because the cost of arming is not going to be borne until a threat is clear.

The role of repeating crises or militarized disputes is best depicted as an engine that fuels the taking of the next step, whatever that would be. Repeating crises also increase the number of hard-liners and, through this process, tend to make bargaining behavior escalate across crises until there is a sense that the only way to handle the situation is to go to war. Rivalry is mostly a function of perception, which in turn is a function of crisis involvement. Alliances will probably come in the early stages of a rivalry, whereas arms racing will come after numerous crises. Nevertheless, in some cases, arms racing can lead to a sense of rivalry, the best example being the Anglo-German naval race (see Kennedy, 1980: 252–53).

In a simple two-actor world starting at the beginning of history, the above sequencing would make sense, but the world is not confined to two actors, and history has a long record. The most obvious element disrupting the stipulated pattern is that no ally may be available. Territorial disputes will not give rise to alliances if no allies are to be had. In addition, alliances may pre-date the emergence of a territorial issue. Such an alliance, which was made to deal with some other issue and target some other state, may now become relevant, even though the current territorial dispute may have nothing to do with the initial formation of the alliance. Likewise, military buildups directed toward one state may now be useful in a conflict with another. Finally, the domestic leadership and changes in that leadership have an impact on these processes and how they might be perceived by an opponent. All of this is a way of specifying in a limited fashion the kind of noise in the system that makes it difficult to test and empirically document the sequence of the steps to war. Nevertheless, the logic of the steps and how they increase the risk of escalation to war (regardless of their sequence) by setting off conflict spirals through the ways states interact (and indirectly through the internal effects of the interactions) is clearly specified.

The Relative Impact of Specific Steps

A second question raised by concerns of sequence and order is whether certain steps have a greater impact than others on the probability of war erupting. Part of this has already been answered by specifying territorial issues as an underlying cause and power politics as a proximate cause. Ultimately the answer must be empirical, but can anything theoretical be said about the relative impact of alliance making, arms racing, and recurring crises and/or rivalry?

Theoretically, the steps-to-war explanation draws upon two logics to explain why war occurs. The first is the logic of realist prescriptions, and the second is the psycho-logic of the security dilemma and how people deal with the unanticipated consequences of the failure of realist prescriptions to bring about the desired result. As discussed earlier, realist folklore can be seen as a set of constructed rules that guide diplomats and leaders. In this sense, they are similar to the rules of chess, and just as knowledge of the rules of chess can lead one to anticipate what moves players might take, so too can a knowledge of realist prescriptions be used to anticipate the moves that leaders and diplomats might take in a competitive interstate relationship involving the threat or use of force. Of course, for most realists, these rules are not seen as constructed, but reflect the structure of a material and objective reality.

The steps-to-war explanation, however, maintains that the projected outcome of following realist prescriptions and adopting realpolitik strategies and tactics in a crisis between relative equals often leads to a failure to prevail. In these circumstances, the security dilemma predicts a rise in threat perception and hostility. Psychologically, among leaders and their audience, this touches upon a host of powerful emotions, including fear and anxiety, which touch upon honor and insecurity, as well as fight and flight syndromes. These emotions affect decision making, although we do not fully understand how.[18] Suffice it to say here that threat perception and hostility combine with realist prescriptions to encourage escalatory behavior producing conflict spirals. Both psychologically and consistent with realist prescriptions of minimizing

---

[18] For some intriguing propositions on the role of emotions in foreign policy, see Crawford (2000). She employs findings from cognitive psychology to argue that emotional reactions to certain events make them more memorable and more apt to give rise to analogies that influence subsequent decisions (cf. Jervis, 1976: 228–82; Khong, 1992). She also uses evolutionary theory to point out that humans are predisposed (maybe even "hard-wired") to detect and react to threats to such an extent that we may be sensitive to even very low thresholds of threat. This may give hard-liners an edge in getting their recommendations accepted (see some of the suggestive evidence from psychology in Kahneman and Renshon, 2007). Some analyses have been done on how neuroscience findings might be applied to decision making, including the decision to go to war. For an analysis of how these findings might augment and perhaps even supplant rational choice models, see Rosen (2005) and Damasio (1995). For a similar application to American politics, see Marcus et al. (2000).

costs, actors order their reactions from least costly and risky to most, and thereby climb a latter of escalation. This is true for both specific realpolitik tactics and the taking of larger actions, like making alliances and building up one's military. Given relative equality of capability and highly salient issues, like territorial issues, following realist prescriptions leads to a series of steps to war. The only way to avoid war is for one side to capitulate or get off the realist road to war and adopt a very different set of diplomatic practices that handles the issue in a less coercive manner.

On the basis of this theoretical rubric, one would expect that the least costly practices and tactics would be tried first. In terms of interstate actions, one would expect probes in the forms of threats and limited uses of force to be tried first with more escalatory actions to be tried later only if the former failed.[19] In terms of adopting power politics practices, like alliances and military buildups, one would expect alliance making to be less costly and a faster solution to implement in most circumstances than building up one's military, if outside allies are available. Because realist prescriptions outline a rough order or ladder of escalation, it can be anticipated that those steps that come earlier will have less impact on the probability of war, since there are still other options left short of war that can be adopted. This means that, normally, there will be a longer time lag between the adoption of certain practices, like alliance making, and escalation to war. In addition, since there are more options to be tried, fewer wars should arise fairly soon after the taking of these early steps to war, and thus by definition these steps will have a lower probability of war.

Previous empirical research before the formulation of the steps-to-war explanation is consistent with these expectations. For instance, Levy (1981) (see also Ostrom and Hoole, 1978) finds that alliances are made several years before the outbreak of war, which implies that their impact is not strong in the sense that it is not immediate. Even though Levy (1981) finds that sometimes 100 percent of the alliances involving great powers are followed by war within five years, the fact that there can be up to a five-year lag suggests that whatever occurs to bring about war in this five-year period has more of an impact on the probability of war.[20] Thus, alliances seem to have the impact the steps-to-war explanation posits—they increase threat perception and hostil-

---

[19] Of course actors may anticipate this failure and move to more escalatory actions. However, in order to prevent this from being an ad hoc explanation, perceptual evidence along these lines must be found in the relevant cases. Evolutionary theory and neuroscience, when combined with recent findings from cognitive science, provide a set of logics on threat that might be usefully mined for the steps-to-war explanation. This has not been done here since the purpose is to test the theory as it was originally presented in 1993.

[20] In other words, alliances may increase the probability of war from 10 to 20 percent, but that still leaves an 80 percent chance of avoiding war, whereas some other factor might produce a 70 percent chance of war.

ity, which leads states to take additional actions that further increase the probability of war (e.g., from 20 to 40 percent).

The additional actions that presumably bring about war are repeated militarized confrontations in which the bargaining tends to escalate across each crisis. Each of these crises (in terms of the theoretical explanation) becomes more difficult to manage, even if decision makers want to avoid war, because the dynamics of bargaining leave progressively fewer realist options to be tried short of war, and hard-liners push for war. Some evidence on this action-reaction pattern is provided by Leng (1983) (see also Wilkenfeld et al., 1980, and Holsti, North, and Brody, 1968). Since the publication of the steps-to-war explanation, the research on rivalry by Goertz and Diehl (2000) has shown that pairs of states with six or more militarized disputes have a high probability of having at least one war. This research supports the steps-to-war explanation in that it shows that six or more militarized disputes act as an important threshold for increasing the probability of war, thereby supporting the notion that it is the *recurrence* of disputes that helps bring about war. The strength of the impact of this variable is further underscored by the fact that Goertz and Diehl (1992a) show that most wars fought since 1816 are fought between rivals (see also Diehl and Goertz, 2000: 61). These findings also support the claim that recurring disputes are a much greater risk factor than garnering outside allies. According to the steps-to-war explanation, this would be expected, especially with recurring territorial disputes.

Is the impact of rivalry greater than that of arms racing? This is difficult to answer, because in principle, making an alliance or building up one's military is different from crisis initiation and involvement. Nevertheless, early crisis initiation would seem to be less costly than alliance making and more readily available as a probe. It seems unlikely that without at least one or two crises a state would feel the need to build up its military vis-à-vis an opponent (or to make an alliance against them) without testing the other's resolve. This suggests that having a limited number of crises (Diehl and Goertz, 2000, would say under six) would have a weaker impact on the probability of war than having a large number of crises. Repeated crises (anywhere from 5 to 10), because they would reflect a climbing of the ladder of escalation, should be the most war prone. In principle, since these later crises also bring about arms racing, the two may be intertwined. Nevertheless, if one had to choose on the basis of the theory, arms racing would be seen as slightly more dangerous, because involvement in an arms race might be perceived as being at the top rung of the escalation ladder; however, this is a more difficult inference to make during any particular crisis in a pattern of crises. Arms races are also more dangerous because losing an arms race could make one very vulnerable (or might encourage a preemptive strike).

Theoretically, it is expected that when arms races do occur, they raise both threat perception and hostility to very high levels. At some point (and for hard-liners this point is reached a lot earlier than for accommodationists), arms racing becomes no longer a realist strategy for avoiding war by peace through strength, but a way of preparing for war and winning it if it comes about.[21] Such a shift in thinking helps bring about a self-fulfilling prophecy and a diplomacy that is less likely to avoid war. Of course, for those with long-term plans for war, like Hitler, building up one's military is a way of preparing for war from the beginning. All of these factors suggest, theoretically, that arms racing will have a strong impact on the probability of war and especially so if they occur after a pattern of recurring disputes.

The research on arms races often shows that most crises that erupt in the presence of an ongoing arms race eventually lead to a crisis that escalates to war (Wallace, 1979, 1982; Sample, 1997). At the same time, it must be kept in mind that this effect does not seem to be present after 1945 (Sample, 2002). This suggests that other factors can mute the effect and/or bring about war before actors have a chance to become involved in an arms race (as currently measured). In fact, since many dyadic wars occur in the absence of an arms race, arms races are not responsible for most wars (see Diehl, 1983: 209).

While it is possible to delineate the relative weight of each of the steps, the important factor in the explanation is that *each step produces a "step-level" increase* in threat perception and hostility that both increases the probability that another step will be taken *and* the probability of a crisis emerging that will escalate to war. In the end, the steps-to-war is a developmental model, with one thing leading to another. The steps fuel each other and become a syndrome of behavior, so that in the end, it is really all of them together that bring about war, with each doing its part.

Endogeneity

This raises the question of endogeneity, which some have posed as a potential problem with the steps-to-war explanation. The question of endogeneity is a complicated one (King et al., 1994: 185–99), but with regard to this analysis such a perspective would ask whether the steps produce war or whether war (or the anticipation of it) produces the steps (see King et al. [1994: 197–98], who look specifically at the endogeneity problem in analyzing the role of arms races and alliances in bringing about war).

---

[21] Wayman (1990) describes this switch as the Phillips curve of insecurity; see also Vasquez (1993: 215).

One approach to this problem can be taken from Diehl and Goertz (2000). Endogeneity is not a problem in their model, because it is assumed to exist. Applying this to the steps-to-war approach, one could say that what one wants to study is when enduring rivalry, alliances, arms races, and war are collectively present and when they are absent, and not whether they produce war or vice versa. The main prediction of this approach, as well as Diehl and Goertz's (2000), is that the presence of enduring rivalry, alliances, arms races, and territorial disputes will be associated with war, and the absence of all these factors will be associated with peace.[22] To a certain extent we will test something like this in chapter 5.

Nevertheless, even though the steps could be treated this way, the explanation does not present them this way, but as factors increasing the probability of war. Even if some of the variables have to be treated as endogenous, this does not mean that their sequencing and mutual impact could not be studied individually. Even such unmeasured variables as "anticipation of war" could be observed and studied through the use of case studies and process tracing. Process tracing could also be used as a way to collect more data that would give us a way of looking at the steps in terms of a developmental model rather than simply as a syndrome of behavior.

Thompson's (2001) data on rivalry, which is not based on recurring militarized disputes but on the perception of decision makers, illustrates how this can be done. From his perspective, it is a decision makers' perception (hostility) that makes for militarized disputes and wars. Since Thompson determines perception of rivalry separate from recurring disputes, he can use the former to predict the latter. For him, the two comprise a syndrome of behavior that can be disentangled. It may be possible to build on his data to determine when such perceptions occur in the sequence of interstate interactions and thus to see whether they follow certain foreign policy practices (such as the steps) or precede them, and whether they follow or precede a certain number of militarized disputes. Such data would help ensure that the independent and dependent variables are separate. Such data would be particularly important with regard to the role "anticipation of war" plays in the steps to war and whether such anticipations are uniform in a state's leadership or differ with regard to hard-liners and accommodationists (see Hagan 2003).

To address the question of endogeneity, it is important to recognize that research is a process (see James, 2002: ch. 3) and that even though current re-

---

[22] Likewise, it could be argued that the presence of two or more of these factors leads to an anticipation of war (especially among hard-liners), which in turn fuels the taking of further steps. From a steps perspective, anticipation of war is really a reflection of fear coming out of increasing threat perception.

search cannot solve all endogeneity problems, future research may. There are, after all, econometric techniques for dealing with endogeneity if a proper measurement instrument can be identified. Likewise, "matching" techniques have been employed when instruments are not available (see Simmons and Hopkins, 2005).

A related criticism of the steps-to-war explanation is spuriousness. Some critics argue that it is not the particular step—alliance making or arms racing, for example—that brings about war, but some other (X) factor that leads states to take these steps and at the same time bring about war. This, of course, is logically possible, but just because something is logically possible does not mean it is true or, on the surface, a better scientific explanation.

Taking the latter first, the main competitor to the steps-to-war explanation is the broad set of realist theories. None of these see alliance making and arms racing as inherently war prone. Indeed, some, like peace through strength and the deterrence model, often see them as a way of preventing an attack or of "deterring" war, if they can marshal sufficient strength. For a realist, the making of an alliance should reduce the probability of war, if it balances power. Likewise, a military buildup, even an arms race, should not increase the probability of war and might avoid war if it is made clear to the revisionist state that the war will be lost because of the overwhelming power the status-quo state has marshaled (see Morgenthau, 1960: 30, cited in Wallace, 1982: 37).

In contrast, the steps-to-war explanation rejects these claims, even if the conditions realists expect (like balancing power) come to fruition. It uses the logic of the security dilemma to show why it is so difficult to create peace through strength and focuses on the negative effects of threat perception and hostility that automatically arise from adopting the practices of power politics. These bring about three conditions that make a competing relationship ripe for war: (1) The various options short of war offered by realpolitik strategy become exhausted; the opponent has not capitulated and so one must live with a stalemate or take the ultimate step and go to war. (2) The number and influence of hard-liners in each side increases, which leads them to advocate that the only way to handle the situation they face is to go to war. (3) The increasing threat perception and hostility create a psychological atmosphere of fear and anxiety (and other emotions), where it becomes increasingly difficult to manage crises to avoid war, even if that is what is desired. Eventually a crisis goes out of control either through design, mismanagement, or some stochastic process.

In terms of philosophy of science questions, what is important in the testing process is that a given explanation have testable differences between it and its main theoretical competitors. The steps-to-war explanation does make different predictions about the effect of alliances and arms racing on the probability of war compared to realist theories. If evidence is uncovered that shows that these practices encourage war and do not confirm a peace-through-strength expectation, then this must be counted as evidence in favor of the steps-to-war explanation and against the peace-through-strength explanations. To then explain away that finding as spurious without actually empirically showing it to be so by identifying and measuring the missing "X" factor is simply producing an ad hoc explanation.

To the extent that there might be an unobserved variable(s) producing both the steps and war, two variables have in fact already been identified: threat perception and (psychological) hostility. One could argue that these two variables are the real underlying factors and that alliances and arms races are spurious. This may in fact be the case, but at this stage of research, identifying alliance making and arms racing as factors that produce threat perception and hostility is useful in that it tells us where these factors come from, especially since both threat perception and hostility are unobserved given current data.

Differences between This Explanation and Realism

The last question that is raised, and sometimes even posed as a criticism, is just how different the steps-to-war explanation is from realism (with the implication sometimes being that it might be able to be subsumed by realism). There are three aspects of this question that deserve elaboration and clarification on our part: the relationship between the steps and anarchy, the role of the security dilemma in bringing about war, and the connection between the territorial explanation of war and realism's notion of vital interests.

The steps-to-war explanation does build upon realism and uses aspects of its insights to map out a realist road to war. It does differ from realism in what it sees as increasing the likelihood of peace and the limited role it sees power playing in the onset of war. To begin with foundations, realism, as stated in classical realism (Morgenthau, 1960), sees international politics as a struggle for power, with war being a natural side effect of that struggle. The steps to war are derived from what classical realists see as the key actions major states take toward each other to deal with security, which we describe as power politics behavior. Neorealists, like Waltz (1979), add the notion that such power politics behavior (especially the balancing of power) comes out of anarchy. In both cases, such behavior is natural, lawlike, and grows out of material conditions. Failure to adopt such behavior, for both Morgenthau and Waltz, results in failure and, in extreme cases, destruction. One of the main differences between the steps-to-war explanation and that of both classical and neorealism are over the nature of the factors that give rise to the steps in the first place and their likely consequences.

The differences with neorealism are more easily described because it sees power politics behavior as a consequence of the anarchic system (see Waltz, 1979: 117–19). Whenever the system is anarchic (which it has always been), such behavior is present and cannot be avoided, if one wants to survive. The steps-to-war explanation differs with this at the most basic level in that it does not see the system as always anarchic. Rather than treating anarchy as a dichotomy it sees it as a continuous variable with the system having various levels of order. Empirically, it accepts Bull (1977; see also Alker, 1996) over Waltz as a more accurate account of the system since 1815 (see Vasquez, 1998:a 197–202, for elaboration). The kind of anarchy Waltz describes is fairly rare in the modern global system and certainly does not come close to a Hobbesian notion of anarchy where there is no industry, no navigation, no arts, no letters, and continual fear and danger of violent death (Hobbes, 1651, part I, ch. 13). Conceptually, our explanation agrees more with Wendt (1992, 1999) that anarchy is what states make of it (see also Ashley, 1984). The world, including a world without government, provides the opportunity for constructing different types of politics, and while certain forms may be privileged in certain material conditions, Hobbesian anarchy is not the only form of politics possible in the absence of government—Grotian forms of politics are possible as Bull (1977) maintains, as are other forms, like a Kantian order (Deutsch et al., 1957; Russett and Oneal, 2001; Wendt, 1999). The steps to war do not come from anarchy because the kind of Hobbesian anarchy Waltz stipulates is too rare to account for them.

If the steps to war do not come from anarchy, as neorealists would argue, where do they come from? Morgenthau (1960) is probably closer to the truth in that he sees them coming out of the experience of struggle. As stated earlier in the chapter, we hold that war is learned from experience and changes with experience. Our main difference with classical realism on this question is one of nuance; we see the institution of war as being learned and constructed in history and not simply a reflection of material conditions. War involves rules and expectations and not just raw power, so war as an institution changes in history (see Vasquez, 1993: ch. 1). Likewise, we see the steps to war as a process learned over the course of history, and that realism, itself, helped institutionalize in the system. Historically, since at least 1648, realist thinking and practice have created an ideational system that guides diplomats and tells them when to handle certain situations by a resort to arms. We do *not* disagree that such a system, and its attendant behavior, exists; our disagreement is that realism fails to see this as a constructed system that can change, and that it underestimates how many of the policies it recommends to avoid war actually backfire and make war more likely.

A realist construction of the system and the predominant diplomatic culture in which decision makers (and followers) often operate create an ideational structure,[23] that encourages realist practices and hence indirectly war (see Vasquez, 1993: appendix: 309–10). These are deep background factors, however, and the steps-to-war explanation *should not be seen as positing these deep background factors as the main causal process by which war comes about.* They are after all fairly constant over time, and war is not, so they cannot be the main factors for bringing about war. For the steps-to-war explanation, it is the actual taking of the steps—the way states behave toward each other—that brings about war. The steps-to-war explanation is primarily a dyadic explanation of war that works at the interaction level of analysis and not at the systemic level.

A second question deserving clarification has to do with the logic of the security dilemma and its relationship to the steps to war and how this differs from realism. The explanation uses the security dilemma to explain the origins of the steps and why they have negative consequences that lead to war. The main difference with realism is that the steps-to-war explanation argues that, while certain realists analyze the security dilemma and sometimes incorporate it into their analyses (see Jervis, 1978, in particular, but see also Van Evera, 1999: 117n), realist theory does not see the making of alliances and the building up of militaries as steps to war. On the whole, realist theory accepts the peace-through-strength hypothesis. Likewise, although some defensive realists, like Jervis (1976: ch. 3), have worked on elaborating the spiral model, most realists place greater emphasis on the deterrence model. This, of course, is true of offensive realists, like Mearsheimer (2001), but also of more mainstream realists, like Waltz (1981). At any rate, the steps-to-war explanation maintains that these steps generally do not create the consequences they are intended to create within realism—winning without going to war—but actually set off a series of additional steps that increase threat perception and hostility, and eventually lead to a crisis that results in war.

Some defensive realists may come close to saying the latter—the closest is Jervis (1976: ch. 3) when he discusses the spiral model—but most do not. Even with Jervis however, the spiral model is not a full-blown explanation of war. The steps to war embody the spiral model logic in critical parts of the explanation, but the explanation is broader than that model and places emphasis on other steps and not just the repetition of crises. In addition, it moves

---

[23] On this concept and how ideas form a structure that shapes behavior, see Legro (2005).

beyond the spiral model that looks primarily at a hostile spiral within a single crisis (as in the early 1914 studies of Holsti, North, and Brody, 1968) and looks at how behavior spirals across crises (as with Leng, 1983), thereby bringing in the concept of rivalry, something absent in the spiral model.

The main reason realists do not use either the spiral model or the security dilemma as a full-blown explanation of war is that these concepts do not produce an explanation that gives much of a role to power. For most realists, and certainly for the peace-through-strength hypothesis and the deterrence model, the onset of war is closely related to power. For the security dilemma and for the spiral model, war is related to psychological variables, a far cry from objective power. A theory of war that does not give power a central role is not much of a realist theory. This should come as no surprise because the original concept of a security dilemma was put forth by John Herz (1950), a nonrealist.

Another important criticism that is sometimes leveled at our use of the security dilemma concept is to deny that realists actually think that power politics (and hence the steps) are actions that will prevent war. Real realists, the argument goes, are less concerned about avoiding war than being in a position to win it if comes about. This has been noted in the original explanation (Vasquez, 1993: 215). The difference here is that the steps-to-war explanation maintains that in most situations, at least one side in a conflict would like to avoid war, and it attempts to do so by following realist advice to increase power. The peace-through-strength hypothesis does explicitly say that war can be avoided by having sufficient power to in effect "deter" the other side from aggression. The steps explanation recognizes that as various actions fail to accomplish goals and the other side escalates, one or both sides may begin to fear that war will come about, regardless of what they do, and they shift from an orientation of war avoidance or "deterrence" to preparing for war. The steps explanation sees this shift as a consequence of the failure of realist strategy and as part of the process that leads states to a decision for war. Some critics want to deny that war avoidance or deterrence is ever the main goal of one or both sides and that therefore these steps or policies do not "backfire." While such a characterization of realist theory, if it were true, would not make this evidence contradict certain realist versions, it would not prevent it from contradicting the peace-through-strength hypothesis or the claims of the deterrence model.

Nevertheless, in making this argument, another testable difference arises between the steps explanation and these critics—namely, whether or not decision makers try to avoid war by making alliances, building up arms, and demonstrating resolve through the use of realpolitik tactics. The more instances found where some decision makers are actually trying to do this early on in the process, the more times the steps backfire and the more contradictions with realist expectations. Conversely, if in fact it is frequently the case that decision makers are not trying to avoid war through increases in power, then the steps explanation would fail to pass this test.

A third question that sometimes arises is that realism also places great emphasis on territory, so how is the main prediction of the territorial explanation of war that different? Is it not the case, after all, that territorial integrity is part of Morgenthau's (1952: 968–78) definition of the national interest and considered a "vital interest" over which a state might go to war (see Gochman and Leng, 1983)? This is true, but having said that, it is equally true that classical realists and all other realists do not see territory as a unique issue that shapes politics and interstate relations the way the territorial explanation of war does. For realists, all issues can be reduced to the issue of power (Morgenthau, 1960: 27), and this includes territory as well. What is important about territory for realists is that it is a source of power. For us, what makes territory important to decision makers is that they have, like all mammals, a proclivity to defend it.

This proclivity, which is part of our evolutionary inheritance, makes territory special and makes states' behavior on territory different from what realists would expect. For the territorial explanation of war, territorial concerns make wars between neighbors more likely to occur, but once territorial boundaries are settled and mutually accepted (even if this occurs through war), neighbors can go on to have long periods of peace, even if other salient issues arise. For realism, such periods of peace are not predicted. For realists, new issues can give rise to a new struggle for power. As noted earlier in the chapter, this is a central and important testable difference between the territorial explanation of war and realism. For the former, peace is not only possible, but likely under certain conditions. Indeed, generally the steps-to-war explanation is much more optimistic about the possibility of peace than is realism, and it offers specific propositions as to when war (and when peace) is likely.

The steps-to-war explanation involves a number of propositions (the appendix in *The War Puzzle* [Vasquez, 1993] lists seventy-six), and Senese and Vasquez's (2003) unified explanation of territorial conflict has added several more. Not all of them can be tested at the same time, nor are data always available to test them in a manner that gets at the dynamic aspects embodied in the explanation. This does not mean that there cannot be tests with data that can be collected with reasonable effort that would provide a way of subjecting certain hypotheses to falsification.

In this study, a number of propositions will be derived from the theoretical explanation and tested. While they do not get at all the aspects of the explanation, they all should be true if the theory is true. In other words, if they are found to be false, then the theory from which they are derived is false, if not in its entirety, then at least in the areas specified by the hypotheses. The next chapter will outline the aspects of the explanation that we plan to test and why we have selected these rather than other propositions. It will also report on research that we and others have done prior to this book that is relevant for assessing the empirical accuracy of the explanation, and we will discuss how this prior research, including criticisms, has led the steps-to-war research program to evolve in the almost twenty years that have elapsed since it began. Chapter 2 will also present the research design for this book as a whole, and detail the data sets, measures, and statistical techniques we will employ, although details of specific tests will be discussed in the chapters where they are conducted.

2

The Evolution of a Research Program:
Research Design

Theories are fine, but facts are better.

In any discipline theories are golden and theorists typically occupy a high, and at times heady, position. Newton, Einstein, and Freud are remembered for their theories and not so much for their empirical work. Yet a theory is only as good as the evidence that supports it, and theories that command belief in the absence of much evidence quickly become doctrine. The hallmark of science is not to even consider accepting theories until they have been subject to testing. This chapter outlines the tests of the steps-to-war explanation that have been conducted to date and the tests we plan to undertake in this book.

The-steps-to-war explanation has had its fair share of adherents. Some have been attracted to it because it is a consciously nonrealist explanation of war. Others have liked that it explains and makes sense of a large number of empirical findings. Still others have appreciated the extent to which it builds on realist insights and combines them with the logic of the security dilemma to delineate a realist road to war. More recently, constructivists have been attracted to it because of its conceptualization of war as an institution that is a cultural invention that is learned and changes in history. Many critics have taken these same reasons as a basis to question, and at times even reject, the explanation. Some critics do not like the explanation because it is not realist. Others object that it is too inductive and that its "logic" is not formal. While it is fine to evaluate theories on the basis of their theoretical characteristics— their logical coherence, explanatory power, and parsimony, for example—the more important criterion for science is that theories pass empirical tests, which means that in principle they must be falsifiable (Popper, 1959). It is not a surprise, therefore, that the steps-to-war explanation did not begin to gain influence until its claims about territory, which were somewhat unusual at the time, began to be supported by research, some of which was guided by the explanation and some of which was independent of it.

In the next section, we review the early research on the explanation and give an overview of how the research program has evolved in light of external criticism. We do this in the form of a narrative or brief intellectual history of the research program, pointing out how the early tests were constructed, why they were questioned, and how the research program shifted to address those questions, while at the same time other propositions from the theory were being tested with new data. In the second section of the chapter, we use this review as a backdrop for presenting and justifying the research design of the studies in this book.

The Steps-to-War Research Program

The standard view of philosophy of science (Nagel, 1961; Hempel, 1966; Popper, 1959) is that propositions are logically derived from theories to test them; theories are rejected if after a reasonable time these propositions turn out to be false. Kuhn (1970), and more importantly Lakatos (1970), point out that this view of science does not always conform to what practicing scientists do. Theories are rarely falsified because they keep being reformulated in light of evidence. Thus, instead of a single theory, one can get a family of theories. Verbal theories already embody a family of theories in that several different mathematical models can be consistent with a set of propositions given the ambiguity of words over numbers. What is more troubling is when new propositions are created or different versions of the theory are constructed in order to deal with unexpected experimental outcomes (or findings), as often happens with realist theory. The failure to falsify in light of discrepant evidence can lead to problems (see Lakatos, 1970; Vasquez, 1997).

Up to this point the kinds of problems discussed by Lakatos regarding several theories that might lead to a degenerating research program have not been relevant to steps-to-war theory because the research has been limited and consistent with hypotheses that were tested. Instead, the problem has been with some critics refusing to accept tests and evidence as supportive of the explanation. This raises the question of what kinds of tests need to be conducted. This process within the project led the program to evolve and to produce the kinds of studies presented in this book.

What was unique about the steps-to-war explanation (at the time it was published in Vasquez, 1993) was its emphasis on territory. Many mainstream international relations scholars had talked about the importance of territory (Weede, 1976; Goertz and Diehl, 1992b; Holsti, 1991; Luard, 1986) but none had given it such a central causal role in a theory of war. Those that did were typically outside the mainstream and often dismissed as biological determinists (e.g., Ardrey, 1966; Shaw and Wong, 1989). Given some of the constructivist assumptions in Vasquez (1993: ch. 1), this criticism was not made early on, but scholars were and remain skeptical of placing too much causal significance on territory. Initially, then, what was unique about the explanation did not attract scholars to it.

In addition, one of the major claims of the steps-to-war explanation—that most wars occur between neighbors because they have territorial disputes—was dismissed by the counter-explanation that most neighbors fight because they are contiguous and nearby. Just as automobile accidents are more apt to occur within fifty miles of home (because that is where most driving occurs), so wars are most apt to be fought with neighbors. Such an explanation was attractive because it was parsimonious, was consistent with what we know about related phenomena (like car accidents), and had a touch of brilliance in that it is non-obvious and looks beneath the surface. Given this competition and the theoretical bias against territorial explanations, it is not likely that the steps-to-war explanation, or at least the territorial aspect of it, would have gotten very far. Then something serendipitous happened—the release of the long-awaited Militarized Interstate Dispute (MID 2.1) data set by the Correlates of War project, which records all instances of a militarized threat or use of force among states from 1816 on. Unbeknownst to just about everyone except those closest to the data set, the data had a variable related to the threat or use of force over territorial questions. Here, in effect, was a data set of territorial disputes along with other kinds of militarized disputes that could be used as a basis for comparison.

These data were seized upon to provide the initial tests of what was called the "territorial explanation of war" (embedded in the broader steps-to-war explanation) and to answer empirically some of the criticism being put forth. It was the ability of the territorial explanation to pass these tests that began to attract the attention of scholars.

The data turned out to be ideal for the research program for three reasons: First, the data were independent of those who developed the theory and pre-dated the construction of the theory. Second, the collectors of data were not aware of the theory, which was not published until long after the data collecting began. Indeed, the collection of the information on territory and two other types of disputes was not theory driven, but almost an afterthought to make the coding more systematic. Both of these factors greatly reduce the problem of bias in that if one thinks that territorial questions are related to war, that might unconsciously affect the coding. Third, these data were separate and different from the war data that gave rise to findings that influenced the construction of the broader steps-to-war explanation (Vasquez, 1987) in the first place. The evidence that was used to inform theory construction was based on a data set that looked at interstate wars primarily from 1816 to 1965. It then developed a set of propositions that could be used to test the explanation. The data on militarized disputes are quite different from the war data with the former containing several thousand cases, most of which do not escalate to war, as opposed to the fewer than one hundred cases of interstate wars in the war data. The initial versions of the new MID data also went through 1992, whereas most of the analyses used with the war data ended in 1965. Most importantly, the new data on militarized interstate disputes permitted us to test core propositions unrelated to findings derived from the earlier data. The latter included all the propositions dealing with territorial disputes. The new data also permitted us to examine the factors that increase or decrease the probability of war by systematically comparing the many interstate militarized disputes that do not escalate to war to the few that do.

The MID data became useful early on in dealing with the very first criticism made of the explanation, which was that it was tautological. It was argued that every war is fought over and on territory, so that does not really tell us anything and the explanation is nonfalsifiable. Part of this criticism misconstrues the nature of the territorial explanation of war. Even if most interstate wars are fought on territory, this does not mean that they are fought *because of* territorial issues or grievances. The territorial explanation of war maintains that issues that claim and dispute who owns certain parcels of land are more apt to precipitate war than issues that make nonterritorial claims. The manner in which the war is fought is different from the issue that gives rise to it (before the war breaks out).

The explanation has always maintained that territorial issues must clearly precede the onset of war and that territory is a source of conflict that leads to war (Vasquez, 1993: 125, 127). This is important because territorial disputes cannot be a cause of war if they arise after the war starts. The latter often occurs and may be a reason to continue the war or not accept a settlement, but this should not be seen as a causal factor in bringing about war in the first place. Analytically, there can be wars fought on other issues—regime questions or other foreign policy issues—and we expect this to be the case since the steps-to-war explanation does not maintain that territorial disputes are a necessary condition of war.[1]

A second question related to the tautology criticism concerns the elasticity of the concept. Everything that precedes a war cannot be seen as somehow related to territory—what is and is not must be specified. If the explanation

---

[1] For the position that territory is a necessary condition of war, see Heldt (1999: 451, 453).

is to be falsifiable and nontautological, territorial issues must be defined narrowly enough that they can be distinguished from other issues and claims. On both this question, and the one that territorial disputes must come prior to the outbreak of war, the MID 2.1 data provided useful solutions that put an end to the tautology criticism.

It did this by collecting data that was able to clearly distinguish territorial claims from questions about the legitimacy of a regime and from a host of other general foreign policy disagreements. Rather than code issues directly, the data set identifies instances of the threat or use of force between legally recognized nation-states, records the names of the parties to the dispute, and classifies them into revisionist states trying to revise and change the status quo, and nonrevisionist states. Revisionist states are coded in terms of the *type* of revision they are trying to bring about by the threat or use of force—whether one or both sides are disputing claims to the same territory; challenging a regime or trying to topple it from power; opposing the foreign policy of state; or contending over some "other" miscellaneous question (Jones, Bremer, Singer, 1996: 178). Since not every dispute has revisionist actors or a clear revisionist claim, the revision type is sometimes coded as "nonapplicable." The data also took care of the temporal problem by requiring that revisionist claims be made by official representatives of the state *prior* to the onset of the threat or use of force.

Here were data that showed that not only was it possible to distinguish territorial disputes from other types of disputes, but data that could be used in tests that would, in principle, falsify the territorial explanation of war, thereby demonstrating it was not tautological. To do this first, it had to be shown that there are in fact militarized disputes that are not associated with territory. This was done in Vasquez (2000: 385, table 2). He showed that only 28.7 percent of the militarized disputes in the data are over territory and that the modal type of dispute is over policy—46.3 percent (number of cases = 2034). This seems to make for plenty of variance to conduct a test of the territorial explanation of war. Second, it had to be shown that while wars arising out of territorial disputes are quite prevalent, as predicted, there are plenty of wars arising from policy and regime disputes. A little over half the wars come out of territorial disputes, with the rest coming from policy disputes (30.4%), regime disputes (8.8%), other (3.9%), and non-applicable (4.9%) (N = 102) (Vasquez, 2000: 384–87, see table 2 for the statistics). If the explanation is tautological or nonfalsifiable, then one could not get this sort of distribution.

The key benefit of the data, however, was that they permitted the core propositions on territorial disputes and the steps to war to be tested empirically. The major test conducted in the research program was by Vasquez and Henehan (2001), one of the first articles published after the project received

Table 2.1

Probability of Territorial Disputes Going to War: Comparison of Revision Types, 1816–1992

Dispute sample from MID 2.1 data: revision type by hostility level

	Wars		MID Total	Cond.P(War)	Z	p
	Observed	Expected				
Territory	53	33.8	583	0.091	3.408	<0.001
Policy	31	54.6	941	0.033	−3.280	<0.001
Regime	9	6.7	115	0.078	.918	0.179
Other	4	1.9	32	0.125	1.622	0.053
Total	97		1671			

Base probability of war = 97/1671 = 0.058
(nonapplicable coded cases excluded)
Source: Vasquez and Henehan (2001: 128). Reprinted with permission of Sage Publications from the *Journal of Peace Research* (2001) 38 (March): Table IA.

the NSF grant.[2] A number of tests were conducted, but the key and most straightforward one is reproduced in table 2.1. The analysis in the table looks at each MID, regardless of the number of parties in the dispute,[3] and compares their probability of going to war according to whether the revision type of the dispute is territory, policy, regime, or other. Probabilities are calculated as simple frequencies. If the proposition that territorial disputes are more war prone than other disputes is true, then the data should show that the likelihood of territorial disputes escalating to war should be greater than expected by chance, that territorial MIDs should have a higher probability of escalating to war than the other types of disputes, and that this difference should be statistically significant.

These expectations are borne out. Disregarding the small and statistically insignificant "other" category, it can be seen from the table that territorial disputes do have the highest (conditional) probability of going to war (.091), followed by regime disputes (.078), and then policy (.033). A comparison of the observed number of war escalations to the expected number (if war escalation were distributed randomly) reinforces this conclusion since roughly only thirty-four war escalations are expected when territorial is being disputed but fifty-three actually occur (compare this to the nine observed and seven expected for regime disputes). A more rigorous way of making this same point

---

[2] This study was based on the earlier analysis of Vasquez (1996b).

[3] The unit of analysis in table 2.1 is the dispute as a whole and does not break down the MID into its dyadic pairs. Thus, the 1938 Munich dispute is one observation, including Germany, Czechoslovakia, the United Kingdom, and France.

is to compare the base probability of war for this sample, which is .058, with the (conditional) probability of each type of dispute escalating. The probability of territorial disputes escalating is higher (.091), and the Z score in the table indicates that this difference is statistically significant. The probability of regime disputes escalating to war is also higher (.078), but not statistically significantly higher (p = .179). Interestingly, policy disputes are significantly less likely to escalate to war (as indicated by the fact that their probability of escalation, .033, is lower than the base probability of war, as well as the negative Z score).

A separate test (Vasquez and Henehan, 2001: 130, table II) used a logit analysis to see if the differences among territory, policy, and regime with regard to the probability of escalating were statistically significant. For the sample of disputes reproduced in table 2.1, the difference between territorial MIDs and policy MIDs is significant, but the difference between territory and regime is not. However, two subsequent tests—one that looks at dyadic disputes and one that compares the long-term relations of dyads (e.g., France and Germany) according to whether their history of MIDs are mostly over territory, policy, or regime questions—show a significant difference between territory and both policy and regime MIDs.

This study also introduced a number of controls to see whether territorial disputes are also highly war prone in the pre-1946 and post-1945 periods and for major-major, major-minor, and minor-minor dyads. Regime disputes are found to more likely to escalate than expected by chance only in the post-1945 period and for minor-minor dyads. This study concluded that the territorial explanation of war passed a series of important tests, and, indirectly, so had the steps-to-war explanation, since the territorial explanation basically constituted the first step to war in that explanation.

This research is also consistent with previous research that had been conducted on territory, even though these were not direct tests of the territorial explanation of war. Hensel (1996), analyzing the same MID data set but combining policy, regime, and other disputes into a single category of nonterritorial disputes, also found territorial MIDs to be significantly more war prone. In an early study of Latin American states, Hensel (1994) also found that about two-thirds of territorial MIDs are followed by a subsequent MID between the same two parties. This is important because it is known that as MIDs between the same parties recur they are apt to escalate to war (Goertz and Diehl, 1992a).

In addition, Senese (1996) showed that territorial MIDs are more apt to result in fatalities than nonterritorial MIDs. This implies that decision makers and their publics are more willing to fight (and die) for territory than other issues, something entirely consistent with the logic of the territorial explanation of war.

Lastly, Ben-Yehuda (1997, see also 2004) added to the robustness of the finding on the war proneness of territorial disputes by showing that this pattern also holds for another data set—the international crisis behavior (ICB) project data on twentieth-century crises. She found that crises dealing with territorial questions are more apt to escalate to war than other crises.

At about the same time that these studies were being conducted, interest in territorial disputes was given a great spur by the publication of Huth (1996b), which contained a data set of all territorial disagreements between nation-states from 1950 through 1990. Although he did not compare territorial disputes to nonterritorial disputes, he did classify territorial issues into different types based on whether they involved ethnic questions, strategic territory, economic resources, and so forth. He found that territorial issues involving ethnic claims (including bordering minorities) are most apt to escalate to the use of force (i.e., something similar to having an MID) and to war.

This body of evidence and research helped bring work on territory back into the mainstream of international relations, but there were still two important obstacles to accepting the kinds of findings presented in Hensel (1996), Senese (1996), and Vasquez and Henehan (2001). The first was that in terms of explaining why neighbors fight, most scholars were still enamored of the contiguity explanation and several scholars had established a link between contiguity and conflict/war (see Gleditsch and Singer, 1975; Bremer 1992, 2000; Senese, 1996). Vasquez (2001) proposed and conducted a fairly straightforward crucial test. He argued that if the contiguity explanation is correct then contiguous states should be more apt to go to war than noncontiguous states regardless of whether they have territorial disputes. Conversely, if the territorial explanation is correct, dyads with territorial disputes should be more apt to go to war than dyads without them, regardless of whether they are contiguous or noncontiguous. The results of this test are reproduced in table 2.2.

The data here are based on comparing the long-term history of dyads with each other from 1816 through 1992. The unit of analysis is the dyad where the history of relations between two states (e.g., Germany and the United Kingdom) is a single case. Dyads are compared on the basis of whether they have ever been contiguous and whether 25 percent or more of their MIDs have been over territory.[4] It can be seen that dyads that have more territorial disputes are always more likely to have a war than those with fewer territorial disputes ($<25\%$). This is indicated in the upper part of the table by the negative Z score, which shows that the dyads with <25 percent territorial disputes have a significantly lower probability of having a war than the base probability of

---

[4] Using a 50 percent threshold does not change the outcome of the test.

Table 2.2

Crucial Test of Territorial and Contiguity Explanations of War (Dyad-History Data)

Noncontiguous Dyad

	Wars		MID Total	Cond. P(War)	Z	p
	Observed	Expected				
< 25% Terr	69	143	311	.222	−8.42	<.01
≥ 25% Terr	200	126	274	.730	8.97	<.01

Base Probability = 269/585 = .460

Contiguous Dyad

	Wars		MID Total	Cond. P(War)	Z	p
	Observed	Expected				
< 25% Terr	26	37	113	.230	−2.22	.013
≥ 25% Terr	49	38	116	.422	2.16	.015

Base Probability = 75/229 = .328

Rank Order by Conditional Probability (War)

	Cond Pb(War)	Z score
Noncontiguous ≥ 25% Terr	.730	8.97
Contiguous ≥ 25% Terr	.422	2.16
Contiguous < 25% Terr	.230	−2.22
Noncontiguous < 25% Terr	.222	−8.42

Terr. Based on < 25% Terr MIDs or ≥ 25% Terr.
(Nonapplicable coded cases excluded)
Source: Vasquez (2001: 161). Reprinted with the permission of Taylor and Francis Inc. from *Conflict Management and Peace Science* (2001)18 (2):Table 4.

war. It is also shown by the rank order of the conditional probabilities (reported in the lower part of the table), which show that those dyads with more territorial disputes having higher ranks (.730 and .422) than those with fewer territorial disputes (.230 and .222). What is crucial however in demonstrating that the territorial explanation is superior to the contiguity explanation is that territorial disputes always have a higher probability of going to war *regardless* of whether the dyads are contiguous or noncontiguous. In fact, noncontiguous dyads with territorial disputes have an even higher probability of having a war than contiguous dyads with territorial dispute (.730 versus .422). This is impressive evidence against the contiguity explanation.

    Working independently, Hensel (2000) has also looked at the relative impact of contiguity and territorial disputes on the likelihood of a MID having fatalities. His unit of analysis is the MID where each case is a dispute involving two states. He finds that territorial MIDs are more likely to result in fatalities than nonterritorial MIDs, again regardless of whether the actors involved are contiguous or noncontiguous. Specifically he finds that MIDs between noncontiguous adversaries where territorial issues are at stake result in fatalities about 52 percent of the time compared to only 24 percent of the time when territorial issues are not at stake. Similarly, MIDs between contiguous adversaries where territorial issues are at stake result in fatalities about 42 percent of the time compared to only 26 percent when they are not at stake (Hensel, 2000: 73, table 4.4). Explicitly comparing the proximity/interaction explanation with the territoriality explanation, he concludes that the "territorial explanation appears to be the strongest" (Hensel, 2000: 77), but that does not mean that proximity has no impact on conflict.

These two studies went a long way toward undercutting the contiguity explanation of why neighbors fight and gaining support for the territorial explanation of war. In addition, they also explain why contiguity, which is a constant, does not always give rise to war. War is more likely between contiguous states when they dispute territory, and less likely when they do not. The evidence from these two tests helped displace the contiguity explanation in favor of the territory explanation. In light of other research studies on territorial disputes, the idea that territorial disputes are highly war prone became more accepted within mainstream international relations, a far cry from the half-decade before.

These studies, although an important turning point, are far from definitive. There are two reasons for this. First, the role of contiguity and proximity in conflict has not been precisely delineated. Second, all the studies reviewed to date look at empirical relationships once a militarized dispute emerges. It is entirely possible that the factors that make a MID emerge in the first place may be more important in bringing about war than the presence of a territorial dispute. In fact, contiguity or a host of other factors could operate in this manner. Such a line of criticism became very popular in international relations as the research on territorial disputes was being published. This was particularly the case after Reed (2000) published a two-stage model on the democratic peace demonstrating the presence of selection bias in previous studies. Even though this problem had been raised earlier in the literature, especially with regard to deterrence studies and with the role of alliances (see Levy, 1989b; Siverson, 1996; Garner and Siverson, 1996; Smith, 1995, 1996; Bueno de Mesquita, 1996: 61–63), after Reed (2000) the problem of selection effects or selection bias became an important basis for questioning lots of research on MIDs, including the kinds of findings reported in Vasquez and Henehan (2001). As a result, the research program took an important turn—an investigation of some of the factors related to the onset of militarized conflict that might have an impact on their proclivity of war.[5]

In order to advance research on war it is necessary to get a better understanding of just how much, if any, selection bias might be operating when using MID data. This question becomes the focus of the two empirical studies in part II of this book. Chapter 3 addresses a criticism made of the findings in Vasquez and Henehan (2001) and in Hensel (1996) that it is the factor(s) that brings about a territorial MID in the first place that makes for war, and that without controlling for this factor(s) it cannot be confidently concluded that territorial disputes are more war prone than nonterritorial disputes. The factor that is most likely, theoretically, to bring about a territorial MID in the first place and be more related to the escalation to war, is the presence of a territorial claim or issue. A *territorial issue* is a claim to a piece of territory and reflects a disagreement (in opinion). A *territorial dispute* is the threat or use of force over that issue. What could be possible is that both a MID and war are being brought about by the presence of a territorial issue (the first stage) and that the resort to force (i.e., the second stage) is a meaningless intervening variable. Theoretically, what this criticism is saying, contrary to the territorial explanation of war, is that it does not matter how territorial issues are handled, they are inherently war prone. This criticism was given some empirical weight because Huth (1996b: 137–38, 267–68) had found some evidence of a selection effect operating along these lines in a random sample of cases related to his data (as opposed to the MID data) from 1950 through 1990. If the research on the steps to war is to go forward, then this issue has to be studied systematically. Chapter 3 presents the results of our tests. In doing so, it establishes the relationship between territorial disputes and escalation to war on a firmer footing.

A second factor that is apt to bring about a territorial MID in the first place and to propel it to war is contiguity. Selection effects play a role in the analysis of both contiguity and territorial disputes. Conducting a two-stage analysis provides an opportunity to specify and delineate more clearly how contiguity and territory work in the conflict process from the onset of a MID to its escalation to war. Senese (2005) tackled this problem, and chapter 4, below, extends his earlier analysis. The end result of these analyses is a much more definitive assessment of the comparative role of contiguity and territory, one that demonstrates the importance of contiguity in conflict (MID) onset, and of territorial disputes in the escalation of MIDs to war, as stipulated in the territorial explanation of war.

---

[5] While this question might lead to a full-blown focus on MID onset, at this point the research program is still placing an emphasis on the factors that bring about war and only looking at the earlier stage of conflict as, in effect, a control variable.

Both of the studies in part II of the book strengthen and deepen the research on territory and war in the field. The territorial explanation of war, however, captures only part of the steps to war. The other steps involve arms racing, alliance making, and rivalry. The research related to these factors as it was conducted within the research program will now be reviewed. The variables will be treated in the chronological sequence in which the research was conducted.

Research on Arms Racing, Alliances, and Rivalry

Of all the propositions within the steps-to-war explanation, the most controversial is the claim that an ongoing arms race increases the risk that a MID will escalate to war. At the time the explanation was first published, the scientific debate between Wallace (1979, 1982, 1990) and Diehl (1983, 1985a, 1985b) on arms races had deadlocked, although some ways out of this were suggested by Vasquez and Henehan (1992: 105). Susan Sample (1996) took on this question and her work has played a major role in delineating the effect of arms races on the escalation of MIDs to war. Her major breakthrough, in retrospect, looks simple, but at the time, no one had done it. What she did was to examine the mutual military buildups using Diehl's measure (and later Horn's 1987 measure) to see which arms races do not increase the likelihood of escalation. She found that most of these "safe" arms races prior to 1946 produce a MID between the same parties within five years that escalates to war. Militarized disputes after 1946 are not more likely to escalate to war in the presence of an ongoing arms race.

Her initial studies (Sample, 1997, 1998b) looked at only major states, which is what Diehl and Wallace had done. She also introduced a number of other variables, mostly related to capability (relative equality, power transition, rapid approach), but also to territorial disputes to see how they might affect the relationship. None of the capability variables wipe out the relationship prior to 1946 even when they have a separate impact. She also looked at the effect of territorial disputes in this context and showed that they remain a significant risk factor (although at times at the .10 level) (Sample, 2000: 176–78). Next, she collected arms-race data on minor states so the relationship could be tested on all states from 1816 through 1992. Again this was groundbreaking work. The results also showed that arms races during 1816–1945 increase the risk of a MID escalating to war within five years. This is not the case in the post-1945 era. Her work provides important evidence consistent with the steps-to-war explanation, while at the same time limiting the domain of the arms race proposition to the 1816–1945 period.

As with other research at the time, the question of selection effects was raised. In this case, scholars asked whether the arms-race data was confined to dyads that had MIDs (Diehl and Crescenzi, 1998; see also Sample's 1998a response). Gibler, Rider, and Hutchison (2005) shared this concern and collected arms race data for a sample of strategic rivals from 1816 to 1993 (whether or not they had a MID) to overcome this problem. They then were able to test the proposition on arms racing as a step that increases the risk of a MID escalating to war using a very different research design. The results were still supportive of the steps-to-war explanation with most of the evidence in favor of the hypothesis coming from the periods surrounding World War I and World War II.

In light of these findings, it can be concluded that arms races do increase the probability of a militarized dispute escalating to war in the 1816–1945 era, but not in the Cold War period. What remains to be researched is the relationship between arms races and other steps to war, like alliance making and rivalry. In particular, one would want to know if the relationship is spurious, especially with regard to some of the other steps to war. One way of testing for this is to control for these other steps. Another question is whether some steps, like alliance making, pose a greater risk of a MID escalating to war than arms racing. This question can also be probed by controlling for the other steps and then calculating predicted probabilities to see which steps increase the probability of war the most. At the same time, the predicted probabilities can be examined to see how combinations of various steps affect the probability of war. Lastly, one would want to know whether arms races interact with any of the other steps. Each of these questions will be investigated in part III of the book.

The role of alliances has been another area that has been studied within the steps-to-war research program. Alliances, and whether they encourage or prevent war, have long been a research question within international relations (see, among others, Liska, 1962; Bueno de Mesquita and Singer, 1973; Ward, 1982; Levy, 1981). Douglas Gibler was the first, however, to research the war proneness of alliances systematically from the steps-to-war perspective. He began by taking seriously the call in Vasquez (1993: 171) to develop a typology of alliances that would discriminate between those alliances that are followed by war and those that are followed by peace. In the process of collecting alliance data, Gibler (1996) noticed that certain types of alliances—those that settle territorial disagreements—tend not to be followed by war. These alliance treaties are very different from the typical way in which IR (international relations) theories view alliances—namely, as ways of balancing power. Instead, they are treaties that settle territorial disagreements and seal that settlement with an alliance. Using the logic of the territorial explanation of war, Gibler argued that such alliances would not be followed by war because they do not pose a threat and they eliminate a major source of conflict leading to war. His empirical analysis of such alliances shows that all but one (and none, if one takes into account measurement error) of these alliances are followed by war within five years (Gibler 1996). He also finds, consistent with the expectations of the territorial explanation of war and the previous findings of Kocs (1995), that settling territorial disputes can have a clear pacifying effect on future conflict when such settlements are cemented by an alliance between the former contenders (Gibler, 1997a).

The territorial settlement treaty identified by Gibler (1996) is important because it has been ignored by IR theorists and because it has an irenic effect, but such alliances are comparatively few in number. Gibler (1996) finds only 27 such alliances out of 193 from 1815 through 1980. What of the vast number of other alliances? How are they to be classified? Using the logic of the steps to war, Gibler (1997b) hypothesized that alliances that increase threat perception are more apt to increase the risk of war. In a highly original move, he then argued that the characteristics of states that comprise an alliance signal the level of threat involved in the formation of alliance to the likely targets. He maintained that alliances composed exclusively of states successful in their previous war, of major states, and/or of those dissatisfied with the status quo are signaling a higher level of threat and are more likely to be bellicose than those with the opposite characteristics. In theory, alliances of the first type are not only more likely to be followed by a MID escalating to war, but are more apt to be followed by increased armament levels, more involvement in crises, and the formation of counter-alliances, that is, additional steps to war (Gibler, 1997b: ch. 6; see also Gibler, 2000: table 7.3, 160). An empirical analysis of alliances classified according to these types does show that each of the three kinds of alliances and their combination increase the probability of war (Gibler, 1997b, 2000; see also Gibler and Vasquez, 1998).

Of equal importance is that the typology can discriminate between the alliances followed by war from those followed by peace, thereby solving the puzzle posed by Levy's (1981) findings that 56–100 percent of great power alliances are followed by war from 1495 to 1975 except in the nineteenth century. Using the typology, Gibler (1997b, 2000: table 7.2, 156) is able to explain why alliances in the nineteenth century are more likely to be followed by peace while alliances in other centuries are followed by war. The alliances in the nineteenth century are of a type that signals considerably fewer threats.

Gibler's research on alliances helped advance the research program on the steps to war in that it showed that alliances that increase threat perception are more apt to be followed by war. In doing so, he eliminated the nineteenth-century anomaly that shows alliances to be less war prone. At the same time, his identification of the territorial-settlement treaty added evidence in support of the claim of the territorial explanation of war that settling territorial disagreements increases the prospect of peace. As with the work on arms races, this research also needs to look at the relationship between alliances and the other steps to war in more detail and by controlling for the impact of the other steps. Both of these questions will be foci of the tests in part III.

The most extensive work related to the steps to war that has been conducted since the publication of the explanation has been on rivalry, although most of it has been conducted outside the steps-to-war research program. The engine that keeps states along the realist road to war is the recurrence of disputes. Theoretically, it is the onset of a major crisis that increases insecurity, and the repetition of crises that leads to attempts to increase power by making alliances and building up armaments. In addition, as crises repeat, they increase the influence and number of hard-liners domestically, which in turn leads states to escalate across crises. This logic suggests that recurring disputes increase the probability of war, and a substantial amount of research shows that rivalry, as measured by the repetition of MIDs, is associated with war. Goertz and Diehl (1992a) demonstrated that about half the wars fought since 1816 involve rivals, and that rivalry itself increases the probability of war (Diehl and Goertz, 2000: 61–63). Wayman and Jones (1991), using a different threshold (of the number of MIDs) to indicate rivalry found a similar pattern. Wayman (1996) also found that rivals among major states in the context of power transitions are highly likely to be embroiled in war with each other.

Given that so much of the existing research has demonstrated the relationship between the recurrence of MIDs and the escalation of MIDs to war, the steps-to-war research program has been able to concentrate on linkages between rivalry and the other steps. Vasquez and Leskiw (2001) argued that pairs of states that have territorial disputes are more apt to become rivals since territorial disputes recur. They found that dyads that dispute territory do have a greater likelihood of becoming an enduring rivalry than expected by chance (see also Tir and Diehl, 2002).[6] This research uncovered an important link between rivalry and territory, showing that territorial MIDs produce rivalry, which we know increases the likelihood of war.

Early on, Vasquez (1996a) used the logic of the steps-to-war to distinguish between those rivals that go to war and those that do not. He argued that there are two distinct paths to war, one between contiguous rivals that erupts over territorial disputes and one by which noncontiguous rivals are brought to war.

---

[6] They also add to our knowledge base by listing all enduring rivalries from 1816–1992 according to whether their relations are dominated by territorial, policy, or regime MIDs and measuring the extent to which at least 25 percent of a dyad's MIDs are over territory regardless of the issues that dominate their relations.

Noncontiguous rivals that are not centered on territorial disputes tend to become embroiled in war through contagion and diffusion factors. Otherwise, they remain at peace, as in the Anglo-American rivalry of the nineteenth century. Typically a major state is dragged into a war because of its alliance with a state in a territorial dispute. As in Britain's coming to the aid of Poland in 1939, the allied states (Britain and Poland) both share a common rival (Germany) but the states that go to war initially are those that have the territorial dispute and are often contiguous (Poland and Germany), while the third-party noncontiguous dyad (Britain and Germany) becomes involved later on (and usually does not have a preceding territorial dispute). The idea of two paths to war underlines the complexity of the war onset process; the ability of the steps-to-war explanation to elucidate it speaks to its explanatory power.

Vasquez (1996a) examined twenty-three cases of major-state dyads to test propositions derived from the analysis of the two paths to war, and the evidence is consistent with the predictions of the propositions. Rasler and Thompson (2000) also looked at the two different paths to war using a perceptual definition of rivalry and found evidence consistent with this aspect of the steps-to-war analysis as well. In addition, Rasler and Thompson (2006), using ICB data, examined the interaction of contiguity, strategic rivalry, and contested territory and found that the combination is strongly related to war onset. Their analysis provides further evidence on contiguity, rivalry, and the different paths to war (see also Colaresi, Rasler, and Thompson, 2008).

Valeriano (2003) extended the research program further by making rivalry the dependent variable and asking what steps states take that make them rivals. Using Correlates-of-War data, he found that states that engage in power politics are apt to have recurring disputes and become proto- or enduring rivals. He also found that alliances tend to precede arms races with the latter coming late in the relationship. Valeriano's theoretical extension of the research program to an examination of the steps to rivalry adds to our knowledge of how the various steps are interrelated.

The research in part III looks at the relation between rivalry and the other steps to war. It does this primarily by examining the impact of rivalry on the probability of war while controlling for the effect of the other steps. A focus of the research is the extent to which rivalry increases the probability of war in the presence of other steps and whether the impact of rivalry might be curvilinear. Two different measures of rivalry are utilized—Diehl and Goertz's (2000) categorical measure of rivalry and a more continuous measure. One comparison of these measures is used to see whether the risk of war is more associated with the sheer number of recurring disputes (especially the highly war prone territorial disputes) or some sense of rivalry that emerges once a certain threshold (or number) of MIDs is crossed (as implied by the Diehl and Goertz measure).

Two other areas that have been investigated in the research program, although they are not directly relevant to the studies in this book, are the impact of multiple actors in a crisis on the probability of war and the impact of dispute settlement on the duration of peace. Petersen, Vasquez, and Wang (2004), testing a hypothesis from Vasquez (1993: 192, 318), found that disputes with multiple actors are more apt to escalate to war than disputes confined to two parties. This is particularly true of multiparty territorial MIDs. Senese and Quackenbush (2003) examine the impact of the type of settlement in a MID and the recurrence of conflict in light of various deterrence models. Their study is relevant to what might stop disputes from recurring and the relationship of force to rivalry termination (see also Werner, 1999).

In light of the research to date how should the steps-to-war explanation presented in chapter 1 be tested? We address this question in the next section by outlining the rationale for the tests we present in this book and by discussing the research design that guides the analysis. In this chapter we present an overall research design for the entire book, and in later chapters, we supplement this with details specific to the chapter at hand. Below we present the rationale for the tests and the data, measures and statistical techniques we employ that are common to the book as a whole.

Research Design

Rationale for Tests

The tests we conduct in this book come out of the research to date and reflect a plan for systematically testing the steps-to-war explanation. In this sense, each chapter is connected to and builds upon the previous one. Up to this point there has been a fairly substantial amount of research, both within the program and outside of it, on the individual components of the explanation. Much of this research has shown at the bivariate level that there is some positive association between territorial disputes, arms racing, having alliances, and being in rivalries and having an increased risk that a militarized dispute will escalate to war. The next task is to examine whether the steps accumulate in the fashion described in the explanation to increase the probability of war. It is important to establish sound bivariate relationships, but as those patterns begin to emerge, it is also important to move to more multivariate analyses to gauge the relative potency of variables and whether any drop out. In addition, it is important to establish the domain of the explanation to determine how generalizable it is and whether it fits all historical periods. Previous research has established a good foundation for each bivariate hypothesis for a substantial period of time (at least 1816–1945 for arms races) and in some cases the entire post-Napoleonic period (as for territorial disputes and for rivalry).

We divide our tests into two parts—those dealing with territorial disputes and those dealing with the use of power politics (making alliances, building up armaments, and engaging in repeating militarized confrontations). Part II deals with territorial disputes. Although there is a growing body of empirical work demonstrating that territorial disputes increase the probability of war, there remain two major obstacles to accepting this fundamental claim of the steps-to-war explanation. As discussed earlier, these are the criticisms based on selection effects and on the alternate explanation that contiguity not territory is the most important factor bringing about war. Chapters 3 and 4 will be devoted, respectively, to testing and assessing these two criticisms.

Despite the evidence presented both within and outside the research program (see Vasquez and Henehan, 2001; Senese, 1996; Hensel, 1996, 2001) that territorial disputes are a key factor in bringing about war, the criticism based on selection effects tries to undercut and dismiss this evidence by raising the logical possibility that it is not territorial MIDs themselves that increase the likelihood of war, but some other X factor that brings about both the territorial MIDs and war. This argument is buttressed further by pointing out that the MID data are a nonrandom sample of interstate behavior, in that they record only the behavior of states already engaged in militarized disputes and exclude behavior where the threat or use of force is absent. Even though one could make a strong argument that empirical evidence should not be dismissed because of an untested logical possibility, the best way to deal with this criticism is to test it directly, which we do in chapter 3. If the territorial explanation of war can pass such a test, then a major obstacle will be removed.

Chapter 4 deals with the second major objection to the claim that territorial disputes are a key to understanding why war occurs—the contiguity explanation. Earlier tests (Hensel, 2000; Vasquez, 2001) provide some evidence that it is the presence of territorial disputes and not contiguity that is the key, but these do not look at the role contiguity plays in the onset of MIDs and whether controlling for contiguity at the first stage might demonstrate that contiguity is the key factor. In a way, this is a variation of the selection bias argument that identifies contiguity as the X factor. Chapter 4 not only tests for this possibility, but also expands the theoretical analysis of the steps to war to incorporate some of the steps to conflict that precede the onset of militarized disputes. If this test is passed, then the territorial explanation of war will demonstrate its superiority over the contiguity explanation of war in a much more definitive fashion than to date.

The studies in part II buttress the existing work on territory by providing two sophisticated tests dealing with major criticisms that have provided impediments to accepting one of the fundamental claims of the steps-to-war theory. They do not, however, get beyond what is, in effect, the first proposition in the theory. Nor do they look in detail at the claim that it is not territorial issues, per se, that bring about war, but handling them in a power politics fashion that is crucial. To get at this question one must go beyond the territorial explanation of war to the broader steps-to-war explanation in which it is embedded. The three empirical studies in part III do that.

Each looks at how adopting the practices of power politics—specifically the making of alliances, repeatedly resorting to the threat or use of force (to produce MIDs), and arms racing—increases the probability that territorial disputes will result in the outbreak of war. The focus on what states do to each other while they contend on issues gets at the heart of the steps to war; for this explanation maintains that it is what states do to each other—how they interact—and not just the system or their attributes that is a key to explaining the onset of war.

Chapters 5 and 6 derive and test propositions from the steps-to-war explanation that look at how the presence of each step in combination with one or more of the others affects the probability of war. Thus, propositions are derived on the probability of war occurring when territorial disputes are present, regardless of how they are handled. This base proposition is then compared with propositions that look at: (1) the probability of war when territorial disputes are present and states also have outside allies to aid them, (2) the probability of war when territorial disputes, outside allies are present and the states are also rivals, (3) and so on and so forth until all the logical possibilities embodied in the steps to war are exhausted. The steps-to-war explanation maintains that while territorial issues that are handled in this manner are most likely to end in war, any issue handled in this manner will have an increased likelihood of ending in war, albeit not as high as territorial issues. Hence, the probability of war in both territorial and nonterritorial disputes will be examined.

Chapters 5 and 6 differ from each other in the units of analysis on which their tests are based. Chapter 5 looks at the probability of war between nation-states from 1816 through 2001. Each pair of states is compared in terms of whether they have ever had a war in a particular period within the larger temporal domain. Specifically, the chapter compares those dyads that have gone to war with those that have always been at peace, even though they have had at least one MID in a given historical period. It is predicted that dyads that have territorial disputes and have handled them through the practices of power politics are more likely to have had a war. It is also expected that the probability of war increases as more power-politics steps are taken by the two contending actors. The unit of analysis (i.e., the entity or observation on which data is collected) is the dyad. Each dyad's history provides one case or observation.[7] Some dyads, like France and Germany, will have all the steps present in their history—territorial disputes, outside alliances, rivalry, and arms racing. Some will have only one or two, and others none. The more steps present the more likely the dyad will have had at least one war in its history. The fewer steps, the more likely the dyad will have been at peace.

MID data cover 1816–2001, and often scholars test their hypotheses on the full period. We will also do this for some tests, since our explanation is meant to explain war for long periods of time. However, it could be the case that in certain specific historical eras our explanation might not hold. To test for this possibility we break down the full period into certain subperiods to see how generalizeable the explanation is or whether it fails to hold for certain historical periods. The data are divided into three historical eras—1816–1945, 1946–89, 1990–2001. Doing so permits an examination of the historical domain of the explanation. Breaking down the full period into subperiods also makes the tests in chapter 5 more rigorous and precise, because it provides a narrower temporal domain by which to match the presence of the steps to war and whether states go to war or remain at peace. In addition, each proposition is tested three times.

A number of temporal demarcations could be employed. Here we focus primarily on the difference introduced by nuclear weapons, so our first cutoff point is 1945. Numerous scholars have argued that nuclear weapons ushered in a new era that fundamentally changed the way international politics was conducted and lowered the likelihood of war between nuclear states (Brodie, 1945; Herz, 1959; Jervis, 1989). Given this line of thinking it makes sense to divide the post-Napoleonic era at 1945. Of course, it may be the case that it is not only nuclear weapons that made for a change, but also the particular policies the United States and the Soviet Union adopted for dealing with the threat of nuclear annihilation. In retrospect, these policies seemed to have lowered the prospect of war between the two blocs. To see if nuclear weapons really ushered in a fundamental change in history or the changes that did occur with

---

[7] This unit of analysis—the dyad—should not be confused with the dyad-year. The latter typically has one observation for each dyad for every year and often ends up with 500,000 cases, whereas the dyad has only one observation for the entire period under scrutiny in a given test and ends up with usually under 1,000 cases.

regard to the probability of war were fairly unique to superpower relations in the Cold War, we separate out the post–Cold War period of 1990–2001.[8]

Chapter 5 provides a good understanding of the factors in the long-term relations of states that increase the probability of war. It does not, however, get at the precise timing of the steps; all that one knows is that a pair of states adopted certain steps and had or did not have a war. It is a reasonable assumption that the steps precede the outbreak of a war (and spot checking indicates that this is the case), but it is not *known* that this is always the case. Nevertheless, this is still a good test because if the explanation failed to pass such a test it would be falsified, and passing it, while it gives credence to the explanation, still leaves open the question of whether the explanation could pass a more precise test.

Chapter 6 provides this more precise test by switching the unit of analysis from the dyad to the MID. Here a given dispute is the focus of observation. Data are collected on the type of dispute—whether it is a dispute over territory, policy, or regime—whether the contending parties have outside alliances, whether they are rivals at the time of the MID, and whether there is an ongoing arms race. Each MID is broken up into its dyadic pairs (see below). Since the dyadic dispute (MID) is the unit of analysis, it is known that certain steps have been taken prior to the onset of a MID and hence prior to the onset of a war. It is also known how many MIDs have occurred between the two contenders before one emerges that escalates to war. When using the dyadic dispute as the unit of analysis, what is explained are the characteristics of the MID that make it escalate to war and how these differ from the characteristics of MIDs that do not go to war. This differs from the analysis in chapter 5, which compares how two states that have gone to war have interacted over their history (in a given period) compared to states that have never gone to war in a given period. Together the two chapters complement each other and provide a more comprehensive test in that we know something about the long-term interactions of states associated with war and the types of MIDs (or crises) that are apt to escalate to war. A theory of war that can explain and pass tests related to both of these units of analysis is a powerful and useful theory.

Up to this point in the book, the multivariate analyses will have treated the steps to war as if they are merely additive. The explanation, however, implies that there is a statistical interaction between some of the steps to war that would enhance the likelihood of war more than would be expected from just the added combination of steps. Chapter 7 examines whether certain combinations of steps reflect more multiplicative processes by including interaction

---

[8] For an alternative and more precise periodization, see Henehan and Vasquez (2006), which is based on Wallensteen (1984).

terms in the tests. The logic of the steps to war is utilized to determine which combinations are most apt to have multiplicative processes at work. Statistical interaction is expected mostly with territorial MIDs, next with rivalry, and least with arms races. Interactions are examined for three historical periods—1816–1945, 1946–89, 1990–2001. By comparing the results in this chapter with those in chapter 6, a determination is made as to when the steps to war are better seen as following an additive or multiplicative model. The analysis of interactions among the steps to war provides the most sophisticated tests of the explanation to date and is the capstone chapter of part III.

The specific propositions that will be derived and tested in the book are listed in the individual chapters. In general they look at the impact of the presence of one or more step on the risk that war will break out. The more steps, the greater the risk for war. This is the heart of the explanation and this is what will be tested in this book. Not all aspects of the explanation can be tested, however. In particular, we lack data on the dynamic aspects of the steps. As a result, our tests are static in that we look at dyads in a particular condition. Nevertheless, they are still valid tests because we assume that the underlying dynamic has placed the actors in this condition. Our tests can be seen as indirect, but from a philosophy-of-science point of view this is acceptable because the key thing is that if the predictions derived from the propositions are not upheld, then the explanation is falsified. At the same time, it must be recognized that in passing an indirect test, we are not attempting to make inferences about the underlying dynamics that put dyads in this condition. We now turn to a description of the data, measures, and statistical techniques we will use in the various tests that we conduct.

Data, Variables, Statistical Techniques

To test the steps-to-war explanation, we use the updated Militarized Interstate Dispute (MID 3.02) data of the Correlates of War project as our main data base for the dependent variable. These data go from 1816 through 2001. The MID data purport to record every instance of the threat or use of force between legally recognized nation-states.[9] For a disagreement between states to be considered a militarized dispute, at least one of the following events or confrontations must have occurred: (1) an explicit threat to resort to military force; (2) a mobilization, deployment, or other display of military force; or (3) an actual resort to military force. For these acts to be included, they "must be

---

[9] Gleditsch and Ward (1999) provide an alternative (and supplement) to the standard Correlate of War list of nation-state actors. These are not incorporated into the MID data, since the data collection pre-dates that article. It is not likely, however, that a broader list of dyads would change the outcome of the tests used in this or other analyses studying the escalation of MIDs to war.

explicit, overt, nonaccidental, and government sanctioned" (Gochman and Maoz, 1984: 586).

These data were collected over a long period of time, first beginning with doctoral dissertations at the University of Michigan under the direction of J. David Singer.[10] These data were then cleaned and updated under the direction of Stuart Bremer and released as MID 2.1 data going from 1816 through 1992 (see Jones, Bremer, and Singer, 1996). Most analyses of MIDs, including all of our previously published studies, have used the 2.1 version of the data. The MID 3.02 data have been updated through 2001 and also include some corrections and slight changes to the 1816–1992 data, as well as some new measures for the 1993–2001 period (see Ghosn, Palmer, and Bremer, 2004; Ghosn and Palmer, 2003).[11] All the data analyses in this book are updated by using the MID 3.02 data.

The MID data list all disputes and the characteristics they have, such as the names of all the participants, who is on which side, the beginning and end dates of the dispute, the level of hostility reached (including war), which participants are revisionist states, the type of revision (change in the status quo) they are trying to bring about, and so forth. Most scholars have not analyzed the disputes in this form, but have taken them and divided them into several disputes so as to produce a sample of *dyadic disputes*. This sample is derived by taking the 2,332 MIDs in the set for the entire 1816–2001 period and breaking them down into each pair of states in the dispute. This increases the number of cases to 3,511 dyadic disputes. Such a dyadic analysis is justifiable since each state involved in a dispute must decide for itself whether to escalate its involvement to the war stage, and therefore should be treated individually.[12] In addition, breaking up large disputes gives them more weight in the data analysis, which is not necessarily unwarranted; otherwise World War II would have the same weight as a simple tuna-boat chase.

All the data we employ in this book start with dyadic disputes, but we configure them in various ways so that we end up with three different *units of analysis*—dyadic disputes, dyad-year, and the dyad (or dyad-history). When employing dyadic disputes, each observation is a militarized dispute, and the research design compares those militarized disputes that go to war with those

---

[10] These include, among others, Gochman (1980) and Maoz (1982), as well as the earlier study by Wallace (1979).

[11] The new measures for the post-1992 period that affect our analysis incorporate the switch from coding MIDs into just one primary category for type of dispute—territorial, policy, or regime—to permitting them to have more than one code for revision type if appropriate; see the discussion of independent variables below.

[12] For a comparison of using just the disputes without breaking them into dyadic disputes, see Vasquez and Henehan's (2001: 127–31) analysis of the MID 2.1 data. The tests of their propositions generally produce the same outcomes on both the dispute and dyadic dispute samples.

that do not. Many scholars, however, want to know what a given dyad does in every year, so they generate an observation for every dyad for each year, hence the label—dyad-year. Thus, France and Germany will have observations for every year they are in existence recording when they have MIDs and when they do not. Such a data set can produce up to 500,000 observations. What is compared here is when dyads (regardless of proper names) in a given year go to war and when they do not. There are certain advantages in using such a research design, namely one compares dyads not only when they are in a MID, as with a dyadic dispute design, but also when they are not in a MID. In addition, if MID onset is the dependent variable, as it typically is in a two-stage analysis, the dyad-year is the conventional unit of analysis that is employed.

There are certain disadvantages to the dyad-year unit of analysis, however—all related to basically taking a couple of thousand MIDs and deriving from that 500,000, most of which involve the absence of any dispute. The disadvantage that concerns us the most is that MIDs between the same pair of states, especially when they are close in time, are probably not statistically independent observations. In addition, our theory includes the concept of rivalry, which explicitly posits a connection between MIDs. These are also problems with using the dyadic dispute as the unit of analysis, but they are greatly accentuated when expanding the data to the dyad-year as the unit of analysis. This problem has been recognized in the field and there are ways of controlling for temporal dependence either statistically, using the technique developed by Beck, Katz, and Tucker (1998), and/or by introducing the number of peace years between MIDs as a variable in the model.[13]

These modifications make the dyad-year usable, especially when there are few other options. Nevertheless, even with these corrections, we are wary of placing much emphasis on getting a significant chi-square using 500,000 cases. This is not a difficult test for a proposition to pass, even though some variables in a model fail it. The best one can say about this sort of test, is that if there is anything to a relationship, such a sample will find it. We believe the considerably smaller dyadic-dispute sample provides a more difficult test for propositions. The end result is that in part II, where we conduct a two-stage analysis and our dependent variable is the onset of a MID, we use the dyad-year as the unit of analysis. In part III, in chapters 6 and 7, where we focus solely on the characteristics of MIDs that put them at risk of going to war, we use the dyadic dispute as the unit of analysis.

[13] The other major problem with using the dyad-year as the unit of analysis is that when including all "peaceful" dyads without any MIDs, some of these are not so much free of conflict as they are free of contact with no opportunity to fight. One way of handling this problem is to look only at politically relevant dyads (see Lemke and Reed, 2001a; Maoz, 1996, 2004; Clark and Regan, 2003).

As mentioned before, dyadic disputes are not completely free from problems of temporal dependence, although they do not suffer from the problem of an inflated N (number of cases) the way a dyad-year sample does. To correct this problem we use "the dyad" as the unit of analysis in chapter 5. Here, each observation records the interactions of a pair of states (e.g., France and Germany): the data record, among other things, the number of MIDs; how many are over territory, policy, or regime questions; whether they have ever been enduring rivals, and so forth. Each observation provides a miniature history of the dyad's interactions. This sort of research design compares dyads that go to war to those that never have. The nature and pattern of the interactions between the two states is seen as the source of war. Employing these three separate units of analysis—dyad-year, dyadic disputes, and dyad-history—we believe, provides a more robust evidentiary base for the theory than using just one.

There are two versions of the MID data—the first, the MID 3.02 data released by the Correlates of War project and available on their website (http://cow2.la.psu.edu/), and the second, by Maoz, also available on the Correlates of War website, and at his own website (at http://psfaculty.ucdavis.edu/zmaoz/dyadmid.html). The latter is commonly referred to as the Maoz (MID) data. There are important differences between these two data sets. The two most significant differences for our purposes are that the Maoz data eliminates dyadic disputes that he believes never really engage in any militarized behavior with each other (including threats) but merely appear on two different sides. This is particularly problematic for World War II, where certain states are listed as being engaged in war with each other when in fact they are not fighting each other (e.g., the Netherlands and Italy). The second difference is that Maoz sometimes changes the code for revision type when he believes that is warranted. Those scholars who opt to use the Maoz data usually do so for the former reason.

Our position is that a good theory should be able to pass tests using either set of data, and we have employed both from time to time in our previous analyses. Here for the sake of efficiency we do the following: In part II, on territory and war, we use the MID 3.02 data in chapter 3, and the Maoz data in chapter 4. Since both these chapters deal with territory, they allow us to see if Maoz's shift of revision type codes or his deletion of certain cases will have any substantial impact on the outcome on propositions dealing with the propensity of territorial MIDs to escalate to war. As will be seen, both chapters produce results that are consistent. In part III, we employ several data sets in addition to the MID data that would make it time consuming to always use two MID data sets. We opt to use the standard (Correlates of War) MID 3.02 data, but we make adjustments to these data by removing superfluous dyadic disputes associated with World War II, so they are more in line with the Maoz data. This is by far the most important case accounting for the differences in the number of observations across the two data sets. We make the adjustment by a careful analysis of this case based on Valeriano and Vasquez (2005).[14] Through this procedure over twenty cases are eliminated.

Our *temporal domain* is the post-Napoleonic era from 1816 through the end of 2001. Except where we lack data for certain independent variables, we use this full period. In addition to examining the full time span, in some of the chapters we control for historical era by breaking down the full sample into three periods—the classic international politics era of 1816–1945, the Cold War 1946–89 nuclear era, and the post–Cold War period 1990–2001. We separate the periods before 1946 and after 1945 because it is widely believed that nuclear weapons brought about a new era. Now that we have lived through over sixty years of the nuclear era we can see that nuclear weapons have in fact raised the provocation threshold for total war. What would have provoked a war between major states in the pre-nuclear era, no longer does so (Lebow, 1981: 277). This conservatism on the part of nuclear states may have also led them to restrain their minor allies. In addition, the East-West alliance system may, because of the danger of escalation to the nuclear level, have actually limited mutual superpower intervention during the Cold War into ongoing wars, such as in the U.S. war in Vietnam (1965–75) and the Soviet invasion of Afghanistan (1979), rather than encourage the expansion of war as alliances had in the past. Given this line of reasoning, we think that the Cold War era is fundamentally different in important aspects from the more classic and longer 1816–1945 era. In particular, the power politics aspect (as opposed to the territorial aspect) of the steps-to-war explanation may find its more natural domain in the pre-nuclear era. Because of the impact of nuclear weapons, using just the full span is likely to produce misleading results and mask interesting differences across the subperiods.

We examine the post–Cold War, 1990–2001 period simply to see if the absence of a superpower conflict and rivalry makes this period more closely resemble the non-nuclear, 1816–1945 period, or the nuclear 1946–89 period. We have been somewhat torn over when to start the post–Cold War period. One could easily start it in 1992, since the Soviet Union collapses on December 31,

---

[14] Cases are purged by first going to the war data of the Correlates of War project (available at the Correlates of War2 website—http://cow2.la.psu.edu/; see Small and Singer (1982) for a published version); dyads that do not meet their threshold for participation in the war, typically because of insufficient troop commitments, are eliminated. Note a number of dyads in the MID data are purged for this reason. Of the remaining, those dyads that are either not in the Maoz data set or in Wright's (1965: appendix A, 1538–40) list of participants are purged. This rules means that those dyads that made the war data threshold could stay in only if they are listed in either the Maoz or the Wright.

1991. We have decided, however, to end the Cold War period in 1989, since that is the year of the fall of the Berlin Wall, which is often taken as the symbol of the end of the Cold War, and 1990 is frequently taken as the start of the post–Cold War period (see, e.g., *The World Almanac and Book of Facts, 2005*: 524–25). By 1990 it was clear that the Soviet Union and the United States were no longer "at war." George Herbert Walker Bush refers to the period as a "new world order," and the United States and Soviet Union exhibit a high degree of cooperation in 1990, especially in opposing the Iraqi invasion of Kuwait, which cannot be seen, in any manner, as a Cold War war. Instead, the United Nations operates as Franklin Delano Roosevelt envisioned with foreign ministers seated at the Security Council and each of the five permanent members acting in concert to decide questions of war and peace to maintain this new world order.

Our *dependent variable* typically is whether the current MID under contention or any other between the same two parties escalates to war within five years. While most studies utilizing MID data examine whether the dispute under question goes to war or not, the steps-to-war model sees the outbreak of war as a process, with the probability of war increasing as disputes recur. Specifically, it is hypothesized that as crises recur the dyad is more apt to be plunged into war. Because this is the case, it could be misleading to count disputes that do not immediately go to war, but do eventuate in war within a reasonable time frame, as evidence against the hypothesis.[15]

This can be seen by looking at a hypothetical case. Let us assume three dyads that each have exclusively territorial MIDs and only one war in a five-year period, with no disputes after that war. Let us assume further that Dyad A has four disputes, Dyad B has six disputes, and Dyad C has ten disputes. In this example, seventeen observations (3 + 5 + 9) would count against the hypothesis, and only three in favor. Yet in each dyad, the pattern of repeated territorial disputes, with one resulting in war, is correctly predicted by the hypothesis. This indicates that a research design that looks only at whether the current MID escalates to war is a misspecified test. It cannot be overemphasized that a properly specified test requires a window of opportunity; otherwise important patterns might be suppressed.

---

[15] Of the 3,511 dyadic dispute cases in the MID 3.02 data for the full 1816–2001 period, 320 MIDs escalate to war in the current MID, whereas our measure of going to war within five years has 568 escalating to war. This is an additional 248 cases out of 3,511 that count as going to war. However, if this were not done all these cases would count against the propositions, even though the dyads involved in them go to war in a relatively short period of time.

For the subperiods that we use in the analysis the differences are: 1816–1945, current MID to war = 233 out of 1,335 versus 390 with the five-year window; 1946–89, current MID to war = 69 out of 1567 versus 159 with the five-year window; 1990–2001 current MID to war = 18 out of 609 versus 19 with the five-year window. These increase the subperiod number of cases respectively by 157, 90, and 1.

This being said, in previous work we have used dependent variables with and without the five-year window, and the results show no important differences; see, for example, Senese and Vasquez (2003: appendix, 295–96) and Senese and Vasquez (2004: 202). Thus, for this analysis, unless otherwise stated, the results we report will be for whether the current dispute or any dispute within the next five years between the parties, escalates to war.[16] Nevertheless, to make sure there are no differences between using these two dependent variables with the updated data, we also employ in chapters 3, 4, and 7 the escalation of a MID to war without the five-year window.[17] While this conception of the dependent variable differs from the typical study using MID data, the use of a five-year window (or sometimes longer) has a long history in the field (see Organski and Kugler, 1980; Levy, 1981; Sample, 2002; Lemke, 2002).

The dependent variable in this analysis is whether the dyad has ever had a MID with the other party that has escalated to a *war between the two of them*. The latter is important to keep in mind because often dyadic analyses of MIDs use the "hostility level 5" code in these data (indicating that at least one side has gone to war in the dispute) (see Jones, Bremer, and Singer, 1996) as a way of operationalizing the dependent variable. One of the problems of doing this is that when MIDs are broken down into dyadic disputes some cases can be coded as going to war (since the dispute as a whole goes to war) when in fact not every party on the two sides of a dispute might enter the war. To avoid this problem the data used for the dependent variable in this analysis is constructed by comparing all "hostility level 5" MIDs with the interstate war data of the Correlates of War project and coding a case as a war between the two states only if they are listed as opposing belligerents in the war data.[18]

The four major *independent variables* in our tests will be the type of dispute, the type of politically relevant alliance, measures of rivalry involving the number of disputes, and whether there is an ongoing arms race. The best way

---

[16] The five-year rule is the year of current MID plus the next four. For those replicating the analysis, it is important to not just add five years to the start year because that would make for a six-year window. Also, note that the start date of the MID that goes to war is taken for the measure; the MID may often start before the year the war occurs.

[17] As will be seen in chapter 7, in some instances elimination of the five-year window strengthens certain findings.

[18] It should be noted that even if one corrects for the above problem by making sure both sides have a level 5 hostility score, as many scholars do, using the war data to determine if both sides are in a war produces fewer cases of war than the MID data. The reason for this is that the war data employ certain thresholds of involvement, such as troop commitments, to determine who are participants in a war, whereas the MID data do not. For alternatives to the war data of the Correlates of War project, see Gleditsch (2004). The most recent war data of the Correlates of War project may be found in Wayman, Sarkees, and Singer (2005); see also Sarkees (2000) and Sarkees, Wayman, and Singer (2003).

to determine whether territorial issues are more war prone than other types of issues is to have data that distinguish the different types of issues states fight over (see Diehl, 1992; Mansbach and Vasquez, 1981; Coplin, Mills, and O'Leary, 1973). There are no such data sets going back to 1816. However, the MID data do provide information on the *type of revision* in the status quo that states are trying to bring about by the threat or use of force, and these do provide useful data on territorial disputes. The MID data classify actors involved in militarized disputes in terms of revisionist and nonrevisionist states. The revision the former is trying to bring about by its resort to force is then classified in terms of whether a state is openly "(1) making claims to territory, (2) attempting to overthrow a regime or (3) declaring the intention not to abide by another state's policy" (Jones, 1993: 30; Jones, Bremer, Singer, 1996: 178). This revision-type variable allows us to compare the war proneness of territorial disputes to regime and policy disputes and thereby test one of the fundamental set of propositions in the steps-to-war explanation.

Examples of territorial disputes are those between France and Germany over Alsace-Lorraine, or Germany and Poland over Danzig. Policy disputes are the broadest category; these include the British seizing of Brazilian ships engaged in slave trading, as well as Britain and France's objection to Nassar's nationalization of the Suez Canal in 1956. Regime disputes are attempts to overthrow a given leader or administration; examples include the Allied intervention in Russia in 1918 and the war between North Vietnam and South Vietnam starting in 1965.

The MID data up through 1992 only code revision type in terms of the primary claim being made, which means coders are forced to make a decision as to what is the main claim when more than one may be present. It turns out, however, that sometimes coders of the MID 2.1 data did record a secondary revisionist claim, but these data were not released by Stuart Bremer, because he was not convinced that all coders systematically approached each MID with the possibility that more than one code could be applied.[19] Nevertheless, the presence of the 187 out of 2,034 disputes in the MID 2.1 data with two codes provides an opportunity to review how valid giving a single primary code to revision type is. An analysis of these double-coded disputes reported in Vasquez and Henehan (2001: 126, note 3) convinces us that the primary code does have face validity and that the coders are able, even in difficult cases, to distinguish between whether territorial, regime, or policy disputes are primary. We expect territorial disputes to be more war prone than policy or regime disputes.

After 1992, the MID 3.02 data can have up to two codes for revision type.

---

[19] Personal communication to John Vasquez from Stuart Bremer, 1995.

To manage these data we create two variables—"primary revision type," which look only at the primary code (which is comparable to the MID 2.1 data), and "ever territory," which looks at whether territory is present as either a primary or secondary revision. Initially, analyses were run with both variables, and the results were the same, but this was due to the fact that in our samples (after dropped cases and so forth), there are no cases where territory is a secondary code in the 1993–2001 period. For our purposes, we opted to use only the primary code.[20]

The revision-type variable also codes MIDs into a miscellaneous "other" category, as well as non-applicable (when no revisions are being sought). We report the findings on "other" disputes, but do not place great emphasis on them because they tend to mirror territorial disputes. This is not an accident. A previous analysis of these disputes in the MID 2.1 data reveals that although they are coded correctly, three of the four "other" disputes that go to war (out of the thirty-two disputes for which there are complete data for all variables in the analysis) have an underlying territorial element (see Vasquez and Henehan 2001, 127–33, especially footnotes 9 and 15 for a detailed discussion of these cases).[21]

Nonrevisionist states on opposing sides of a MID by definition do not have any revision type and hence their revision type is coded as "nonapplicable," and these are dropped from our analysis. Dropping these cases from the full 1816–2001 sample of 3,511 MIDs reduces that sample by 558 disputes. These cases often involve joiners to opposite sides in a MID, for example, the United States versus Spain, Hungary, and Romania in 1941, and Cuba versus Germany, Italy, and Japan in the same year. In our view, dyadic disputes that have a nonapplicable revision type do not really have an issue under contention and therefore should not be grouped with nonterritorial disputes as is sometimes done. Dropping these cases makes for a more rigorous and difficult test for our propositions.

The second independent variable we will examine is whether the disputants have outside *politically relevant alliances*. We compare MIDs according to whether the dyadic contenders (a) have no alliance ties with anyone, (b) are allied to each other and only in the same alliances, (c) have one side with an outside alliance, (d) have both sides with outside alliances, or (e) are allied to each other, but at least one side has an outside alliance that the other does

---

[20] The new coding scheme, however, would still be useful for comparing the war proneness of "ever having a regime dispute" or "ever having a policy dispute."

[21] The four wars are the Franco-Prussian War, the Football War between Honduras and El Salvador, the Spanish-Peruvian/Chilean War of 1866—all of which we see as having strong territorial elements—and the Lopez War, which we do not see as having a large territorial element before the start of the war.

not share. We expect dyads with outside alliances to be more likely to have a war than those that have no alliances.

For this variable, we generate a new measure based on the Correlates of War formal alliance data that determines for any given case whether the alliance ties of each disputant are politically relevant to any dispute that might occur between them. Simply put, an alliance with a major state is always relevant because it is assumed that a major state is able to project its capability beyond its own region.[22] An alliance with a minor state, however, is only seen as relevant if the alliance partner is in the same region as the "target" in the dyad, because it is assumed that an ally that is a minor state cannot easily project its capability beyond the region in which it is located and/or that it may not be inclined to do so. The only exception to this is when an alliance partner is in a different region, but contiguous by land to either side A or B in the dyad.[23] A minor state outside the region but contiguous by land presumably could still reach one of the parties to the dispute.

A hypothetical example may make this rule clearer: if the United States and Brazil are in a dispute and the United States has an alliance with Argentina, then that alliance is relevant, since Brazil (the "target" in the dyad) is in the same region as the United States' ally. If Brazil has an alliance with Portugal, this is not relevant, because Portugal is a minor state and is not in the same region as either Brazil or the United States. However, if Brazil had an alliance with the Soviet Union, the latter would be relevant because the Soviet Union is a major state. In order to make this determination, first side B is treated as the target and the relevant alliances for it are computed and then side A is treated as the target and its relevant alliances are computed. Regions are determined by the state membership list of the Correlates of War project with a couple of emendations to include some states in more than one region.[24]

More formally, an alliance is classified as politically relevant if any of the following conditions are met:

1. If the state in question is a minor state, then any alliance it has with a major state is relevant.
2. If the state in question is a minor state, then any alliance it has with another minor state is relevant, if that minor state is in the same region as

[22] Major and minor states are classified according to the conventional listing of major states by the Correlates of War Project (see majors2004.csv at http://cow2.la.psu.edu/; see also Small and Singer [1982: table 2.1, 47–50] and Ray [1998: 197–200]).

[23] The contiguity rule is new and hence makes this measure slightly different from the one by the same name, which we used with the MID 2.1 data in Senese and Vasquez (2004).

[24] The Ottoman Empire and Turkey are included in both Europe and the Middle East. Russia is included in both Europe and Asia.

the "target" in the dyad or contiguous by land to either side in the dyad in question. This has the effect of dropping those minor states as politically relevant allies if they are not contiguous or in the region of the target of the dyad, which might happen in a large multilateral alliance.

3. If the state in question is a major state, then any alliance it has with a major state is relevant.
4. If the state in question is a major state, then any alliance it has with a minor state is relevant only if that minor state is contiguous by land to one party in the dyad or in the same region as the target in the dyad.

Once the data on the politically relevant alliance measure were collected, each dyadic MID[25] was coded on the basis of:

(0) No [politically relevant] alliance in the dyad.
(1) Both states in the dyad are allied to each other and have no allies outside the alliances of which they are joint members, that is, they are all in the same alliances.
(2) One side has an outside alliance of which the other is not a member.
(3) Both sides have an outside alliance.
(4) Allied (and in the same alliances as each other), but also having a separate outside alliance of which the other is not a member (any combination of 1 and [2 or 3]).

Given the theoretical discussion in the previous chapter, it is predicted that states that are allied to each other, but have no outside allies independent of the other, should not pose a threat to each other, all other factors being equal, and therefore should have the lowest probability of war. Conversely, states that are not allied to each other should have a higher probability of war, all other factors being equal. On the basis of this assumption, dyads without a politically relevant alliance would be ranked second in their probability of going to war. For all the reasons outlined earlier, a considerably higher probability of war is assumed to occur if one side has an outside alliance. Lastly, if both sides have an outside politically relevant alliance, this is assumed to have the highest probability of going to war, because each side is threatened by the other.

Category four was originally included to make the classification mutually exclusive, in a manner that would distinguish states that were allied with each other from dyads that also had an outside ally that the other did not have. It was felt that states that fell into this category might be of a different sort than those that were allied only with states that had the very same allies as it did.

---

[25] We code dyadic MIDs in terms of their politically relevant alliances; however, the same rules could be used to code a dyad's politically relevant alliances whether or not they have MIDs.

States that also had an outside independent alliance might be states that were not really "friends" but foes that were using the practice of alliance making to control their rival (as in a *pacta de contrahendo*, see Schroeder, 1976: 230–31). Having an outside alliance while being allied to a state might be seen as hedging one's bet. Having developed this indicator, however, it was unclear on the basis of the theory where such dyads might rank in their probability of war. Obviously, it would be above two (those without outside allies), but how much above could not be logically derived.

The Correlates of War formal alliance data (version 3.03) (Gibler and Sarkees 2004) are used as a basis for calculating all our alliance measures. These data go from 1816 through 2000 and are based on earlier data collections by Singer and Small (1966), Small and Singer (1969), and Gibler (1999b). This permits us to have alliance data for all the years we have MID data except the last one, 2001. In order to capture the correct theoretical sequence posited by the explanation, a politically relevant alliance must precede a territorial dispute; otherwise it could not be seen as increasing the probability of war. Therefore, any alliances that came into effect after the first day of the MID are dropped from the analysis of the given MID. We also follow the Correlates of War convention of dropping any alliance formed three months prior to the outbreak of a war on the rationale that such alliances are more apt to be a product of the coming war than a possible cause of it. While not eliminating the problem of endogeneity (see chapter 1 above), it does help to manage one of its more severe forms.

Our third major independent variable refers to the extent to which states are engaged in a *rivalry*. We define *rivalry* as "a relationship characterized by extreme competition, and usually psychological hostility, in which the issue positions of contenders are governed primarily by their attitude toward each other rather than by the stakes at hand" (Vasquez, 1996a: 532). It is assumed that rivalry is brought about by persistent disagreement and conflict over salient issues, which usually means a series of militarized disputes. The repetition of disputes is a typical indicator of rivalry, and we use two indicators of rivalry, both based on the repetition of disputes.[26]

---

[26] It is possible, as Thompson (1995, 2001) maintains, that the psychological condition of rivalry may not result in a series of militarized disputes. Even if this is the case, we assume that dyads that have repeated disputes become rivals, so that any measurement error resulting from this indicator would be one of omission rather than of including nonrivals. In this analysis, we do not use a more perceptual measure of rivalry such as that of Thompson (2001). We are only just beginning to probe the impact of that measure on the steps to war. However, his work suggests that this purely perceptual measure is consistent with the thrust of the steps-to-war explanation outlined in chapter 1; see Colaresi and Thompson (2005); Rasler and Thompson, (2006); Colaresi, Raseler, and Thompson (2008).

The first measure we use is a categorical classification based on the work of Diehl and Goertz (2000: 45, 145–46) that classifies dyads as engaged in isolated conflict, a proto-rivalry, or an enduring rivalry depending on the number of MIDs they have with each other within a certain time span. Briefly, isolated conflict refers to dyads with one or two MIDs in their history, enduring rivalry to those dyads with six or more disputes within twenty years, and proto-rivalry as those dyads in between, as long as more than two MIDs occur within ten years (see Diehl and Goertz, 2000: 45, for details). The Diehl and Goertz idea of rivalry is based on the notion that after a certain threshold of MIDs is crossed the psychological condition associated with rivalry is locked in and does not really change much in terms of its impact on the probability of war.

Our second indicator is an integer variable that simply looks at the number of disputes that occur and assumes that the more disputes a dyad has before its current one, the greater the likelihood of war, ceteris paribus. To measure this we determine how many disputes have occurred previously between the same pair of states. We call this variable, number of prior MIDs, and we assume that as disputes recur a greater sense of rivalry emerges, resulting in a greater risk of war with each dispute that occurs. By operationalizing the concept as an integer variable, we can examine the precise effect of each additional dispute on the probability of war.

The idea that repeated disputes encourage the emergence of a dispute that will escalate to war is at the heart of the idea of rivalry. In that sense our measure of prior disputes can be seen as an indicator of the degree of rivalry. Treating it as an integer rather than a categorical variable assumes that crossing a particular behavioral threshold (especially six disputes and above) or perceptual threshold is not crucial and does not make for a marked change in a relationship at that specific number of disputes, but that rivalry emerges in a continuous pattern across disputes as hostility increases from one engagement to the next. An integer variable (and the concept of repeated disputes) sees each dispute as increasing the probability of war (see Leng, 1983), even after a particular threshold has been passed. For example, the tenth dyadic dispute is seen as more likely to go to war than the seventh.

Using repeated disputes as an indicator raises the question of whether just the repetition of territorial MIDs is driving the relationship between rivalry and war. In chapter 5 this hypothesis will be tested using a variable that simply counts the number of territorial disputes that occur between two states during their history. Measuring rivalry as an integer variable also raises the question of whether the marginal risk of war might decline after a certain point for dyads that have a large number of MIDs. This hypothesized curvilinear relationship will be tested in chapter 6.

Our fourth, and final, independent variable is the presence of an *arms race*. We use data collected by Susan Sample (2002) for both major and minor states. These data record arms races for each dyad in a MID based on the measure developed by Horn (1987), which essentially examines the increase in military expenditures of two states over time.[27] We employ Sample's categorical data to determine whether there is an ongoing arms race for each dyadic dispute.

We also utilized several other variables in the analysis, and these will be detailed in the specific chapters. Suffice it to say here that the two major independent variables used in the two-stage analyses conducted in chapters 3 and 4, respectively are *territorial claims* (taken from a data set collected by Huth [1996b] and Huth and Allee [2002: appendix A], which record all territorial disagreement between states from 1919 through 1995 regardless of whether they give rise to the threat or use of force)[28] and *contiguity* (a data set from the Correlates of War project [Stinnett et al., 2002] that records when two states are contiguous by land or sea from 1816 on). In addition, we employ several standard *control variables* (although not all in every analysis)—the level of democracy or regime type (from POLITY data, see Jaggers and Gurr [1995]), capability ratios, major state status, the level of economic development, and the number of peace years between MIDs. These control variables, unless otherwise indicated, are taken from the Correlates of War data files provided through EUGene (Bennett and Stam, 2000).

Since we are concerned with the probability of war, we have relied on standard maximum-likelihood techniques in our various tests. In our tests for selection bias in chapters 3 and 4, we conduct two stage-analyses utilizing probit estimation procedures (see Greene 2000: 926–37). In our multivariate tests in chapters 5–7, we utilize logistic regression (see Liao, 1994), since we have a binary dependent variable (no escalation to war/escalation to war). We should note that for convenience all our significance tests are reported as two tailed tests, but since almost all our propositions posit direction, one-tailed tests are perfectly acceptable, which means that the reported significance levels can be cut in half. This usually is not an issue, but when it is we make it

---

[27] We have, at times, also used her categorical data based on Diehl's (1983) measure of arms races. The Horn measure can be regarded as more conservative in that it identifies fewer arms races, but at the same time it shows a greater percentage of MIDs escalating to war than the Diehl. Both, however, produce statistically significant relationships between ongoing arms races and the escalation of MIDs to war within five years. We do not report results in this book using the Diehl measure; for a more detailed comparison of the two measures, see Sample (2000: notes 3, 7).

[28] Our labels differ from Huth's (1996b), who refers to his data as "territorial disputes." His data, however, include territorial disagreements that never become MIDs, so we call them territorial clams, and reserve the term "dispute" for MIDs.

clear that we are resorting to one-tailed tests. To get at the strength of the relationships we calculate predicted probabilities using CLARIFY, a software program (Tomz, Wittenberg, and King, 1999, 2003; King, Tomz, and Wittenberg, 2000) that runs simulations to calculate the predicted probabilities. We now turn to our first set of tests.

II

Territory and War

3

From Territorial Claims to Territorial Disputes: Testing for Selection Effects

What starts a militarized dispute may not be the same thing that makes it escalate to war.

Before territorial issues become militarized they need to be raised and put on the agenda. Territorial claims on a state usually lead to disagreement. Whether they become militarized and give rise to the threat or use of force (a MID) is an important threshold that if crossed increases the probability of war. The stages or phases of conflict from disagreement through war have received only limited research in international relations (Braithwaite and Palmer, 2003), although they have attracted theoretical attention for some time (Rummel, 1979; Bremer and Cusack, 1995; Cioffi-Revilla, 1998). The steps-to-war explanation focuses primarily on the stage of conflict once states are involved in a MID, with emphasis on what separates MIDs that escalate to war from those that do not (Bremer, 1992). In this chapter, however, we look at the prior stage of conflict—the onset of a MID in the first place and its effect (theoretically and empirically) on the likelihood of war.

One of the earliest criticisms made of the finding that territorial MIDs have a greater probability of going to war than other types of disputes is that the data analyses on which this finding is based fails to examine whether the factor(s) that get states into a MID in the first place are also the factor(s) that bring about war. Another way of making the same criticism is that a sample of states involved in MIDs is a nonrandom or biased sample and that before placing a great deal of emphasis on inferences from this sample it would be wise to consider the issue of selection effects.

Unfortunately, it is not always clear what factor(s) actually give rise to a MID that would also be responsible for the escalation of the MID to war. The steps-to-war explanation outlined in chapter 1 maintains that territorial MIDs have a greater probability of going to war than other types of disputes. It does not explicitly consider what factor(s) make states have a MID in the first place. In this chapter, we ask if the factors associated with the onset of conflict also have an impact on the escalation of conflict to war. One obvious factor that might have an impact on both stages is the presence of a territorial issue, that is, a claim on the territory of another state. States that have disagreements over who owns what pieces of territory might also be more likely to have a MID. A considerable amount of research in international relations focuses on the movement of lower-level conflicts across various increasingly intense thresholds to the point of war (see, for example, Bremer and Cusack, 1995). The research focusing specifically on the relationship between the onset of conflict and its escalation to war further underlines the importance of looking at process models of war since they make it easier to recognize in theories possible selection effects due to sampling bias (Huth, 1996b: 267–68; Smith, 1999; Reed, 2000; Lemke and Reed, 2001b; Braithwaite and Palmer, 2003; Rasler and Thompson, 2006).

We begin by constructing a new unified territorial explanation of conflict and war. This explanation broadens the scope of our previous work (Vasquez, 1993; Senese, 1996) and the analysis in chapter 1 by accounting for the influence of territory at the dispute onset stage. Here we seek to investigate the relationship between territorial claims and the effect they have on states' resorting to the threat or use of force and the subsequent likelihood of war. We use the unified explanation of conflict to specify the impact of territory on both dispute and war onset, while considering the potential role of sampling bias. Next, we discuss the problem of making inferences from a possible nonrandom sample, particularly as it relates to the Militarized Interstate Dispute data set. Third, we test this expanded territorial explanation against the empirical record from 1919 through 1995, specifically examining the possibility of sample selection bias. Finally, we conclude by reviewing the findings and discussing their relevance to furthering an understanding of interstate conflict onset and escalation to war.

A Territorial Explanation of Conflict and War

The question of selection bias focuses on the nonrandom sampling of cases for theoretical and empirical consideration. In international relations, this problem manifests itself in a variety of ways. One of the most prominent pertains to an examination of various stages in relations between nation-states. When looked at in isolation, each of these phases is neatly characterized by its own set of features. However, the presence of these particular traits may not be randomly assigned. Instead, some of the traits may be at least partially attributable to the sequence of relationship phases that have preceded the one being looked at presently. In this fashion, decisions or circumstances that have guided a set of relations in the past may have an important impact on the features associated with present and future dealings.

One way this might occur with territorial issues is by one state's making a claim on another state's territory and thus affecting the decision of a state's leaders to get involved in a MID. A logical extension of the steps-to-war explanation can be used to delineate when and what kinds of influences territory will have on the onset of disputes, as well as their escalation to war. Such a two-stage analysis would provide a comprehensive and precise explanation of the relationship between territorial claims, the rise of militarized disputes, and the escalation of territorial militarized disputes to war.

Table 3.1 portrays the possible effects territory might have in a two-stage analysis of dispute and war occurrence and how they might be consistent with, or falsify, the territorial explanation of conflict and war presented here. Testing such a two-stage model involves first examining whether the impact of territorial claims is positively or negatively related to the onset of a MID and then whether a territorial MID is positively or negatively related to the escalation of a MID to war, while accounting for the potential presence of selection bias in the second stage. Table 3.1 portrays four possible outcomes associated with the joint estimation of the effect of territorial claims on dispute onset and the presence of territorial disputes on escalation to war. When both models reveal a relationship in the same direction (cells *a* and *d*) there is no evidence of a sample selection bias, as it relates to the influence of territory across the two stages of conflictive intensity.[1]

The logic of the territorial explanation of conflict and war can be used to predict various effects, and these are presented as hypotheses just below the matrix in the table. The theoretical question posed by testing for selection effects is whether territory has a differential effect in terms of pushing states to enter a MID compared to pushing states to a war. The logic of the explanation maintains that territorial issues are very salient to leaders and followers, so much so that, all other factors being equal, they will be willing to incur costs and take risks on territorial questions that they would not on other matters—such as regime or policy issues.

According to the steps-to-war explanation, territorial issues, while they may increase the risk of war, will only go to war depending on how they are handled. Territory is an underlying cause in that it does not immediately pro-

---

[1] It is also possible to construct a 3 × 3 table that would include a null category that posits a random relationship at each of the stages. We presented such a model, along with more detailed discussion of the various possible hypotheses, in a previous paper (Senese and Vasquez, 2000). However, we have dropped the null category here, as it provided no additional empirical import.

Table 3.1

Theoretical Expectations Based on a Territorial Explanation of Conflict and War

		Territory Impact at the Escalation to War Step	
		Increase Prob War	Decrease Prob War
Territory Impact at the Dispute Onset Step	Increase Prob MID	Most Consistent a	Mixed Results b
	Decrease Prob MID	Mixed Results c	Exact Opposite d

a = Territorial claim increases the likelihood of a MID and a Territorial MID increases the likelihood of escalation to war.

b = Territorial claim increases the likelihood of a MID and a Territorial MID decreases the likelihood of escalation to war.

c = Territorial claim decreases the likelihood of a MID and a Territorial MID increases the likelihood of escalation to war.

d = Territorial claim decreases the likelihood of a MID and a Territorial MID decreases the likelihood of escalation to war.

duce war, but rather sets off a train of events that eventually results in war. The proximate causes are assumed to lie in a foreign policy that relies on the practices of power politics to resolve the territorial issue in one's favor. Such practices include the threat, display, and use of force; the making of alliances and building up of one's military to increase power; and the escalation of realpolitik tactics within and across crises to compel an opponent. Each of these practices, including the initial resort to a threat or use of force (as recorded in the onset of a MID), increases the probability of war. Without a resort to this minimal level of coercive diplomacy, power politics is not really being used. Put another way, what greatly increases the probability of war is not the presence of a territorial disagreement in terms of one or both sides having conflicting territorial claims, but the resort to a threat or use of force to back up those claims.

One reason territory becomes politically salient is that leaders may use territorial issues to ride to power, but these issues also are highly susceptible to creating their own domestic hard-line constituencies, so leaders could find themselves being pushed to take increasingly hard-line actions until the issue is resolved in favor of the state (see Huth, 1996b; Roy, 1997).[2] Such a logic is consistent with existing evidence that territorial MIDs are more prone to fatalities (Senese, 1996) and to war (Hensel, 1996; Vasquez and Henehan, 2001; Vasquez, 2001) than other types of MIDs. Given these findings, it is plausible to expect that leaders who do engage in a territorial MID are going to be less

---

[2] For a general analysis of the role of domestic contention or audience costs in democracies and their impact on conflict see Schultz (1999, 2001); see also Braumoeller (2004: 812–15).

hesitant and less able to resist escalation to war, compared to leaders who initiate a nonterritorial MID, who will be more willing *and* able to "bail out" if pursuing the dispute seems too costly.

In a two-stage analysis, we expect to find that the major impact of territory on war will come not from the mere making of a territorial claim (at the first or dispute onset stage), but instead from the resort to the threat or use of force and the initiation of a territorial militarized interstate dispute (at the second stage). Nevertheless, we do believe that territorial claims are sufficiently salient that they have the potential to sour relations between states, so that these states have an increased probability of ending up in a MID (whether over territory or not) compared to states that have no territorial disagreement with each other. Thus, our main expectations with regard to dispute onset and escalation to war are that territorial claims increase the likelihood of a MID and territorial MIDs increase the probability of war.

While the initiation of a territorial MID increases the probability of war, it would be a mistake to think that this results immediately in war. War is a highly costly and uncertain venture. It can be assumed that states do not resort to war unless less costly means for gaining their way fail. Therefore, it is reasonable to expect that the first MID would not necessarily escalate to war. However, given that territorial disputes usually become a domestic political issue in both sides, it is unlikely that the use of force without many fatalities would result in one side giving in. The end result is that territorial MIDs will recur (Hensel, 1994), that the conflict will fester, and that eventually a crisis between states disputing territory will come along that escalates to war. Given highly salient stakes, war eventually occurs because actors are apt to increase escalation across crises.

The onset of war in this explanation is seen as a process whereby leaders learn to go to war on the basis of failed past attempts to get what they want. The territorial explanation of conflict and war sees the outbreak of war as a process in which an initial crisis or militarized dispute creates a certain level of hostility that is insufficient to result in war, especially among prudent and powerful actors, like the major states. As disputes repeat, leaders learn from their previous interactions with their opponent that war is the best, or perhaps the only, way of handling the situation facing them. For this reason, it would be expected that as disputes recur, they have a greater probability of going to war.

While the number of disputes it will take to bring about war cannot be known precisely, it can be predicted that once a territorial MID occurs, it will set off a train of events—including the repetition of territorial MIDs and progressive escalation across disputes—that increases the risk of war. Here, as in the other chapters, a five-year window of opportunity for war to occur is provided in order to place a reasonable limit on this process so that it is amenable to empirical testing. Although any single number can be seen as arbitrary (why five and not four?), five years is neither so short that war need occur in one or two years, nor so long that the question of nonfalsifiability need be raised.

On the basis of this discussion, we would expect that the effect of territory is positive at both the onset and escalation-to-war stages. This is the situation in cell *a* of table 3.1, which portrays the various logical possibilities in terms of hypothetical predictions and possible findings:

> *Proposition (a)*: A dyad with an outstanding territorial claim is more likely to engage in a MID than a dyad with no outstanding territorial claim and, once engaged in a MID, those characterized by a territorial dispute are more likely to escalate to war (within five years) than MIDs over policy or regime questions.

The exact opposite of what the explanation would expect is found in cell *d*. A finding consistent with this cell would mean that territorial claims are not only less likely to give rise to a MID, but also that territorial MIDs, once they arise, have a lower probability of going to war than any of the nonterritorial MIDs. Such an outcome would warrant a rejection of proposition (a) and the territorial explanation of conflict and war presented here.

Cells *b* and *c* illustrate mixed results. A finding in cell *b* is mixed, in that the anticipated positive effect between territorial claims and the resort to a MID is supported, but the predicted second-stage effect, namely that territorial MIDs have a higher likelihood of going to war, does not receive support. Such a finding would call for considerable reformulation of the territorial explanation of conflict and war, and would limit the bellicose impact of territory to the conflict onset stage.

Cell *c* also portrays mixed results, although these are less damaging to the territorial explanation of conflict and war. A finding that fell into this cell would mean that a dyad with an outstanding territorial claim is less likely to engage in a MID, but once engaged in a territorial MID is more apt to go to war than those involved in regime or policy MIDs. In other words, states with territorial issues would not be likely to have a war (because territorial claims do not often result in MIDs), but if they initiated a territorial MID, then the probability of war would increase sharply. A finding consistent with cell *c* would require the territorial explanation of conflict and war to explain why leaders would be less likely to press their territorial claims by the threat or use of force in the first place.

If the data analysis produced mixed results, a rejection of the original formulation of the steps-to-war explanation in chapter 1 would be required, but not an abandonment of the idea that territory is a key variable, since territory would be considered important in at least one of the stages (conflict in cell *b* and war in cell *c*). The logic of the territorial explanation of conflict and war could be used to explain why these two disparate outcomes might occur. If we assume not only that territory pushes collectivities (leaders and followers) toward conflict and war, but also that leaders (and their followers) can learn from this pattern to change their behavior, then it is possible to explain why there might be mixed results for some or a large number of dyads. It can be assumed that in the presence of a persistent pattern (e.g., stronger states winning over weaker ones), leaders learn and incorporate this knowledge into their strategic calculus. If leaders learn patterns of behavior and change their behavior based on those lessons, as some critics of "positivist" social science argue (see Winch, 1965), we might expect the kinds of mixed results depicted in cells *b* and *c* of table 3.1.

Thus, an outcome in cell *b* might be explained by arguing that contenders on territorial issues realize from history that territorial MIDs are war prone, and therefore if they become involved in them, the risk of war has just gone way up. This could make them very cautious once a MID erupts and make them think twice before engaging in further escalation. Conversely, an outcome in cell *c* might indicate that leaders learn from history that territorial MIDs are very war prone and therefore they become much more hesitant to initiate any MID, territorial or not. If they cannot avoid a territorial MID, then the normal pattern takes over. We must emphasize, however, that the unified territorial explanation of conflict and war, which we are testing here, does not predict this sort of learning in the absence of much knowledge about the role of territory in conflict and war.

The above discussion uses the logic of the theoretical explanation to predict outcomes, at the two stages of escalation. The analysis permits an examination of alternate theoretical formulations and shows how the logic of the original theory can or cannot account for the outcomes in the various cells. It should also be pointed out that these theoretical explanations were constructed (and presented in Senese and Vasquez, 2000) before any probing of the data, so it is not a result of an inductive or "curve-fitting" analysis of empirical findings.

Before turning to how the above hypotheses can be tested, one final theoretical point must be clarified and emphasized: The territorial explanation of conflict and war maintains that while territorial MIDs increase the probability of war, they are not a sufficient condition of war. Indeed, most individual territorial MIDs do not escalate to war. The effect of territorial MIDs on war can be thought of as similar to the effect of cigarette smoking on getting lung cancer—it increases the probability of getting cancer, but is far from sufficient for getting that disease. Indeed, many territorial claims, in the right context—such as the presence of an arbitration procedure—can be settled without escalating to a MID or going to war (see Simmons, 1998, 1999).

Selection Effects and the MID Data Set

One of the reasons we have been drawn to developing a unified explanation of dispute onset and escalation to war derives from criticism directed at the MID data set. The most extreme form of this criticism holds that valid inferences cannot be made about the probability of war by comparing MIDs that go to war with those that do not without controlling for possible sampling bias. One conceivable problem with analyses utilizing MID data is that they only record actual militarized episodes of conflict, while not including political conflict at levels below that of a threat to use military force. The problem specifically is that the variables that may affect the onset of the dispute in the first place may also affect whether it escalates to war, and a number of studies provide a compelling theoretical logic for the importance of a proper consideration of selection effects in models of conflict dynamics (Levy, 1989b; Morrow, 1989; Bueno de Mesquita, 1996: 61–63; Gartner and Siverson, 1996; Huth, 1996b; Siverson, 1996). In the area of dispute onset and escalation, a developing line of work suggests the importance of considering decisions made at each stage of increasingly hostile state interactions (Bueno de Mesquita and Lalman, 1992; Fearon, 1994; Smith, 1999). In terms of our theoretical analysis, attempts to change the territorial status quo could have two impacts on escalation: one directly after the dispute has begun, and one indirectly through the process whereby the territorial claim occurs in the first place. If one examines only the direct effect, inferences about the impact of territorial disputes on escalation to war may not tell the entire story, since the indirect effect is not observed through inclusion in the statistical model. One might see this as a potential selection bias leading to an incorrect inference.

This suggests the need to take potential sample-selection effects into consideration. One of the earliest treatments in political science of sample-selection bias is presented by Achen (1986), who describes the theoretical rationale for considering the importance of sample selection, in addition to providing an extensive discussion of the various pros and cons attached to feasible statistical estimation options.

Reed (2000) follows this general line of reasoning in his discussion of the merits of statistically modeling the impact of selection effects. He argues that the factors that affect the onset of a MID need to be taken into account when modeling the factors that affect the escalation of a MID to war. Comparing only MIDs that go to war with those that do not fails to examine the indirect effect of independent variables on conflict escalation through their direct effect on dispute onset (Reed, 2000: 91). Reed, therefore, argues for the need to test a unified model of conflict onset and escalation to war. His empirical tests, examining the influence of joint democracy and status quo satisfaction on the onset and escalation (to war) of interstate conflict, reveal disparate effects for the independent variables across the two dependent variable thresholds. Reed's use of a bivariate probit model, capable of assessing and incorporating the impact of selection effects, allows him to discover interesting empirical patterns. His analysis of the indirect and direct effects of joint democracy is particularly important for "the democratic peace." He finds that joint democracy reduces the likelihood of a MID, but has no (statistical) effect on whether a MID will escalate to war (Reed, 2000: 91). This latter result is in line with findings reported by Senese (1997) using single-stage estimation techniques. However, Reed's use of a two-stage method allows him to provide an empirical explanation for Senese's initially surprising results—namely that the rarity of war between democracies is largely due to the paucity of jointly democratic MIDs in the first place. Without examining the indirect and direct effects of joint democracy and testing for selection effects, such a finding would not be uncovered. Thus, testing for selection effects is important not only for methodological reasons, but also because it can enrich our empirical knowledge and theoretical understanding.[3]

Huth (1996b: 137–38, 267–68), in his analysis of the role played by territorial claims on conflict, includes in his tests a consideration of selection effects. Huth (1996b) was the first to recognize that research on territory and war needed to test for the effect of lower-level territorial disagreements on militarized dispute onset, along with the influence of territorial militarized disputes on war onset. Our analysis builds on his work, but instead of using his modified realist explanation to derive theoretical expectations about the dynamics of dispute onset (at the first stage), we use the logic of the nonrealist territorial explanation of war (Vasquez, 1993) to construct an expanded unified explanation of conflict and war.

---

[3] Of course, one of the fundamental rules of inquiry is that one should only make inferences outside of the population sampled with great hesitation. However, statistical inferences derived from analyses focused exclusively on a nonrandom sample are potentially biased and inaccurate (Achen, 1986; Greene, 2000: 926–37). Through the proper statistical consideration of potential sampling bias, we can substantially increase our confidence in the accuracy of our empirical results.

Research Design

While we are interested in the methodological issue of selection effects in interstate dispute data, we are also concerned with the theoretical question of how the emergence of territorial claims affects the probability of a MID arising and of a territorial MID eventually escalating to war. Consequently, we will justify our research design in light of both these concerns.

Modeling Potential Sample Selection Bias
through a Two-Step Estimation Procedure

The need for a two-stage estimation procedure stems from the presence of unobserved (and observed) explanatory factors that may influence actors' choices at more than one point in a multistep process. These unobserved factors are statistically subsumed within the error term in single-step models. For instance, if one chose to statistically model the effect of foul weather on the propensity of states to engage in militarized disputes, a standard specification would list weather type as the independent variable, and dispute as the dependent variable. Such a model specification would estimate the impact of weather on dispute propensities, while relegating the unobserved influences of all other explanatory components (e.g., territory and power status) to the error term. Thus, the effects of territory and power status would, since they are left unspecified in the statistical model (thereby creating an underspecified model), be subsumed within the error term. Now if, on the other hand, one decided to examine the influence of foul weather on pushing states from lower-level disputes to war, the single equation specification would list weather type as the independent variable, with war occurrence as the dependent variable. Again, this model would be underspecified due to the exclusion of such potentially integral explanatory factors as territory or power status. In addition to being underspecified, this second model could also be misspecified if the unspecified influences of the unobserved explanatory factors have meaningful, yet unobserved, effects in the first model. Statistically, this would be true if the error terms in the two models are correlated to a significant degree. The presence of correlated error terms may lead to biased coefficient estimates in the outcome (second-stage) equation (Heckman, 1979; Achen, 1986; Greene, 2000: 926–37). Theoretically, this would be true if territory or power status had a significant, but unspecified, impact at both the dispute- and war-onset points.

While it would be fairly easy to add independent variables for territory or status into our statistical models, there are often other meaningful explanatory factors whose influence cannot be explicitly modeled. Resolve and risk propensity are two examples of variables frequently left unobserved (see Morrow, 1989). A two-step estimation procedure allows us to assess how the unobserved (and omitted) variables that affect dispute onset also affect their eventual escalation to war. It does this by directly estimating the statistical connection, ρ (rho), between the two error terms. In the analyses below, we utilize a maximum-likelihood probit estimation procedure that accounts for selection and, thus, the potentially linked nature of dispute and war occurrence. In explicitly estimating this statistical connection, we can severely reduce the possibility of faulty conclusions that may come about if the two conflict phases are connected, but modeled as if they are not.[4]

Testing a Territorial Explanation of Conflict

Given that the first step in the analysis will examine the effect that the presence of territorial issues has on the probability that states might threaten or use force on these issues, it is necessary to compare dyads with territorial disagreements (claims) to dyads that do not contend over these issues. The most systematic manner in which to proceed is to begin with a data set of all possible dyads for each year within our temporal domain. Next, it is necessary to obtain data on territorial issues so as to distinguish dyads with such claims from those without them. This test will be called the "all dyad-year test" and will be our main test. The unit of analysis in all tests in this chapter is the dyad-year.

Such an analysis compares all dyads for all years in which a state was a recognized member in the system in terms of the effect of (a) the presence of territorial issues (claims) on the onset of a MID and (b) the presence of a territorial MID on the probability that war will eventually break out between these two states. Theoretically, such a test permits us to examine whether states that make territorial claims are more likely to resort to the threat, display, or use of force than states that do not make such claims, and whether states that have territorial MIDs have a greater probability of going to war than states engaging in nonterritorial MIDs. A number of questions need to be addressed, however, in constructing a research design that allows for the joint estimation of MID and war occurrence, while also accounting for the potential presence of sample selection effects.

The first problem is that of data availability. There have not been, until recently, any long-term data on conflict short of militarized disputes or crises

---

[4] We also considered using a newly developed method designed for analyzing strategic interaction models (Signorino, 1999, 2002), but ultimately decided that our theoretical explanation, as well as the data available, was more appropriately tested using a two-step estimation procedure; see Senese and Vasquez (2003: 283) for a more detailed discussion.

that cover a significant temporal span. Most data of this sort have been event data, like COPDAB (Azar, 1980) (see also Schrodt and Gerner, 1994; and Gerner et al., 1994). These data do not go back before World War II and have been criticized for not providing adequate coverage of all "Third World" states, although such data are better than "no data," if used in a sophisticated manner. One source that does exist and can be made compatible with the MID data set is Paul Huth's Territorial Dispute data, which have been extended back to 1919 (see Huth and Allee, 2002).

Huth's data record all territorial claims between recognized states whether or not they give rise to the threat, display, or use of militarized force. Huth (1996b: 19) defines a territorial dispute as either a disagreement over "where their common homeland or colonial borders should be fixed, or . . . contesting the right of another country even to exercise sovereignty over some . . . of its homeland or colonial territory." A territorial disagreement, then, involves one state not accepting a boundary, claiming a piece of territory, or occupying it and refusing to relinquish control (Huth, 1996b: 20–21). To establish such disagreement, Huth (1996b: 23) relies on written documents or public and official statements by state leaders in which they question the location of a border, call for revisions of the border, or contest the right of a state to exercise sovereignty over a piece of territory. He also provides explicit rules for determining when a territorial disagreement comes to an end and for excluding certain types of disputes, such as maritime episodes (Huth, 1996b: 23–26).

Huth (1996b:195–96) comprehensively searches numerous sources to compile a complete list of all territorial disagreements between 1950 and 1990, and these same procedures are followed in the extension of the data in Huth and Allee (2002) to cover the 1919–95 time span.[5] In addition, the potential cases that might be a subject of debate and why they are excluded or included are discussed. A variety of information on each case is recorded, including the duration of the dispute, a description of the territory over which there are competing claims, whether it ever produces a militarized confrontation, whether the territory is strategically located or economically valuable, and two indicators of whether ethnic questions are involved. Huth's data are primarily useful for comparing how conflict prone these three types of territorial disputes are vis-à-vis each other. Because these data are confined to only territorial disputes, they do not provide a basis for assessing whether territorial issues, as a class, are more conflict prone than nonterritorial disputes.

---

[5] See Huth and Allee (2002) for a discussion of the data for the 1919–49 and 1991–95 periods. Our thanks to them for permitting us to use their data early on.

For our purposes, the data are of interest primarily for determining whether and when a given state in a dyad has a territorial disagreement with the other side. We use his data to create a simple dichotomous variable whereby we are able to distinguish the years that dyads have a territorial claim from the years the dyads do not. Huth's data permit scholars to analyze whether certain factors associated with the onset of a MID are also associated with its possible escalation to war. His data provide a basis for seeing whether there is an important selection effect between territorial claims and the population of cases recorded in the MID data set.

Huth (1996b) has already conducted tests designed to assess the existence and feasible influence of selection effects, for the 1950–90 time period. Since he records whether a state has a territorial claim and whether that claim escalates (in terms of diplomatic disagreement, political pressure, and conflict), Huth can test for selection effects within his own data. He does find such a selection effect operating for the 1950–90 period and discusses its meaning (Huth, 1996b: 137–38, 267–68). Our analyses differ from his in that we will be using his data on territorial claims to see whether there is a selection effect within the MID data with regard to territorial issues. Such a test has never been conducted.

It is important that it be conducted because all the analyses in the literature that have found that territorial MIDs are generally more prone to war than nonterritorial MIDs are based on MID data (Hensel, 1996; Senese, 1996; Vasquez and Henehan, 2001). Huth (1996a, 1996b), because he does not have data on explicit disputes over nonterritorial questions, never compares the propensity of territorial disputes to escalate to war with the propensity of other types of disputes to escalate to war; rather, he is more concerned with comparing different types of territorial disputes (such as strategic territory, economically valuable territory, and territory related to ethnic concerns) with each other. Criticism of the existing findings—that territorial MIDs are more war prone than nonterritorial disputes—rests on the assumption that the MID set itself may represent a nonrandom sample, and, as such, the finding may be a result of a selection effect. Our analysis explicitly tests this criticism of the findings and the MID data set, in addition to testing relevant propositions in the unified territorial explanation of conflict and war. It should also be noted that our test of selection effects differs from Huth's (1996b) in that he uses a random sample of dyads without territorial claims to run his tests, whereas we look at the entire population of dyad years. Lastly, Huth's release to us of his extended data permits an expansion of the temporal domain to include the entire 1919–95 time span.

A second problem in constructing the research design is that the theoretical explanation does not simply posit that a state with a territorial claim will have an increased probability of having a MID and, if a territorial MID occurs, an increased probability of going to war. The territorial explanation is more precise than that model. It maintains that while states having territorial claims are more apt to have a MID, a MID is most likely to escalate to war if the militarized dispute repeats. In terms of a research design, therefore, it is not a fair test to predict that a dyad-year in which a territorial MID is present is going to result in that particular MID escalating to war. War, especially among major states, is often preceded by more than one crisis (see Leng, 1983; Vasquez, 1993:186–87, 316; Colaresi and Thompson, 2002). In order to take account of this, as discussed in chapter 2, our test provides a five-year window of opportunity for war to occur after a MID appears. Thus, states that have competing territorial claims are more apt to engage in MIDs, and states that engage in territorial MIDs are more apt to go to war within five years compared to states not possessing these characteristics. Nevertheless, as a check on the consistency of findings across alternative dependent-variable specifications, we also conduct analyses that look specifically at whether or not an individual MID escalates to war (with no five-year window), which will be reported in the appendix to this chapter.

A potential problem with looking at all dyads is that when comparing states with territorial issues to those without territorial issues, the category of "without territorial issues (or claims)" consists of two distinct types of dyads—those that have no outstanding issues between them and those that have specific nonterritorial issues that divide them. In order words, the nonterritorial category consists of dyads with some level of political conflict, along with dyads that are comparatively conflict free. Using a conflict-free sample may not be as difficult a test for the territorial explanation to pass as using a sample confined to states that are known to have outstanding nonterritorial issues. The problem with using the latter sample is that there are no data. In such a circumstance, it may be possible to provide an estimate of which dyads are conflict free and which might have some nonterritorial conflict. One way to do this is to make the assumption that states that have very limited opportunity to press claims may have a reduced tendency to disagree about any issues. The concept of politically relevant dyads is based on this notion that some pairs of states simply have a greater opportunity for war than do others (see Most and Starr, 1989; Maoz and Russett, 1993). Politically relevant dyads are defined as those that are contiguous (including within 150 miles by sea) or have one major state (see Lemke and Reed, 2001a). We perform additional analyses confined only to politically relevant dyads to help us eliminate those cases that are most apt to be conflict free.

Operationalization and Measurement

Our full set consists of 498,854 dyad years from 1919 through 1995.[6] Dispute onset observations are taken from the Correlates of War Project's MID data set (version 2.1) for 1919–92 and from the MID 3.02 data for 1993–95. War onset observances are drawn from the Project's interstate war set (see Sarkees, 2000; Sarkees, Wayman, and Singer, 2003).[7] For our first stage-dependent variable, we code dyads as having a dispute onset when a MID begins in a year. Our core dependent variable at the second stage considers a dispute dyad as escalating if that particular MID advances to war or if the pair engages in a war within five years (while our secondary dependent variable at this stage (results in appendix) measures only whether the current individual MID escalates to war). There are 1835 dyadic MID onsets across the 498,854 dyad-years in our full set. Fully 312 (17%) of these 1835 MIDs are followed by war within five years.[8] Our two key dependent variables are dichotomous indicators coded as one when a MID or war occurs, and zero otherwise.

There are two core independent variables, the first of which is the territorial-claim variable derived from Huth (1996b), and Huth and Allee (2002). Huth's (1996b) data provide information on territorial claims that is independent of MID occurrence and therefore permit an examination of selection effects. The claim variable is coded as one when two states engage in conflict over disputed territory (see Huth, 1996b, especially chapters 2, 5, and appendix A, for a more complete description). He then has additional data on distinguishing claims that escalate from those that do not, but we are not utilizing that variable. Among the 498,854 observations in our full set, 4,407 (0.9%) are characterized by the presence of a competing claim to territory.

The second key independent variable is what type of MID is under contention in terms of whether it is over territory, policy, or a regime question (or some miscellaneous "other" question). These are a set of four dummy variables derived from the revision type variable in the MID data, which was described in chapter 2. Suffice it to say here that revision type refers to the kind of change in the status quo that the revisionist actor in a dispute is trying to bring about (see Jones, Bremer, and Singer, 1996). As in all our data analyses of this variable, cases that do not have any revision type coded because such a code is "nonapplicable" are dropped. These are typically dyadic disputes in-

---

[6] Data for the final three years were obtained through the EUGene (version 3.04) software program (Bennett and Stam, 2000). These additional three years of data (encompassing 51,925 dyad-year observations) distinguish this analysis from that presented in Senese and Vasquez (2003).

[7] The war data and all of the individual Correlates of War sets utilized here are available at http://correlatesofwar.org, which also has the coding rules.

[8] Among these 312 war observations, 196 stem from the original MID and the remaining 116 follow within five years.

volving exclusively joiners. Since our purpose here is to differentiate territorial from nonterritorial disputes, we designate the cases characterized by a territorial revision attempt as the reference category and create separate dummy indicators for the other three dispute types (coded as one when the condition is present, and zero otherwise). Among the 1835 dyadic MIDs in our full set, 728 (40%) comprise territorial, 870 (47%) policy, 193 (11%) regime, and 44 (2%) other disputes.

While we are concerned primarily with the effects of dyadic territorial claims, MID revision types, and potential sampling bias in this study, we do introduce five control factors to see whether the relationships expected in Proposition (a) hold while controlling for the potential influences of dyadic power status, contiguity, domestic governing structure, mutual alliances, and economic development. Each of these controls is fairly standard, and we include them here as a control for possible overlap with our revision-type dummy variables. We anticipate that such controls will not change the test results found for the base model. A very brief description of these controls will suffice for the purposes of this study.[9]

The status of actors is operationalized based on the list of major states in the Correlates of War Project (http://cow2.la.psu.edu). We include two dummy variables that allow us to distinguish among jointly major, jointly minor, and mixed-status dyads. Data on contiguity are also taken from the Correlates of War listing (Stinnett et al., 2002). We have considered states that are adjacent or separated by 150 or fewer miles of water as contiguous; all others are treated as noncontiguous. Our democracy measure, adopted from Jaggers and Gurr (1995), is constructed as the difference between the Polity III democracy and autocracy indices (i.e., democracy *minus* autocracy). To parsimoniously represent this joint democracy effect we rely on what has been termed the "weak link principle" by assuming that the norms and expectations most likely to promote or discourage dispute onset and escalation are those of the *less* democratic party to the conflict (Dixon, 1993; Senese, 1999; Russett and Oneal, 2001; Senese and Quackenbush, 2003). In order to distinguish disputants that are allied from those that are not, we use the alliance data in EU-Gene, which are based on the Correlates of War formal alliance data (Small and Singer, 1969; Gibler and Sarkees, 2004). The separation of alliances into the categories of mutual defense pacts, neutrality agreements, and ententes is not utilized. Instead, all three are gathered into a general alliance category.[10]

[9] The introduction of controls makes the use of a politically relevant sample less pressing, since we control for status and contiguity. Therefore, the tests on the politically relevant sample will be discussed primarily in the footnotes.

[10] Bremer (1992) finds evidence suggesting that the type of alliance characterizing a dyad has some importance, but the major effect of dyadic alliances on dyadic conflicts can be captured by a

This coding decision accurately captures whether or not pairs of states have committed to mutual agreements with one another. The alliance term codes each dyad year as 1 when the parties are allied to each other, 0 otherwise. We measure economic development using logged energy production per capita taken from the Correlates of War capabilities data base (Singer, 1987).[11] In line with our democracy indicator, we introduce the minimum of the two development measures into the equation. Finally, because there may be temporal dependence in any dyad-year analysis (such as that in the first stage of our analyses), we test and control for this by using the cubic spline technique developed by Beck, Katz, and Tucker (1998).

Findings and Interpretation

Since, in addition to testing the unified territorial explanation of conflict and war, we are interested in unearthing the possible presence of sample selection bias, we begin with a single-stage probit analysis. This model is estimated without consideration of a possible correlation of unobserved explanatory factors across the two levels of conflict onset: MID and war occurrence. By presenting these findings first, we allow for comparison with the two-stage estimation discussed subsequently. Also, we begin with a base model specification, followed by a model that accounts for the various controls. The test results reported in the text are for the population of all dyads, with results for other samples reported in the notes.

The first column in table 3.2 depicts the effect of having a policy, regime, or other (revision-type) MID on the probability of a pair of states going to war within five years. These estimates are in direct comparison with the reference category—territorial MIDs. Since territorial MIDs is the reference category, if they are positively related to war (as hypothesized), then the policy and regime variables (listed in the table) will appear as negatively related to war. The findings show that the policy and regime MID estimates are indeed negative and statistically significant (in bold) at the $p < .001$ level, indicating that militarized disputes fought over policy or regime revisionist goals are significantly less likely to lead to war than those fought over territory, and that therefore territorial disputes are more war prone than policy or regime dis-

---

simple allied–not allied dichotomy. This alliance variable is the standard one used for controls and is different from the politically relevant alliance variables discussed in chapter 2, which we use in part III of the book.

[11] For treatments of the importance of economic development in conflict studies, see Mousseau (2000) and Russett and Oneal (2001).

Table 3.2.
Effect of Territory on Dispute and War Onset (within five years), 1919–95
(Probit Estimates)

Variables in Model	Base Model		Model w/Controls	
	War Onset	Joint Model	War Onset	Joint Model
Y₁: MID Onset				
MID Constant	—	−2.194 (0.017)	—	**−1.530** (0.033
Territorial Claim	—	1.583 (0.024)	—	**0.710** (0.035
Minimum Democracy	—	—	—	**−0.033** (0.002
Allies	—	—	—	0.046 (0.032
Contiguity	—	—	—	**0.988** (0.030
Economic Development	—	—	—	**0.177** (0.020
Major-Major Status	—	—	—	**0.495** (0.067
Minor-Minor Status	—	—	—	**−0.619** (0.025
Peace Yrs[a]	—	−0.157 (0.007)	—	**−0.190** (0.008
Y₂: War Onset				
War Constant	−0.411 (0.048)	−0.528 (0.121)	0.077 (0.105)	−0.356 (0.230
Policy MID[b]	−1.176 (0.084)	−1.192 (0.089)	−1.063 (0.096)	−1.047 (0.099
Regime MID[b]	−1.046 (0.144)	−1.065 (0.145)	−1.062 (0.173)	−1.039 (0.173
Other MID[b]	−1.590 (0.419)	−1.606 (0.422)	*−1.166 (0.476)*	*−1.118 (0.474*
Minimum Democracy	—	—	*−0.028 (0.011)*	*−0.026 (0.01*
Allies	—	—	*−0.254 (0.117)*	*−0.236 (0.116*
Contiguity	—	—	*−0.224 (0.099)*	*−0.396 (0.152*
Economic Development	—	—	**−0.451** (0.103)	**−0.442** (0.10
Major-Major Status	—	—	**0.606** (0.171)	*0.533 (0.180*
Minor-Minor Status	—	—	*−0.314 (0.101)*	*−0.239 (0.119*
P	N/A	0.053 (0.051)	N/A	−0.121 (.090
Wald χ² (df)	**225.79** (3)	**204.45** (3)	**211.95** (9)	**201.74** (9)
# of Observations	1,835	498,854	1,505	353,047

Note: **Bold** = p < .001, *Italics* = p < .05 (all two-tailed). Robust standard errors in parentheses.
[a] The spline coefficients are not reported.
[b] As compared to the reference category of territorial MID.

putes. Disputes categorized in the "other" (miscellaneous) category are also negatively related to war when compared with territorial MIDs.

While the single-step results reported in the first column of table 3.2 are in line with our theoretical expectations, they were produced without consideration of potential sample selectivity. In order to assess and control for the possibility of selection bias in the single-stage model, we estimate the two-step process of dispute and war occurrence utilizing a probit estimation procedure with sample selection.[12] The results for the two-stage probit analysis of the base model are depicted in the second column (Joint Model) of table 3.2. Jointly estimating MID and war onset produces a positive and significant impact for territorial claims and MIDs, while controlling for sample selection bias. This means that dyads that have a territorial claim against each other are more apt to become involved in a militarized dispute. Further, if disputants are involved in a territorial MID, this increases the probability of their going to war within five years as indicated by the negative policy, regime, and "other" estimates in the war-onset stage of the joint model.[13]

The negative and significant policy and regime MID coefficients for the joint model (with territorial MID as the reference category) are consistent with our theoretical expectation that territorial militarized disputes are more likely to be followed by war. This finding is congruous with that reported for the single-stage war estimation in the first column of table 3.2. Further, this positive territory influence is in evidence even while controlling for sample selection. Thus, including an explicit consideration of the potential presence of correlated disturbances between the two single equation models does not alter the direction or significance of the policy and regime estimates, meaning that the positive impact of territorial disputes on war remains. Another way of putting this is that it is not the mere presence of a territorial claim that leads to war, but whether the claim is handled by an actual threat or use of force. The relationship modeled in the second stage is not eliminated by the relationship modeled in the first stage. These findings are supportive of a unified territorial explanation of conflict and war and consistent with the proposition depicted in cell *a* of table 3.1.

---

[12] Stata was used for all of the data analyses presented in this chapter. For more information on the maximum-likelihood probit-estimation procedure that accounts for selection, see the Stata 9 Reference Manual A–J (2005: 468–74).

[13] Since the consideration of disturbance correlation in the joint model should only affect the war-onset parameter estimates (the policy, regime, and other coefficients and significance levels), one should expect the MID onset estimates (territorial-claim and temporal-dependence controls) derived from a single-stage model to be virtually identical to those derived from a joint model. A comparison of the joint model (table 3.2, column 2) and a single-stage MID onset specification (results not shown) confirms this expectation.

In the first column of table 3.2, we assume that MID and war onset are independent processes (the value of ρ constrained to zero). The insignificant ρ coefficient in the joint version of the base model indicates that the MID and war-onset phases are independent. This insignificant ρ estimate implies no meaningful correlation of unmeasured factors across the MID and war-onset phases of conflict. Of central importance for us, however, is the fact that the significance and signs of the policy and regime MID coefficients are perfectly in line across the first and second columns of table 3.2, indicating the absence of a selection effect when assessing the impact of revision type in the MID data. In fact, even the magnitude of these estimates is only slightly altered in the joint model.

Next, we introduce control variables as a check on the robustness of the base model findings. We do this by estimating single and two-stage models inclusive of controls for democracy, alliance, geographic proximity, economic development, and power status. The results for the War Onset and Joint Models with controls are shown in the third and fourth columns of table 3.2. The core finding when viewing the four models depicted in table 3.2 is the consistency in the direction and magnitude of the policy and regime MID estimates across base and control specifications, as well as across single and two-stage designs, which indicates that territorial disputes (the reference category) are positively related to war onset. The consistency of these results once again points to the war-engendering influence of territorial MIDs, compared to regime and policy-militarized disputes.

At the MID onset phase of conflict, we see that the presence of a territorial claim, once again, increases the likelihood that a dyad will engage in a militarized dispute even in the presence of the control variables. Interestingly, the magnitude of this estimate for the model with controls is less than half that for the base model, suggesting some explanatory overlap between territorial claims and the control variables. However, the territorial-claim influence is still highly significant (and substantively nontrivial, as we show below).

In looking at the impacts of our control factors, we see that as the democracy level of the less democratic member of a pair increases, the probability of dispute onset decreases.[14] This conflict-dampening influence for increasing levels of dyadic democracy is also in evidence at the escalation-to-war phase, though only at the ($p < .05$) level. These findings are nicely in line with the dominant findings in the extant literature that point to a strong pacifying impact for joint democracy on dispute onset (e.g., Russett and Oneal, 2001),[15]

---

[14] For a detailed look at the related effects of democracy and territory on conflict (in the twentieth century), see Huth and Allee (2002).

[15] While most do agree with this point, some dispute the direction of the causal arrow between

and a borderline or insignificant influence on the escalation of MIDs to higher levels of conflict (e.g., Senese, 1997; Reed, 2000).[16] The presence of a shared alliance has no statistically meaningful effect on dispute onset, but does significantly lower the likelihood of their escalation to war.[17] Interestingly, both the geographic contiguity and economic development impacts are nonmonotonic across the two conflict thresholds, as contiguous and increasingly developed pairs are more likely to engage in MIDs, but less likely to escalate these disputes to war compared to noncontiguous and less developed pairs.[18] Our status variables reveal consistent and significant effects at both the MID and war-onset points, as jointly major dyads are more likely, and jointly minor dyads less likely, to engage in militarized disputes and wars than are major-minor pairs. These findings for economic development and status make intuitive sense as economically developed and/or major states, almost by definition, have improved capability to participate in militarized disputes, with neighbors or distant foes (a point which we return to in the next chapter). The negative-coefficient estimate for the peace years temporal-dependence-control variable is congruent to that reported for the base model in the second column of table 3.2, suggesting that peace (i.e., the absence of MIDs) is a reinforcing process. Finally, the ρ estimate for the model including controls is statistically insignificant, just as it was for the base model.

In order to ascertain the robustness of our main findings, the analyses shown in table 3.2 were also run without the five-year window of opportunity for war. These results are reported in table A3.1 of the appendix. For these tests, the dependent variable in the second stage is whether the current MID escalated to war, whereas in table 3.2 the dependent variable is whether the given MID escalated to war or a war fought between the same pair of states anytime within the next five years. A comparison of table A3.1 and table 3.2 for our core variables of interest reveals that the results are substantively the same for both specifications of the war-dependent variable. In the war-onset stage it makes no difference if the five-year window of opportunity is removed; policy and regime disputes are still significantly less likely to escalate to war than territorial disputes. The same is true for the joint model when controlling for the effects of territorial claims, but "other" is insignificant. These additional analy-

---

peace and democracy. For more on this debate, see James, Solberg, and Wolfson (1999, 2000); Thompson (1996); Gibler (2007) (cf. Mousseau and Shi [1999], and Oneal and Russett [2000].

[16] Of course, different spatial and, especially, temporal domains across these studies complicate direct comparisons. Further, the exact definitions and operationalizations of conflict escalation also differ across these works.

[17] For a more detailed look at the effects of various alliance configurations (including the affect of having outside allies) on conflict, see chapter 6 below.

[18] Both of these findings and their implications deserve further investigation. The next chapter provides an in-depth examination of the contiguity effect.

ses should allay any concerns that the revision-type findings reported in table 3.2 might be a function of the particular dependent-variable specification employed in the second stage of the statistical estimation.[19]

The estimate for the ρ disturbance correlation in the base model of table A3.1 is positive and statistically significant, in contrast to the insignificant estimate reported in table 3.2. Inclusion of the control variables, however, renders ρ insignificant, indicating that a good proportion of the omitted variables are captured by the joint model with controls in table A3.1. Apparently, our selection of control variables has tapped into a substantial portion of the unmeasured factors that were being picked up by the significant error-correlation estimate shown for the base model.

The significant and positive territorial-claim estimates, along with the significant and negative policy and regime-MID estimates, shown in tables 3.2 and A3.1, evince the escalation-enhancing influence of territory at both the dispute and war-onset stages of interstate conflict. To more properly illustrate and describe the probit results, predicted probabilities were calculated based on the findings reported for the models with controls in table 3.2.[20] We estimate two sets of predicted probabilities, one for the likelihood of a dyad engaging in a MID in a given year (MID onset), and the other for the likelihood of war occurring between this pair of states within five years (war onset). The two sets of predicted probabilities, along with 90 percent confidence intervals, are presented in table 3.3.

The first two rows compare the likelihood of a pair engaging in a MID, depending on whether or not the dyad is characterized by an outstanding territorial claim, while the final three rows compare the probability of a MID eventuating in war, based on whether the dispute was fought over territorial-, policy-, or regime-oriented revisionist goals. Viewing the MID Onset column in table 3.3, we can observe the magnitude of the territorial-claim impact. Among all dyads in a given year, those with an outstanding territorial claim are almost eight times (.0085 versus .0011) as likely to engage in a MID com-

---

[19] All of the analyses reported here were also conducted on a politically relevant sample. The findings for the revision-type and territorial-claim estimates within this sample for both the base model and the model with controls are perfectly in line with those reported in the text for the full set.

[20] Maximum-likelihood estimation can be used to calculate the probability of the dependent variable taking on a certain value, in this case the probability of war onset. These probabilities are normally called "predicted probabilities" to distinguish them from "actual probabilities," which are the simple frequencies that war has occurred within a given sample. Here, we use an alternative procedure to calculate the probabilities, which runs a thousand Monte Carlo simulations to derive a "probability" from the probit model estimates (for the advantages of this approach, see King, Tomz, and Wittenberg [2000]). The predicted probability estimates derived from simulations in CLARIFY are almost identical to standard predicted probabilities (not shown).

Table 3.3
Probability Estimates of MID and War Onset (within five years), 1919–95

Conditions	MID Onset	War Onset	90% Confidence Interval	
Presence of a Territorial Claim	.0085		.0070	.0100
Absence of a Territorial Claim	.0011		.0010	.0012
Presence of a Territorial MID		.283	.250	.316
Presence of a Policy MID		.051	.039	.064
Presence of a Regime MID		.053	.029	.085

Note: Predicted probabilities are calculated using CLARIFY software developed by Tomz, Wittenberg, and King (2001). Probability estimates for MID onset are derived from a single-stage probit estimation (coefficient estimates almost identical to those shown for the Joint Model w/Controls in table 3.2); estimates for war onset (within five years) are derived from the single-stage War Onset w/Controls estimation in table 3.2. CLARIFY (version 2.0) does not yet accommodate the estimation of predicted probabilities for a two-stage model. However, since the ρ estimate for the Joint Model w/Controls (table 3.2) is not statistically significant, predicted probabilities based on the single-stage estimation will be quite similar (as is suggested by the nearly identical policy and regime MID estimates across the third and fourth columns of table 3.2). The values of all control variables are set to their means.

pared to those without such a claim. These estimates are statistically quite stable, as even the most conservative approach to assessing the confidence intervals (comparing the .0070 and .0012 bounds) reveals a plain difference. Clearly, the presence of an outstanding territorial claim imparts a meaningfully increased tendency toward state pairs involving themselves in militarized disputes.

A look at the War Onset probabilities attached to the three main MID revision-type classifications allows us to more easily grasp the tendency for territorial militarized disputes to result in war. The probit model estimates that the probability of territorial MIDs escalating to war within five years is about .28. Among all dispute dyads, territorial MIDs are more than five times as likely as policy MID (.283 versus .051) and as regime disputes (.283 versus .053) to be followed by war within five years. Further, we can have a high level of confidence in the difference between the territorial and nonterritorial estimates, as the lower confidence bound (.250) of the territorial MID to war estimate is quite distant from the upper bounds of both the policy and regime MID estimates (.064 and .085, respectively). These predicted probabilities lend clear support to a territory-based explanation of conflict and war, and fit neatly within cell *a* of table 3.1, indicating support for proposition (a).[21]

[21] Findings for politically relevant pairs are also quite supportive of proposition (a). Within the politically relevant sample of dyad-years, pairs with an outstanding territorial claim are four times (.048 versus .012) as likely to engage in a MID compared to those without such a claim. Among all politically relevant dispute dyads, territorial MIDs are more than four times (.272 versus .062) as

The escalation-enhancing influence of territory is also plainly evident when the dependent variable is whether the current MID goes to war, as can be seen in table A3.2 in the appendix. This table also reveals a clear hierarchy among the three revision-type categories. The findings show that the probability of territorial disputes escalating (immediately) to war is .176; whereas, the probability for regime disputes is .021, and for policy disputes, .004. As expected, these probabilities are lower than those shown in table 3.3 for the five-year-window variant, since all the MIDs that escalate to war five years afterward are not included. Tables 3.3 and A3.2 clearly reveal the significant and substantively nontrivial impact of territorial MIDs on the likelihood of war, compared to policy and regime disputes. Moreover, they suggest the utility of the five-year-window concept, especially for the examination of policy disputes, in that the latter are as war prone as regime disputes with a five-year window, but appear more peaceful than regimes without that window (cf. tables 3.3 and A3.2).

These results also have important implications for making inferences about the probability of war by comparing only MIDs and not looking at what factors make states have a MID in the first place. Our tests show clearly that controlling for the effects of territorial claims at the first stage does not change the direction or significance of the relationship between territorial MIDs and the probability of war at the second stage. Territorial disputes have a higher probability of going to war than policy and regime disputes, as earlier tests by Hensel (1996), Senese (1996), and Vasquez and Henehan (2001) showed. Our tests demonstrate (1) that states that have a territorial MID have a greater probability of going to war within five years than states that have a policy or regime dispute, and (2) that territorial MIDs have a greater probability of going to war immediately than policy or regime disputes.

These findings also demonstrate that using the MID data set to make inferences about the probability of territorial MIDs going to war was not a misguided venture. Of course, this could not be known definitely until after the hypothesis was tested, but this is true of any counter-hypothesis—for example, the claim that a given finding demonstrates a spurious relationship. Logical possibilities should not be confused with empirical accuracies. While we have no objections to testing whether a selection effect might remove the significance of a given relationship when data are available, data are often not available. To automatically dismiss findings simply because they *might* be due to a selection effect or a spurious relationship is to reject a hypothesis that is supported by evidence and has passed an important test in favor of one that

---

likely as policy MIDs, and over nine times (.272 versus .0293) as likely as regime disputes, to be followed by war within five years.

may have no empirical evidence supporting it and has not been tested. Such a tack can undermine and divert research programs by undercutting confidence in existing data sets.[22] It also evinces an overconcern with Type I errors without balancing that concern with the possibility of making a Type II error. Critics who use the selection-effect argument need to be more modest and cautious in making their claims. Selection-effects criticisms of research designs that rely exclusively on MID data should be treated as possible counter-hypotheses and not as proof of a logically flawed research design warranting the automatic dismissal of findings.

These judgments about selection effects have been substantiated further by research conducted since our original tests in Senese and Vasquez (2003). Rasler and Thompson (2006) find territory to be a consistent engine of conflict at both the dispute- and war-onset points using a seemingly unrelated probit technique. Using this method, which allows them to control for and assess the presence of sample-selection bias, produces results that are substantively in line with those we present here. The fact that their study uses a different design further substantiates the general robustness of the territory-conflict link predicted by the steps-to-conflict and -war explanation.

Braithwaite and Palmer (2003) confirm that territorial MIDs are more prone to escalation, including escalation to war, than other types of disputes, even when controlling for several factors (at the first stage) that might bring about a MID in the first place. Although they do not look at the impact of a territorial claim, they do examine the impact of contiguity, joint democracy, joint satisfaction with the status quo, peace years, capability ratio, shared defense pact, and shared civilization on the onset of a MID. Only the first four factors are significantly related (positively or negatively) to having a MID. In terms of selection effects, however, they show that controlling for the effects of the first stage never changes the sign or statistical significance of the territorial MID variable at the second stage for the five dependent variables of escalation they employ. They conclude that territorial MIDs are more apt to be reciprocated, more apt to involve mutual force, more apt to have fatalities, more apt to have fatalities greater than 250, and more apt to escalate to war. None of these relationships are subject to a selection effect, although other independent variables in their study, namely contiguity, are.

---

[22] It should be remembered that the MID data set was created in part to address complaints that the war data omitted cases of under one thousand battle deaths and that to understand war one should look at the threats, displays, or uses of force that give rise to war.

Conclusions

We began this inquiry with two major goals in mind. First, we sought to develop more fully a territorial explanation of conflict onset and escalation. This extended explanation led to a set of testable propositions not only at the point where interstate conflict erupts into war, but also at less intense stages of disagreement. Second, we endeavored to include a specific theoretical and statistical consideration of potential sampling biases that may come into play when one isolates a single stage in any multistage process. Specifically, we sought to address the criticism that statistical analyses that show a relationship between territorial MIDs and escalation to war might be flawed because they fail to take account of possible selection bias within the MID data set. We addressed this issue by considering the potentially varied role of territorial issues at both the conflict and war-onset points by comparing (Huth) data on territorial claims with MID data.

The results produced by our analysis lend strong support to the unified territorial explanation of conflict and war. It was found that pairs of states with an outstanding territorial claim are significantly more likely to engage in militarized disputes than are dyads with no outstanding territorial claim. Further, among the set of interstate disagreements that escalate to militarized disputes, those over territory are significantly more likely to escalate to war (either immediately or within five years) than those characterized by nonterritorial questions. These findings are consistent for both base models and models with controls, and robust across both single and two-stage estimation analyses. The two-stage model explicitly assesses the potential presence and biasing role of a selected sample for observation. Although some evidence was found (for the analysis of immediate MID escalation to war without controls) that sample selectivity should be considered in general tests of conflict escalation, there is no evidence that sample bias affects the results on territorial claims or MIDs.

This last point raises an interesting issue. Selection effects should always be addressed from two perspectives. The first refers to the possibility of *general* issues of sample selectivity when modeling single estimation stages in a multistep (theoretical or statistical) process. Evidence supporting such a general selection effect may be ascertained if the associated disturbances are correlated (as evidenced by a statistically significant ρ estimate). The presence of such a general sample-selection issue does not necessarily lead to the conclusion that estimates derived from a single-stage model are biased. It only means that they may be biased. A more *specific* selection effect is only in evidence when the sign and/or magnitude of a coefficient's influence are/is markedly different when comparing single and two-stage model results. One base-model analysis we present in this research (see table A3.1) reveals such a general selection mechanism, which does not specifically modify the estimates for the substantive influence of territory. In our model (with controls) even this general selection effect as evinced by ρ is nonsignificant, indicating that most of the omitted variables that produced a significant correlation among the error terms are captured by the control variables included in our second model.

The analyses reported herein have provided one of the most stringent tests of a territorial explanation of conflict and war to date. Along with Huth (1996b), it is one of the few analyses to take seriously and to test for the effects of selection bias with regard to territorial issues. We build on Huth (1996b) by looking at all dyad years and not just a random sample, and by using his expanded data on territorial claims to assess sampling bias within the MID data set. The results show that having a territorial claim increases the probability that the contending states will become involved in a MID. In addition, they show that the presence of a territorial MID between states increases the probability that they will go to war, even while controlling for the effect of a previous territorial claim. No one else has shown this before, through a systematic comparison of territorial disputes with policy or regime disputes. Indeed, our study is the first examination of whether the MID data set is prone to selection effects, in terms of its sample of territorial, policy, and regime disputes. The end result is a rigorous test that fails to falsify the territorial explanation of conflict and war.

On the basis of this test, we now have evidence indicating that (at least since 1919) (a) territorial disagreements between two states increase the probability that they will become involved in a militarized dispute, (b) once in a territorial MID, states will have an increased probability of becoming involved in a war (compared to states involved in nonterritorial disputes), and (c) the latter finding holds even while controlling for the effects of the original territorial disagreement (i.e., it is not the presence [or absence] of a territorial claim or disagreement per se that increases [or decreases] the probability of war, but how it is handled).

By showing that selection bias is not having an effect, these tests should put to rest one of the major criticisms of the finding that territorial disputes increase the probability of war. The next chapter examines the second major criticism of the finding on territorial disputes and the probability of war—namely, that contiguity, not territorial disputes, is the main factor explaining the escalation of MIDs to war.

Appendix

Table A3.1
Effect of Territory on Dispute and War Onset (no five-year window), 1919–95 (Probit Estimates)

Variables in Model	Base Model		Model w/Controls	
	War Onset	Joint Model	War Onset	Joint Model
Y$_1$: MID Onset				
MID Constant	—	−2.195 (0.017)	—	−1.530 (0.033)
Territorial Claim	—	1.583 (0.024)	—	0.709 (0.035)
Minimum Democracy	—	—	—	−0.033 (0.002)
Allies	—	—	—	0.047 (0.032)
Contiguity	—	—	—	0.989 (0.030)
Economic Development	—	—	—	0.177 (0.020)
Major-Major Status	—	—	—	0.495 (0.067)
Minor-Minor Status	—	—	—	−0.619 (0.025)
Peace Yrs[a]	—	−0.155 (0.007)	—	−0.189 (0.008)
Y$_2$: War Onset				
War Constant	−0.679 (0.051)	−1.559 (0.139)	−0.043 (0.129)	−0.503 (0.313)
Policy MID[b]	−1.848 (0.165)	−1.869 (0.156)	−1.776 (0.198)	−1.750 (0.190)
Regime MID[b]	−1.000 (0.164)	−1.067 (0.161)	−1.139 (0.223)	−1.136 (0.219)
Other MID[b]	−1.322 (0.420)	−1.368 (0.413)	−0.647 (0.497)	−0.695 (0.482)
Minimum Democracy	—	—	−0.041 (0.015)	−0.043 (0.015)
Allies	—	—	−0.308 (0.159)	−0.320 (0.156)
Contiguity	—	—	−0.741 (0.142)	−0.441 (0.207)
Economic Development	—	—	−0.264 (0.136)	−0.274 (0.134)
Major-Major Status	—	—	−0.115 (0.214)	0.006 (0.224)
Minor-Minor Status	—	—	−0.208 (0.130)	−0.329 (0.147)
ρ	N/A	0.399 (0.061)	N/A	0.194 (.124)
Wald χ^2 (df)	158.35 (3)	184.12 (3)	139.20 (9)	148.57 (9)
# of Observations	1,835	498,854	1,505	353,047

Note: **Bold** = p < .001, *Italics* = p < .05 (all two-tailed). Robust standard errors in parentheses.
[a] The spline coefficients are not reported.
[b] As compared to the reference category of territorial MID.

Table A3.2

Probability Estimates of War Onset (no five-year window), 1919–95

Conditions	War Onset	90% Confidence Interval	
Presence of a Territorial MID	.176	.148	.206
Presence of a Policy MID	.004	.001	.008
Presence of a Regime MID	.021	.007	.043

Note: Predicted probabilities are calculated using CLARIFY software developed by Tomz, Wittenberg, and King (2001). Probability estimates for MID onset are identical to those shown in table 3.3 and, therefore, are not repeated here; estimates for war onset (no five-year window) are derived from the single-stage war Onset w/Controls estimation in table A3.1. CLARIFY (version 2.0) does not yet accommodate the estimation of predicted probabilities for a two-stage model. However, since the ρ estimate for the Joint Model w/Controls (table A3.1) is not statistically significant, predicted probabilities based on the single-stage estimation will be quite similar (as is suggested by the nearly identical policy and regime MID estimates across the third and fourth columns of table A3.1). The values of all control variables are set to their means.

4

Territory, Contiguity, and Their Interaction:
A Contingent Model of Interstate Conflict

Good fences may make good neighbors, but they
need to be built first.

While the previous chapter focused largely on territory and its role in interstate conflict dynamics, this chapter expands that focus by looking at a second key element that might produce selection bias—the role of contiguity. We examine two questions. First, we want to know if controlling for contiguity at the first stage (conflict onset), affects the relationship we have found between territorial MIDs and war onset (the second stage). Second, as in the previous chapter, we want to do more than just test for selection bias. We also want to explore further the relationship between MID onset and war onset by more fully specifying a unified explanation of conflict that embodies both the insights of the contiguity and territorial explanations. As stated in chapter 2, we still believe that in terms of war onset, the territorial explanation is superior to the contiguity explanation of war, but we also think that contiguity plays an important role at the MID onset stage. Since we spent considerable time on the selection-bias question in the previous chapter, here the emphasis will be on theoretically formulating and testing a unified explanation of conflict and war, although we will test systematically for selection bias.

Throughout the history of the international system, the significance of geography in understanding conflict has been undeniable. Whenever one hears such phrases as "land for peace" or "the sanctity of sovereign borders," one is hearing the unmistakable overtones of geopolitics. We as a discipline have unearthed some key pieces of the conflict puzzle by focusing on two fundamental components of geography—territory and contiguity. But while research on each of these factors has mounted, the resulting two streams of literature have ultimately tended to talk past one another. This is not to say that theoretical explanations based on either territory or contiguity are mutually exclusive—in fact, there is nothing logically inherent in either that would preclude the other from also being true. Instead, it is to say that little systematic attention has been paid to the *concurrent* impact of these two critical variables across varied phases of peace and conflict and how their effects might be related to one another. This chapter focuses precisely on this important gap by theoretically and empirically examining the potentially contingent roles that territory and contiguity play in pushing state pairs across two distinctive thresholds of conflict—the onset of militarized disputes and their subsequent escalation to war.

A small but significant number of works have begun to lay the groundwork for this current investigation. Lemke and Reed (2001b), for instance, examine the impact of contiguity on the onset of great power rivalry and then war. Work by Huth (1996b), meanwhile, looks at various aspects of competing territorial claims and their roles in pushing states toward overt disputes with one another. These two studies highlight some of the important individual effects of contiguity and territory at particular stages of conflict. They do not, however, address the potential interactive effects of these two variables, nor do they consider contiguity and territory together within the same model. Other works (e.g., Hensel, 2000; Vasquez, 2001) do take promising initial steps in considering the potentially linked impacts of territory and contiguity, but only in a preliminary way and on a single level of conflict. These latter studies do not intend to, or provide a comprehensive and appropriately sophisticated methodological examination of the contingent effects of territory and contiguity on both dispute and war onset, two junctures widely seen as critical in the study of conflict. Nevertheless, taken together these works do provide a solid grounding of inquiry for the cumulative and novel next step taken in this chapter—one that considers the roles of *both* contiguity and territory in pushing state pairs into disputes *and* wars.

The analysis begins by briefly reviewing expectations derived from prior work looking at the independent influences of geographic contiguity and territory. The review is then used to develop a new explanation that goes beyond these existing studies in two essential ways. First, this joint contiguity-territorial account sees both contiguity and territory as important precipitators of conflict. Second, it considers the consistency of the territory and contiguity impacts at different stages of conflict; that is to say, are their conflict-enhancing effects limited to a particular phase of dispute, or are they uniformly applicable across various levels of interstate discord? Finally, a test of the joint explanation is conducted, controlling for economic development, power status, alliance ties, regime type, relative capability, temporal dependence, and sample selection bias. These analyses provide a "crucial test" to decipher the relative importance of both territory and contiguity within any geography-based account of conflict behavior, and, in doing so, also provide answers to several related questions discussed in more detail below.

Contiguity, Territory, and International Conflict

Since good, general treatments of the importance of contiguity and territory have been offered elsewhere (e.g., Most and Starr, 1980; Diehl, 1991; Hensel, 2000; Senese, 1996; Vasquez, 1995), they will only briefly be discussed here. The main purpose is to develop a new theoretical account that effectively incorporates the roles of both contiguity and territory into a single explanation. In developing this new account, Starr's (1978) opportunity and willingness framework is utilized, as it provides some useful organizing concepts for the discussion to follow (see also Most and Starr, 1989; Cioffi-Revilla and Starr, 2003). In particular, his notion of opportunity resonates well with any analysis of geographic contiguity, while his idea of willingness provides a useful conceptual lens through which to view territory and its particular effects on conflict (see also Starr, 2005).

The geographic contiguity of states, not taking into consideration the particular nature of any grievances between them, has consistently been cited as a key variable in explaining conflict. Bremer (1992), for one, finds contiguous states much more prone to fight one another than noncontiguous ones. In putting together a fairly short list of the most important factors affecting "who fights whom," he places contiguity at the top (Bremer 2000). Earlier empirical studies also find support for the general notion that contiguity tends to be associated with higher levels of conflict. Both Gleditsch and Singer (1975) and Garnham (1976), for instance, show that warring states tend to be closer together, or more proximate (in terms of the distance separating their capital cities), than their nonwarring counterparts. Diehl (1985c) and Gochman (1990) also find statistically significant relationships between contiguity and conflict, looking at the escalation and intensity of disputes, respectively. Most recently Bennett and Stam (2004) reconfirm Bremer's (1992) findings on contiguity.

One particularly useful way to think about contiguity is provided by the idea of opportunity. Drawing on work by Boulding (1962) and Sprout and Sprout (1965), Starr (1978) highlights the importance of contiguity in providing a more ready *occasion* for conflict. Occasion here, to be clear, refers to what is often called interaction opportunity, or the extent to which a certain policy is possible for a state and, if it is, how feasible its implementation would be. For instance, it is almost impossible, as well as inconceivable, for Ecuador to target a major military action against Ghana—impossible because Ecuador simply does not have the capacity to target such a distant foe; inconceivable because the lack of interactions between the two countries makes it highly unlikely that they would experience a disagreement that is both intense and important enough to warrant such an action. On the other hand, it is possible for Ecuador to launch a border raid against Peru, as the nearness of this foe allows Ecuador (and Peru, for that matter) to more effectively implement military action.[1] A later work by Siverson and Starr (1991) puts an even finer point on the relationship between contiguity and opportunity by explicitly conceptualizing contiguity as a factor that promotes the diffusion of war.

At its most basic level, a contiguity-based account argues that while states may choose not to fight, the geographic nearness of contiguous states provides a setting amenable to conflictual interactions. Since higher levels of conflict require increased degrees of participant commitment, it is also reasonable to expect that great distances between disputants will not only quell their propensity for engaging in conflict, but also lower the chances that they will continue fighting at increasingly intense phases of dispute. In other words, a contiguity-based explanation argues that states are less constrained in their opportunities for all levels of interaction and participation, including militarized disputes and wars, when the venue of combat is geographically nearby.

While this account is fine as a starting point, ideally, it would also be desirable to know what makes conflict and its escalation more or less likely in the presence of contiguity and the interaction opportunity it provides. Herein lies the weakness of the contiguity/conflict literature. In short, though interaction opportunity is sometimes posited as a necessary condition for conflict,[2] either little is said or a random process is assumed about conflict beyond that. The random-walk notion supposes that proximate states will simply interact with one another more frequently and, just like those who drive in traffic are more apt to get into accidents, frequently interacting states are more likely to have conflictual (as well as cooperative) interactions (Bre-

---

[1] Boulding's (1962) depiction of a "loss of strength gradient," nicely captures states' declining ability to project power over greater distances. In order to distinguish the individual effects of power projection versus contiguity, controls for state status (i.e., major or minor power) and relative capability are included in the data analyses below.

[2] Sometimes the general concepts of opportunity and willingness are posed as necessary conditions of conflict since if there is no opportunity for conflict and no willingness (by either side), there cannot be any conflict. This is only true by definition and thus is more tautological than explanatory. When specific variables, like contiguity and territory (see below), are used as indicators it is clear that neither are truly necessary conditions since noncontiguous and distant states can fight and, as noted in all our work, nonterritorial issues can and do give rise to conflict and war. Rather, what we find useful about the opportunity and willingness framework is that it delineates the different roles the two variables play in the "causal" process. We see both contiguity and territory as neither necessary nor sufficient, but simply as increasing the probability of conflict or war. On necessary conditions, see Goertz and Starr (2003).

mer, 1992, 2000; Gleditsch and Singer, 1975; Gochman, 1990). The reliance on this random-walk idea underscores how underdeveloped this literature is in answering the following question: given ample opportunity to enter into conflict, what specific factors push states to actually do so?[3]

The opportunity and willingness framework suggests that the answer to the above question, and the key to filling the void in the contiguity/conflict literature, lies in "willingness." As Starr uses the term, willingness refers simply to the degree to which an actor desires to pursue a particular policy action; that is, peaceful states may be perfectly able to engage a potential foe (they have an apt level of interaction opportunity), but clearly unwilling to do so because they deem the issue at hand insufficient to justify such engagement. For example, the United States certainly has the opportunity to launch an aggressive military strike against Surinam, but its willingness to do so has been quite low as it has found no issue meaningful enough to warrant an initiation of hostilities. On the other hand, both Argentina and Britain clearly possessed sufficient levels of willingness to engage militarily over the Falklands/Malvinas in 1982. In fact, Britain's hearty response to Argentina's initiation, in spite of great distance, is a prime example of the role of territory in promoting willingness, and demonstrative in part, of why territory is an attractive indicator of the important concept of willingness.

While there are a number of possible factors that can affect willingness (see below), the most prominent, rooted in geography, focuses on territory and the role of territorial grievances. This general conception of territory as a strong impetus for militarized action is at the heart of a territory-based explanation of conflict (Vasquez, 1993; 2001; see also Huth, 1996b; Senese and Vasquez, 2004, 2005). As shown in the previous chapter, this is true in terms of both onset and escalation. A basic tenet, for instance, of the territorial account is that domestic populations are more concerned with preserving the integrity of land and more willing to fight in defense of it than in defense of an ideological or policy stance. Additionally, a territorial disagreement may become a foundational threat to a state's security since, by definition, nation-states comprise well-defined and controlled areas of land. Given this, any threat to such a basic element of a state's makeup will be given high priority by that state's leadership. For these reasons, states are simply more willing to resort to the initial use of military force when the issue at stake involves territory. With specific regard to escalation, the territorial explanation maintains that territorial disputes will have a greater probability of escalation, as both sides have ample willingness to stay the course and not back down. In these

---

[3] Another way of looking at the random-walk rationale is through a realist lens. From this perspective, war is inherent in any struggle for power, and contiguity simply increases its probability.

ways, territorial disagreements are expected to raise the chances of both militarized dispute onset and escalation, relative to nonterritorial disagreements.

Taken together, it appears that contiguity and territory fit nicely within an opportunity and willingness schema. While previous work has marked each separately as an important predictor of conflict, an advance of the joint contiguity-territorial explanation developed here lies in its explicit consideration of *both* contiguity and territory as important precipitators of conflict. Unlike prior work, we consider the impacts of both within the same theoretical model.

A second advance in the joint explanation is its expectation that the effects of contiguity and territory are disproportionate across the two phases of conflict, as opposed to a nondifferentiation between dispute and war onset shown in most prior work. In this way, the joint explanation approximates more closely the notion of Kinsella and Russett (2002), who also build on the work of Starr, that the effects of causal factors may not be consistent along the range of international conflict.

In line with the first of these two advancements, we can begin to derive theoretical expectations for a joint account. Owing to the posited conflict-enhancing potential of both contiguity and territory, a joint version expects *the least* dispute and war-prone dyads to be noncontiguous with no outstanding territorial disagreements. Such cases represent situations where the mutual absence of contiguity and territorial grievances generally reduces both opportunity and willingness, respectively. Logically, the flip side of this produces an expectation that the *most* dispute and war-prone dyads will consist of contiguous states with territorial disagreements. These cases will often be characterized by one or both states feuding over their own or bordering territory. Examples representative of the high salience attached to such disagreements include the Iran-Iraq conflict over the Shatt-al-Arab waterway, Somalia's war with Ethiopia over the Ogaden region, Iraq's war to possess Kuwait, and the continual tensions between Syria and Israel over the Golan Heights. Losing such conflicts would do more than merely hurt the reputation or prestige of a participating state; it could also serve to displace large numbers of indigenous people and submit the loser to partial "occupation" by the victor. Furthermore, implicit in such situations are the tangible, "zero-sum" effects that could directly result from defeat in a dispute fought over bordering land. These increased stakes, then, associated with territorial disagreements between neighbors, raise the likelihood that states will engage in militarized disputes and not back down at successively higher levels of dispute intensity.

The main implications of the joint account's second advancement come into play in differentiating the expected tendencies of the other two scenarios—contiguous pairs without territorial disagreements and noncontiguous pairs with territorial disagreements. Since a lack of opportunity is often seen as a factor that prevents discord from arising in the first place, an opportunity and willingness framework suggests that contiguity is most crucial at the dispute-onset phase. The key rationale behind this expectation is the observation that contiguity is both quite stable and obvious—stable in the sense that states only rarely see change in this aspect of their relationship, and obvious in that both sides clearly know if they are neighbors. Therefore, since information pertaining to whether states are contiguous is public from the beginning, the disproportionate effect of this factor should be included in leaders' conflict choices at the outset. Once a dispute has begun, though, contiguity becomes less important, as the most significant barriers of opportunity have already been weighed and overcome.

It is at this point that willingness becomes relatively more meaningful, leading a joint theoretical explanation to place greater emphasis on the effect of territory in pushing ongoing disputes to war. Contrary to the immediately transparent nature of contiguity, knowledge about an opponent's commitment to fight over a particular issue (such as disputed territory) is less obvious early on. This aspect of willingness starts out more within the domain of private information and, while somewhat apparent at early stages, only becomes more public as a conflict unfolds. Territory fits nicely within this framework, as states become more aware of each other's dedication to stay the course only as persuasive actions (in the form of escalation behavior) are exhibited. Since a good deal of extant theory and empirical findings suggest that contested territory is at the very core of states' priorities, its magnified role in the escalation of militarized conflict is to be expected.

Deriving from this logic of a joint contiguity-territorial explanation, the following two hypotheses naturally follow:

> *Proposition 4.1 (Dispute Onset)*: The expected probability ranking of dispute onset based on the presence or absence of contiguity and territorial claims is (from lowest to highest): non-Contiguous, non-Territorial < non-Contiguous, Territorial < Contiguous, non-Territorial < Contiguous, Territorial, ceteris paribus.

> *Proposition 4.2 (War Onset)*: The expected probability ranking of war onset based on the presence or absence of contiguity and territorial disputes is (from lowest to highest): non-Contiguous, non-Territorial < Contiguous, non-Territorial < non-Contiguous, Territorial < Contiguous, Territorial, ceteris paribus.

While the joint explanation considers both contiguity and territory in explicating dispute and war onset, it weighs their effects unevenly across these two phases of conflict. It does so by placing relatively more emphasis on the impact of contiguity (opportunity) in states' decisions to enter disputes in the first place, while granting a greater relative influence to territory (willingness) on disputants' choices to escalate to war. In this way then, this new joint explanation reflects a form of contingency that reveals itself in disparate expectations across the two phases of conflict, as evidenced in the disparate orderings of the two middle categories across the two hypotheses.

In appraising the above propositions, answers to several related questions are also revealed. For instance, whether or not contiguity affects conflict chances even in the absence of territorial disagreement, and whether or not territory increases the risk of disputes and war even in the absence of contiguity can be assessed. In addition, the possibility that nongeographically based opportunity and willingness factors may supplement, or substitute for, the posited effects of contiguity and territory can be evaluated. For example, major power status and high levels of economic development may provide degrees of interaction opportunity similar to those of contiguity, while the absence of alliance ties and joint democracy may facilitate the willingness of states to engage in MIDs and war in a fashion similar to that of territory. The opportunity and willingness framework certainly expects such supplementation and substitution within its two core concepts, and we will explore their presence in the tests below.[4]

With this set of expectations in place, we now move to the specification of a research design that allows for their direct testing. As mentioned above, earlier work (including the previous chapter) has begun to address the accuracy of theoretical expectations for the independent effects of contiguity and territory. However, none of these studies simultaneously examine the potentially nonmonotonic and connected nature of their influences. The analyses below do just that by using multiplicative terms to estimate interaction effects at both the dispute- and war-onset phases of conflict.

---

[4] The logic of opportunity and willingness has been used to rank the expectations for propositions 4.1 and 4.2. However, other nonspecified variables may alter these rankings. We note here, for example, that Vasquez (2001: 161; see chapter 2, above: table 2.2) and Hensel (2000: 73), using different research designs, find dyads that are noncontiguous and have territorial MIDs have a higher probability of war or deadly conflict than contiguous dyads with territorial MIDs, contrary to the two propositions here. The propositions assume that some states (e.g., major states, trading states, or naval powers) may have interests in more than their own region and therefore will be less constrained by contiguity, but such variables are being held in abeyance in propositions 4.1 and 4.2.

Research Design

How do the expectations of the joint contiguity-territory explanation fare against the historical record? To answer this question, dispute and war observations over the 1919–95 time span taken from the (Maoz, 2005) Dyadic Militarized Interstate Dispute data set (DYMID) will be examined. The DYMID set includes only observations for pairs of states that were actually on opposing sides of an explicit militarized conflict action that took place as part of an interstate dispute.[5] Since the analysis examines both conflict onset and escalation-to-war outcomes, two dependent variables are necessary. For the first dependent variable, dyads are coded as having a dispute onset when a MID begins in a year. The second dependent variable measures whether or not a dispute advances to war. After exclusions for missing data on the independent variables, the number of observations becomes 494,613 dyad-years for the MID onset analyses, and 1,348 MIDs (from which ninety-six war participations emerge) for the war onset tests.[6]

To measure the first key explanatory concept of interest, the Correlates of War Contiguity data are used once again (Stinnett et al., 2002).[7] A slightly different contiguity indicator is used in this chapter compared to the last—the indicator used in the tests below measures whether or not two states *or their colonies* are contiguous by land or within 150 miles or less of water.[8] It could be that there are many territorial disagreements of a colonial nature that the metropole disputes with another colonial power or with a free state in a colonial region, about territory. If such colonial cases were excluded from the contiguity grouping, the impact of contiguity might be inadvertently underrepresent. Such a misrepresentation might artificially strengthen estimates of the territory effect, relative to contiguity, and subtly bias the findings. To avoid this possibility, colonial contiguity is included as part of the contiguity measure in this chapter.[9]

---

[5] The Maoz "DYMID" data can be accessed at http://psfaculty.ucdavis.edu/zmaoz/dyadmid .html. All of the data used in this chapter (with the exception of the Huth and Allee territorial claims data) were obtained through the EUGene (version 3.04) software program (Bennett and Stam, 2000).

[6] The sample size differences between this and the previous chapter are due primarily to differences between the MID 2.1 data and the Maoz data.

[7] All of the individual Correlates of War sets utilized here are available at http://correlates ofwar.org/.

[8] Vasquez (2001) did not include colonies in his measures of contiguity either, thereby putting them in the noncontiguous category. These changes give contiguity a better chance of playing a role and make it more difficult for the territorial explanation of war to pass testing (see below).

[9] In practice, the decision to include colonial contiguity makes little difference for the substantive nature of the findings presented below.

Two operational indicators are used to capture the second key explanatory concept—territorial disagreement. At the dispute-onset stage, a territorial-claim variable derived from Huth (1996b: ch. 2, 5, appendix A) and Huth and Allee (2002: chs. 1, 2, appendix A) is employed. Their data set records all territorial claims between recognized states from 1919 through 1995, whether or not they give rise to the threat or use of militarized force. At the war-onset phase, the DYMID set's revisionist character variable is employed as a measure of territorial dispute. This variable specifies the particular aspect of the status quo the revisionist state seeks to change in the militarized dispute, and four categories are employed to capture this: territory, policy, regime, and other. All these attempts must be characterized by the threat, display, or use of militarized force, and coding of the substantive content of the revisionist claims is based on objectives stated before the initiation of the MID and not on those that occur within the MID (Jones, Bremer, and Singer, 1996: 178).[10] In terms of territorial disputes, this means a claim to territory must be made before the MID.

By using different measures of territorial disagreement across the two levels of conflict, the theoretical concept is more accurately matched to the empirical indicator. The Huth (1996b) and Huth and Allee (2002) measure is ideal for our dispute-onset tests, as it marks the presence of standing claims that may last for long periods of time and may or may not lead to militarized disputes. However, it is not well suited or intended for tests such as those embodied in our war-onset examination. This is true because militarized disputes over *non*territorial issues can and do occur between states that are classified by Huth and Allee as having outstanding territorial claims. In other words, just because states have competing territorial claims does not mean that all of their MIDs will be over territory. In fact, of the 529 MIDs arising between states with Huth and Allee territorial claims, nonterritorial aims principally drive the revisionist actor fully 39 percent of the time. Because of this nuance, the MID-based revision-type measure is more appropriate for the war-onset tests.

While this chapter is concerned primarily with the effects of contiguity and territory, several alternative indicators of opportunity and willingness are considered.[11] Concerning willingness, the absences of alliance ties and dyadic democracy are plausible substitutes or supplements to the influence of terri-

---

[10] As noted in chapter 2, Maoz's coding of revision type can in specific cases differ from that in the MID 2.1 and MID 3.02 data.

[11] The usual "all else being equal" caveat is applied to propositions 4.1 and 4.2 since not every potential "opportunity and willingness" factor is identified. However, extant theory and research (e.g., Gartzke [2005]; Hewitt and Goertz [2005]; Kinsella and Russett [2002]; Siverson and Starr [1991]) are utilized to identify several items that merit immediate consideration.

tory. The alliance control variable (derived from the Correlates of War alliance data) distinguishes allies from non-allies. The democracy variable measures the difference between the Polity IV democracy and autocracy indices (i.e., democracy minus autocracy) and relies on what has been termed the "weak link principle" by assuming that the norms and expectations most likely to affect conflict are those of the less democratic party to the dispute (Dixon, 1993; Dixon and Senese, 2002; Senese, 1999). With regard to opportunity, the contiguity effect may be attenuated when at least one of a pair of states is able to project its influence across great distances. For this reason, two additional variables are introduced—a dummy indicator measuring whether the dyad consists of two minor powers, and a continuous measure of economic development using logged energy production per capita taken from the Correlates of War capabilities data base. In line with the democracy indicator, the lesser-developed actor within a dyad is used as "the weak link." To more fully capture the potentially confounding effect of power, a standard measure of relative capability is included, operationalized by first recording each party's power using the Correlates of War composite index of national capabilities and then computing the natural log of the ratio of the larger to smaller values for each pair of states. Finally, because there may be temporal dependence among dyads across years the cubic spline technique developed by Beck, Katz, and Tucker (1998) is utilized in the MID onset tests.

Since we are interested in explaining conflict behavior at two points of intensity, and the joint explanation makes predictions contingent on conflict phase, we use an appropriate two-stage estimation procedure for our primary analyses. This censored probit technique estimates and controls for potential sample-selection bias, which could otherwise lead to biased coefficient estimates in the war (second-stage) equation (Greene, 2000: 926–37). As its estimate is always insignificant ($p > .05$), the implications of this selection parameter (ρ) are discussed only briefly. Also, to control for the potential non-independence of conflict observations that are not the first to be observed for a particular pair, we adjust the calculations of all standard errors by clustering by dyad.

Within the analyses, the main focus will be on the variables representing contiguity, territory, and their interaction. In fact, the addition of the multiplicative terms is both a crucial and novel component of the tests below, as it permits an estimate of the *particular* conditional relationships among contiguity, territory, and conflict rather than the *general* ones explored in previous work using additive models. Specifically, the results detail the contingent effects of territorial claims and revision attempts based on the presence (or absence) of contiguity, and the contingent effects of contiguity based on the presence (or absence) of territorial claims and revision attempts, at both the dispute- and war-onset points. To more easily illustrate the substantive nature of these effects, and relate them to the theoretical expectations, predicted probabilities are derived from the relevant statistical models.

Findings

Before viewing the censored probit results, the analysis begins with a brief look at the distribution of cases across the MID and war-onset dependent variables. Table 4.1a shows the percentage of dyad-years that experience the onset of a MID, based on the presence or absence of contiguity and territorial claims. As expected, dyad-years characterized by territorial claims are associated with a higher percentage of MIDs compared to those absent such claims; and this is true for both contiguous (4.45–16.6 percent) and noncontiguous (0.15–6.59 percent) pairs. Similarly, contiguity is associated with a higher percentage of MIDs than is noncontiguity, among dyad-years both with (6.59–16.6 percent) and without (0.15–4.45 percent) territorial claims. These positive impacts for territory and contiguity are nicely in line with Proposition 4.1. Also supportive of the joint explanation are the observed rankings for the least and most dispute-prone dyads—the percentage of years with a MID onset is lowest for noncontiguous dyads absent territorial claims (0.15) and highest for contiguous dyads with territorial claims (16.6). The one element in table 4.1a that is not supportive of proposition 4.1 is the observation that noncontiguous dyads with territorial claims experience MID onset a higher percentage of the time (6.59) than do contiguous pairs absent such claims (4.45), a point that we return to shortly.

Table 4.1b shows the percentage of MIDs that escalate to war, based on the presence or absence of contiguity and territorial revisionist aims. Like the MID onset percentages shown in table 4.1a, the war-onset percentages reveal a clear association between territory and conflict—territorial MIDs are linked to a higher percentage of wars than are nonterritorial MIDs, among both contiguous (2.36–11.33 percent) and noncontiguous (3.75–33.33 percent) disputants. Unlike table 4.1a, however, is the observation in table 4.1b that contiguous disputants are actually less likely to escalate their disputes to war compared to noncontiguous foes (a finding similar to those of Vasquez, 2001: 161 [see ch. 2: table 2.2 above], and Hensel, 2000: 74). Contiguity imparts a sharp decrease in the percentage of wars among territorial disputants (33.33–11.33 percent) and a modest lessening for nonterritorial foes (3.75–2.36 percent). The implications of this finding are quite important and are discussed in more detail below.

Table 4.1a

MID Onset by Contiguity and Territorial Claims, 1919–95 (in percentages)

	Geographic Proximity			
	Noncontiguous		Contiguous	
	Territorial Claim		Territorial Claim	
MID Onset	No	Yes	No	Yes
No	99.85	93.41	65.55	83.40
Yes	0.15	6.59	4.45	16.60
(N)	480,597	668	14,260	3,795
	Cramer's V = .06; p = .000		Cramer's V = .19; p = .000	

Note: Cases are dyad years.

Table 4.1b

War Onset by Contiguity and Territorial MIDs, 1919–95 (in percentages)

	Geographic Proximity			
	Noncontiguous		Contiguous	
	MID Revision Type		MID Revision Type	
War Onset	Non-Territorial	Territorial	Non-Territorial	Territorial
No	96.25	66.67	97.64	88.67
Yes	3.75	33.33	2.36	11.33
(N)	347	141	594	450
	Cramer's V = .41; p = .000		Cramer's V = .18; p = .000	

Note: Cases are dyadic militarized interstate disputes (MIDs).

The Two-Stage Model

Turning to the multivariate censored probit estimations, the first column of table 4.2 reports the base model by considering the individual impacts of territory and contiguity on conflict, absent multiplicative terms. The base model permits an assessment of the general effects of territory and contiguity on dispute and war onset. Even more important, though, by comparing these results to those obtained inclusive of the multiplicative variables (second column of table 4.2), an assessment can be made of whether the interaction terms substantially improve the overall explanatory power of the statistical models.

Looking at the base model results, one sees that both territorial claims and geographic contiguity impart significant positive effects on the likelihood of MID onset. This indicates that state pairs with competing territorial claims

Table 4.2

Contiguity, Territory, and Interaction Effects on Dispute and War Onset, 1919–95 (probit with selection)

Variables in Model	Base Model	Model w/Interactions
Y_1: MID Onset		
Geographic contiguity	1.100** (.057)	1.136** (.056)
Territorial claim	0.595** (.085)	1.045** (.160)
Contiguity × Territorial Claim	—	−0.505* (.175)
Minor-minor status	−0.715** (.067)	−0.703** (.068)
ln (Minimum Development)	0.130** (.036)	0.128** (.036)
ln (Relative capability)	−0.095** (.016)	−0.095** (.016)
Peace years[a]	−0.164** (.012)	−0.165** (.012)
MID constant	−1.727** (.098)	−1.745** (.099)
Y_2: War Onset		
Geographic contiguity	−0.828** (.177)	−0.392 (.229)
Territorial MID[b]	0.964** (.154)	1.321** (.192)
Contiguity × Territorial MID	—	−0.629* (.266)
Alliance	−0.286 (.178)	−0.284 (.175)
Minimum democracy	−0.025 (.014)	−0.024 (.014)
ln (Relative capability)	−0.077 (.044)	−0.073 (.045)
War constant	−0.717 (.425)	−1.010* (.417)
ρ	−0.218 (.117)	−0.194 (.123)
Wald χ^2 (df)	62.24** (5)	89.36** (6)
N for MID onset (full)	494,613	
N for War onset (uncensored)	1,348	

Note: Main entries are censored probit estimates, with robust standard errors (adjusted for clustering on the dyad) in parentheses. Estimations were performed in Stata 9.1 (heckprob).
[a]Estimates for the three natural cubic spline variables are not reported.
[b]As compared to the reference category of nonterritorial MID. All tests are two-tailed.
*$p \le .05$; **$p \le .001$

are more likely to engage in MIDs, which is consistent with what was found in chapter 3. The findings also show that geographically contiguous pairs are likely to have more MIDs, which is consistent with proposition 4.1. These results show that both contiguity and territorial claims increase the likelihood of a MID occurring and that their effects are separate and independent.

At the war onset phase, however, there are different effects for contiguity and territory; that is, while territorial MIDs are more apt to escalate to war than nonterritorial disputes, contiguous foes are actually less, not more, likely to push their MIDs to the point of war compared to noncontiguous adversaries. Although the joint explanation does predict a smaller influence for contiguity on war onset, this reversed effect is not supportive of proposition 4.2. Interestingly, these findings for contiguity suggest that one reason why contiguous states are involved in many wars is simply because they are involved in many disputes, not because their disputes are more likely to escalate to war compared to those between noncontiguous states.

To tap into a key question raised by the joint explanation, though— whether the direction and/or magnitude of the contiguity influence differ depending on the presence (or absence) of territory, and vice versa—it is necessary to add multiplicative terms between contiguity and territory to both stages of the statistical model. Prior to looking at the results for this interaction specification, it is first useful to assess whether the inclusion of these multiplicative terms is nontrivial. To do so, one needs to compare the fit of the model inclusive of the interaction terms with the model that does not include them by conducting a hierarchical test of changes in χ^2 values for model fit across the two specifications (Jaccard, 2001: 15–19). Looking at table 4.2, it can be seen that the χ^2 value for the base model is 62.24 (degrees of freedom = 5) and for the interaction model it is 89.36 (df = 6). Referring to a table of critical χ^2 values for $\alpha = 0.01$ and df = 1, the difference in these χ^2 values of 27.1 is highly significant. This significant disparity indicates a consequential improvement in model fit provided by the addition of interaction terms, and therefore recommends the more fully specified model.

In this interactive specification (shown in the second column of table 4.2), once again one sees significant positive estimates for the influences of both territorial claims and contiguity on MID onset. The inclusion of the Contiguity $\times$ Territorial claim interaction makes the interpretation of these two parameter estimates a bit less straightforward, though, as they are conditioned on the value of the other variable equaling zero. For example, the positive territorial-claim estimate applies to a dyad-year characterized by the absence of contiguity (i.e., geographic contiguity equals zero); and similarly, the positive contiguity estimate is pegged to a dyad-year absent a territorial disagreement (i.e., territorial claim equals zero). When assessing the dispute proneness of a contiguous dyad with an outstanding territorial claim, it is important to look at the interaction estimate, as well as the individual estimates for contiguity and territory. And since such renderings are much clearer when presented in the form of predicted probabilities, we will save a full interpretation of the MID onset findings until later. For now, it is sufficient to note that the estimates for the three key variables are all statistically significant at this first stage, and that the significance of the multiplicative term suggests some type of contingency between the contiguity and territorial claim impacts.[12]

At the war onset phase, both the territorial MID and Contiguity × Territorial MID estimates are statistically significant, while the contiguity estimate is not. Comparing these findings from the model with interactions to those shown for the base specification, the importance of including the interaction term is clear. For while the base model results suggest a general negative influence for contiguity on the escalation of disputes to war, the interaction model suggests that an accurate interpretation of the contiguity impact is more particular; specifically, it is contingent on a consideration of the particular type of alteration (territorial or nonterritorial) sought by the revisionist actor in a MID.

This finding, as well as the P estimate, which tests for whether there is a meaningful correlation-of-error terms across the two stages, also allow us to see if selection bias affects inferences about war onset. The insignificant P shows, as in chapter 3, that the error terms are uncorrelated and that therefore there is no significant general selection bias operating. Likewise, controlling for the first-stage processes does not eliminate the significance of the relationship between territorial MID and war onset in the second stage. This suggests that the bivariate territorial explanation of war is superior to the bivariate contiguity explanation and that contiguity plays a role primarily in increasing the likelihood of a MID occurring and not of its escalation to war.[13]

Before moving to the predicted probability estimates for the effects of contiguity, territory, and their interaction, a few words about the control estimates are in order. Recall that the power status and development variables were included at the MID-onset stage as alternative opportunity factors, and the alliance and democracy variables at the war-onset phase were included as auxiliary willingness indicators.[14] These control estimates reveal several

---

[12] The propositions do not necessarily expect the contiguity-territory interactions to be positive (although positive estimates are supportive). A negative interaction may also be supportive if its magnitude is less than that of two positive component term estimates (e.g., the contiguity-territory interaction for MID onset, but not for war onset, in the second column of table 4.2). For further elaboration on this point, see Jaccard (2001); Lemke (2002: 119–20).

[13] Note the lower-order contiguity variable in the second stage loses its significance whereas the lower-order territory MID variable does not. Nevertheless, contiguity still plays a role in war onset through the interaction term, whose impact is best seen in the discussion on predicted probabilities.

[14] Models including a wide mix of interactions between and among contiguity, territory, and the opportunity and willingness controls were also estimated. These alternative specifications, while quite extensive and often cumbersome to interpret (and, therefore, not shown), are noteworthy in

things. First, dyads consisting of two minor powers are significantly less likely to engage in disputes compared to dyads consisting of at least one major state, a finding nicely in line with some recent work suggesting the sometimes singular behavior of minor powers (e.g., Lemke, 2002, 2003; Mousseau, 2000). Second, increasing levels of economic development lead to higher chances of MID onset. Third, the negative and significant peace-years estimates indicate the reinforcing nature of peace—as the number of years since the previous dyadic dispute increases, the probability of another MID onset decreases. Fourth, being allied imparts no significant impact on the probability of MIDs escalating to war. Fifth, increasing levels of dyadic democracy lead to lower chances of war onset among disputants, although this result is only marginally significant ($p = .077$) (similar to the finding in chapter 4). Sixth, increasing levels of disparity in relative capability do reduce the chances of MID onset, but have no significant impact on MID escalation to war. Finally, the estimates for ρ are insignificant, indicating no meaningful correlation-of-error terms across the MID and war-onset stages, just as was found in the previous chapter.

Predicted Probabilities

While the findings shown in table 4.2 indicate the direction and significance of the explanatory variable effects, predicted probabilities illuminate more clearly their substantive effects. The first column in table 4.3 compares the likelihood of a pair engaging in a MID, depending on whether or not the dyad was characterized by contiguity and/or a territorial claim, while the second column compares the probability of a MID escalating to war, based on whether the disputants were contiguous and/or fought over territorial revisionist goals. Viewing the dispute-onset estimates first, there is a clear ordering among the four dyad types that is strongly supportive of proposition 4.1. Noncontiguous dyads absent territorial claims are by far the least likely (.001) to engage in a MID, while contiguous pairs with competing territorial claims are by far the most likely (.038) to experience a dispute onset. The mixed dyad types fall somewhere in between—noncontiguous pairs with territorial claims show a .011 probability for MID onset in a given year, and contiguous pairs without competing claims experience MID onset with a probability of .018.[15] This ranking is nicely in line with two key bases of the joint explana-

---

that they confirm the robustness of the contiguity, territory, and interaction effects displayed in table 4.2.

[15] The ranking of these two middle categories is the reverse from that shown for the MID-onset cross tabulation in table 4.1, suggesting the usefulness of including the theoretically derived opportunity and willingness controls within the model specifications contained in table 4.2.

Table 4.3

Predicted Probabilities of Dispute (MID) and War Onset Based on the Presence or Absence of a Territorial Disagreement and/or Contiguity

Conditions	MID Onset	War Onset
Not Contiguous No Territorial Disagreement	.0010 (.0009–.0011)	.030 (.016–.056)
Not Contiguous Territorial Disagreement	.011 (.008–.016)	.282 (.203–.374)
Contiguous No Territorial Disagreement	.018 (.016–.020)	.020 (.011–.037)
Contiguous Territorial Disagreement	.038 (.033–.044)	.094 (.067–.127)

Note: Entries are predicted probabilities derived from the model with interactions in table 4.2; 95 percent confidence intervals are in parentheses. For MID onset, territorial disagreement refers to a Huth and Allee (2002) territorial claim among two states in a year. For war onset, territorial disagreement refers to a territorial militarized interstate dispute. The values of all control variables are set to their means.

tion at the dispute-onset stage—first, both contiguity and territory will increase MID onset chances and, second, the contiguity effect will be stronger than that of territory.

Moving to the war-onset estimates, there is only partial support for proposition 4.2. The proposition does correctly predict that territorial MIDs will encompass the two most war-prone categories and, conversely, that nonterritorial MIDs will make up the two least war-prone groupings. However, its predictions *within* each of these two classes are not supported, mostly due to the unexpected impact of contiguity. Contiguity imparts no significant effect among nonterritorial disputes and, even more surprisingly, it actually has a comparatively weak effect on war compared to noncontiguous dyads—territorial MIDs. Contiguous pairs are three times *less* likely (.094 versus .282) to escalate their territorial disputes to war than are noncontiguous foes. So, while this probability ranking for war onset does support the joint explanation's prediction that the territory effect will be stronger than that of contiguity, it does not support the explanation's notion that contiguity will have some positive impact on the likelihood of MIDs escalating to war.

Beyond showing clear support for the MID onset expectations (proposition 4.1) of the new joint explanation, and only partial support for its war-onset predictions (proposition 4.2), the predicted probabilities in table 4.3 also reveal several related and interesting findings. For one, at the MID onset phase, contiguity influences both dyads with and without territorial claims—contiguity raises the likelihood of MID onset from .011 to .038 among those with territorial claims and from .001 to .018 among those without. This is strong evidence supporting the joint explanation's idea that contiguous states enjoy more interaction opportunity, especially at the earlier MID onset stage, as the contiguity effect is present regardless of whether the bone of contention is territorial or not.

The joint explanation's posited willingness-enhancing role for territory is also clearly evident—territorial claims increase MID onset among both contiguous and noncontiguous dyads, while territorial MIDs are more likely to go to war for both contiguous and noncontiguous disputants. Particularly intriguing here are the war-onset findings. When territory is not in disagreement, MIDs are unlikely to escalate to war. When territory is in disagreement, war is more likely, but it is most likely when borders are not contiguous. This is clearly not in line with the contiguity explanation of war. This pattern, which was also found by Vasquez (2001) and Hensel (2000), is now found to hold even while controlling for the processes in the first stage. This provides further evidence that contiguity is playing, at best, a secondary role to territory in bringing about war.[16]

Taken together, the findings for the effects of contiguity and territory on the onset of disputes and wars provide strong support for the joint account's expectations at the dispute-onset stage, but only partial support at the war-onset phase. In line with one of the explanation's key notions, territory always imparts a conflict-enhancing influence, with territorial claims raising the likelihood of MID onset and territorial MIDs raising the likelihood of war. Thus, the conflict-heightening effect of territory is not contingent on a particular phase of conflict. The same cannot be said for the impact of contiguity, however, as contiguity tends to promote the onset of disputes, but is associated with a lower probability of their escalation to war. In this fashion, the influence of contiguity is not consistent across the two thresholds of conflict. Instead, a proper description of its effect is plainly contingent on the particular phase of conflict being examined.[17] In this sense, territory is a much more potent a factor for explaining war than contiguity—as predicted by the territo-

[16] An explanation for this result is not immediately obvious. The results suggest that the 141 territorial MIDs between noncontiguous states are somehow different from the average of the 591 territorial MIDs. What makes them different is a subject for further investigation.

[17] All of the predicted probabilities and confidence intervals were also estimated on a subsample of "politically relevant" dyads. The resulting rank orderings of probability estimates do not differ from those shown in table 4.3. This politically relevant subsample only includes dyads that are contiguous by land or less than twenty-four miles of sea and/or include at least one major power. The full set of cases is preferred for two reasons. First, by including variables for contiguity and power status, the models are explicitly estimating their role as opportunity factors, instead of assuming them. Second, use of the subsample would exclude more than two hundred disputes and twenty war participations from the analysis, certainly not what a "politically relevant" selection rule would intend.

rial explanation of war in contradistinction to the contiguity explanation of why neighbors fight.

Conclusion

This chapter began this investigation by developing a new theoretical account that simultaneously considered the roles of both contiguity and territory in pushing state pairs into disputes and wars. This joint contiguity-territorial explanation goes beyond prior work in two essential ways. First, it explicitly regards *both* contiguity and territory as important precipitators of conflict. Second, it predicts that the effects of contiguity and territory will be disproportionate across varied phases of conflict. After deriving hypotheses for the joint account at both the dispute- and war-onset points, we proceeded to an empirical evaluation spanning the years from 1919 to 1995.

The empirical analysis sheds significant new light on the exact nature of the territory and contiguity impacts, while controlling for a host of alternative explanatory factors. For instance, while the direction of the territory influence is consistently positive, its magnitude is markedly greater among noncontiguous pairs than among contiguous ones for war onset. Evidence regarding the impact of contiguity has also been found. The presence of contiguity consistently increases the likelihood of dispute onset, with this effect gaining strength in the absence of territorial claims. This contingency of magnitude at the dispute-onset phase is quite minor, however, when compared to the contingency of direction shown at the level of war onset. By itself, contiguity exhibits little influence on the escalation of nonterritorial disputes to war, while imparting a strong *negative* impact on the likelihood of war among territorial MIDs. Taken together, these findings perfectly support the joint explanation's predictions for dispute onset, while partially supporting its expectations for the onset of war. Further, the joint account's dual consideration of contiguity and territory enables it to more accurately explain the results compared to theoretical explanations based on contiguity or territory alone, but not in tandem.

Second, this analysis provides a crucial test to decipher the relative importance of territory and contiguity in pushing states toward or away from international conflict and whether controlling for the effect of contiguity eliminates the significance of territory. Territory appears to be more important in terms of war onset. The finding that noncontiguous dyads with territorial disputes are more war prone than even contiguous dyads with territorial disputes is especially damaging to the contiguity explanation. It is not opportunity that is the key to war, but territorial grievances. These apparently will even overcome the loss-of-strength gradient present in noncontiguous dyads. This conclusion is further enhanced by the tests that show no general or specific selection effect to be operating.

Finally, two additional points are worth noting. First, the examination here indicates that the use of an opportunity-and-willingness framework (Starr, 1978) has proven useful. Specifically, geographic contiguity, and territory in particular, appear to operate according to their respective role of providing interaction opportunity and willingness. Second, this analysis suggests that future research should carefully weigh the contingent nature of various causal processes.[18] This may prove to be especially true for the conditional impact of contiguity. In this way, we can move forward by explicitly incorporating the possibility of contingent linkages among explanatory factors into our theoretical and statistical modeling choices.

By showing that territory is still a potent engine of conflict onset and escalation while giving full consideration to the role played by geographic contiguity, these tests should put to rest another of the major criticisms of the finding that territorial disputes increase the probability of war. They show in a more definitive fashion than Vasquez (2001) or Hensel (2000) that a bivariate territorial explanation of war is superior to a bivariate contiguity explanation of war. At the same time, despite the only partial support for proposition 4.2, the analysis shows that a joint explanation that delineates the respective effects of contiguity and territory in a unified model is the best explanation of conflict across the MID onset and war-onset stages.

Part II of this book has not only dealt with two of the major obstacles to accepting the finding that territorial disputes are more war prone than other types of disputes, it has also added to our empirical knowledge about the onset of militarized disputes in the first place. This chapter has shown that contiguous states (i.e., neighbors) are more apt to have militarized confrontations than non-neighbors. This chapter, along with the previous chapter, has shown that states that have territorial disagreements with each other are also likely to have militarized confrontations with each other. Although it has not been tested directly in these two chapters, it is a plausible inference that these MIDs will be over territory. At any rate, it has been shown in the last two chapters that if states have territorial MIDs, they are more likely to go to war than states that have nonterritorial disputes. All of this is consistent with the notion that neighbors are prone to war because of territorial disagreements, a key proposition in the territorial explanation of war. Having territorial disputes increases the probability of war; however, it does not make it inevitable—that

---

[18] Bennett and Stam (2004: 219) come to the same conclusion following an in-depth empirical examination of the origins of war.

depends on how these MIDs are handled in the future, and in particular whether they recur. In part III, we build on these territory findings by examining whether handling issues through the practices of power politics—alliance making, recurrent disputes, and arms racing—increases the likelihood of war.

III

Power Politics and War

5

The Probability of War between Nation-States

War is a process and the most important thing in that process is what nation-states do to each other.

Up to this point in the book, we have concentrated on testing the relationship between territory and war. In this next part of the book we look at how the practices of power politics affect the probability of war. While territory is seen as an underlying cause of war, the use of the foreign policy practices of power politics is seen as a proximate cause of war. It must be remembered that it is not the mere presence of territorial issues that produces war, but how they are handled. Because the major practices of power politics (the making of alliances to promulgate one's claims, the repeated use of realpolitik tactics, and arms racing) involve states in a security dilemma, each of these is seen as embodying a series of steps toward war, rather than a way of achieving peace through strength, as Vegetius said.[1]

In the next three chapters we will test a series of propositions that claim that as states handle their territorial disagreements through power politics, they are more likely to go to war. Conversely, territorial disputes that are not handled in this manner are considerably less likely to result in war. Since power politics is a proximate cause of war, any issue handled in this way will have a higher risk of ending in war. Thus, the proposition that nonterritorial disputes have an increased probability of war when handled by power politics will also be tested, although it is expected that nonterritorial disputes do not have as high a probability of going to war as territorial ones.

The chapters in part III each test aspects of the steps-to-war explanation and employ different research designs. Nevertheless, each complements, and sometimes overcomes limitations, of the other. Chapter 5, the current chapter, asks the basic question of whether states that resort to power politics to

---

[1] The actual quote is *Si vis pacem, para bellum*, If you want peace, prepare for war.

contend over territorial issues have their overall relations so soured that they become involved in a syndrome of hostile behavior that makes war highly likely. It asks what kinds of behavior increase the probability of war between nation-states. Chapter 6 moves away from looking at the long-term behavior of states and examines the specific disputes between pairs of states. It asks what factors increase the likelihood that a crisis will escalate to war. Chapter 7 analyzes the extent to which the steps to war are best seen in terms of statistical interactions or simpler models.

This chapter, like the steps-to-war explanation itself is based on the assumption that the most important factor in bringing about wars is what states do to each other, that is, their pattern of interaction. Put another way, the key to understanding why war occurs is to analyze the issues that states have with each other and how they contend over those issues. The focus is on the overall relations of states. The emphasis is on what distinguishes the relations of states that go to war from those that do not. The answer lies in the kinds of issues and foreign policy practices that dominate the relations of the two states (a dyad).

Except for the study of interstate rivalry, this sort of theoretical analysis is missing from most quantitative analyses. While the move toward studying dyads is an important return to studying relations (away from the system and states' attributes), it has been drowned by using dyadic disputes, not to mention dyad-years, as the unit of analysis. These perspectives look at what distinguishes the MIDs that go to war from the MIDs that do not. They fail to look at the underlying relations that shape the kinds of MIDs that come to the fore. This chapter begins to correct that by complementing our study of MIDs with a study of the long-term relations between states that increase the probability of war.

One way of testing the steps-to-war explanation is to use a cross-sectional design that compares the long-term relations of a pair of states to see whether those that have taken one, two, or three of the steps are progressively more likely to have gone to war. Put another way, the study compares dyads that have the condition (or treatment) of having adopted certain foreign policies with those that have not.[2] Dyads that have this condition are expected to be at a greater risk of going to war; those that do not have this condition should not ever have a war.

Six propositions derived from the steps-to-war explanation will be tested by comparing pairs of states that go to war with each other at least once in

---

[2] Studying war by comparing dyads has been fairly successful in producing findings compared to the earlier approach, which tried to explain wars by looking at system characteristics such as the number of alliances in the system (e.g., Singer, Bremer, and Stuckey [1972]); see Vasquez (1993: 43–45).

their history (in a given period after 1815) with those that do not. The language of "steps" is meant to convey that the pursuing of certain objectives by adopting realist practices—such as the making of alliances, buildups of the military, and resorting to the threat and use of force—increases the probability of war each time one of these is adopted. Although these steps may follow a particular order for many pairs of states (of a certain type),[3] no specific sequence is seen as being immune from a risk of war. Alliances may precede or follow military buildups, and militarized disputes are likely to punctuate the entire relationship, thereby occurring before and after certain practices are adopted. While there might be a sequential pattern to the steps that can be theoretically derived and/or inductively established, such precision is not necessary when looking at the overall relations between two states. What is important is that the presence of more than one step, regardless of its order, results in an increase in the probability that this pair of states is apt to go to war. What is crucial is not the sequence of the steps, but that they are mutually reinforcing.

The focus on the long-term relations of a dyad advances the research program on the steps to war in two ways. First, most research typically examines only one step with control variables or, at the most, two steps (see respectively, Vasquez and Henehan, 2001; Senese and Vasquez, 2004). Second, most studies to date on the steps have been on dyadic disputes. Research on territorial disputes, even when not directly testing the steps explanation, has followed this pattern (see Hensel, 1996, 1998, 2000; Senese, 1996; Huth, 1996b; Henehan, 2001; James, Park, and Choi, 2006). Similarly, research on the war proneness of alliances has looked at individual alliances (Levy, 1981; Gibler, 1996, 1997b; 2000; Gibler and Vasquez, 1998; Leeds, Long, and Mitchell, 2000; Leeds, 2003a, 2003b; Walker, 2000). Likewise, the studies on military buildups and arms races have examined whether these have resulted in war by comparing whether in any given MID they are present or absent (Wallace, 1979, 1982; Diehl, 1983, Sample, 1997, 1998b, 2000, 2002). With few exceptions, mainly the work on interstate rivals (Diehl and Goertz, 2000; Thompson, 1995; Wayman, 1996; but see also Vasquez and Henehan, 2001) and that on recurring crises (Leng, 1983, 1993; Brecher and Wilkenfeld, 1997), quantitative research has not looked at how steps to war have affected the long-term relations of two states.

The propositions below identify what it is about the relations of the dyads that experience wars that distinguish them from the dyads that have militarized confrontations but never go to war. For the full time period there are 1,003 dyads, 251 of which go to war at least once in their history. The propositions below identify what it is about the relations of these 251 dyads that distinguish them from the 752 that have had militarized confrontation but have

---

[3] For example, major-major dyads or democratic-nondemocratic dyads.

never gone to war. Since 1816–2001 is such a long period of time, separate studies for three historical periods are conducted: 1816–1945, 1946–89, 1990–2001.[4]

Because data on the dynamics of state interaction and the timing of the steps are not always available, each proposition is expressed in terms of whether states in a dyad have taken certain steps sometime during their relationship and whether these steps distinguish the interstate relationships that go to war from those that do not. Five propositions deal with the effect of territorial disputes on the probability of war in light of the various realist foreign policy practices that a state might adopt in contending over these issues, and one proposition deals with the effect of using power politics to handle nonterritorial issues. Each proposition stipulates whether the probability of a dyad going to war, at least once in its history, is higher or lower, depending on whether the dyad has ever adopted one, two, or three of the foreign policy practices or steps (i.e., an outside alliance, repeated confrontation, or arms racing) specified in the models.

Proposition 5.1: Dyads whose relations are dominated by territorial disputes have a greater probability of going to war than the typical dyad that has militarized disputes.

Proposition 5.1 has to be true if the steps-to-war explanation is true, because the explanation maintains that territorial disputes are highly prone to war. Therefore, a pair of states whose relations are dominated by territorial disputes should have a greater probability of going to war than a pair of states that are not.

Proposition 5.2: Dyads whose relations are dominated by territorial disputes and have politically relevant outside allies have a greater probability of going to war, especially if both sides have outside alliances, than dyads whose relations are dominated by territorial disputes but have no outside alliances.

Proposition 5.2 has to be true if the theory is true because the theory maintains that when disputants make an alliance with a politically relevant third party (i.e., one that can reach the target either because it is a major state, contiguous, or in the region of the target), this increases the probability of war. Therefore, dyads whose members have outside allies should have a higher probability of going to war than those that do not have outside allies.

---

[4] The justification for this periodization is presented in chapter 2. When the subperiods are employed, the number of cases is reduced to: 456 for 1816–1945, 464 for 1946–89, and 291 for 1990–2001. There are two reasons for this. First, some dyads do not exist in a period, especially in the early period, and second, dyads that have an MID in one period may not have one in another period, and therefore are not included in the sample. This is especially the case in the two most recent periods.

This is especially the case if one side makes an alliance and the other forms a counter-alliance, which the theory expects is likely to happen if such allies are available. This prediction flows from the idea that the formation of a counter-alliance increases threat perception and thereby the probability of war. This goes against realist logic, which sees both sides having an outside ally as reducing the probability of an attack if the alliances balance power, as well as going against some existing findings (see Geller, 2000, for a review).

Proposition 5.3: Dyads whose relations are dominated by territorial disputes, have politically relevant outside allies, and have had repeated disputes to the point of being in an enduring rivalry have a greater probability of going to war than dyads whose relations are dominated by territorial disputes, have outside allies, but have not been enduring rivals with each other.

Proposition 5.3 assumes that, as militarized disputes and crises repeat, they increase the level of threat perception and hostility between the contending parties, as well as generating hard-liners within the domestic polity of each side. This in turn can lead to more disputes. At some point in the repetition of disputes, each side begins to see the other as a rival and significant enemy. Such perceptions are assumed to have an effect on behavior and the likelihood of war. Given this logic, a dyad whose members are enduring rivals should have an increased probability of war. The proposition implies that recurring disputes—regardless of the nature of the grievance (e.g., whether they are over territory or not)—will increase the probability of war.

Proposition 5.4: Dyads whose relations are dominated by territorial disputes, have politically relevant outside allies, and have had recurring territorial disputes have a greater probability of going to war than dyads whose relations are dominated by territorial disputes, have outside allies, and have no or few recurring territorial disputes.

The logic of this proposition flows from the idea that territorial issues are an underlying cause of war. If this is true, then dyads that have repeating territorial disputes, along with outside politically relevant alliances, will have a greater probability of war the more territorial MIDs they have. Also, this proposition implies that dyads dominated by policy or regime disputes, but have recurring territorial disputes are more likely to go to war than dyads dominated by policy or regime disputes without repeating territorial MIDs.

Proposition 5.4 is similar to proposition 5.3 in that it too looks at the role of recurring disputes. The main difference is that proposition 5.4 confines the main variable to the recurrence of territorial disputes—and at a lower threshold than the rivalry variable (operationalized as four instead of six). This is based on the idea that territorial disputes are more war prone in general, and it takes fewer repetitions of them to put a dyad at risk of war. The proposition also permits an analysis of whether dyads that are not rivals, but have recurring territorial disputes, have an increased likelihood of war.

Proposition 5.5: Dyads whose relations are dominated by territorial disputes, have politically relevant outside allies, are enduring rivals (or have recurring territorial disputes), and have an arms race have a greater probability of going to war than dyads that have these conditions, but do not have an arms race.

The logic of proposition 5.5 comes from the idea that as states feel threatened, they will build up their militaries, which will lead them to become involved in arms races. Arms races are seen as highly likely to result in war, especially in the presence of the other conditions. Arms races, however, are not seen as a necessary condition of war and many dyads will go to war without an arms race. However, when they are present, they will increase the probability of war.

The steps-to-war explanation is not confined just to the effect of territorial disputes, nor are territorial disputes seen as a necessary condition of war. Dyads that do not have territorial disputes or whose relations are centered on other sorts of issues can also be expected to go to war under the right conditions. According to the steps-to-war explanation, the probability of war occurring over these nonterritorial questions will increase if the issues are handled in a power politics manner. However, nonterritorial disputes are generally not as war prone as territorial disputes, so the probability of war will be expected to be lower. Therefore, the following proposition can also be derived from the explanation and will be tested:

Proposition 5.6: Dyads whose relations are dominated by nonterritorial disputes, have politically relevant outside allies, have had repeated disputes to the point of being in an enduring rivalry, have recurring territorial MIDs, and have an arms race have a greater probability of going to war than dyads whose relations are dominated by nonterritorial disputes, but do not have outside allies, have not been enduring rivals with each other, do not have recurring territorial MIDs, and do not have an arms race. The probability of war for these dyads will be lower than those whose relations are dominated by territorial disputes and have the other conditions present.

Proposition 5.6 flows from the notion that the practices of power politics tend to increase the likelihood of war, rather than prevent it. The steps-to-war explanation posits only that territorial disputes are most likely to go to war when they are handled in a power politics fashion, and not that other issues will not go to war when handled in a power politics fashion. As each of the power politics practices becomes more prevalent in the relations of two states contending primarily over nonterritorial disputes, their probability of going to war will also increase, although not to the level of dyads handling territorial disputes with power politics practices.

Research Design

The steps-to-war (Vasquez, 1987, 1993; Senese and Vasquez, 2003) and other explanations of war (Bremer and Cusack, 1995) that look at war as a process that emerges out of a set of interactions assume that the underlying relationship of two states, their prior history if you will, is a key to understanding and explaining why war comes about. To test explanations of this sort, it is important to have data that compare all the MIDs between two states; that is, it is important to take an historical approach to configuring one's data. It is possible to do this, as Maoz (2004) points out, by treating the relations of a dyad (for example, from 1816 through 2001) as the unit of the analysis.

Studying individual dyadic disputes or dyad-years misses how one dispute or crisis between states is related to their subsequent behavior. Such research tends to reduce relations between states to a series of independent atomistic interactions, which of course they are not. The popularity of dyad-year data has had the negative consequence that too many IR scholars are failing to examine the overall relations between two states and how their behavior may be a function of their underlying relationship.[5] Methodologically, looking at dyad-years inflates the number of cases to the point of several hundred thousand. The result is that small differences will be statistically significant. Yet these cases are not independent cases. France-Germany in 1937 is not independent from France-Germany in 1936 and in 1938.[6]

The data set used in this analysis is intended to overcome these problems and capture an overview of the long-term relations of a pair of states without breaking it down into a yearly analysis. The unit of analysis can be thought of as the "true dyad" because it looks at the entire history of relations between the two sides in much the same way as data on interstate rivalries have attempted to do.

In the data collected for this study, the unit of analysis has one observation for each dyad in a given historical period, so we refer to these data as a dyad-history data set. The following information on the relations between the pair of states over this long period of history is included:

[5] This is not to say that long-term relations have not been studied before; see the early study by Zinnes, Zinnes, and McClure (1972), for example, as well as the work of Leng (1983) or much of the work on conflict resolution, such as that of Burton (1990) and Kriesberg, Northrup, et al. (1989).

[6] For other possible negative effects, see James (2002: 21–24).

The number of MIDs the pair of states has experienced

Whether they have ever had a war with one another

The dominant questions or issues over which the two states have contended

The number of territorial MIDs, policy MIDs, and regime MIDs

The dominant alliance pattern that has characterized their relations—for example, whether they both have mostly had outside allies when facing each other, or only one side has had allies, or whether they have mostly been allied to each other, and so forth

The extent to which their territorial disputes recur

Whether they have engaged in an enduring rivalry

Whether they have ever engaged in an arms race

A problem in constructing a data set of dyads is to determine when a pair of states has sufficiently changed that one should no longer consider it the same dyad. This is primarily a theoretical problem; for example, in a study of the democratic peace if both sides should become democratic, the researcher might want to regard them as sufficiently different to generate a new dyad. In the construction of the dyad data set used here, two rules were followed in ending one dyad and beginning a new one: First, any system-membership change within the Correlates of War project that ended a state and replaced it with a new one generated a new dyad. For example, in 1945 Germany is replaced by East and West Germany, so after 1945, all German dyads end and a new set of East and West German dyads are generated. Second, the data in this study generate a new dyad whenever there is a change in the major state status of a state, according to Correlates of War criteria (see Singer, Bremer, Stuckey 1972: 22, and http://cow2.la.psu.edu/). For example when the United States becomes a major state in 1898, this generates a new set of dyads for the United States.[7] Major state status is used as a demarcation for dyads because major states are thought to behave differently in much of IR theory, especially realist theory, and there is some empirical evidence (Bremer, 1980) to indicate that this is the case.

The logic of the explanation maintains that states whose relations are dominated by certain kinds of militarized disputes and behavior are more apt to go to war than states that are dominated by other kinds of disputes and behavior. To test this notion, this chapter will compare dyads that go to war with

---

[7] The dyad data set is discussed further in Vasquez and Henehan (2001: 131–33). For purposes of replication, it should be reported that when this procedure is used, some split dyads (like Germany-Italy), where both have their major state status change during a given period, will have fewer than six MIDs but still be labeled by Diehl and Goertz (2000), and herein, as having had an enduring rivalry sometime during their history.

those that have never gone to war in a particular period. One of the problems with the latter sample is that it can include those that may have no real risk of war either because they have no contact or because they have few disagreements. To make for a more rigorous test, this chapter focuses on a sample of states that are known to have had serious disagreements, at least one of which resulting in a militarized dispute in a particular period.[8] It then compares those dyads that have gone to war with those that have never gone to war for a large number of years even though they have had a militarized confrontation.

The original dyad-history data set had one observation for the entire post-Napoleonic period (Vasquez, 2004). This analysis breaks down the data into three subperiods (1816–1945, 1946–89, 1990–2001). This permits a more refined historical analysis, especially since a number of dyads (e.g., in Western Europe) that have gone to war in 1816–1945 never have a war after that. If the steps-to-war explanation is correct, these dyads should no longer exhibit a power politics syndrome of behavior.

The dyad-history sample is an important sample that has been underutilized in international relations. It has major advantages over a dyad-year sample and a dyadic-dispute sample—the two typical samples used in the study of war. A dyad-year sample compares dyads that go to war and those that do not in a given year. The advantage of looking at the entire history of dyads that have at least one MID and comparing them with each other rather than looking at all dyads whether or not they have a MID is that the reference group (for the dyad-history data) is one where each side in the pair truly avoids war with the other in the presence of some serious confrontation. This sample better captures a history of no war/war than looking at all dyads or even just politically relevant dyads because the sample does not include any dyads that are free of serious conflict. This makes for a more rigorous test of the explanation because it says that among the pool of those who have at least some risk of war (in that they have shown a willingness to threaten and use force), it is able to distinguish those that go to war from those that never have done so.[9]

A dyad-history sample has an advantage over the dyadic-dispute sample in that the former more clearly identifies and therefore is able to predict those pairs of states that do not have wars. A dyadic-dispute sample compares MIDs—those that go to war with those that do not. The latter can tell us noth-

[8] We have used the minimal threshold of one MID. The rivalry literature refers to such dyads as having isolated conflict (one or two MIDs). For an analysis and discussion of such dyads, see Diehl and Goertz (2000).

[9] This issue is separate from the question of selection bias, which we treated in the previous two chapters and which we discuss again at the end of the research design. We make the kind of natural "bias" present in this sample work for us to construct a more difficult test. The sample assures that dyads that are at peace because they have no serious conflict (for whatever reason) are excluded.

ing about the history of peaceful relations between two states. It only tells us that in this one instance war has been avoided; war could erupt in the next MID or five years later. The dyad-history sample provides a more difficult test because the explanation must predict a no-war outcome across all MIDs that occur between the two states and not just the failure of a single MID to escalate to war.

The dyad-history data set will be used to test the six propositions derived from the steps-to-war explanation. To test these propositions, it is necessary to calculate the probability of war under each of the specified conditions and then to see if that probability increases when each proposition expects it will. To get an idea of how much of an impact the variables will have, a series of analyses utilizing maximum likelihood estimation will be conducted that delineates how the presence of each additional factor increases the probability of war. Thus, first an overall benchmark, the probability of at least one war breaking out in a dyad, will be calculated. Next, statistical models will be used to derive how much of an impact the presence of territorial disputes dominating the relations of two states has on the probability of their having at least one MID that escalates to war. This latter probability will then be compared to the probability of having at least one war when each of the various conditions outlined in propositions 5.2–5.5 are added (outside politically relevant alliances, rivalry, recurring territorial MIDs, and arm races). Lastly, those dyads that have all the steps present are expected to have the greatest likelihood of going to war.

If the steps-to-war explanation is correct, the presence of each factor posited to increase the probability of war should be above the overall (base) probability of a dyad having a war, and as each factor is added, this should produce incremental increases in the probability of war.[10] This prediction makes it clear that the explanation anticipates that there is an increased effect on the likelihood of war as each of the conditions are combined. In order to keep an already complicated set of hypotheses from becoming unduly complex, each of these combined effects is treated as additive rather than multiplicative.[11] Probabilities will be derived from a logit model (given the binary nature of the dependent variable) using CLARIFY, a software program (Tomz,

---

[10] It should be noted that the test proposed here is static in that it looks only at whether the condition has occurred in the history of relations between the two states and thus does not test the dynamic quality of the explanation in terms of seeing when the steps occur and their effect on taking the next step. Thus, when we say that a factor is "added," we simply compare cases having two factors with those having three, using a cross-sectional design. Also, the order in which the factors are added is not a concern in this test.

[11] For an analysis that tests for statistical interaction, see chapter 7.

Wittenberg, and King, 2003; King, Tomz, and Wittenberg, 2000) that runs simulations to calculate the predicted probabilities.

To derive the predicted probabilities, it is necessary to posit a logistic regression model that specifies the various factors thought to have a statistically significant impact on the overall probability of war. To test the propositions, six different logit models will be examined for each period when data are available. Each of these models is based on the general steps-to-war explanation, which offers propositions not only on the probability of dyads dominated by territorial disputes going to war, but on the probability of any dyad going to war.

The first test that will be conducted is of model 1, a base model that compares the effect of dyads whose relations are dominated by territorial disputes with dyads that have other types of dispute (e.g., policy or regime disputes) or combinations of disputes dominating their relations. Model 2 adds a set of alliance dummy variables that look at the effect that various alliance configurations within a dyad have on the probability of war while simultaneously controlling for the effect of the issue dummy variables. Model 3 adds a variable on whether the dyad has had an enduring rivalry. Model 4 substitutes for rivalry, a variable that measures the number of recurring territorial MIDs. Model 5 includes both rivalry and recurring territorial MIDs to see if they have separate and independent effects. Model 6 adds the arms-race variable along with the other variables in model 5.

What is important to keep in mind about these logit analyses is that the coefficients do not examine the combined effects of the variables; these effects are best ascertained by calculating the predicted probabilities. What the logit coefficients indicate is whether a given variable has a significant impact on the probability of war while controlling for the effects of all the other variables included in the model. In model 2, for example, they indicate whether a dyad with an outside alliance has a separate and independent effect on the probability of war regardless of the kinds of disputes that dominate a dyad's relations. The combined effects of territory, outside alliances, et cetera, can be ascertained when the predicted probabilities are calculated.

The dependent variable in this analysis is whether the dyad has ever had a war with the other party in a given period. As noted in chapter 2, wars between two states are derived from the interstate war data of the Correlates of War project and are coded as a war between the two states only if they are listed as opposing belligerents in the war data.

The key independent variables in the analysis are: the issues dominating relations; the type of alliances dominating relations; whether states have ever been enduring rivals; the extent to which territorial disputes have recurred, and whether the dyad has ever had an arms race. It must be emphasized that each variable tries to capture a snapshot of the entire history of two states in a given period and compare the salient characteristics of its history with the history of other pairs of states. Each of the independent variables is measured in the following manner:

ISSUEDOMinance: This is a classification intended to tap the dominant disputes that have characterized the relations of two states. MIDs are classified within the Correlates of War data as to the claim revisionist states are making according to five categories (nonapplicable, claims on territory, disagreements over the foreign policy of a state, claims pertaining to the nature of the current regime of another state or its type of government, and a miscellaneous category [see Jones, Bremer, and Singer 1996: 178–79 for details]). The ISSUEDOM measure is built by examining every MID that occurs within a dyad from 1816 through 1945, 1946 through 1989, 1990 through 2001. If 50 percent or more of the MIDs that occur between the two states in a given period are of one type (territory, policy, regime, other), then relations are said to be dominated by that issue. If none of the types reach 50 percent, then the modal type is taken as dominant. In cases of ties, the combination is seen as dominant. Policy disputes dominate the relations of most dyads, followed by territory, and then regime. This holds for the entire 1816–2001 period and each subperiod.[12] The most frequent combination (for the entire period and for each subperiod) is territory and policy. Dyads dominated by nonapplicable MIDs are dropped.[13] Further information on the ISSUEDOM measure is provided in Vasquez and Henehan (2001: 132–33) and Leskiw (2000).[14]

To run the logit analysis, each of the categories of ISSUEDOM is broken into dummy variables. There are three dummy variables relevant to territory,

---

[12] For the entire period, the numbers are: Policy (400, 39.9%), Territory (201, 20%), Regime (53, 5.3%), N = 1003. For the subperiods, the numbers are: for 1816, Policy (150, 33%); Territory (84, 18.4 %); Regime (9, 2%); for 1946, Policy (218, 47%); Territory (78, 17%) ; Regime (44, 9.5%); for 1990, Policy (138, 47%); Territory (74, 25.4%); Regime (8, 3%). Subperiods do not equal the sum of the entire period, because of overlapping and changes in major state status. The nonapplicable categories range from 3.4% (10) (1990–2001) to 12% (57) (1946–89) to 30% (135) (1816–1945).

[13] These are dyads that tend to be joiners to a dispute and are not matched with a revisionist state. Thus, two states, neither of which is revisionist, but join on opposite sides of a dispute, would have a nonapplicable code for that given MID. For the number of cases whose relations are dominated by MIDs coded as nonapplicable for each subperiod, see note 12 above.

[14] For data on the ISSUEDOM of Diehl and Goertz's enduring rivalries, see Vasquez and Leskiw (2001: 311–12). For variations on the measure, see Leskiw (2001). The ISSUEDOM measure was developed in consultation with Chris Leskiw. Our thanks to him for his work on this measure. The update of the dyad-history data using MID 3.02 data and the calculation of ISSUEDOM for each subperiod was done by Choong-Nam Kang. Our thanks to him also.

Terr Dom, which is the main indicator, and two combination variables—Territory and Policy (Terr&PolDom), and Miscellaneous Territory (MisTerDom (which combines seven categories: Territory and Regime, Territory and other, Territory-regime-other, Territory-policy-regime, Territory-policy-other, Territory and Nonapplicable, Terr-Policy-Nonapplicable).[15]

ALLIANCEDOMinance: This measure is constructed by looking at the kinds of alliances within the dyad each state has had over its history that are relevant to its relations with the other state in the dyad. The variable measures whether one disputant has an outside ally and the other none; whether both have outside allies; whether they have been allied to each other and have exclusively been only in the same alliances as each other (i.e., they do not have any outside allies that are not simultaneously the ally of the other); whether both have been allied to each other but have had at one point a simultaneous outside alliance that was not shared by the other, or whether the states have had no politically relevant alliances.

Politically relevant alliances are defined as those alliances that contain one or more states that can project their capability to the primary area(s) where one of two sides of the dyad are located. Such states are seen as any major state or any minor state in the region or adjacent country where one of the sides of a dyad is located. This measure originally was calculated for each dyadic MID. The data used to derive politically relevant alliances are the updated and revised Correlates of War alliance data (version 3.0) collected by Gibler and Sarkees (2004).

To determine the overall alliance pattern of a pair of states, a procedure similar to the construction of the ISSUEDOM variable was followed.[16] Each MID within the dyad is coded for the type of alliance present *on the first day* the MID was initiated. Note that alliances formed after a MID was initiated, or three months before a war broke out, are not included in this measure. If 50 percent of the MIDs between a pair of states have the same alliance type present (e.g., both sides have an outside alliance), then this pattern is said to dominate relations in a given historical period. If 50 percent of the MIDs have no one type, then the modal category is employed. In cases of ties, a combination is employed. The latter cases are combined into a Miscellaneous Out-

---

[15] The coding rules for combined issues are: (1) if any territory, then code as Misc Terr, (2) if no Terr and Policy present in combination, then code as Misc Pol, and (3) if none of the above and Regime present, code as Misc Regime (to date these cases consists of Regime & other, Regime and Non-applicable).

[16] This procedure was initially developed by Chris Leskiw in consultation with us (see Senese and Vasquez, 2004). Choong-Nam Kang refined this measure for the updated data.

side Alliance category (Misc Out).[17] Each of the alliance types are then broken down into dummy variables.

ENDURING RIVALRY: This variable is constructed from Diehl and Goertz's (2000: 45) categorical measure of enduring rivalry. They classify dyads with one or two MIDs as having isolated conflict, those with six or more within twenty years as enduring rivals, and those in between (so long as they occur within ten years) as proto-rivalries. Any given isolated conflict, proto-rivalry, or enduring rivalry can come to an end if there has been no MID activity for a ten- to fifteen-year period (the scale slides requiring more time for termination of those dyads with more MIDs). It is thus possible for a dyad to have more than one episode of an isolated conflict or enduring rivalry. In the dyad-history data each dyad is coded on the basis of the maximum rivalry level it reaches in a given period. These codes are used to create a dummy variable indicating whether a dyad ever had an enduring rivalry (six or more MIDs within a twenty-year period).

RECUR4: This index measures the extent to which territorial disputes recur within a dyad. It simply counts the number of territorial MIDs that occur in the history of relations of a pair of states in a given period and then codes them as to whether the dyad has four or more territorial MIDs. Unlike the RIVALRY variable, it does not measure all MIDs that occur, but only those related to territory. RECUR4 is included because the steps-to-war explanation assumes that, while the recurrence of any dispute increases the probability of war, the recurring of *territorial* disputes is even more prone to war.

There is a moderate association between the RIVALRY and RECUR4 measures,[18] but they do measure different things. Logit model 4 employs the RECUR4 index to see if it has an impact. Model 5 employs both the RIVALRY variable and RECUR4 index to see if controlling for one will eliminate the effects of the other.[19]

---

[17] There are 123 cases coded in the Miscellaneous category across the three subperiods; all but two of these involve outside alliances, so they are labeled Miscellaneous Outside alliances. The two exceptions are both in the 1816–1945 period and both involve the combination of no alliance and allied to each other. One case goes to war and the other does not.

[18] For the period beginning in 1816, Phi = .448; for 1946, Phi = .468; and for 1989, Phi = .317. All are significant at the .01 level.

[19] It should be noted that since Diehl and Goertz see any particular episode of isolated conflict, proto-rivlary, or enduring rivalry terminated if there is no MID for a ten- to fifteen-year period, it is possible to have dyads with several periods of isolated conflict and hence more than just two MIDs. Since RECUR4 looks only at the number of recurring territorial MIDs, it is possible that dyads with isolated conflict can score a 3 or 4 on the RECUR4 index, if these do not cluster. These

ARMS RACES: Arms races have traditionally been measured by comparing the rates and levels of military expenditures of two states (see Wallace 1979, Diehl 1983, Horn 1987, and Sample 1997), although the specific formulas vary. Sample's (2002) data using the measure developed by Horn (1987) are employed here. A dyad is coded according to whether members "ever have had an arms race" with each other in the period in question.

Classification of an entire history of a dyad even for a given period using the above measures is always, at best, an indirect measure because it does not examine the precise times at which the variables co-occur. For example, it is assumed—but not demonstrated—that at least one of the wars that occur in a dyad that has had an enduring rivalry occurs either at the enduring rivalry stage or because the relationship between the states is approaching that level. Diehl and Goertz (2000) and Hensel (1998) do provide evidence that this is the case, but such precise inferences cannot be made from the research design presented here.

Such problems are not uncommon in a variety of research designs—for example, research conducted at the system level. As with the latter, the research based on the history and patterns found in a dyad over time can be subject to errors of "ecological inference" if findings uncovered for the dyad are assumed to necessarily hold at the dyadic dispute level or for any specific MID involving the pairs of states. All that can be inferred from an analysis of dyads is that the presence of these variables in the relationship of these two states makes them prone to go to war at least once. It is assumed that the variables in the model brought about this war or others because they were present prior to or at the time the war occurred. It is known from previous research that the independent variables included in the model (territory, outside alliance, and rivalry) precede the dependent variable in dyadic disputes involving the states in the dyad sample (see Levy, 1981; Leng, 1983; Hensel, 1996, 1998; Huth, 1996b; Senese, 1996; Gibler, 1997b, 2000; Sample, 1997, 1998b, 2000; Vasquez and Henehan, 2001; Senese and Vasquez, 2003, 2004), so that is not a real concern. In addition, the ALLIANCEDOM variable is constructed so that only alliances present before the first day an MID is initiated are counted. Likewise, the Correlates of War project alliance data that are employed do not record intrawar alliances, nor are alliances formed three months prior to the outbreak of a war counted.

---

three or four territorial disputes are not seen as a proto-rivalry because at best only two of them occur within a ten-year span. For the full period, there are eleven cases that have three or four territorial disputes, but are classified on the rivalry scale as having only "isolated conflict." Some examples include: Haiti-Dominican Republic, Venezuela-UK, Bolivia-Peru, Chile-UK, Argentina-Uruguay, UK-Spain.

What is not known is if the specific MID that escalates to war has the variables present or preceding it. So long as the conditions existed some reasonable time before the states went to war, even if they did not exist in the specific MID, this would still be evidence consistent with the steps-to-war explanation because the presence of these variables would indicate a kind of poisoning of the relationship that makes war highly likely at some point, even if it does not erupt in that particular dispute. This is another way of saying that the entire history of relations between two states may be more important than just the specific factors associated with the current disagreement that escalates to war. Nonetheless, based on previous analyses using a dyadic dispute sample, it is highly likely that dyads that have these factors present have them in at least one MID that escalates to war. To make sure that this is the case, the next chapter analyzes the dyadic dispute data that were employed to construct the dyad-history data used in this chapter to see if wars arise from the MIDs that embody the risk factors identified by the steps-to-war explanation.

The data utilized in this research design, however, generally do not measure timing (with the partial exception of the ALLIANCEDOM variable), but simply whether the variables were ever present. Measurement of the timing would require much more precise data than is currently available. Nevertheless, the tests in this analysis are valid and useful, because they are based on the logic of falsification (see Popper 1959; Lakatos, 1970). Based on this approach not every aspect of a theory need be tested, but only a plausible prediction. Here, the prediction is that dyads that have had these foreign policies will also have a war. If the propositions are falsified using this research design, the larger explanation from which they are derived can be rejected. It is also unlikely the explanation could pass the tests involved in a more complicated design. In addition, without passing the tests in this design, the expense and effort in creating data on timing would not be warranted (for an initial attempt at creating data on timing relevant to the steps-to-war explanation, see Valeriano [2003]). Conversely, if the propositions fail to be falsified, this adds credence to the explanation, but still leaves open the possibility that more precise data on timing will lead aspects of the explanation to be falsified or reformulated.

Still one would like to know the extent to which the evidence on dyads conforms to the overall expectations of the steps-to-war explanation or whether the steps occur at a time when they are not likely to have a causal impact. To get some idea of how the data look, we derive a sample of cases from the data to probe this question, and we provide the results after the main body of findings.

In the end, the dyad-history data used in this chapter, while overcoming some of the problems with dyad-year data, limits the inferences that can be made to general tendencies, such as: if power politics is used sometime during the interactions of two states, this increases the probability that they will go to war; the more power politics practices they utilize, the greater the probability of war. Conversely, the absence of any resort to power politics greatly reduces the risk of war. The latter prediction, of course, is not subject to any limitation on inferences since timing is not at issue (i.e., power politics is not utilized to handle issues, so war is not likely to ever occur).

Findings

As noted in the previous sections, the steps-to-war explanation sees the outbreak of war as a process whereby what states do to each other (in terms of the claims they make and the foreign policy practices they engage in to support those claims) increases the probability of war by making it more likely that eventually a MID will emerge that escalates to war. To test this explanation, several models are examined adding one variable (or cluster of related dummy variables) at a time to get an idea of the effect of each. The findings for each subperiod will be reported separately beginning with the 1816–1945 period.

1816–1945

The six most important models are reported in table 5.1. Model 1 is the base model and consists simply of comparing dyads that have different types of disputes dominating their relations. It can be seen from the table that dyads whose relations are dominated by territorial disputes are significantly more likely to have a war than dyads whose relations are dominated by policy disputes (the modal and reference category).[20]

The positive impact of territorial disputes on escalation to war remains significant even when most of the other steps to war are included—outside alliances, enduring rivalry, and recurring territorial disputes. Only when the arms-race variable is included in model 6 do territorial disputes lose significance, but here recurring territorial disputes are significantly related to escalation to war.[21] On the basis of these findings, proposition 5.1 and the territorial aspects of propositions 5.2–5.4 fail to be falsified.

[20] The analyses were also run with territorial dominance as the reference category. It was found that dyads dominated by territorial disputes are also more likely to go to war than regime disputes in model 1 in a one-tailed test (p = .0645). This statistically significant result disappears in the other models, although the coefficient for regime disputes is negative in all the models except that with arms races (model 6).

[21] This implies that only when dyads have four or more territorial MIDs will territory have a separate impact from arms racing on the likelihood of war.

Table 5.1

Logit Estimates: Likelihood of a Dyad Going to War, 1816–1945
Never a War/One or More Wars (reference category = policy disputes, no alliance),
Dyad-History Data

Variables	Model 1	Model 2	Model 3	Model 4	Model 5	Model 6
Terr Dom	.65	.84	.94	.76	.86	.29
	(.28)**	(.31)***	(.31)***	(.31)**	(.31)***	(.38)
Regime Dom	−.16	−.06	−.01	−.04	−.01	.26
	(.24)	(.28)	(.28)	(.29)	(.28)	(.46)
Other Dom	−.22	−.01	−.03	−.02	.04	.15
	(.21)	(.23)	(.23)	(.23)	(.23)	(.24)
Misc Terr	−.56	−.48	−.33	−.40	−.31	.11
	(.52)	(.52)	(.53)	(.52)	(.53)	(.66)
Terr & Pol	.58	.50	.52	.47	.47	1.02
	(.46)	(.47)	(.49)	(.47)	(.48)	(.58)*
Misc Pol	−1.17	−1.42	−1.39	−1.35	−1.35	−1.34
	(.53)**	(.55)***	(.53)***	(.55)**	(.54)**	(.62)*
Misc Regime	−.88	−.67	−.59	−.60	−.55	perfect
	(1.17)	(1.11)	(1.12)	(1.12)	(1.12)	predictor[c]
Allied Each Other		.91	.77	.94	.85	−1.09
		(.61)[a]	(.64)	(.68)	(.69)	(1.23)
One Outside Ally		1.03	.99	1.10	1.05	1.01
		(.35)***	(.35)***	(.36)***	(.35)***	(.41)*
Both Outside Ally		.67	.68	.67	.69	.59
		(.21)***	(.20)***	(.21)***	(.20)***	(.26)*
Allied Each Other + Outside		1.08	1.03	1.17	1.11	.82
		(.51)**	(.50)**	(.52)**	(.51)**	(.74)
Misc Out		1.34	1.45	1.40	1.47	1.24
		(.43)***	(.43)***	(.43)***	(.43)***	(.49)*
Enduring Rival			1.28		.98	1.03
			(.50)***		(.54)*	(.60)*
Recur Terr4				1.47	1.04	1.25
				(.60)**	(.64)[b]	(.66)*
Arms Race						1.04
						(.39)*
Constant	−.21	−1.20	−1.37	−1.33	−1.41	−1.28
	(.16)	(.32)***	(.32)***	(.34)***	(.33)***	(.38)*
Chi-Sq (df)	18.7	31.0	35.4	36.0	35.5	35.6
	(7)***	(12)***	(13)***	(13)***	(14)***	(14)***
Pseudo R^2	.047	.081	.100	.098	.107	.142
Number of Cases	321	321	321	321	321	238

Entries are logit coefficients; robust standard errors in parentheses.
*$p \leq .10$ level **$p \leq .05$ level ***$p \leq .01$ level.
All tests are two-tailed unless otherwise indicated.
[a]$p = .134$ [b]$p = .106$ [c]N = 2 and these are placed in the reference category.

The findings on "outside politically relevant alliances" are also consistent with the steps-to-war explanation. In general all dyads that have outside alliances, especially those for both sides or one side with outside allies, have a significant likelihood of going to war. The only exception is in model 6, when arms races are included; here one variable, "allied to each other but at least one side has an outside alliance," now becomes insignificant, although the other three outside alliance variables remain significant. Thus, for the 1816–1945 period the expectations regarding outside alliances are fulfilled for propositions 5.2–5.5, which can be seen as failing to have been falsified with regard to the alliance aspects of the propositions.[22]

The three other variables included in the models—enduring rivalry, recurring territorial disputes, and arms races—also work in the way hypothesized by the steps-to-war explanation. Models 3 and 4 examine the impact of repeated disputes by employing two different measures—(1) the repetition of MIDs that reach a level indicating that states are in an enduring rivalry according to Diehl and Goertz (2000: 45) (regardless of whether that rivalry is spurred by territorial or nonterritorial disputes) and (2) the repetition of territorial disputes (measured as four or more territorial MIDs regardless of whether there is an enduring rivalry or whether nonterritorial MIDs dominate relations).

The findings for model 3 show that enduring rivalry has a statistically significant impact on the likelihood of war. The steps-to-war explanation posits that a dyad that has sufficient disputes to move up the Diehl and Goertz scale from isolated conflict to proto-rivalry to enduring rivalry will experience an increased probability of going to war. The test results of model 3 are consistent with this expectation. This means that, when a pair of states has six or more MIDs in twenty years, they will have an increased likelihood of going to war, a finding first established by Goertz and Diehl (1992a). Here, the enduring rivalry variable is statistically significant even when controlling for the effects of the issue and alliance variables. The effects of type of disputes and the alliance variables remain the same as in model 2.

Model 4 substitutes for the measure of enduring rivalry a measure of recurring territorial disputes. As noted in the research design, these measures differ from each other in two ways: First, recurring territorial disputes (RECUR4) examines only territorial MIDs and not all disputes, and second, unlike the Diehl and Goertz measure, it has no requirement that a certain number of disputes need occur within a specified period. The results show

[22] The findings related to states that are allied to each other and belong only to the same alliances are nonsignificant and in the wrong direction (positively related to war). This finding, however, is a function of the Seven Weeks' War of 1866; otherwise this variable would be negatively related to war as generally expected in the literature; see the discussion in chapter 6, below.

that dyads that have four or more recurring territorial disputes will have an increased likelihood of going to war, even if the pair of states does not reach Diehl and Goertz's (2000) enduring rivalry stage.

Since there is some overlap between the recurring territorial-dispute index and the Diehl and Goertz enduring-rivalry classification, model 5 was run including both variables to see whether one will eliminate the other. Even though further research will be needed to disentangle the effects of these two variables, the test results indicate that each has independent and separate effects, although recurring territorial MIDs are just barely significant. These findings imply that both recurring *territorial* disputes and recurring disputes of all kinds increase the probability of war.

Model 6 includes all five sets of variables in the model. It adds the effect of arms races and includes both the enduring-rivalry and the recurring-territorial-disputes variables. When this is done the thrust of the steps-to-war explanation is supported, although some variation in significance is revealed. First, the major new finding is that arms races have an independent and separate effect that increases the likelihood of war. Second, both recurring territorial disputes and enduring rivalry increase the likelihood of escalation to war even in the presence of each other and the other steps.[23] Third, territorial disputes lose their significance, but it must be kept in mind that recurring territorial disputes still play a significant part in the onset of war. This implies that once arms racing starts states either have or require at least four territorial disputes in order to be at great risk of war. When arms racing is not included in the model, this "requirement" need not be met.[24]

The above tests suggest that all of the five variables relevant to the explanation—territorial issues dominating relations, both sides having outside alliance, enduring rivalry, recurring territorial disputes, and arms races—play important roles in distinguishing the pairs of states that go to war from those that have never gone to war in the 1816–1945 period. All five variables in all but one of the models are consistently found to have an effect. The exception is in the arms-race model where the territorial impact is captured solely by the recurring territorial MIDs variable.

What the logistic regressions do not test is the cumulative and combined effects of each of the variables that are posited by the steps-to-war explanation and the extent to which they each increase the probability of war. These

[23] This also holds in the arms-race model when enduring rivalry and recurring territorial disputes are included separately (not shown).

[24] While including the recurring territorial disputes may reduce the impact of the territorial MID variable, the elimination of its significance appears to be more a function of including the arm race variable. It should be remembered that in model 3, when recurring territorial disputes is first introduced, it reduces the Z score for territorial MIDs but does not eliminate its significance.

Table 5.2

Probability of War Occurring at Least Once in the History of Two States, 1816–1945

Conditions	Territorial MID	Policy MID	Regime MID
Issue Dom only	.368	.201	.204
All others set to 0	(.241–.494)	(.123–.297)	(.109–.331)
Issue Dom +	.532	.328	.330
Both sides with	(.407–.649)	(.240–.421)	(.211–.462)
outside allies			
Both sides with	.732	.554	.552
outside allies +	(.511–.892)	(.344–.753)	(.311–.768)
Enduring Rivalry			
Both sides with	.755	.581	.580
outside allies +	(.546–.904)	(.347–.801)	(.320–.818)
Recurring Terr MIDs			
Both sides with outside	.875	.764	.761
allies + Recurring Terr MIDs	(.699–.971)	(.530–.930)	(.496–.936)
+ Enduring Rivalry			
Both sides with outside allies +	.935	.917	.930
Recurring Terr MIDs +	(.827–.986)	(.799–.982)	(.798–.988)
Enduring Rivalry			
+ Arms Races			

Note: Main entries are predicted probabilities with 90 percent confidence intervals in parentheses. The predicted probabilities are derived from model 5 in table 5.1 for all the rows except for the last, the model including the arms-race variable, for this row, model 6 in table 5.1 used. The base probability of war for this period (including all missing data for arms races, but not dropped MIDs labeled nonapplicable) is .461.

effects are most directly and simply tested by comparing the probabilities that can be derived from the logit models. An overview of these is provided in table 5.2.

Table 5.2 highlights the major findings from the analysis (with confidence intervals in parentheses). The probabilities reported in this table are predicted probabilities derived by using CLARIFY (Tomz, Wittenberg, and King 1999). Each of the probabilities reported in the table is based, respectively, on model 5 (which includes both recurring territorial disputes and enduring rivalry, but excludes arms racing) for all the probabilities without arms races and model 6 for the probability that includes arms racing.[25]

The most important result of the tests reported in table 5.2 is that the probability of war increases as each variable is added to a model. The overall

[25] The reason for this is that in model 5, the inclusion of the arms-race variable reduces the number of cases to 238 (from 321), and the "territorial disputes dominating relations" variable is insignificant; see the analysis reported in table 5.1 for details.

(base) probability of war in this sample is .461.[26] This is a very high base probability of war. It means that during this time period almost half of all dyads have gone to war at least once. A good deal of this warfare, of course, is concentrated in the first half of the twentieth century around the world wars. The base probability can be used as a benchmark for comparing the predicted probabilities.

On the basis of model 5, it can be seen that dyads whose relations are dominated by territorial disputes but have taken none of the other steps to war have a .368 probability of going to war at least once. This probability of war is higher than for the dyads whose relations are dominated by policy and regime disputes—.201 and .204.[27] This is consistent with proposition 5.1.[28]

When both sides in a dyad have an outside alliance while they are contending on territorial disputes, the probability of war increases to .532. This supports the expectation of the steps-to-war model in that states contending primarily on territorial disputes where both have outside alliances in most of their MIDs will have a significant increased probability of war.[29] These two sets of findings are consistent with propositions 5.1 and 5.2. They are also consistent with previous research on the steps to war using MID 2.1 data (Vasquez and Henehan, 2001; Senese and Vasquez 2003, 2005; see also Gibler, 1997a, 2000), even though the specific tests and/or techniques used are different.

The biggest jump in the probability of war occurs when dyads have either an enduring rivalry and/or recurring territorial disputes (at least four). If a pair of states is involved in an enduring rivalry, the likelihood of war increases to .732.[30] As states go from one to four or more territorial disputes, the likelihood of war increases accordingly, going from the .368 for dyads that have fewer than four to .755 when a dyad has four or more territorial disputes.[31] In-

---

[26] The base probability of war is derived from the sample of 321 MIDs used in models 1–5. Since 148 of these go to war, this makes for a base probability of $148/321 = .461$.

[27] It can be seen from an examination of the confidence intervals that the .201 for policy and the .204 for regime falls below the lower bound of the territorial confidence interval (.241–.494). The same is also true for the probability of war when "both sides with outside alliances" is included in row 2, .328 for policy and .330 for regime, with the territorial confidence interval being .407–649.

[28] It should also be noted that the .368 is lower than the base probability (of .461), but all this means is that territorial MIDs require some use of power politics before they exceed the base. When the other steps to war are taken, it can be seen from table 5.2 that the predicted probabilities exceed the base probability.

[29] This is a significant difference in that the .532 predicted probability falls above the upper bound of the .368 (.241–494) confidence interval and the latter is below the lower bound of the .532 (.407–.649) confidence interval, as can be seen in the table.

[30] This is also significantly different from the .532 in that the probability of .732 is above the upper bound of the confidence interval (.407–.649) of dyads being dominated by territorial MIDs with both sides having outside alliances, but note that the .532 fall just within the lower bound of the .732 (.511–.892) confidence interval.

[31] The jump from .532 to .755 is statistically significant in that .755 is above the upper bound

dividually, when recurring territorial disputes are present (and an enduring rivalry is absent), the probability of war is slightly higher (.755) than when there is an enduring rivalry and not at least four territorial disputes (.732); these differences are not statistically significant, however. They do, though, underline that recurring territorial disputes put a dyad at a risk of war as great as if it had an enduring rivalry, something not previously known.

As shown in model 5 (in table 5.1), the effects of recurring territorial disputes and enduring rivalry are separate and independent. Thus, when both are present, we would expect an increase in the probability of war, and this is evident in table 5.2, which shows that in this condition the predicted probability of war increases to .875.[32] This is a very high probability of war. The latter finding shows that when all three of the major steps to war have been taken by a pair of states, very few manage to avoid war; only 15 percent or so are able to escape. These results provide evidence highly consistent with the steps-to-war explanation.

Lastly, table 5.2 uses model 6 to examine the effect of all five conditions (territory, both having outside alliances, recurring territorial disputes, rivalry, and arms races) on the probability of a dyad having a war. It can be seen that when these conditions are present (at their maximum value) the highest probability of war is reached for territorial MIDs—.935. This is consistent with the expectation of proposition 5.5 in that it is in the correct direction and there is a substantial increase in the absolute size of the probability, but the increase over model 5 is not quite statistically significant, as can be seen from an examination of the confidence intervals.

These findings, although weaker, are similar to Sample's (2000, 2002) findings on the danger of arms races. Likewise, the general increase in the probability of war from .368 to .532 , to .732 and . 755, to .875 and to .935 (beginning with a base probability of .461) is the sort of progression anticipated and predicted by the steps-to-war explanation.[33] This is highly consistent with the overall logic of the steps-to-war explanation. Of equal importance is that the probabilities from each of the models is consistent with propositions 5.1–5.5, even if there may be some overlapping in the confidence intervals.

---

of the .532 confidence interval (.407–.649) and the .532 falls below the lower bound of the .755 confidence interval (.546–.904).

[32] The .875 indicates that when both recurring territorial disputes and enduring rivalry are present this does significantly increase the likelihood of war compared to when both are absent in that the .875 is well above the upper bound of the .532 (of both sides with outside alliances) (.407–.649), and the .532 is below the lower bound of the .875 (.699–.971).

[33] While this is the case, that does not mean that the confidence intervals of these probabilities do not overlap; in fact they do overlap on two occasions, as discussed in the text, but to make this criterion the basis of a decision on the hypotheses in light of all the other results poses the greater risk of accepting the null hypothesis when it should be rejected, that is, a Type II error.

Table 5.2 has presented an overview of the predicted probabilities that highlight their progression as outside alliances, rivalry, recurring territorial disputes, and arms races are present in a dyad's relations. The table also presents evidence on the probability of nonterritorial disputes going to war. These findings can be used to test proposition 5.6. These results support several points. First, as stated in the proposition, dyads whose relations are dominated by disputes other than territory (or the combination of territory and policy) generally have a lower probability of going to war than dyads dominated by territorial disputes. This is indicated primarily by the top three rows of table 5.2.[34] The predicted probabilities for policy and regime MIDs are always lower than those for territorial MIDs, but note that sometimes there is an overlap with the confidence interval. These findings provide support for proposition 5.6.

Second, the resort to (at least some practices of) power politics (as exemplified by the presence of outside politically relevant alliances, interstate rivalry, and arms racing) to handle disputes increases the probability of war, as proposition 5.6 predicts. In other words, when both states resort to making outside alliances and handle policy or regime disputes in such as way that they are enduring rivals; they have a higher probability of going to war. These findings support the claim within the steps-to-war explanation that power politics is a separate path to war from the territorial path to war.

Third, the biggest jump in the probability of war for dyads dominated by regime and policy disputes is reached when they have an enduring rivalry *and* four or more territorial disputes (even though these disputes need not be dominant in the numerical sense). This implies that at times there may be a territorial element in their proneness to war that deserves further attention.[35] Similarly, when arms racing is present, the probability of war jumps again. From these results, it is clear that the classic international politics era of 1816–1945 generally fits the steps-to-war explanation. The findings of the 1946–89 period will be examined next.

1946–1989

The post–World War II period is distinguished by two interrelated characteristics—the presence of nuclear weapons and the Cold War. Even the most cur-

---

[34] The bottom three rows include recurring territorial disputes as a variable in the models, so these results cannot be used to test proposition 5.6.

[35] Analyses by Vasquez (2001) show that dyads with 25 percent or more of their MIDs over territory have a greater likelihood of going to war than would be expected by chance. In addition, Vasquez and Leskiw (2001) show that dyads with 25 percent or more of their MIDs being over territory have a greater propensity of becoming enduring rivals than expected by chance.

sory understanding of history makes it clear that this period is considerably less warlike than the first half of the twentieth century. The major rivals of the Cold War era—the United States and Soviet Union—do not fight each other, unlike the major rivals of the nineteenth and early twentieth centuries. Given these stark historical differences, it remains of interest how well the steps-to-war explanation will be able to account for behavior in this period.

Table 5.3 presents the same six models that were tested for the previous period. Model 1 shows that when territorial disputes dominate the relations of two states, they have an increased likelihood of going to war (compared to policy disputes, the reference category), as do states whose relations are dominated by a combination of territorial and policy disputes. Also of interest, given that this is the Cold War period, is that states whose relations are dominated by regime disputes also have an increased likelihood of going to war, a pattern absent in the previous period.[36] These findings on territorial and regime MIDs hold for all the models even when all the other steps are included. This makes the fit slightly tighter than for the previous period, where territorial MIDs drop out when arms races are included. On the basis of this, proposition 5.1 and all the territorial aspects of propositions 5.2–5.5 fail to be falsified.

The findings on alliances, however, are not confirmed. As can be seen in model 2 none of the outside alliance patterns significantly increase the likelihood of war. The two variables on being allied with each other are perfect predictors of peace in this period (N = 24 for allied with each other and N = 41 for allied and an outside alliance). The former is consistent with conventional and steps-to-war expectations, while the latter is not. In general, proposition 5.2 and all the expectations about alliances in propositions 5.3–5.5 are falsified.

The only relationship that approaches significance (.15) is when both sides have outside allies (in models 3 and 5).[37] In these models, which include the enduring rivals variable, states are less likely to go to war if both sides have outside alliances. This relationship is the opposite of what is expected by proposition 5.3 and 5.5, but it is consistent with what we know about the Cold War, namely that rivals, like those in the East and West, did not go to war when they both had outside allies. This finding will be explored in greater detail in the next two chapters.

---

[36] However, dyads whose relations are dominated by regime disputes are less likely to go to war than dyads dominated by territorial disputes (not shown), even though they increase the likelihood of war. The latter relationship is statistically significant only for model 1; in models 2–5 the direction is still negative but not significant. In the arms-race model (6), the relationship changes direction. The findings are produced by making territorial MIDs the reference category.

[37] This is not significant using a two-tailed test. It is significant at the .10 level in a one-tailed test, but a one-tailed test cannot be used because the predicted direction is positive and not negative.

Table 5.3

Logit Estimates: Likelihood of a Dyad Going to War, 1946–89
Never a War/One or More Wars (reference category = policy disputes, no alliance),
Dyad-History Data

Variables	Model 1	Model 2	Model 3	Model 4	Model 5	Mode'
Terr Dom	2.40 (.40)***	2.55 (.41)***	2.53 (.42)***	2.32 (.46)***	2.52 (.47)***	1.60 (.60)
Regime Dom	1.68 (.50)***	1.96 (.53)***	2.05 (.52)***	1.98 (.53)***	2.05 (.52)***	2.33 (.53)
Other Dom[c]	perfect predictor	perfect predictor	perfect predictor	perfect predictor	perfect predictor	perfe· predic·
Misc Terr[d]	perfect predictor	perfect predictor	perfect predictor	perfect predictor	perfect predictor	perfe· predic·
Terr & Pol	2.01 (.61)***	1.81 (.67)***	1.78 (.72)**	1.73 (.69)**	1.78 (.73)**	1.71 (.81)
Misc Pol	−.10 (1.07)	−.28 (1.13)	−.14 (1.16)	−.29 (1.14)	−.14 (1.16)	.11 (1.16)
Misc Regime	1.09 (1.12)	.56 (1.15)	.68 (1.16)	.51 (1.15)	.68 (1.16)	1.17 (1.23)
Allied Each Other[e]		perfect predictor	perfect predictor	perfect predictor	perfect predictor	perfe· predic·
One Outside Ally		.16 (.44)	−.03 (.48)	.12 (.46)	−.03 (.48)	.74 (.81)
Both Outside Ally		−.45 (.52)	−.86 (.60)[a]	−.54 (.53)	−.86 (.60)[a]	.07 (.87)
Allied Each Other + Outside[f]		perfect predictor	perfect predictor	perfect predictor	perfect predictor	perfe· predic·
Misc Out		.82 (.70)	.79 (.74)	.87 (.70)	.79 (.74)	1.35 (1.01)
Enduring Rival			1.72 (.53)***		1.71 (.58)***	1.66 (.54)
Recur Terr4				.95 (.64)[b]	.02 (.71)	.81 (.77)
Arms Race						.46 (.79)
Constant	−3.03 (.32)***	−2.89 (.45)***	−2.98 (.47)***	−2.87 (.46)***	−2.98 (.48)***	−3.88 (.79)
Chi-Sq (df)	39.2 (5)***	48.3 (8)***	53.7 (9)***	54.7 (9)***	55.6 (10)***	51.4 (11)***
Pseudo R^2	.154	.197	.242	.208	.242	.238
Number of Cases	391	326	326	326	326	296

Entries are logit coefficients; robust standard errors in parentheses.
*$p \leq .10$ level   **$p \leq .05$ level   ***$p \leq .01$ level.
All tests are two-tailed unless otherwise indicated.
[a]$p = .152$ [b]$p = .070$ one-tailed test   [c]N = 2 and these are dropped   [d]N = 14   [e]N = 24   [f]N = 41

The findings on model 3 show that states involved in an enduring rivalry are more likely to go to war than those that are not. When the recurring territorial disputes and the arms race variables are added, respectively, in models 5 and 6, enduring rivalry remains significant. Rivalry, then, is a consistent factor in the Cold War period that increases the likelihood of war, even though the most famous rivalry of the period (the Soviet-American) never ends in a direct war. This consistent result warrants the conclusion that proposition 5.3 and all the aspects related to enduring rivalry in propositions 5.4–5.5 fail to be falsified.

Model 4 drops the enduring rivalry variable and includes only the recurring territorial-disputes variable. When this is done it becomes clear that dyads that have recurring territorial disputes during the post–World War II period have an increased likelihood of going to war (significant at the .07 level in a one-tailed test).[38] This lends support to proposition 5.4. However, when rivalry is added to recurring territorial disputes, as in model 5, then enduring rivalry wipes out the effect of recurring territorial disputes, which means that any effect of recurring territorial MIDs is included in the phenomenon of rivalry itself. Unlike in the 1816–1945 period, there is no separate and independent effect for recurring territorial disputes; it is the recurrence of MIDs that are important rather than their content per se.[39] This same finding holds for model 6. On the basis of this finding, the aspects dealing with recurring territorial disputes in proposition 5.5 must be modified to emphasize the potency of enduring rivalry.

Lastly, model 6 shows that arms races have no significant impact on the likelihood of war in this period. This is not consistent with the steps-to-war explanation, although it is consistent with earlier research on arms races and the Cold War (see Sample, 2002). Therefore, proposition 5.5 is falsified. Further investigation, not presented in the table, however, shows somewhat surprisingly that arms races do significantly increase the probability of war in a simple bivariate model or when the arms-races variable is added to models 1 and 2. In other words, arms races are positively related to war onset, except when controlling for rivalry or repeated disputes, in which case their effect is lost. Thus, it may not be that the logic of the steps is incorrect, but that the sequence of the steps listed in the propositions is not correct. At any rate, it is clear that, in the Cold War period, rivalry and recurring disputes eliminates the independent effect of arms races whereas in the 1816–1945 period they do not.[40]

[38] Since proposition 5.4 specifies direction, a one-tailed test is legitimate. The p level for a two-tailed test is .141.

[39] Given the findings on model 1, it would be expected that regime disputes are probably recurring as well as territorial disputes in this period.

[40] Further investigation of the effect of arms races in the 1816–1945 period also shows that arms

Table 5.4
Probability of War Occurring at Least Once in the History of Two States, 1946–89

Conditions	Territorial MID	Policy MID	Regime MID
Issue Dom only	.394	.053	.294
All others set to 0	(.217–.600)	(.022–.101)	(.156–.455)
Issue Dom +	.221	.024	.157
Both sides with	(.109–.382)	(.009–.050)	(.060–.299)
outside allies			
Both sides with	.242	.034	.185
outside allies +	(.066–.517)	(.005–.107)	(.030–.492)
Recurring Terr MIDs			
Both sides with	.588	.118	.482
outside allies +	(.328–.804)	(.043–.227)	(.251–.728)
Enduring Rivalry			
Both sides with outside	.590	.135	.487
allies + Recurring Terr MIDs	(.319–.836)	(.030–.324)	(.188–.808)
+ Enduring Rivalry			
Both sides with outside	.652	.327	.775
allies + Recurring Terr MIDs	(.342–.890)	(.073–.687)	(.432–.961)
+ Enduring Rivalry			
+ Arms Races			

Note: Main entries are predicted probabilities with 90 percent confidence intervals in parentheses. The predicted probabilities are derived from model 5 in table 5.3 for all the rows except for the last, the model including the arms-race variable; for this row model 6 in table 5.3 is used. The base probability of war for this period is .130.

Table 5.4 presents the predicted probabilities. Most of the probabilities are derived from model 5 in table 5.3; the only exception is for the probabilities involving arms races (in the last row), which are derived from model 6 in table 5.3.[41] The base probability of war in this period is .130,[42] considerably lower

---

races were positively related to war onset in a bivariate model and to all of the models in table 5.1 to which it was added including model 4 for rivalry. In other words, in the earlier period rivalry does not eliminate the significance of the arms-race variable.

[41] In table 5.2 the main reason for using two models in calculating predicted probabilities was that in model 6 one of the variables became insignificant and there was a loss in the number of cases. Here, however, neither reason is of concern since all the variables retain the same significance level in both models and the number of cases lost are fewer; rather, the same procedure is used simply to remain consistent.

[42] The base probability is derived from the sample of 407 MIDs used in models 1–6 in table 5.3. This sample drops all dyads dominated by nonapplicable MIDs. The base includes all the relevant observations including those dropped because they were a perfect predictor. For example in model 1 there are 391 cases and 16 dropped "perfect predictor" cases for a total of 407. Only 53 of 407 dyads go to war during the Cold War: 53/407 = .130.

than the .461 for the 1816–1945 period, which supports the idea that at least among the major states the Cold War was a "long peace" (Gaddis, 1986, see also chs. 6 and 7 below). This means that approximately 87 percent of the dyads during 1946–89 never go to war, compared to approximately 54 percent for the 1816–1945 period. Of course, the latter has fewer dyads (321 versus 407) in its sample.[43]

It can be seen from the table that dyads whose relations are dominated by territorial MIDs have a much higher probability of going to war, .394, than the base probability of war. In fact, this probability is comparable (in absolute numbers) to that in the 1816–1945 period (.368). This suggests that the more "peaceful" profile of the Cold War period is not due to a lowered probability of territorial disputes, but to some other factor. One of those factors is clearly illustrated in the second row of table 5.4—both sides having outside alliances. Contrary to steps-to-war propositions and the findings for the previous period, we see that when both sides have outside alliances, this lowers the probability of war, whereas before it increased it. The probability of war for dyads dominated by territorial MIDs is reduced from .394 to .221. Similar reductions occur for dyads dominated by policy and regime disputes.[44] The findings on outside alliances are anomalous for the steps-to-war explanation and falsify the alliance portion of propositions 5.2–5.5.

The "both sides having outside alliances" finding is particularly anomalous. From what we know about the Cold War, this alliance pattern, which reflects in many ways the centrality of the Warsaw Pact–NATO and East-West polarization of the system into two hostile blocs, seems to be responsible for the irenic effect. How and why this alliance system reduces the probability of war (as opposed to the 1816–1945 period where both sides having outside alliances increases the probability of war) deserves further research. Two possibilities are suggested. First, the superpowers, out of fear of war with each other including escalation to nuclear war, tightly controlled their allies. Second, this was an alliance system that dominated the entire Cold War period from roughly 1949 on, and this "long-term impact" is what is picked up by the "both sides have outside alliance" indicator; whereas, in the earlier period there is no single alliance system dominating the entire period and most alliances were not as global and centered on the same rivalry, so no single alliance type could have such a long-term impact. Together these two factors reduce the amount

---

[43] The earlier period actually has fewer dyads than indicated, because as will be recalled from the research design, when a state becomes or ceases to be a major state, this generates a new set of dyads, which results in more "double counting" in the 1816–1945 period.

[44] As can be seen by an examination of the confidence intervals, the .394 is outside the upper bound of the .221, but the latter falls just inside the lower bound of the .394.

of war in the system.[45] Because this seems to be the case, this finding implies that of the various steps to war, alliances politics may have complicated underlying processes that can either push parties toward war or away from it.

Table 5.4 also shows that the irenic effect of both sides having an outside alliance is wiped out if the pair of states is engaged in an enduring rivalry. Here the probability of war increases from the low .221 to a significantly higher .588.[46] A similar jump occurs with regime disputes, but not policy disputes. Thus, despite the lack of a war between the United States and Soviet Union, enduring rivalry still significantly accounts for the onset of war in this period. Put another way, the presence of territorial MIDs or regime MIDs and a pattern of enduring rivalry distinguish dyads that go to war from those that do not. These results are sufficiently strong that the rivalry aspects of propositions 5.3–5.5 fail to be falsified by this test.

Recurring territorial disputes are a different matter. The results in the table show no statistical difference over just having territorial disputes dominate relations. More important, inclusion of both the enduring-rivalry and the recurring-territorial-dispute variables in the same model does not really add much to the strength of the predicted probability (.588 versus .590). On the basis of this evidence, then, the recurring-territorial-disputes aspects of the propositions must be rejected. Any effect recurring territorial disputes has in the 1946–89 period is subsumed under the effect of enduring rivalry, unlike the previous period where there is a separate and independent effect.

Lastly, when arms races are present along with the other steps there is a substantial increase in the probability of war from .588 to .652, although this is not significantly different, indicating that enduring rivalry and arms racing may be intertwined in terms of their impact on the probability of a pair of states going to war. Of the two, however, rivalry seems to be the more important.

Where does this leave us? Two constants appear across the two periods— territorial disputes and enduring rivalry. Both of these place dyads at risk of war. Of the various steps to war these are consistently the most dangerous. Arms races also may have an impact in both periods, although their impact during the Cold War period is tenuous and seems to be intertwined with rivalry. Recurring territorial disputes are more important in the 1816–1945 period. They are also important in the Cold War period, but their effect is wiped

---

[45] Further evidence that it is the nature of the specific Cold War alliance system that reduced war is indicated in the findings related to one side having an outside alliance. Here the probability of war remains the same (.394 versus .382) (not shown in the table).

[46] This is also a substantial increase over the .394 for just territorial MIDs, but it is not quite statistically significant since there is an overlap with the confidence intervals, as can be seen in table 5.4.

out by enduring rivalry. Whether this is more than just a historical coincidence will need a deeper analysis than provided here. Lastly, outside alliances provide an effect contrary to that expected by the steps-to-war explanation. Indeed, they may hold a key to understanding why the Cold War period was a long peace (along with the effect of nuclear weapons).

Of the propositions, only those dealing with the effect of territorial MIDs dominating relations and of enduring rivalry have clearly failed to be falsified. Conversely, those regarding outside alliances must be rejected, and those regarding arms races left somewhat in abeyance with the suspicion that their effect may be a function of rivalry. Nevertheless, with the exception of alliances, table 5.4 evinces a progressive increase in the probability of war as additional steps to war are taken with most of the weight being carried by territorial MIDs dominating relations, enduring rivalry, and to a lesser extent, perhaps, arms races. Concentrating on these three steps we see an increase in the probability of war going from .394 to .588 to .652.

Finally, nonterritorial disputes during the post–World War II period will be briefly examined. The most significant contrast with the previous period is that policy and regime disputes are quite different in their propensity for war. Dyads whose relations are dominated by regime disputes are simply more likely to go to war. Regime disputes seem to become dangerous when they are embedded in an ongoing rivalry. Here the probability of war goes from .294 when all factors are held at zero to .482 when rivalry is added. When arms races are present, regime MIDs have a very high probability of going to war—.775.

The table also shows that the use of power politics with regard to non-territorial disputes results in a progressive increase in the probability of war. This, however, follows the same pattern as that of territorial MIDs; namely, having both sides with outside alliances reduces the probability of war and the effect of recurring territorial disputes seems to be a function of enduring rivalry. On the whole, both policy and regime disputes have a lower probability of war than territorial disputes; the one exception is when dyads dominated by regime disputes have an enduring rivalry and an arms race, in which case they have a higher probability of going to war than those in similar circumstances but whose relations are dominated by territorial disputes. This is a substantial difference, but it is not statistically significant. Given this caveat, we can say that the thrust of proposition 5.6 fails to be falsified.

Of the two periods, the steps to war, then, best fits the longer 1816–1945 period, and only partially fits the post–World War II (Cold War) period. The Cold War period fits in that territorial disputes and the presence of rivalry increase the probability of war during the Cold War as they did in the previous period. What is most different is that war did not break out between the two superpowers despite their rivalry. In addition, outside alliances no longer increase the probability of war, and arms races may have only a tenuous impact, if any. These two findings contradict the steps-to-war explanation. The conventional wisdom would assume that nuclear weapons played a role in preventing a superpower war and in making the Cold War a kind of long peace. They also may have stripped alliances of their belligerent effect and encouraged arms control to keep arms races from getting out of hand—thereby helping to bringing about the statistical anomaly for the steps-to-war explanation. Why the Cold War was as peaceful as it was will be the subject of further analysis in the next two chapters. For now, the question is how well the steps-to-war explanation fits the post–Cold War period.

1990–2001

The post–Cold War era is a label that implies that this is a transitional period, and indeed it turns out to be that way. It begins with high hopes for superpower cooperation and a resolution of outstanding issues, many going back to the end of the World War II. It ends on September 11, 2001, with the attack on the Twin Towers in New York City. The MID data on which the analyses in this chapter are based end in the calendar year of 2001 so the entire post–Cold War period is encompassed.

The post–Cold War period is of intrinsic interest, in that it is recent, and of theoretical interest, in that it provides a basis for comparison with the other two periods, which reflect different patterns. Intrinsically, one is always drawn to the immediate past to see what kinds of patterns are reflected. The post–Cold War era saw many peaceful resolutions of difficult and sensitive issues. Germany was reunited, the Baltic states and Eastern Europe underwent radical transformation and would eventually link with the West. Both NATO and the EU would come up to the border of the former Soviet Union, something unthinkable during the Cold War without war. In the immediate aftermath of the Cold War, peace broke out in several places, including such disparate conflicts as those in Cambodia and Northern Ireland. At the same time, it must be remembered that the post–Cold War period and its hope for a New World Order was born in war. The Persian Gulf, which heralded a new United Nations and superpower cooperation, was an important multilateral war in the period and set the stage for later conflict and war in the area. So one of the questions of interest is just how peaceful the post–Cold War period was.

More theoretically, but on the same note, given the disparity between the findings for the Cold War with those for the longer 1816–1945 period, one asks whether the most recent period will continue trends established in "the long peace" or return to old patterns. Historically, one wonders if the advent of nuclear weapons and the bipolar structure of the Cold War have profoundly changed international politics or whether the removal of the centrality of the Cold War issue, tightly linked with nuclear rivalry, will see a resurrection of the politics of the past. Theoretically this is important because the steps-to-war explanation fits the earlier 1816–1945 period quite nicely, while the 1946–89 period reflects only a partial fit with some anomalies. A focus of the data analysis will therefore be on whether the post–Cold War period, and presumably the future, will be more like "the long peace" or the classic international politics period of 1816–1945. Put another way, just how relevant is the steps-to-war explanation today? Can it provide a full explanation of war for the most recent past and for the future, or must it be adapted, as the implications of the findings on the Cold War suggest?

The first piece of evidence to address several of these questions is a simple statistic—the base probability of war, which, for this period, is .064,[47] considerably lower than the .130 of the Cold War period, and much lower than that for 1816–1945, which had a base probability of .461. This means that the notion that peace broke out after the Cold War has some merit. We know that a number of important transitions were accomplished peacefully, such as the complete reversal of the Soviet buffer zone that Stalin had created at great risk. What this statistic indicates is that even when militarized confrontations emerged after 1989, fewer went to war than before.

Of course, it must be kept in mind that this low base probability of war reflects the activity of only a little over a decade, and there have been many decades with low probabilities of war. This does not mean a new progressive trend to peace per se, albeit one can be a little more optimistic about the waning of major state war in the near future (see Vayrynen, 2006, and Henehan and Vasquez, 2006).[48] Such a low base probability of war does mean, on this measure at least, that the post–Cold War period is more like the Cold War than the 1816–1945 period. The key however is whether the process of war onset in the post–Cold War period follows the patterns outlined by the explanation. In other words, of the wars that occur, do they follow the pattern expected by the steps-to-war explanation?

The analyses reported in table 5.5 provide evidence on this point. The table tests the propositions in this chapter for the 1990–2001 period and can be used to provide a systematic comparison across the three periods to see if the post–Cold War period is more like classic international politics (1816–

---

[47] The base probability is derived from the starting sample used in table 5.5, which has 281 observations of which 18 have a war, 18/281 = .064. Note that the logits in table 5.5 have 249 (or fewer) cases because perfect predictors have been dropped.

[48] There has not been a major state war (a war with a major state on each side) since the end of the Korean War in 1953, although there have been plenty of major-minor-state wars.

Table 5.5

Logit Estimates: Likelihood of a Dyad Going to War, 1990–2001 Never a War/One or More Wars (reference category = policy disputes, no alliance), Dyad-History Data

Variables	Model 1	Model 2	Model 3	Model 4	Model 5
Terr Dom	.67	.57	.77	.32	.53
	$(.56)^a$	(.57)	$(.62)^d$	(.62)	(.68)
Regime Dom	perfect predictor	perfect predictor	perfect predictor	perfect predictor	perfect predictor
Other Dom	perfect predictor	perfect predictor	perfect predictor	perfect predictor	perfect predictor
Ter&Pol	1.08	1.42	1.74	1.16	1.48
	$(.73)^b$	(.79)*	(.86)**	(.95)	$(.96)^c$
Misc Terr	perfect predictor	perfect predictor	perfect predictor	perfect predictor	perfect predictor
Misc Pol	.29	.45	.77	.53	.74
	(1.11)	(1.13)	(1.18)	(1.13)	(1.16)
Misc Regime	perfect predictor	perfect predictor	perfect predictor	perfect predictor	perfect predictor
Alliance Index1		.90	.90	.95	.93
		(.35)***	(.36)**	(.38)**	(.38)**
Enduring Rivalry			2.27		1.82
			(.83)***		(.74)**
Recurring Terr				1.69	1.21
				(.82)**	$(.78)^c$
Constant	−2.93	−5.26	−5.56	−5.45	−5.63
	(.39)***	(1.18)***	(1.27)***	(1.28)***	(1.33)***
Chi-square	2.7	7.2	14.3	10.7	17.7
	(3)	$(4)^c$	(5)**	(5)*	(6)***
Pseudo R^2	.021	.071	.121	.109	.138
Number of Cases	249	235	235	235	235

Entries are logit coefficients; robust standard errors in parentheses.
*$p \leq .10$ level; **$p \leq .05$ level; ***$p \leq .01$ level.
All tests are two-tailed unless otherwise indicated.
$^a p = .114$ one-tailed test $^b p = .070$ one-tailed test $^c p = .060$ one-tailed test $^d p = .108$ one-tailed test

1945) or the Cold War's long peace. Unfortunately, because arms-race data are only available through 1992, proposition 5.5 (and model 6) cannot be tested.[49]

[49] Looking only at the three years reduces the number of cases to eighty-four with the arms-race variable being dropped due to collinearity. For the entire period, there are ninety-four cases with arms-race data. Of these cases only fourteen dyads have an arms race and none of them have a war.

Model 1 examines whether dyads dominated by territorial MIDs are more likely to go to war. The findings are not very strong, but the Terr Dom variable approaches significance in a one-tailed test, and the combination of territorial and policy MIDs is significant at the .10 level in a one-tailed test.[50] Generally, however, it does not seem that having one's relations dominated by territorial disputes is a key. What is crucial is if territorial disputes recur. This variable, as can be seen in model 4, significantly increases the likelihood of war. This conclusion is underlined by the fact that model 1, as a whole, is not significant, see the chi-square at the bottom of table 5.5,[51] whereas model 3 with recurring territorial disputes is. This means that issue dominance is not by itself a good predictor of war likelihood, but that recurring territorial disputes are.

On the basis of this evidence, it can be concluded that there is some limited support for proposition 5.1, but much more robust support for proposition 5.4 with regard to recurring territorial disputes. This means that in the most recent period territorial disputes must recur at least four times for there to be a statistically significant likelihood of war. However, given that there is some support (albeit weak) for territorial dominating relations increasing the risk of war, it is important to keep in mind that this conclusion may very well be a function of the limited number of years on which the data are based.

Model 2 is very important for determining whether the post–Cold War period is similar to the Cold War period or the classic international politics period. The Cold War period, it will be recalled, showed that outside alliances were not positively related to war, and in one instance, both sides having outside alliances, were actually negatively related to war. Indeed, this negative statistical relationship seems to be very consistent with what is known historically about the role of alliances being associated with the absence of war between the East and West during the Cold War.

It is of great theoretical interest then to see whether model 2 shows that outside alliances are positively associated with dyads going to war.[52] Unfortunately, a collinearity problem prevented this model or any of the others from being run with the alliance dummy variables used in the two previous subperiods.[53] The strong suspicion, however, is that outside alliances are positively

---

[50] One of the problems with model 1 is that there are several perfect predictors, which reduce the number of cases to 249. If these perfect predictors are placed in the reference category, the number of cases is raised to 281 and Terr Dom is significant at the .054 level in a one-tailed test (Z score = 1.60).

[51] The same is true when the perfect predictors are placed in the reference category.

[52] It should be noted that the alliance data goes through the end of 2000, which means data for 2001 are dropped after model 1.

[53] The "allied to each other and an outside alliance" dummy was the culprit, and when this was dropped from the sample, the "allied to each other" became collinear and prevented the model

Table 5.6

Alliance Index 1 by War in a Dyad, 1990–2000

Dep	No Alliances	Misc Alliances	Allied each Other	Outside Allies	Total
NO WAR					
Count	31	28	21	168	248
Expected	28.9	26.1	22.4	170.6	
% War/No war	12.5	11.3	8.5	67.7	100
% Alliance	100	100	87.5	91.8	93.2
WAR					
Count	0	0	3	15	18
Expected	2.1	1.9	1.6	12.4	
% War/No war	0	0	16.7	83.3	100
% Alliance	0	0	12.5	8.2	6.8
TOTAL					
Count	31	28	24	183	266
% War/No war	11.7	10.5	9.0	68.8	100
% Alliance	100	100	100	100	100
Chi-square (df)					6.13[a] (3)
Gamma					.464**
Cramer's V					.153[a]

Significant at: *.10 level   **.05 level   ***.01 level
All tests are two-tailed unless otherwise indicated.
[a]$p = .054$ one-tailed test

related to war. This suspicion is warranted given that "no alliances"—the standard reference category—for the alliance dummy variables is a perfect predictor of peace. This not only makes it highly likely that the other alliance patterns will be positively related to war, but also demarks this period as different from the Cold War period, where "no alliances" had a higher probability of going to war than certain alliance patterns.

To deal with the problem of collinearity, the alliance dummy variables were replaced with an index that grouped the three outside alliance dummy variables into one category at the highest point in the index. The other vari-

---

from being run. Dropping that variable, as well, so reduced the cases that the remaining outside alliance variables became insignificant.

ables were then ranked below it in terms of their alleged threat perception, as follows: No alliances, Misc. alliances, Being Allied to each other, and Having some sort of Outside alliance.[54] Model 2 shows that the alliance index is positively related to war, which means that as one goes from no alliance and miscellaneous alliance to allied to each other, and to having an outside alliance, the likelihood of war increases significantly.

To get a better idea of how this is the case and how the different alliance groupings are related to the likelihood of war, a bivariate cross tabulation is presented in table 5.6. Two major conclusions can be made from the table. First, the chi-square indicates a significant positive relationship (.054 for a one-tailed test). The gamma is fairly high for this sort of sample—.46 (significant at the .02 level). Second, the observed number of wars for outside allies is higher than the expected, although these are not large numbers. Still the conditional probability of war (the frequency or percentage of cases with outside alliances having a war) is .082 compared to the base probability of .068. It is true that the conditional probability of war for outside alliances is lower than for states that are "allied to each other"—.125. Nevertheless, outside alliances produce most of the war observations—fifteen of the eighteen dyads (83.3%) that go to war in this period have an outside ally. Only three dyads that go to war are allied to each other with no independent allies. All the dyads that are at peace have either no alliance or a combination of miscellaneous alliances, This evidence indicates that in this period outside alliances are positively related to war and that this period is more like the 1816–1945 period than the Cold War period, where having alliances seem to reduce the likelihood of war (although not always significantly).

Models 3–5 in table 5.5 also show that the alliance index is positively related to war and that dyads that have outside alliances have an increased likelihood of going to war even while controlling for enduring rivalry and recurring territorial disputes. On the basis of these findings, it can be concluded that proposition 5.2 in terms of the aspects dealing with the general phenomenon of outside alliances and these aspects in propositions 5.3–5.5 fail to be falsified. This means that for the post–Cold War period outside alliances in-

[54] Theoretically, "no alliances" and "being allied to each other" are expected to pose a lower level of threat perception than having outside alliances, so these are placed at lower ranks, and "no alliances" as the lowest rank, since it has been the reference category in the previous analyses. The only open question is how to deal with the "misc. alliances." The theoretical explanation has nothing to really say about these, and the collinear analysis had already shown them to be a perfect predictor of peace in this period, so these are ranked second. In the Cold War period this category was insignificant and in the 1816–1945 period positively related to war. What seems to be occurring in this period, is that having more than one type of alliance in such a short time does not send much of a signal to an opponent and does not pose much of a threat—at least this seems to be the case behaviorally.

crease the risk of war and that one of the major irenic factors bringing about peace during the Cold War has returned to the belligerent pattern predicted by the steps-to-war explanation. An important process that brings about war, according to the steps-to-war explanation, is now again in place, which makes this period much more like the classic international politics period of 1816– 1945. Nevertheless, having concluded this, one must make the caveat that only a few years have been examined and that the test design, because of problems of collinearity, has had to substitute a different measure of outside alliances, one that groups all the outside alliance types into a single category.

Models 3–5 also look at the effects of enduring rivalry, recurring territo- rial disputes, and the combination of the two. Model 3 shows that enduring rivalry has a statistically significant effect on the likelihood of war; so do re- curring territorial disputes (see model 4), as noted earlier. Lastly, model 5 shows that each of these variables have separate and independent effects on the risk of war, something that was present in the 1816–1945 period, but not during the Cold War.[55] On the basis of these findings, propositions 5.3 and 5.4 fail to be falsified.

It is clear from these findings that the post–Cold War period is more like the 1816–1945 period than the Cold War period. This is particularly the case with the effect of outside alliances, but also with the consistency of the other steps-to-war factors. This means that whatever contributed to the relative peace of the Cold War, it was not the start of a new trend, but most likely some- thing unique to that period and its politics. The findings on the post–Cold War period indicate that the steps-to-war explanation is relevant to current history and is likely to remain so. The explanation is not limited to a particu- lar domain, but generalizable across several periods. What needs to be done is not to come up with a new explanation or theory of war to deal with the Cold War, but to identify what factors made "the long peace" an exception to an overall pattern in history going back at least to 1816. The findings in this chap- ter suggest that it may have something to do with the peculiar alliance struc- ture of the Cold War system, perhaps coupled with the presence of nuclear weapons. The Cold War will be a focus of attention in the next two chapters where the reasons for its peaceful nature will be explored in greater detail.

Table 5.7 presents the predicted probabilities for the steps-to-war so it is possible to see if, when each factor is present in a dyad's interaction, the prob- ability of war increases. It can be seen that for dyads whose relations are dom- inated by territorial disputes, this is not the case, since their probability of

---

[55] During the Cold War, rivalry wipes out the effect of recurring territorial disputes. This is yet another similarity between the 1816–1945 period and the post–Cold War period, although as noted in the table, recurring territorial MIDs are only significant at the .06 level in a one-tailed test.

Table 5.7
Probability of War Occurring at Least Once in the History of Two States, 1990–2000

Conditions	Territorial MID	Policy MID
All others set to 0	.011	.008
	(.001–.036)	(.000–.030)
Outside allies	.097	.060
	(.043–.181)	(.025–.110)
Outside allies + Recurring Terr MIDs	.274	.208
	(.105–.516)	(.036–.520)
Outside allies + Enduring Rivalry	.395	.277
	(.122–.748)	(.117–.487)
Outside allies + Recurring Terr MIDs + Enduring Rivalry	.658	.547
	(.361–.895)	(.228–.842)

Note: Main entries are predicted probabilities with 90 percent confidence intervals in parentheses. The predicted probabilities are derived from model 5 in table 5.5. The base probability of war for this period is .064.

going to war is .011 and the base probability of war for the period is .064. Given that the probability of dyads dominated by policy disputes is also below the base probability of war, this means that the kinds of issues that dominate relations in the post–Cold War period do not have much impact on the likelihood of war. What is important is if these issues fester; when they do, the probability increases significantly, as will be discussed below.

If states have outside alliances and are focused on territorial disputes, the probability of war increases to .097.[56] This provides further evidence that outside alliances increase the probability of war and do not decrease it (cf. table 5.4). This makes this period more like the 1816–1945 period than the Cold War period.

What greatly increases the probability of war, however, is whether issues fester and MIDs repeat. If states have recurring territorial disputes (four or more), the probability of war increases significantly, to .274. If dyads are engaged in an enduring rivalry, the probability of war increases further to .395, and if they have both an enduring rivalry and recurring territorial disputes, the probability of war reaches a high of .658.[57] Overall, once outside alliances are in place, the probability of war goes from .097 to .658. This progression is

[56] The .097 is outside the upper bound of the confidence level for the .011, and the latter is outside the lower bound of the .097, as can be seen in table 5.7. This makes the .097 significantly different from the .011.

[57] The .658 is significantly different from the .097, as is the .274, but the .395 overlaps slightly with the .658; see the confidence levels in table 5.7. The .274 and the .395 overlap each other.

consistent with the steps-to-war explanation and propositions 5.2–5.4. One caveat that should be noted with regard to this conclusion is that dyads dominated by territorial disputes do not have an increased probability of war as expected by proposition 5.1 This finding, however, is offset by the fact that as territorial disputes recur, there is a significant increase in the probability of war.

Table 5.7 also presents the findings on nonterritorial MIDs. The first thing to note is that regime disputes are perfect predictors of peace. This is different from the Cold War period where regime disputes actually have a higher probability of going to war than the base probability of the period. It is also interesting to note that only twelve dyads have their relations dominated by some form of regime disputes compared to fifty-two in the Cold War.[58] The second important finding is that dyads dominated by policy MIDs have a lower probability of going to war than dyads dominated by territorial MIDs (.008 versus .011), although there is an overlap in the confidence intervals. As the other variables are added, policy disputes always have a lower probability of war, although the confidence intervals again overlap. As a whole, the evidence is not inconsistent with proposition 5.6, but no decision on the proposition can be made because only the direction is established and not the significance of the findings.

Since most of the steps-to-war propositions fit this period, the post–Cold War period can be seen as more like the 1816–1945 period than the long peace of the Cold War. This is particularly the case with the role alliances play in increasing the probability of war, whereas during the Cold War they are negatively related to war. The one note of caution in making this conclusion is that the size of the predicted probabilities is below that for the 1816–1945 period and closer to that of the Cold War period. Nevertheless, the underlying forces bringing about war seem to be identical to those of the early period. The thrust of the evidence suggests that the steps-to-war explanation fits both the 1816–1945 and the 1990–2001 periods. Given the findings on the post–Cold War period, it is fair to conclude that the steps-to-war explanation is relevant to current history and is likely to remain so.

Making Inferences and Further Explorations

As discussed at the close of the research-design section, an analysis of dyad histories can only demonstrate that when a pair of states have had territorial

---

[58] After 1989 these include eight dyads with regime disputes and four dyads with misc. regime combinations. In the Cold War these include forty-four dyads with regime disputes and eight with misc. regime combination.

disputes dominating their relations and have made alliances with outside states, have had a history of recurring territorial disputes and rivalry and an arms race, they have a higher probability of going to war than dyads that have taken none or fewer of these actions. What cannot be demonstrated from this snapshot view of their history is whether the particular MID that escalates to war is one that embodies the above steps. In other words, in the worst-case (and least likely) scenario many of the alleged steps to war could have occurred in the history of the two states but long after the war happened. Given this logical possibility, what inferences can be made from the findings in the preceding section, and can any empirical probes be taken to ease possible concerns?

To begin with, it is important to point out that certain inferences are unaffected by this quasi-ecological inference problem. The problem is confined to making inferences about the findings related to war and does not affect the findings related to peace. There is no problem of inference about associating the absence of all of the steps or several with an increased probability that a dyad will never have a war in a given historical period. Because there is *never* a war, one only needs to know that certain steps are never present or generally are not dominating relations. Therefore, this inference is on fairly solid ground.

Nor is that conclusion insignificant, since most of the cases in the sample are peaceful dyads. For example, in the 1816–1945 period, 53.9 percent (173 cases out of 321) never have a war (compared to 148 that do). The 1946–89 period consists of mostly peaceful dyads—87 percent (354 cases out of 407) never have a war (compared to 53 that do).[59] In the very brief post–Cold War period, 1990–2001, there are only 18 of 281 dyads that have a war, meaning that 93.6 percent do not (263). We are on solid ground then for most of the sample for inferring that the absence or few steps to war correctly predict the absence of war.

Next, whatever problem of quasi-ecological inference might exist in the data, it is a reasonable assumption that it is systematic across the subperiods. If we assume any error is constant, then differences across subperiods cannot be produced by it. This means that we can have confidence that the 1816–1945 better fits the steps-to-war explanation than the Cold War, and that the Cold War is fundamentally different. Likewise, the ways in which the Cold War is different is likely to be an accurate portrayal. In other words, during the Cold War both sides having outside alliances is no longer positively related to war as in the earlier period. Lastly, the analysis of whether the post–Cold War period is more like the classic international politics period of 1816–1945 or the Cold War, should not be affected.

[59] Note that the number of cases listed in column 1 of table 5.3 is 391 instead of 407 because 16 cases have been dropped as perfect predictors.

What is affected is our confidence about whether it is actually the steps to war that bring about war. One way of looking at the tests in this chapter is that they fail to falsify the propositions, and they could, in principle, have done that. Thus, the tests are one stage in the larger research plan of the book with timing addressed in the next chapter. While this is all well and good, it is also the case that the tests do not present much "confirmatory" evidence about dyads consistent with the propositions. To do that we would need greater assurance that the steps are embodied or prior to the MIDs that escalate to war. Although that kind of refined data is not available, it is possible to look at a sample of cases and see if the steps occur when they are supposed to occur and not at a time when they could not have a causal impact on bringing the dyad to war. Such an empirical probe would give us a better idea as to whether the problem of timing is a serious empirical problem.

Rather than pick a random sample, we decided to concentrate on an in-depth examination of the cases that are most important for supporting the proposition. In other words, we decided to examine cases that are most likely driving the positive relationships in the statistical analyses that have been presented. As noted above, only dyads having war need be investigated, so this cuts down the sample immediately. Since the 1816–1945 period best fits the steps-to-war explanation and is also the longest period in which the problem of inference is apt to occur, this was selected as the focus of the probe. In addition, since territory is the foundation of the explanation, it was decided to look only at dyads whose relations are dominated by territorial MIDs. These dyads must embody the steps before a war, if the evidence is to provide any "confirmatory" support.

Taking all the above selection criteria into account reduced the sample to 84 dyads where territorial MIDs dominated relations. Of these, 84 cases, about 61 percent (51) go to war out of a total of 321 cases that go to war. Looking at these 51 dyads on a case-by-case basis would still be a daunting task and not completely necessary. What is most important is to examine the cases where territorial disputes are handled in a power politics fashion, so it was decided to look at dyads where territorial disputes are coupled with: (1) one or both sides having outside alliances, (2) arms races, and (3) enduring rivalry. This made for a total of 41 cases, although there is overlap among them. These cases will serve as the sample for our empirical probe.

Table 5.8 presents the findings on outside alliances. There are seventeen cases in table 5.8a where territorial disputes dominate relations and *one side* had an outside alliance sometime during the history of relations. The question is does the MID that escalates to war or one five years prior have that alliance pattern or is the presence of one outside alliance occurring outside that window (i.e., after the war or too long before it to have a causal impact)? It

Table 5.8a

Outside Alliances in Dyads Dominated by Territory and That Go to War, 1816–1945

Dyad	One Outside Alliance Prior to War?	Year	Territory Prior to War?
Thai-France	Yes	1893	Yes
Hung-Czech	Allied & Outside	1919	No
Canada-Germany	Yes	1939	Yes
Canada-Italy	Yes	1940	Yes
Canada-Japan	Yes	1941	Yes
Belgium-Germany	Yes	1940	Yes
SoAfr-Germany	Yes	1939	Yes
Austrl-Germany	Yes	1939	Yes
New Z-Germany	Yes	1939	Yes
Aus-Hun-Modena	Yes	1848	Yes
SoAfr-Italy	Yes	1940	Yes
Austrl-Italy	Yes	1940	Yes
New Z-Italy	Yes	1940	Yes
SoAfr-Japan	Yes	1941	Yes
China-Japan	Both Outside	1941	Yes
Austrl-Japan	Yes	1941	Yes
New Z-Japan	Yes	1941	Yes
Correct Predictions:	15 of 17		16 of 17

can be seen in the top section of the table that fifteen of the seventeen cases fit the expectations of the propositions, that is, the one side having an outside alliance occurs where it should occur to have an impact. Neither are the two deviations very damaging since the MIDs that escalate to war have outside alliances (allied with an outside ally, both sides have outside allies), but not this specific pattern. It is also interesting to note that the MID that escalates to war is in all but one instance over territory. It will also be noticed that most of these cases are related to the different phases of World War II, but not all. They also include the 1848 Italian war of independence against Austria, a war between Hungary and Czechoslovakia, and an imperial war between Thailand and France in 1893.

Table 5.8b presents the findings on dyads dominated by territorial disputes and by an alliance pattern where *both* sides have outside alliances. There

Table 5.8b

Outside Alliances in Dyads Dominated by Territory and That Go to War, 1816–1945

Dyad	Both Outside Alliance Prior to War?	Year	Territory Prior to War?
Hanover-Italy	Yes	1866	Yes
Bavaria-Italy	Yes	1866	Yes
Baden-Italy	Yes	1866	Yes
Saxony-Italy	Yes	1866	Yes
Wuerttem-Italy	Yes	1866	Yes
HesseElect-Italy	Yes	1866	Yes
HesseDucal-Italy	Yes	1866	Yes
Russia-China	Allied & Outside	1900	Yes
	One Side Outside	1929	No
Mongolia-Japan	Yes	1939	Yes
		1945	Yes
Correct Predictions:	8 of 9		9 of 9

are sixteen such cases in the data for this time period, but only nine go to war. Of these, eight of the nine cases have the alliance pattern occurring where it should. Only one case, Russia-China, is deviant, and here it simply has other outside alliance patterns for the two MIDs that escalate to war. Territory was also present (or in one case five years prior) in the MID that went to war in all but one of the two wars (the 1929 war) between Russia and China. Unlike in table 5.8a, most of the cases in this table are related to Italian participation in the 1866 Seven Weeks' War.

Table 5.9a presents the results for enduring rivalry. There are only five cases in the test sample that have territory dominating their relations that go to war and have an enduring rivalry. All five wars occur during the enduring rivalry of the dyad, which supports the proposition. With regard to territory, four of the five have territory present in a MID that escalates to war and one (again the 1929 Sino-Soviet War) does not. However, it should be noted that China and Japan have four wars that fit this condition and two have territory present in the MID and two do not (1894, 1900) but since territory is present it is counted as a successful prediction. Although few in number, the cases in this table include some well-known enduring rivals over a good span of time and across different geographical regions.

Table 5.9b presents the findings on arms races. There are ten cases of territory dominating relations and a dyad having an arms race. Of these, nine of

Table 5.9a

Enduring Rivalry in Dyads Dominated by Territory and That Go to War, 1816–1945

Dyad	Enduring Rivalry Prior to War?	Year	Territory Prior to War?
Greece-Turkey	Yes	1896	Yes
		1912	Yes
		1919	Yes
Italy-Yugoslavia	Yes	1941	Yes
Italy-Ethiopia	Yes	1934	Yes
		1941	Yes
China-Japan	Yes	1894	No
		1900	No
		1931	Yes
		1937	Yes
Russia-China	Yes	1929	No
Correct Predictions:	5 of 5		4 of 5

Table 5.9b

Arms Races in Dyads Dominated by Territory and That Go to War, 1816–1945

Dyad	Arms Race Prior to War?	Year	Territory Prior to War?
Bolivia-Paraguay	Yes	1931	Yes
Hung-Czech	After	1919	No
Canada-Germany	Yes	1939	Yes
Canada-Japan	Yes	1941	Yes
Nethld-Germany	Yes	1940	Yes
Poland-Germany	Yes	1939	Yes
Austrl-Germany	Yes	1939	Yes
SoAfr-Japan	Yes	1941	Yes
China-Japan	Yes	1941	Yes
Austrl-Japan	Yes	1941	Yes
Correct Predictions:	9 of 10		9 of 10

the ten cases have the arms race at the time the MID escalates to war or within five years prior (Bolivia-Paraguay), and only one (Hungary-Czechoslovakia) have it long after. This pattern again satisfies the expectations of the steps-to-war explanation. Also, all but the Hungary-Czechoslovakia dyad have territory present in the MID that escalates to war. As with most of the findings on arms races, these also are associated with the world wars, here World War II, in particular.

This review of forty-one cases derived from the 1816–1945 period is very encouraging for the steps-to-war explanation. In each of the four sets only one and at the most two deviations exist, and with outside alliances, these deviations are minor. This suggests that the steps are operating in the temporal manner the explanation expects. In the samples that were examined, the MID that escalates to war is typically a territorial MID. Dyads that have a pattern of one or both sides with outside alliances have them prior to the MIDs that escalate to war. Dyads that go to war are enduring rivals at the time of the war. Similarly, states that have an arms race typically have it when their MID escalates to war. All of this is consistent with the propositions. This should allay some of the concerns about "ecological inference." However, only a sample of cases has been examined and more systematic tests will need to be conducted, one of which will be presented in the next chapter.

Conclusion

One of the keys to understanding interstate war is to understand how states relate to each other and how and why they resort to force. This chapter has shown that among pairs of states that resort to the threat or use of force there are two fundamentally different ways of interacting. In one category are those dyads who despite the use of force never cross the brink of war. In the other category are those who do. What distinguishes these two patterns of relations? Why do some pairs of states remain at peace even though they have sharp conflict, while others do not? The underlying theory has been premised on the assumption that how states behave toward each other shapes their proclivity toward war. Certain behaviors, especially when coupled with certain issues, place states at greater risk of war. Dyads that are prone to war, therefore, should exhibit a certain behavioral profile in the history of their relations. This chapter has specified theoretically what that profile might be and documented the extent to which it has been able to distinguish those dyads that go to war from those that never have in one or more of three historical periods—1816– 1945, 1946–89, and 1990–2001.

The fundamental factors that distinguish states that never go to war from those that do center on the issues that divide them and, more importantly, how they handled those issues. This is not to deny that the national attributes of states, such as whether they are both democracies, has an impact on behavior, but that the behavior itself is characterized best by focusing on issues and how they are handled.[60] As expected, when territorial disputes dominate relations, they put dyads at greater risk for eventually going to war than when other types of disputes dominate relations. This is especially the case when territorial disputes recur, regardless of whether they dominate relations. This finding holds for all three time periods. This is an important constant across history, although in the most recent period this finding holds only when territorial disputes recur.

This is not to say that other types of issues cannot result in war; all the different types of disputes in the data produce wars—territory, policy, and regime disputes. They just do so at very different rates. Sometimes certain kinds of nonterritorial issues are more apt to go to war in a given historical period. This happens with regime disputes in the Cold War, but as a class they are still less likely to result in war than territorial disputes.

When all is said and done what really increases the probability of war is not the mere presence of territorial issues, but how they are handled. The data sample in this chapter is already confined to pairs of states that have handled their disputes by resorting to threats or the use of force, so in one sense all states have resorted to a minimal level of force. How do states handle issues that make war more likely? One pattern across all three historical periods that increases the likelihood of war is handling issues so as to make for an enduring rivalry. When states engage in at least six militarized confrontations in a twenty-year period this increases the probability of war. This finding supports the idea that violence tends to encourage violence, but it also documents something that is too often overlooked—the repetition of force eventually encourages its escalation to war. The actual finding is not new. Leng (1983) and more recently Diehl and Goertz (2000) have documented this pattern (see also Wilkenfeld et al., (1980), for conflict short of war). What is new is the theoretical context of the steps to war, *which sees rivalry not in isolation but connected to territorial disputes and other practices of power politics.*

While rivalry is a key factor in and of itself, the repetition of territorial disputes, alluded to earlier, is also important even if it does not produce a technical state of rivalry and territorial disputes do not dominate relations. Recurring territorial disputes play a significant role in all three periods, although in the Cold War period, their effect is wiped out when controlling for enduring rivalry. This means, though, that in the two other periods, recurring ter-

---

[60] A number of studies have already shown that democratic states tend to handle issues and behave toward each other differently from other types of dyads and especially democratic-nondemocratic dyads (see for example, Dixon [1993], Raymond [1994]). It is also the case that one of the reasons democratic states may be at peace is that they avoid territorial MIDs; see Mitchell and Prins (1999) and Gibler (2007).

ritorial disputes and rivalry have separate and independent effects, something that was not known before.

The steps-to-war explanation sees repeated confrontations as a resort to the practices of power politics, specifically as the use of realpolitik to coerce the other side to adopt one's issue position or as a way of defending oneself through a demonstration of resolve. The repetition of violence, then, is not seen as just a pattern, but as reflecting an attempt to implement some sort of realist strategy, although how refined that strategy might be would vary considerably given this very general indicator. The indicator, however, does not really tap this nuance, just as it does not tap the presumed underlying hostility that drives rivalry (see Thompson, 1995; Vasquez, 1996a: 532). Nevertheless, the evidence is not inconsistent with these claims and is one example of how issues can be handled in a power politics manner that increases the risk of war.

There are two other indicators of power politics practices used in this chapter—the making of alliances and engaging in arms races. In the 1816–1945 period these factors clearly increase the likelihood of war and sometimes dramatically so. There is also some evidence that arms races might have this effect during the Cold War period, although its impact is wiped out by other factors, in particular, rivalry. Alliances, however, do not always have this belligerent effect. In the Cold War, having outside alliances is not positively related to going to war. It is generally nonsignificant; but it is negative in its impact, and the predicted probabilities show a reduction in the probability of war, albeit a nonsignificant one. This evidence on alliances is contrary to the expectations of the steps-to-war explanation and led to a rejection of the alliance aspects of the propositions tested in this chapter.

In general, the steps-to-war explanation best fits the 1816–1945 period. This is its natural domain. It fits the Cold War period less well, but still territorial disputes and rivalry are documented, important factors in the steps to war during the Cold War. In addition, some evidence has been uncovered that alliances may be a factor in bringing about, or at least maintaining, a long peace in the Cold War.

What remains unanswered is the extent to which the post–Cold War period will be more like the classic international politics period of 1816–1945 or the Cold War. Since there are not sufficient data on arms races, the crucial evidence turns on outside alliances. The analysis shows that outside alliances have a positive impact on war in the post–Cold War period unlike in the Cold War where they tend to be negatively related. Additionally, during the post–Cold War period, having no alliances is related to peace, but during the Cold War this condition is more likely to be associated with war than having both sides with outside alliances. Outside alliances, then, play a role similar to the one they play in the classic international politics era of 1816–1945, making this period conform more to the steps-to-war explanation.

In addition to the above, the evidence on recurring territorial disputes is relevant. The post–Cold War period is similar to that of 1816–1945 in that both rivalry and recurring territorial disputes have an independent and separate effect on war, whereas in the Cold War they do not. Likewise, regime disputes seem to have lost the war proneness they had during the Cold War. All these patterns seem to be indicators that the post–Cold War period will see a return to the politics of the past, which have predominated in most of the post-Napoleonic era. With the exception of the Cold War, the underlying forces that bring about interstate war seem relatively consistent. The next decade will tell the story. For now, however, the future does not bode well for reducing the danger of certain steps to war.

This study provides evidence that handling disputes in certain ways is a series of steps to war and that the more steps taken, the higher the probability of war. Dyads that have a history of having taken one or more of the steps have a higher probability of war than expected by chance than dyads that have not had a history of taking them. As one controls for the various conditions specified in the propositions, the statistical models show that the predicted probability of war generally increases if a dyad's relations are dominated by territorial disputes. Throughout most of the post-Napoleonic era, their probability of war increases further if they both have outside alliances and, further yet, if they are enduring rivals and have had four or more territorial disputes. They typically reach the highest levels of risk if they are also engaged in an arms race. These increases in the predicted probabilities of war (except for outside alliances, which reduce the risk of war during the Cold War) are present in each of the three periods, but are not always significant except during the 1816–1945 period.

Lastly, it is found that in all three periods that policy and regime disputes, if handled in a power politics fashion, increase the probability of war, but generally these are less likely to go to war than territorial disputes. This is also an important finding for the steps-to-war explanation.

All in all, the tests in this chapter have provided considerable evidence consistent with the steps-to-war explanation. With the exception of the Cold War, most of the propositions have failed to be falsified, and even in the Cold War, important parts of the explanation hold. For most years since 1816, the steps-to-war explanation holds, and an analysis of the entire 1816–1992 period shows that it holds for the entire period (Vasquez, 2004). This statistical research on the long-term relations of states shows that the effects of the steps to war can distinguish the dyads in the system that go to war from those that have been at peace since 1815. While this is important evidence particularly with regard to factors other than joint democracy that make for peaceful dyads, it still leaves open the question of the timing of the steps to war, which is best addressed by looking at specific MIDs rather than the historical sweep of relations between pairs of states.

6

The Probability of Crisis Escalation

*Identifying the factors that increase the probability
of a crisis escalating to war is the most fruitful
avenue for understanding why war occurs.*

There are many different ways in which to study the onset of interstate war. One is to ask whether certain systemic characteristics make states more prone to war than others. This was the initial stance of the Correlates of War project, which examined, among other things, whether the distribution of capability, alliance structure, or status were correlates of war (see, respectively, Singer, Bremer, and Stuckey, 1972; Singer and Small, 1966; Wallace, 1972). Another is to ask, as we did in the last chapter, if the long-term pattern of relations between two states, what they do to each other, affects the likelihood that they will go to war. A third approach is to ask if certain characteristics of crises distinguish those that escalate to war from those that do not (e.g., Holsti, North, and Brody, 1968). One of the main effects of the release of the Correlates of War Militarized Interstate Dispute (MID 2.1) data set and its initial analysis by Stuart Bremer (1992) was to move the field away from studying the systemic factors associated with the onset of war to asking what distinguishes the few MIDs that escalate to war from the many that do not.

In this chapter, we ask the same question as Bremer, but we use the steps-to-war explanation to derive what factors promote crisis escalation to war. We ask what characteristics of MIDs increase the risk that they will escalate to war. In this regard, we adopt an approach that has been very successful and widely used within epidemiology—this approach looks at what factors increase the risk of certain health problems, for example getting a heart attack. Our theoretical analysis employs the steps-to-war explanation to identify those factors that, when present in a dispute, will increase the probability that it will escalate to war and, when absent, reduce the likelihood that it will escalate to war. From the steps-to-war theoretical perspective, there are four factors that progressively increase the probability of a crisis escalating to war. It is hypothesized that crises have a higher probability of escalating to war if they are over territorial disputes, one or both sides have outside allies, both have been engaged in an enduring rivalry, and an ongoing arms race is present. It is assumed that disputes that have these characteristics reflect the fact that the contending actors have adopted the kinds of power politics practices outlined in chapter 1. These risk factors are not variables that come together coincidentally, but reflect an interconnected strategy, where each factor progressively increases the risk of war because it reflects that the contending actors have moved further along the realist road to war. It is predicted, therefore, that as each of these factors appears as an attribute of a dispute, the probability of that dispute escalating to war progressively increases.

The analysis in this chapter will test key aspects of this broad explanation of why certain crises escalate to war and others do not. In doing so, it will focus on a set of propositions that link territorial disputes and the use of power politics practices to an elevated likelihood of war. Thus, a territorial dispute between two states where one or both sides have an outside ally that will support them is more likely to go to war than a dispute where neither side has an outside alliance. Likewise, a territorial dispute where outside alliances are present, and the two states have also had a series of recurring militarized confrontations, is more likely to escalate to war than where an outside alliance is present but the states have not had many previous disputes. Lastly, territorial disputes where both sides have outside alliances, a history of prior conflict, and an ongoing arms race are more likely to go to war than those that have all these conditions but are not engaged in an arms race.

This overview of the explanation should make it clear that the dependent variable in our analysis is the escalation of a crisis to war. For the purpose of our data analysis, we treat MIDs and crises as synonymous, although MIDs are a broader category than most conceptions of crisis (e.g., Hermann, 1969; Snyder and Diesing, 1977; Brecher and Wilkenfeld 1997).[1] We test the explanation by breaking down all MIDs into dyadic disputes, which is the unit of

---

[1] We believe that the MID data set includes most of the interstate crises that have occurred between states (for some evidence on this question, see Hewitt [2003], which compares the MID data with the International Crisis Behavior data). While it would be possible to develop measures of MIDs that would make them more like crises, such as requiring that they be reciprocated and last for a certain number of days and/or reach certain levels of force, we have not done so. We prefer to cast our net widely and look at all the disputes included in the data. This has the advantage of allowing our study to be compared with the hundreds of other studies that have been conducted on MIDs. Given the still early stage of research, we assume that the MIDs that are somehow *less* than full-blown crises introduce measurement error that reduces the strength of our statistical associations. Therefore, if anything, the tests in this chapter underestimate the evidence consistent with the steps-to-war explanation. We would expect any findings produced with the MID data to be successfully replicated using the ICB data; see Colaresi and Thompson (2005). The main limitation with ICB data, of course, is that they go back only to the beginning of 1918.

analysis.[2] The independent variables can be seen as a set of risk factors for war that operate in a dynamic and nonlinear fashion. In this chapter, we are interested in seeing whether the mere presence of varied combinations of these risk factors at the beginning of a dyadic dispute will increase tendencies toward war. In this sense, our tests are static rather than dynamic, even though our explanation has clear dynamic aspects. The reason for this is that the data we have available permit only this sort of test. Nevertheless, this is a meaningful test in that the "static" conditions are presumed to be an outcome of the steps-to-war dynamic, and if they do not produce the predicted increase in the probability of war, then the explanation is incorrect and could be considered falsified depending on how inconsistent it is with the evidence. Conversely, if the evidence is consistent with the predictions, all that can be inferred is that the static variables are associated with an increase in the probability of war and that while the presumed dynamic aspects might also be operating in the manner outlined, a different sort of test would be needed to demonstrate that.[3]

One of the advantages of utilizing dyadic disputes as the unit of analysis, as opposed to comparing the long-term relations of a pair of states (the dyad), as was done in the previous chapter, is that we can pinpoint when the independent variables occur in relation to the dependent variable, which could not always be done in the previous chapter. With dyadic dispute data we have a clear idea of the timing of our variables to make sure that each of the independent variables occurs before the dependent variable. We know from the MID coding that a territorial revision claim has preceded the threat or use of force. We also have measured our alliance variables so that the formal alliance must be operating before the first day of the MID. Measuring the number of previous disputes permits us to know when a case crosses what might be considered various thresholds of rivalry. Lastly, an arms race must be ongoing in the year the MID occurs.

---

[2] This means that one of the characteristics of disputes that we suspect might increase the probability of crisis escalation, namely the number of parties in a dispute, cannot be tested here. Elsewhere, this hypothesis has been tested, and it has been found that multiparty disputes have a greater risk of escalating to war than two-party disputes, and that this risk is increased if the dispute is over territory; see Petersen, Vasquez, and Wang (2004); see also Vasquez (1993: 191–92, 318) for the rationale of this hypothesis.

[3] Likewise, the language of "steps" implies a sequence of actions or transitions across phases (on sequences and war, see Cioffi-Revilla [1998]: 140–50, 158–63; see also his discussion of probabilistic causality: 31–34). The various risk factors for war—territorial disputes, relevant alliances, and so forth—may increase the probability of war, however, without necessarily having worked through one specific sequence. To see if the actual steps take place in the sequence implied would require a more case-focused test, which would make most sense after the present sort of analysis is conducted.

A negative effect of using dyadic disputes, of course, is that this is an atomistic perspective that does not capture the overall relationship between two actors. Thus, by using both the dyad as the unit of analysis in chapter 5 and the dyadic dispute here, we are able to provide a very rigorous and complete test of the steps-to-war explanation.

In this chapter, we focus on the following propositions derived from the steps-to-war explanation:

Proposition 6.1: Dyadic territorial disputes have a higher probability of escalating to war than general foreign policy disputes or disputes over one side's regime.

Proposition 6.2: Dyadic territorial disputes where both sides have outside politically relevant alliances have a higher probability of escalating to war than dyadic territorial disputes where neither side has alliances.

Proposition 6.3a: Dyadic territorial disputes where both sides have outside politically relevant alliances and have had a series of recurring disputes have a greater probability of escalating to war than dyadic territorial disputes where both sides have such alliances but have not had a history of militarized disputes.

Proposition 6.3b: The effect of prior disputes is curvilinear. Initially, more prior conflicts steadily increase the probability of war for current disputes, but eventually this relationship reverses as a very high number of prior conflicts will actually engender a ritualization of relations whereby pairs stop their current disputes short of war.

Proposition 6.4: Dyadic territorial disputes where both sides have outside politically relevant alliances, have had repeated militarized disputes, and have an ongoing arms race have a higher probability of going to war than those that have the first three conditions but do not have an ongoing arms race.

As stated in proposition 6.1, we expect territorial disputes to exhibit a higher probability of war compared to nonterritorial engagements. Nevertheless, we also expect that the accumulation of varied power-politics practices (as stated in propositions 6.2–6.4) will tend to increase the chances of nonterritorial disputes going to war, similar to their effects on territorial ones.

In propositions 6.2–6.4 we emphasize politically relevant alliances and not alliances in general because not every alliance is relevant to every dispute or war an ally might be involved in. If a state has an alliance with another state that commits it to fight only in a circumscribed set of conditions, these conditions may not be relevant to a situation that arises in another region or issue area (see Leeds, Long, and Mitchell, 2000). For example, during the Cold War the United States had an alliance with Taiwan, and this alliance is relevant to U.S. relations with China and other Asian states, but having Taiwan as an alliance partner is not relevant to disputes the United States might have with countries in sub-Saharan Africa or Latin America. One of the problems of simply counting formal alliances is that active countries, like Britain and the United States, would be classified as having an ally for many of the years since 1816, even though many of these alliance commitments would not be relevant to the dispute at hand.

The research that we propose and conduct is designed to separate out the impacts of various types of alliance scenarios by focusing on their relevance to the present dispute. The causal logic of realism stipulates that states make alliances in order to increase their power and help balance the power of opponents, which under some versions of realism should lead to a reduction in the probability of war by increasing the risk that an attacker will lose the war. The expectations of the steps-to-war explanation differ with realism on this point. It argues, instead, that when one side makes an outside alliance, this increases threat perception, and in the presence of a subsequent militarized interstate dispute, this increases the probability of war, because it gives the side with an outside ally a potential advantage and in doing so makes it less risk averse. If the dispute stalemates, it is anticipated that the side without outside allies would try to get allies and/or build up its military before the next MID. If both sides have an outside alliance, then this is seen as having a higher probability of war since both sides have now engaged in and reciprocated some highly threatening actions. In addition, they are further along in a realist strategy of coercion and now have fewer options to take before they decide that going to war is the best way of handling the situation they face. For this reason, we expect the alliance configuration where both sides have outside alliances to be the most war prone and have focused on this in our propositions. However, we also anticipate that a dyad having even one outside alliance will be more war prone than a dyad with none at all.

Propositions 6.3 and 6.4 also place importance on the repetition of militarized confrontations. The original construction of the steps-to-war explanation derives this idea from the twin notions that crises between relatively equal states tend to stalemate and repeat, and repeated crises tend to escalate to war (Wallensteen, 1981; Leng, 1983; Vasquez, 1993: 184–90, 316–18; Bremer, 2000: 25). While some targets will back down in the face of a MID, it is assumed that territorial disputes are of such salience that states will tend not to give in, but instead, either allow the current dispute to stalemate (only to be repeated later) or go to war (Hensel, 1994). As MIDs repeat, one or both sides can be expected to escalate their use of force in order to coerce or intimidate the other side into agreeing to its issue position. Such bargaining tends to give rise to hard-liners in each side, which makes the issue more intractable, reduces the prospects of compromise, and encourages more escalation. As both sides climb this ladder of escalation, the external bargaining situation and internal political climate increase the chance that a crisis will emerge that ends in war.

The literature on rivalry assumes that a pair of states that has a history of repeated MIDs is engaged in a rivalry. An enduring rivalry is conventionally operationalized as six disputes within a twenty-year period and is normally seen as an attribute of a dyad and not a dispute (Diehl and Goertz, 2000: 45). If rivalry and the repetition of disputes increase the probability of war, it is important in looking at dyadic conflict to have an idea of whether the current dispute is the first, second, or nth dispute between the same pair of states. We therefore look at how the number of prior dyadic disputes affects the current dispute (proposition 6.3a).

The literature on rivalry, regardless of the particular definition of rivalry employed, basically assumes that once a threshold of repeated disputes or perceived level of hostility is crossed, the probability of war increases (Diehl and Goertz, 2000; Wayman, 1996, 2000; Thompson, 1995, 2001). A key conclusion of this literature is that most wars that have been fought since 1816 have rivals in them. Put another way, war tends to increase in probability as disputes between the same states recur. All of this suggests that rivalry and recurring disputes are a step to war, but little empirical work has been done examining the effect of prior conflict on the probability of war in light of the other steps to war.

However, not all enduring rivalries may be the same. We believe that pairs of states that have a very high number of previous disputes come to learn how to manage their relations and even to a certain extent ritualize their MIDs so that they are not as dangerous as those they had earlier. In effect, at a certain stage, interactions become patterned and generate between the two contenders a set of expectations about how to interact that takes on a ritualized character. Such a depiction is nicely in line with an earlier assertion by Mansbach and Vasquez (1981: 117) that a ritualized stage of relations " . . . involves the continuation of competition and repetitive probing, but within mutually understood limits, and governed by tacit rules in accordance with standard operating procedures that actors develop to prevent surprise and uncertainties. . . . Hostile moves are undertaken by adversaries, but such moves are expected and so can be parried."[4] The Cold War relations of the United States

---

[4] For additional discussion on how dyadic interaction becomes patterned, see Azar (1972). He recognizes a similar process in his normal-relations range, where he maintains that it is not so much the level of hostility that makes for a crisis between two states, but how much that level deviates from the average or typical level of hostility. Thus, a typical negative act between the United States

and Soviet Union provide an illustration of this process. A ritualization process implies that there should be a diminution in the probability of war for dyads that have experienced a very large number of prior MIDs. Put another way, the relationship between recurring disputes and war may not be linear but curvilinear (proposition 6.3b), something that the idea of crossing a "rivalry" threshold misses.[5]

Finally, proposition 6.4 adds the condition of arms racing. The steps-to-war explanation sees arms racing as a way of preparing for war and not avoiding it (see Singer, 1958; Richardson, 1960a; Choucri and North, 1975; Wallace, 1979; Sample, 1997). The rationale for this is that building up one's military produces a security dilemma in which one side's buildup increases the insecurity of the state that is the target of the buildup. This target state reciprocates by building up its military as a way of maintaining and even increasing its own power. This in turn can lead to a full-blown arms race, which in turn increases threat perception and hostility on each side. A militarized dispute that emerges in this atmosphere is more apt to escalate to war than one that occurs in the absence of arms racing.

In addition to these propositions, we will also take note of evidence applying to slight variations on propositions 6.2–6.4, namely looking at the effects of outside alliances, recurring disputes, and arms races on the likelihood of war for nonterritorial disputes. Our basic expectation here is that the use of power-politics practices will also increase the chances of war among nonterritorial disputes—namely, that nonterritorial disputes characterized by two or three of these practices are more apt to go to war than those that have only one, just as we expect with territorial disputes. However, while the probabilities of war should increase with the use of power-politics practices, regardless of dispute type, we expect the chances of war for territorial cases to be higher than for nonterritorial ones.

Research Design

To test the claim that the above steps actually do increase the chances of war among states, we will first look at the probability of war occurring when states

---

and Soviet Union would not have as much impact as the same act would if it transpired between the United States and the United Kingdom. Azar's concept implies that states in long-term rivalries learn to manage their crises so as to make them less dangerous.

[5] An interesting question, raised by Jack S. Levy, is whether recurring territorial disputes, like we examined in the previous chapter, are not also subject to ritualization. Our sense is that they are in principle, though less likely to become ritualized than policy or regime disputes. One reason for this is that they are more apt to go to war before a long pattern can be established.

have territorial disputes as opposed to other types of disputes (proposition 6.1). This test serves as a base model for purposes of comparing whether and how much the probability of war increases with the presence of additional risk factors. Then we see whether the addition of each of the variables specified in propositions 6.2–6.4 increases the probability of war. We examine whether territorial disputes in the presence of both sides having politically relevant outside alliances have a higher probability of war than territorial disputes that do not have any alliances (proposition 6.2). Next, we compare these cases with those disputes that have repeated MIDs (proposition 6.3), and lastly we examine those disputes that have all four conditions present—territorial disputes, both sides having outside alliances, repeated disputes, and an ongoing arms race (proposition 6.4).

Whenever a verbal theory is tested, it must be transformed into a testable model. In doing so, it is found that a single verbal theory often embodies a family of theories in which the variables can be linked in various ways. This introduces a certain ambiguity in the technical sense of that term, in that a series of models can be derived from the same set of variables even before control variables are introduced. In this chapter we emphasize the additive effects of each of the variables, as opposed to an alternative that would treat them as a set of statistical interaction terms, which we will examine in the next chapter. We start with testing additive models because they are simpler and more straightforward; tests involving a number of interaction terms can get quite complex, as we will see later. We expect the steps-to-war explanation to pass a test consisting of additive models; if it does, then the results in this chapter can help to interpret and assess the utility of using more complex interaction models to further examine the steps-to-war approach.

Some might think that a proper theory should only give rise to a single model, yet this rarely occurs, even in the physical sciences. The philosophy-of-science approaches we adopt are those of Popper (1963) and of Lakatos (1970), which assume that a theory will produce not one model but a research program that tests various iterations of a theory. Popper's (1963) approach of conjectures and refutations, where testing leads to a refining of a theory and then further testing, provides the basic justification for the research program we follow. Now that previous research conducted by a number of scholars (Hensel, 1996; Gibler, 2000; Diehl and Goertz, 2000; Sample, 2002) shows an increase in the probability of war when one or two of the "steps" are present in militarized disputes, the next logical step is to assess the effects when all are present. In the past, this has not been done going back to 1816, in part, due to the absence of data.

The models we test here, which combine all the steps, are the ones most closely tied to the logic of the theory. We want to take this more deductive approach rather than just inductively testing the various permutations that could be derived from the steps-to-war explanation (on the dangers of the latter, see Braumoeller and Sartori, 2004). Likewise, we do not report results that include the standard control variables (although we have conducted those tests elsewhere) because our purpose is to test the performance of the models we have derived and not to maximize the amount of variance (or uncertainty) we can account for,[6] *and* we have found when we have done so in an early precursor data analysis to this one that it made no difference in the results in terms of the propositions related to the steps-to-war explanation.[7]

As in previous chapters, we will use the MID data of the Correlates of War project as our main data base for the dependent variable. The sample for the analysis will be all dyadic militarized interstate disputes in the updated MID 3.02 data set, which goes from 1816 through 2001. As will be recalled from chapter 2, the dyadic dispute sample is created by taking the 2,332 MIDs in the dispute sample and breaking them down into each pair of states in the dispute. This increases the number of cases to 3,511 dyadic disputes for the entire 1816–2001 period. Our dependent variable will be whether the current MID under contention or any other between the same two parties escalates to war within five years.[8]

In addition to examining the full time span, we control for historical era by breaking down the full sample into three periods—the classic international politics era of 1816–1945, the Cold War 1946–89 nuclear era, and the post–Cold War period 1990–2001. This approach permits us to assess any differences between the three subperiods and to compare them to findings to the full time period. Given previous findings (Senese and Vasquez, 2004), as well as those in the previous chapter, we have reason to believe that the Cold War period may be different, especially with regard to alliances. Therefore, it is important to control for this subperiod, since the findings for the full time span may mask important differences, which will produce misleading inferences. Controlling for the post–Cold War period permits us to see whether it is more like the 1816–1945 period or the nuclear era of the Cold War.

Our independent variables will be the indicators of the major steps to war. These are whether the dispute is over territory, policy, or regime questions; the

[6] On the overuse and misuse of control variables within the field of international relations, see Ray (2003a).

[7] We report on tests similar to those here, but with controls for joint democracy, power preponderance, and joiners in Senese and Vasquez (2005: 622, note 49). This previous study is based on the MID 2.1 data and goes only through 1992. The controls do not change any of the test results for the four propositions reported without the controls. Joint democracy drops out as a perfect predictor of peace, power preponderance slightly decreases the probability of war, and a sample excluding joiners produces similar results.

[8] For a justification of the five-year window, see chapter 2. See chapters 3 and 7 for tests that run the analysis simultaneously with and without the five-year window, as well as Senese and Vasquez (2003: appendix, 295–96) and Senese and Vasquez (2004: 202). These analyses show no important major difference.

type of politically relevant alliance; rivalry as measured by the number of disputes that have occurred up to the current dispute; and the presence of an ongoing arms race during a MID. For the first of these, we will employ the revision-type indicator in the MID set, which classifies disputes on the basis of whether the revisionist state is trying to change the status quo of a territorial, policy, or regime question or some "other" miscellaneous question (Jones, Bremer, Singer, 1996: 178). Nonrevisionist states on opposing sides of a MID by definition do not have any revision type and hence their revision type is coded as "nonapplicable," and these are dropped from the analysis.

Dropping these cases reduces the 3,511 dyadic disputes in the full period to 2,953. Breaking down the full time span results in the following three samples: (a) for the 1816–1945 period, 1,335 dyadic dispute cases (reduced to 1,040 because of dropped nonapplicable revision type), (b) for the 1946–89 period, 1,567 dyadic disputes (reduced to 1,319 because of dropped nonapplicable revision type), and (c) for the 1990–2001 period, 609 (reduced to 577 because of dropped nonapplicable revision type).

The second independent variable we will examine is whether the disputants have outside politically relevant alliances. As noted in chapter 2, we compare MIDs according to whether the dyadic contenders (1) have no alliance ties with anyone, (2) are allied to each other and only in the same alliances, (3) have one side with an outside alliance, (4) have both sides with outside alliances, (5) are allied to each other, but at least one side has an outside alliance.

Our third independent variable captures the extent to which a pair of states has been engaged in prior conflicts. We hypothesize (in proposition 6.3a) that the more disputes a dyad has had before its current one, the greater the likelihood of war, ceteris paribus. To measure this we determine how many disputes have occurred previously between the same pair of states. We label this variable # of prior MIDs and use it in our analyses across all three time periods. This approach is quite straightforward for the full and pre-1946 spans. For the post-1945 period, however, it assumes that MIDs that occurred prior to 1946 will affect relations after 1945. This assumption has considerable face validity—there is substantial anecdotal evidence suggesting that states have long memories. For instance, most scholars believe that events like the two world wars have had profound effects on the behavior of states since 1945 (see Mueller, 1989). Likewise, the memory of allied intervention in the Soviet Union in 1918 helped shape Soviet attitudes toward the West after World War II.[9] The same issue is present for the post–Cold War period. Here we could continue with the clock started in 1816 or reset it to either 1946 or 1990. In the

[9] For an alternative measure discounting the influence of early disputes, see Crescenzi and Enterline (2001).

end, we have treated each of the rationales for start dates as competing hypotheses about collective memory, so we employ all the measures, where relevant, and report the most useful in the text and the others in the footnotes.

The idea that repeated disputes encourage the emergence of a dispute that will escalate to war is at the heart of the idea of rivalry. In this sense our measure of prior disputes can be seen as an indicator of the degree of rivalry, although we are not directly measuring rivalry in its conventional form as was done in chapter 5. In the previous chapter we followed Diehl and Goertz (2000: 45) by treating rivalry as a categorical variable—using the cutoff points of roughly 1–2 for isolated conflict, 3–5 for proto-rivalry, and 6+ for enduring rivalry, depending on the time frame in which these disputes occur. Here, because we are looking at individual dyadic disputes, we can operationalize the concept as an integer variable and examine precisely the effect of each additional MID on the probability of war.

Treating it as an integer rather than a categorical variable assumes that crossing a particular threshold (especially six disputes and above) is not crucial and does not make for a marked change in a relationship at that specific number of disputes, but that rivalry emerges in a continuous pattern across disputes as hostility increases from one engagement to the next. An integer variable (and the concept of repeated disputes) sees each dispute as increasing the probability of war even after a particular threshold has been passed. For example, the eighth dyadic dispute is seen as more likely to go to war than the third, but less likely to go to war than the seventeenth.[10] Nevertheless, to assess the importance of various thresholds, we will isolate three in our tests of proposition 6.3a—the probability of war when two states are engaged in their first, sixth (a threshold relevant to Diehl and Goertz's measure of enduring rivalry), and fifteenth dispute (which is the mean number of disputes among enduring rivals, i.e., dyads with at least six disputes) for 1816–2001.[11] This last scenario allows us to pinpoint the probability of war for the "average enduring rivalry."

The proposition that as disputes increase, the probability of war also increases, has a ceteris paribus caveat. We think that this relationship is linear for most dyads, but we also expect that pairs that have an extremely large number of recurrent disputes at a certain point become engaged in a kind of ritualized behavior (proposition 6.3b). This pattern would make their militarized confrontations less intense in terms of threat perception. They have somehow

[10] For this reason, we do not start counting the number of prior disputes only at the beginning of a specific enduring rivalry, as defined by Diehl and Goertz (2000: 45).

[11] The mean number of disputes is actually 15.67, but we have rounded down, which makes the average number of MIDs the same as in the MID 2.1 data. This might aid those wishing to compare these results with those in Senese and Vasquez (2005).

learned to manage their militarized confrontations in a way that takes on gamelike characteristics, so these disputes are not at as great a risk of going to war. Their relationship is one of threatening and maybe using limited force, but one where taking the ultimate step is not anticipated. This implies that states that can get through a substantial number of MIDs are at less risk than those that just cross the six-MID threshold. Anecdotal evidence that something like this might be present in history can be seen by looking at East-West relations during the Cold War. The United States, United Kingdom, and France have a very large number of MIDs with the Soviet Union, but none escalate to war. The same holds for China and the United States after the Korean War.

To test this notion of ritualization, we introduce a quadratic specification to see if the relationship between the number of prior disputes and the probability of war is curvilinear and, more specifically, whether it approximates an inverted U shape. We do this by squaring the # of prior MIDs and introducing this new variable (# of prior MIDs^2) into the model. We also graph the relationship to see if the kind of ritualization we hypothesize takes place. This examination of the quadratic specification is then compared to one that simply assesses the impact of # of prior MIDs on its own. Such a progression allows us to test proposition 6.3 to see if the relationship is better depicted as linear or curvilinear.

Our fourth, and final, independent variable is the presence of an arms race. As in chapter 5, we use data collected by Susan Sample (2002) for both major and minor states. These data record arms races for each dyad in a MID based on the measure used by Horn (1987), which essentially examines the increase in military expenditures of two states over time. We employ Sample's (2002) categorical data to determine whether there is an ongoing arms race for each dyadic dispute. Her data, however, do not go beyond 1992, so we are unable to test the effects of arms races in the most recent period.

With these measures in hand, logistic regression is employed to conduct two key tests of our four propositions. The first is to see if each of our four variables—territory, politically relevant alliances, number of previous disputes, and arms races—has a positive and significant impact on the probability of a dispute escalating to war within five years. By using multivariate logistic regression, we have chosen to conduct a very rigorous test of the steps-to-war model; for each step to be seen as a significant factor, it must have a sufficient enough impact so that controlling for the other variables in the explanation does not wipe out the relationship. An alternate and easier test to pass would be to treat the second through fourth independent variables (i.e., outside alliances, repeated disputes, and arms races) as intervening variables. We have not done that here, since we want to have some sense of the relative potency of each variable, and controlling for each gives us an idea of that. Significance levels reported in all the tables and in the text are based on two-tailed tests, but since all the propositions specify direction, these can be cut in half.

The second test focuses on the extent to which each of the steps actually affects the substantive probability of war. We are particularly interested in seeing if the various combinations of the variables specified in the four propositions produce a progressive (and meaningful) increase in the probability of war. To determine the relative probability of war, predicted probabilities are calculated using CLARIFY software (Tomz, Wittenberg, and King, 2003).

Findings

The Full Period, 1816–2001

Table 6.1 reports the logistic regression results for the full 1816 through 2001 period. Each model adds one variable cluster at a time beginning with a base model of the different types of disputes—territory, regime, other (compared to the reference category of policy disputes). The subsequent models introduce cumulatively: politically relevant alliances, the number prior MIDs, the number of prior MIDs^2, and arms races. These models allow us to assess the effects of each of our risk factors, including the precise nature of the relationship between recurring disputes and escalation to war as either linear (# of prior MIDs alone) or curvilinear (adding # of prior MIDs^2).

It can be seen by looking at model 1 in table 6.1 that territorial disputes are significantly more likely to escalate to war within five years than the modal type of dispute (policy MIDs). This provides evidence consistent with proposition 6.1. In addition, a separate model (not shown) finds that territorial disputes are also significantly more likely to eventuate in war than regime disputes.[12]

Model 2 introduces the politically relevant alliance variables (compared to the reference category of "no alliance") to the base model. When states involved in disputes have outside alliances (whether this be one side or both sides having outside alliances or dyads being allied with at least one outside alliance), then this always significantly increases the likelihood of war (at the .10 level) occurring within five years. These results are consistent with proposition 6.2. We also find that when disputes involve two states that are in the same alliance and have no outside alliances, this significantly reduces the like-

---

[12] The Z score for regime disputes escalating to war within five years compared to territorial disputes is -5.81 (p $<$ .000).

Table 6.1

Escalation of the Current or Any MID within Five Years to War, 1816–2001

Variables	Model 1	Model 2	Model 3a	Model 3b	Model 4b
Territorial MID[a]	1.24 (.108)***	1.36 (.110)***	1.36 (.111)***	1.36 (.111)***	1.08 (.137)***
Regime MID[a]	−.07 (.230)	−.05 (.231)	−.05 (.231)	−.07 (.231)	.01 (.288)
Other MID[a]	.21 (.319)	.36 (.323)	.36 (.323)	.41 (.324)	1.05 (.428)**
Allied & only in same alliances[b]		−1.36 (.337)***	−1.34 (.339)***	−1.38 (.340)***	−2.83 (.743)***
One side has outside alliance[b]		.30 (.147)**	.30 (.148)**	.29 (.148)**	.250 (.181)
Both sides have outside alliances[b]		.28 (.161)*	.29 (.164)*	.29 (.163)*	−.03 (.204)
Allied to each other & outside alliance[b]		.35 (.194)*	.35 (.194)*	.36 (.194)*	.06 (.248)
# of prior MIDs			−.00 (.006)	.03 (.016)**	.08 (.020)***
# of prior MIDs^2				−.001 (.000)**	−.002 (.001)**
Arms race					1.61 (.226)***
Constant	−2.16 (.082)***	−2.38 (.147)***	−2.37 (.148)***	−2.49 (.157)***	−2.65 (.195)***
Chi-square (df)	150.55*** (3)	193.12*** (7)	193.37*** (8)	199.55*** (9)	180.32*** (10)
Pseudo R^2	.0568	.0733	.0734	.0757	.1023
Number of cases	2953	2918	2918	2918	1983

Note: Estimations were performed in Stata (logit). Main entries are parameter estimates, with standard errors in parentheses. All tests are two-tailed.
[a]As compared to the reference category of policy MID.
[b]As compared to the reference category of no alliances.
*$p \leq .10$ **$p \leq .05$ ***$p \leq .01$

lihood of war as indicated by the negative parameter estimate, which is consistent with our expectations that allied states tend not to fight each other.[13]

[13] A previous analysis that goes through 1992 (Senese and Vasquez, 2005) found the "allied to each other without any outside alliances" variable a perfect predictor of peace. This analysis has a war occurring after 1992 that violates that pattern—the 1999 Kargil War between India and Pakistan. In addition, a slight change in the coding procedures generates several dyadic disputes as cases

The next two models (models 3a and 3b) test whether the effect of the number of prior disputes has an impact on the likelihood of a MID escalating to war in the context of the other independent variables and whether that effect is better seen as linear or curvilinear. In these models the # of prior MIDs variable is set beginning at 1816.[14] The two models make it clear that while the # of prior MIDs has a positive impact on the likelihood of war (as expected in proposition 6.3a), this effect tends to diminish as a dyad experiences a large number of MIDs (compare models 3a and 3b). This conclusion is indicated by the fact that the parameter estimates in model 3b are significant for both # of prior MIDs and # of prior MIDs^2. The significant estimates show the presence of a curvilinear relationship (in the form of an inverted U curve) that supports proposition 6.3b, which predicts that as two states have a very large number of prior MIDs the probability of any subsequent one escalating to war decreases.

Model 4b introduces the arms-race variable along with the other variables looked at so far. Because the curvilinear model is supported, we report the model with the arms-race variable with both # of prior MIDs and # of prior MIDs^2 (model 4b), although we also ran a model with # of prior MIDs^2 dropped.[15] Model 4b shows that disputes where the contenders are involved in an ongoing arms race are more likely to go to war than disputes in the absence of arms races (controlling for all the other factors). The overall test results for the model provide evidence in line with proposition 6.4 in that arms races have a significant positive impact on the probability of war.

The inclusion of the arms-race variable, however, reduces the number of cases from 2,918 to 1,983. This substantial loss of cases has an impact on the findings for outside alliances. In this model, they now are all statistically insignificant. This undercuts, somewhat, support for proposition 6.2 provided by the previous models. Part of the reduction of cases is due to the fact that the inclusion of the arms-races indicator eliminates the years from 1993 to 2001.

Taken together, these results fail to falsify propositions 6.1, 6.2, 6.3, but not proposition 6.4 with regard to the role of politically relevant alliances. Thus,

---

of states allied only with each other and going to war. These are all associated with the several German states (and Austria) going to war against Mecklenburg-Schwerin, Prussia's ally in the Seven Weeks' War of 1866 (see the findings below for the 1816–1945 period). The only other case of a dyad "allied only to each other" going to war is the 1969 Football War between El Salvador and Honduras, which later drops out because of the lack of arms-race data.

[14] Later tests for the subperiods examine whether resetting the clock at 1945 and 1990 has a different effect.

[15] That model (4a) showed # of prior disputes as significantly increasing the likelihood of war.

the explanation as a whole, while not perfect, is given support by the tests in table 6.1. Next, we consider the performance of the steps-to-war model within the 1816–1945, 1946–89, 1990–2001 subperiods to see if the explanation fits one historical era better than another. We expect that this might be the case due to the advent of nuclear weapons and since an earlier study of just the type of dispute and alliance variables showed that the full period masked important differences regarding the effect of alliances (see Senese and Vasquez [2004]: 211–13).

The 1816–1945 Period

Table 6.2 reports the findings for 1816–1945. The test results for model 1 show, as in the full period, that territorial disputes are significantly more likely to escalate to war than policy disputes. They are also more likely to escalate to war than regime disputes.[16]

The overall findings for politically relevant alliances are even more supportive of the steps-to-war explanation for the 1816–1945 period than they are for the full time period. In contrast to the findings for the full period, outside politically relevant alliances increase the likelihood of escalation to war not only in models 2 and 3, but also for model 4 (a and b), when the arms-race variable is included. These results support our general theoretical expectation that the presence of outside alliances increases the chances of war, presumably by increasing threat perception and hostility. It is also noteworthy that the likelihood of war for a dyadic dispute where both sides have an outside alliance is now highly significant, whereas before it was significant at only the .10 level for models 2 and 3. Thus, proposition 6.2 is supported, as are all our expectations about the role of outside alliances increasing the likelihood of war in the presence of the other variables in the models.

The other difference from the full period for the pre-1946 span is for the condition where states are allied to each other and are in the same alliances. The steps-to-war explanation, as well as the literature as a whole, expects this condition to reduce the likelihood of war. While this was found to be the case for the full period, the results in model 2 suggest that this is not occurring in the pre-1946 period, since the findings are consistently insignificant across all the models.[17]

---

[16] These results are not shown in the table (Z score = −4.63, p < .001).

[17] These findings rest on Mecklenburg's dyadic disputes with eight states (the German princely states and Austria) in the Seven Weeks' War of 1866. These cases go against the hypothesis that allied states (exclusively in the same alliances) tend to not fight each other, but the evidence turns entirely on whether one uses the start date of the original MID or the entry of Mecklenburg into the war. The alliance terminates on June 15, 1866, the same day the war starts, but the original

Another major difference with the full period has to do with the role of the number of prior disputes. For 1816–1945, we find clear support for the more linear expectation specified in proposition 6.3a, compared to the curvilinear notion of proposition 6.3b. So, for the 1816–1945 period, repeated disputes (as measured by # of prior MIDs in model 3a) significantly increase the likelihood of war in a consistent manner, with no hint of a significant curvilinear effect (model 3b). For this period, the number of prior disputes has a linear effect on the likelihood of war—as disputes recur the probability of war goes up. This means that the hypothesized ritualization effect is not occurring.

In light of the results of models 3a and 3b, only the tests of model 4a are reported in table 6.2. Model 4a includes solely the linear number of prior disputes with the arms-race variable.[18] The most important thing about the tests of model 4a is that they provide evidence highly consistent with proposition 6.4—the likelihood of war for disputants in an arms race is significantly higher than for those not engaged in an arms buildup, even while controlling for the effects of the other steps to war.[19]

Taken together then, all of the risk factors spelled out in our propositions—territorial disputes, both sides with outside alliances (as well as any other form of having an outside alliance), repeated disputes, and arms races—have the impact expected by the steps-to-war explanation. A heightened likelihood of war is clearly indicated when each risk factor is present, as well as suggesting a very high chance of war when all four steps combine in the same dispute, although the degree of this likelihood is best assessed by calculating predicted probabilities. Table 6.3 presents such estimates derived from model 4a for the pre-1946 period as they relate to the four propositions under study. The estimates in table 6.3 can be thought of as the probability of war that is predicted by the logistic regression model in the presence of certain risk factors, such as territorial disputes between states with outside alliances, a history of MIDs, and arms races.

MID between Austria and Prussia starts in 1865 with Mecklenburg joining in 1866. In this chapter, we use the MID start date, so the alliance is in effect and fails to prevent the MID from escalating to war. If the war start date is used, then there is no alliance in effect and "allied and only in the same alliances" would be a perfect predictor of peace (cf. Senese and Vasquez [2005]). These findings are relevant to the "friends as foes hypothesis" (see Bueno de Mesquita [1981: 73–83, 159–64]; Ray [1990]). Our analysis suggests that friends are foes primarily when they are allied but also hedge their bets by having outside alliances, which implies that they are not really "true" friends. When they are exclusively in the same alliances, we would expect them to be less prone to war. The Mecklenburg disputes in the sample are the only ones to go against this expectation in the pre-1946 period, but these eight are enough to make the relationship statistically insignificant.

[18] In model 4b, # of prior disputes is negative and insignificant and # of prior disputes[2] is positive and insignificant.

[19] The same is true for model 4b, which includes both the # of prior MIDs and the # of prior MIDs[2].

Table 6.2

Escalation of the Current or Any MID within Five Years to War, 1816–1945

Variables	Model 1	Model 2	Model 3a	Model 3b	Model 4
Territorial MID[a]	.89	1.12	1.11	1.10	.68
	(.143)***	(.159)***	(.159)***	(.159)***	(.199)*
Regime MID[a]	−1.02	−.87	−.96	−1.02	−.39
	(.411)**	(.423)**	(.430)**	(.441)**	(.546)
Other MID[a]	.44	.91	.97	.97	1.07
	(.400)	(.419)**	(.421)**	(.421)**	(.492)*
Allied & only in same alliances[b]		.55	.52	.52	−.63
		(.453)	(.456)	(.455)	(.804)
One side has outside alliance[b]		.61	.62	.62	.50
		(.196)***	(.196)***	(.196)***	(.232)*
Both sides have outside alliances[b]		1.78	1.80	1.81	1.56
		(.217)***	(.219)***	(.219)***	(.277)*
Allied to each other & outside alliance[b]		1.55	1.54	1.54	1.44
		(.262)***	(.262)***	(.263)***	(.347)*
# of prior MIDs			.03	−.01	.06
			(.013)**	(.036)	(.015)*
# of prior MIDs^2				.001	
				(.002)	
Arms race					1.70
					(.325)*
Constant	−1.13	−2.05	−2.20	−2.11	−2.31
	(.098)***	(.186)***	(.200)***	(.218)***	(.241)*
Chi-square (df)	56.44***	145.50***	150.01***	150.94***	118.18**
	(3)	(7)	(8)	(9)	(9)
Pseudo R^2	.0439	.1132	.1167	.1174	.1367
Number of cases	1040	1040	1040	1040	724

Note: Estimations were performed in Stata (logit). Main entries are parameter estimates, with standard errors in parentheses. All tests are two-tailed.
[a]As compared to the reference category of policy MID.
[b]As compared to the reference category of no alliances.
*$p \leq .10$; **$p \leq .05$; ***$p \leq .01$

The first thing to note in table 6.3 is that when policy or regime disputes are under contention and none of the four steps are present (i.e., they do not have territorial disputes, alliances, recurring disputes, or an ongoing arms race), the probability of war is .092 and .069, respectively. These can be taken as benchmarks for purposes of comparison. In order for the evidence in table 6.3 to be consistent with propositions 6.1–6.4, each additional risk factor must

Table 6.3

Probabilities for Escalation of the Current or Any MID within Five Years to War,
1816–1945

Conditions	Territorial MID	Policy MID	Regime MID
No alliances	.165	.092	.069
	(.120–.221)	(.063–.127)	(.025–.140)
Both sides with	.486	.326	.253
outside allies	(.384–.583)	(.248–.407)	(.115–.442)
Both sides with	.572	.406	.320
outside allies, & sixth	(.474–.667)	(.324–.489)	(.158–.525)
MID			
Both sides with	.692	.536	.436
outside allies, &	(.588–.790)	(.426–.640)	(.234–.663)
fifteenth MID			
Both sides with	.921	.857	.788
outside allies,	(.864–.959)	(.766–.922)	(.598–.918)
fifteenth MID, &			
arms race			

Note: Main entries are predicted probabilities derived from model 4a in table 6.2. The base probability of war for this period (including all missing data for arms races, but not dropped MIDs labeled nonapplicable) is .309.

result in increasingly higher probabilities of war; which is to say, the probability of war for proposition 6.2 should be higher than it is for proposition 6.1, the probability of war for proposition 6.3 should be higher than it is for proposition 6.2, and the probability of war for proposition 6.4 should be the highest of all.

Each of these expectations is borne out. Table 6.3 shows that the probability of territorial disputes going to war is .165. In order for proposition 6.1 to pass testing, this probability must be higher than those for policy and regime disputes, which it is.[20]

Adding a second step (both states have politically relevant outside allies before the dispute arose) makes the probability of a dispute escalating to war

[20] The probabilities of war for "other" disputes (not shown) mirror those for territorial MIDs. This is not an accident, as each of these wars has been found to have important territorial elements. "Other" disputes and the four wars that arise out of them (the Franco-Prussian War, the Spanish-Peruvian/Chilean War of 1865, the Lopez War, and the Football War) are discussed at length in Vasquez and Henehan (2001: 129, note 9); see also chapter 2, above. All but two of the twelve dyadic "other" MIDs that escalate immediately or within five years are accounted for by these wars. The two remaining "other" disputes that escalate are a 1900 MID between Russia and Japan, which escalates with the 1904 Russo-Japanese War, which arises out of a territorial MID, and a 1998 MID between Afghanistan and the United States, which escalates with the 2001 Afghan–U.S. war, which arises out of a policy dispute.

rise to .486.[21] This large jump (from .165) clearly supports proposition 6.2.[22] If we add a third step, a history of prior militarized disputes, the chances of war increase still further. For instance, the likelihood of war for territorial disputes between states that both have outside alliances and are in their sixth dispute is .572. If we isolate instead the fifteenth dispute, which is the average number of MIDs (rounded down) among those pairs that have at least six disputes, then the probability of war goes up even higher to .692. We take these as sufficient jumps to warrant support for proposition 6.3,[23] suggesting that disputes between states that have a long history of repeated confrontations, in conjunction with both sides having outside allies, are more war prone than just having both sides with outside alliances.

The test of proposition 6.4 looks at the effect of all four factors being present. As predicted by the steps-to-war explanation, this condition is indeed the most war prone. It has the highest probability of going to war (.921) in the table and in all the analyses conducted related to table 6.3, clearly illustrating the extreme riskiness of bringing all four steps to war together.

Table 6.3 also reports the effects of taking these steps with policy and regime disputes. While it is clear that policy and regime disputes always have a lower probability of going to war than territorial disputes, it can be seen that handling them in a power-politics fashion has the same progressive risk for war as handling territorial disputes in this manner. Thus, policy and regime disputes are more likely to go to war as dyads make outside alliances, have repeated confrontations, and engage in arms races, with the highest probabilities being reached when all four steps have been taken (.857 for policy disputes and .788 for regime disputes).

On the basis of these predicted probabilities for the 1816–1945 period, four conclusions can be reached. First, territorial MIDs are more war prone than policy or regime disputes. Second, as more of the hypothesized risk factors ("steps") are present, the probability of war goes up. Thus, just having outside allies is not as dangerous as having them when also involved in recur-

---

[21] Both sides having outside alliances always has a higher probability of resulting in war than the other alliance patterns, although not necessarily statistically significantly higher. For example, the .486 (confidence interval .384–.583) probability of both sides having outside alliances resulting in war overlaps with the confidence interval of the .453 of each side allied but also having an outside alliance, but does not overlap with the confidence interval of the .247 of one side having an outside alliance.

[22] Unless otherwise stated in the text or notes, comparisons made in the text between predicted probabilities are significantly different in that they do not overlap the 90 percent confidence intervals.

[23] The .572 war probability for the sixth dispute falls just within the upper bounds of the .486 war probability for the first dispute (both sides with alliances), but does not fall within the lower bounds for the fifteenth dispute (.588–.790).

ring disputes, and having allies while involved in recurring disputes is most dangerous if the dyad is also involved in an ongoing arms race. Third, when both sides have an outside politically relevant alliance, dyadic disputes are always more war prone than disputes with no alliances. Fourth, any issue (territorial or not), if handled in a power-politics fashion, will become substantially more war prone. Each of these conclusions is highly consistent with the steps-to-war explanation.

The results in tables 6.2 and 6.3 takes us a long way in identifying key risk factors associated with pairs of states having their disputes escalate to war. These tables present important evidence that in dyadic territorial disputes where both sides have politically relevant alliances with outside parties, have engaged in a history of repeated confrontations, and have an ongoing arms race, the disputes are increasingly likely to go to war, compared to when one (or more) of these steps is absent. This same overall pattern is present when the practices of power politics are employed with policy and regime disputes. Even though territorial disputes are always more war prone when each additional step is present, policy and regime disputes, for their part, also become more war prone as states have politically relevant alliances, have been involved in prior MIDs, and/or have ongoing arms races.

The 1946–89 Period

The steps-to-war model fits the 1816–1945 period with all four propositions failing to be falsified. The analysis of the Cold War 1946–89 period, on the other hand, reveals some disparate patterns, although important parts of the explanation are sustained. The results presented in table 6.4 show this later period differing from the earlier one in two main respects. First, the estimated effects for most of the alliance configurations are reversed. Both sides having outside alliances, which was a distinct step to war for the early time span, is now a step in the opposite direction. The same is true for dyads that are allied to each other but also have an outside alliance. Dyads with one outside alliance remain positively related to war, but not significantly so for the models in table 6.4. On the whole then, outside alliances are not having the same impact in the 1946–1989 period. These patterns hold for all the models, so proposition 6.2 is clearly falsified, as are all the predictions regarding alliances in propositions 6.3–6.4.

The second major difference from 1816–1945 is that the effect of arms races is statistically insignificant in the Cold War 1946–89 period. In part, this may be due to the low number of cases (forty-six) with arms races during these years. While these two differences are contrary to what is expected by the steps-to-war explanation, they are consistent with what we know about the

Table 6.4

Escalation of the Current or Any MID within Five Years to War, 1946–1989

Variables	Model 1	Model 2	Model 3a	Model 3b	Model 4b
Territorial MID[a]	2.27 (.239)***	2.21 (.245)***	2.16 (.246)***	2.12 (.247)***	1.83 (.270)*
Regime MID[a]	1.23 (.333)***	1.39 (.343)***	1.43 (.345)***	1.39 (.346)***	1.26 (.405)*
Other MID[a]	.68 (1.05)	1.16 (1.09)	1.27 (1.10)	1.27 (1.10)	Perfect predictor
Allied & only in same alliances[b]		−3.23 (1.04)***	−3.49 (1.04)***	−3.61 (1.05)***	Perfect predictor
One side has outside alliance[b]		.25 (.266)	.09 (.272)	.04 (.276)	.11 (.374)
Both sides have outside alliances[b]		−1.39 (.365)***	−1.63 (.379)***	−1.66 (.378)***	−1.54 (.463)*
Allied to each other & outside alliance[b]		−1.74 (.566)***	−1.83 (.568)***	−1.87 (.569)***	−1.48 (.625)*
# of prior MIDs			.02 (.009)***	.06 (.028)**	.11 (.032)*
# of prior MIDs^2				−.001 (.001)	−.002 (.001)*
Arms race					.05 (.574)
Constant	−3.39 (.212)***	−3.02 (.317)***	−3.09 (.318)***	−3.15 (.320)***	−3.51 (.402)**
Chi-square (df)	122.42*** (3)	202.37*** (7)	209.99*** (8)	211.80*** (9)	150.85*** (8)
Pseudo R^2	.1316	.2175	.2257	.2277	.2186
Number of cases	1319	1319	1319	1319	1065

Note: Estimations were performed in Stata (logit). Main entries are parameter estimates, with standard errors in parentheses. All tests are two-tailed.

[a]As compared to the reference category of policy MID.

[b]As compared to the reference category of no alliances.

*$p \leq .10$; **$p \leq .05$; ***$p \leq .01$

Cold War period; namely, that the U.S.-Soviet alliance structure and nuclear-arms competition (although technically not an arms race according to most measures) did not result in a war between the major states in the system.

The other results in table 6.4 are similar to the earlier period. First, territorial disputes are significantly likely to escalate to war compared to policy and regime disputes.[24] Second, dyads are more likely to have their disputes go to war within five years if they are involved in repeated confrontations. There is a positive linear relationship (models 3a and 3b), but it becomes curvilinear in (model 4b) when the sample is confined to cases for which data on military expenditures (arms races) are available. Thus, territory and recurring disputes are more consistently potent (and, certainly, less time bound) risk factors than outside alliances and arms races.

The exact nature of the recurrent-conflict influence during the post–World War II period, however, warrants a closer look. Early indications of a curvilinear relationship appear in model 3b in that the # of prior MIDs variable is positive and the # of prior MIDs^2 is negative, although the latter is not statistically significant. When the arms-race variable is added, both prior MID indicators are significant, so it can be inferred that the relationship is curvilinear.[25] Specifically, the results for model 4b in table 6.4 suggest the presence of an inverted U-shaped relationship between repeated disputes and war.

Figure 6.1 is a visual representation of the marginal impact that recurring disputes have on the chances of war. The likelihood of war within five years is shown over the full zero to fifty-five range on the # of prior MIDs measure.[26] As figure 6.1 reveals, the twenty-ninth dispute between a pair is the most likely to eventuate in war.[27] Increasing numbers of prior disputes between zero and twenty-eight positively affect the probability of war, albeit at a diminishing rate. Beyond twenty-nine previous engagements, however, there is an increasingly negative connection between prior dispute propensity and the chances of war.[28] Interstate wars occur less frequently when the number of

[24] For regime disputes (not shown), this is true of models 1, 2, and 3b, but not model 4b (when arms races are included and the number of cases in the sample drops). In the latter model, the difference between regime and territorial disputes has a p value of .116, but recall that these are two-tailed tests.

[25] The "# of prior disputes" variable is based on a start date of 1816. A plausible argument can be made that disputes prior to 1946 have an effect on those in the Cold War; for example, the Allied intervention in the Soviet Union in 1918 certainly played a part in the Cold War, especially for the Soviets. Nevertheless, the models were also run with a prior disputes variable that resets the clock in 1946. The results are highly similar, but slightly less significant for this alternative specification measuring the # of prior MIDs since 1946^2 (p ≤ .10).

[26] Figure 6.1 depicts the probability of a territorial dispute eventuating in war based on the # of prior MIDs, with the other risk factors set to their modal values (i.e., no arms race and one side has an outside politically relevant alliance).

[27] This point represents the maxima where the slope of the line is equal to zero.

[28] Only twelve dyads have more than 28 MIDs from 1816 on: US-USSR (61), Russia-China (52), Russia-Japan (49), Israel-Syria (48), India-Pakistan (43), Greece-Turkey (42), UK-USSR (41), Japan-China (38), Israel-Egypt (36), US-China (35), Russia-Turkey (31), and Ecuador-Peru (30), for a total of 171 dyadic disputes preceded by 28 or more MIDs. In-depth case studies of these dyads would help elucidate whether and how ritualization comes about and the extent to which it is really reducing the likelihood of war.

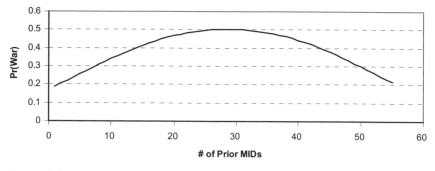

Figure 6.1

Probability of War by # of Prior MIDs

Note: Predicted probabilities derived from model 4b in table 6.4. The maxima point for the probability of war (.503) is at twenty-eight prior MIDs.

prior disputes is both low and very high, with a higher level of war proneness prevalent when the number of previous disputes is intermediate (neither very high nor low). This middle range, where disputants have already gone through a significant number of engagements, but have not yet learned to ritualize their entanglements in a way that limits escalation to war, is clearly the most dangerous during the Cold War period.

Such a finding supports proposition 6.3b, that dyads with a very large number of disputes have a tendency to ritualize and manage their disputes after a period of time, so that the probability of any one of them escalating to war goes down. This result suggests that while more previous disputes generally lead to higher chances of war, there appears to be a point above which subsequent disputes are actually pegged to a lower, not higher, probability of war. This curvilinear effect for the 1946–1989 era, of course, differs from the more linear impact during the 1816–1945 span, implying that ritualization may be a Cold War phenomenon associated with nuclear weapons and thus time bound. The danger of nuclear war may motivate actors to more carefully manage their disputes, but doing so may also inadvertently increase the frequency of repeated disputes.

Given these findings for the two subperiods, what can be concluded about the steps-to-war explanation? First, the steps-to-war model fits the classic international politics 1816–1945 era quite well. This period can be seen as its natural domain. Second, the model fits the shorter Cold War 1946–1989 period less well, but even here some of its core propositions receive substantial support. Third, the insignificance of arms races in the Cold War period may have something to do with attempts to manage arms competitions among nuclear states and their allies, which can reasonably be assumed to reduce the probability of war between major states during the era. If this is true, it may be the case that future non-nuclear arms races in the absence of the kinds of restraints constructed by the United States and Soviet Union will prove once again to be related to war. In this regard, the results for the full 1816–2001 period, which show that arms races are positively related to war, may be more accurate than the analyses of the breakdown of the two periods. This is especially the case since there are so few arms races in the second time period.

Fourth, the Cold War alliance structure was successful in stripping alliances of their belligerent effects—although it did not make them universally a mechanism that prevented war (since one side with an outside alliance is positive, albeit statistically insignificant, in table 6.4). What aspects of the Cold War alliance structure that bring about this effect deserve further exploration; two obvious candidates are nuclear weapons and bipolarity. Whether these Cold War effects will continue or whether arms races and alliances will revert to their earlier bellicose impacts only the future will tell. However, of the two variables—bipolar alliance structure and nuclear weapons—the former is already gone.

Further insights about the chances of war in the 1946–1989 period can be gleaned by examining the predicted probabilities reported in table 6.5. What is most noticeable about table 6.5 compared to table 6.3 is that the probability of war for the Cold War period is considerably lower (ranging from .008 to .178) than it is for the 1816–1945 span (ranging from .069 to .921)—thereby lending statistical sustenance to the appellation, "the long peace." A comparison of the base probabilities of interstate war for the two periods further confirms this conclusion. The base probability of war (looking simply at the number of dyadic disputes that go to war divided by the total number of dyadic disputes) is .309 for the 1816–1945 period compared to a much lower .113 for the Cold War.[29] Nevertheless, it must be remembered that this "long peace" was a peace among major states and not necessarily among major and minor states, which had several wars (See Singer, 1991 and Brecher and Wilkenfeld, 1991).

It is also clear that much of the war fought in this period comes from the escalation of territorial disputes, which are still the most war prone. Their probability of going to war in five years, .178, is higher than the war probability of policy disputes, .034, and regime disputes, .112.[30]

---

[29] This calculation keeps all the other assumptions used in the tables the same; namely, a five-year window and dropping the nonapplicable disputes.

[30] Policy disputes fall comfortably below the lower bound of the 90 percent confidence interval (.102–.281) for territorial disputes, but regime disputes do not. Recall that regime disputes in this

Table 6.5

Probabilities for Escalation of the Current or any MID within Five Years to War, 1946–89

Conditions	Territorial MID	Policy MID	Regime MID
No alliances	.178	.034	.112
	(.102–.281)	(.017–.061)	(.052–.196)
Both sides with outside ally	.045	.008	.027
	(.023–.075)	(.004–.013)	(.012–.049)
Both sides with outside ally, & sixth MID	.069	.012	.042
	(.040–.110)	(.006–.021)	(.020–.073)
Both sides with outside ally, & fifteenth MID	.121	.022	.075
	(.071–.189)	(.012–.040)	(.036–.132)
Both sides with outside ally, fifteenth MID & arms race	.139	.027	.088
	(.047–.285)	(.007–.066)	(.023–.208)

Note: Main entries are predicted probabilities derived from model 4b in table 6.4. The base probability of war for this period (including all missing data for arms races, but not dropped MIDs labeled nonapplicable) is .113.

The major anomaly to note about the post-1945 period is that both sides having an outside ally, which proposition 6.2 predicts as having the highest probability of war, now has the lowest (compared to the reference category "no alliances"). These findings are contrary to proposition 6.2, which must be considered falsified for this period, as must all the other aspects related to both sides having outside alliances in propositions 6.3 and 6.4.

As with the earlier period, when disputes recur the probability of war increases—with it being .045 at the first territorial dispute, .069 at the sixth, and .121 at the fifteenth.[31] We also see that as more steps are taken, the probability of war goes up accordingly with the highest probability of war (.139) occurring when arms races are present (i.e., territorial disputes, both sides with an outside ally, fifteenth MID, and an arms race). While the figures in table 6.5 are not very high and the differences between them are not always statistically significant,[32] they do show a progression from .045 for just territorial MIDs

---

period are significantly less likely to go to war than territorial disputes in all the models except the one with arms races (model 4b), which is the basis of table 6.5.

[31] Of course, as shown in figure 6.1, when the number of prior disputes is greater than twenty-eight, the probability of war begins to decrease. We present the war likelihoods for the sixth and fifteenth dispute in table 6.5 to retain consistency with the estimates for the 1816–1945 period shown in table 6.3. The sixteenth through twenty-eighth dispute would have much higher probabilities of going to war; see figure 6.1.

[32] The confidence levels for each of the predicted probabilities for territorial MIDs are reported in table 6.5. Of these, the .045 is significantly different from the .178, the .121, and the .139 in that they fall below the lower bound of the relevant confidence intervals. The remaining predicted probabilities are not significantly different.

and both sides having alliances (without any additional steps) to .139 with re-curring disputes, and an ongoing arms race. If other alliances variables (not shown in the table) are considered instead, the results are better in terms of the additional steps increasing the probability of war. For example, the likeli-hood of war when there is one outside alliance during a territorial MID goes from .193 to .431, and the no alliance pattern goes from .178 to .404, as recur-ring disputes and arms races are added to the mix. These patterns demonstrate that taking the additional steps posited in propositions 6.3–6.4 increases the probability of war, but that certain alliance patterns in the Cold War reduce the likelihood considerably (compared to having no alliances at all), even in the presence of recurring disputes and arms races.

It is also clear from table 6.5 that it is not that territorial disputes are in-herently war prone, but how they are handled that is the key, even though they are generally more war prone than nonterritorial disputes. The predicted probabilities for policy and regime disputes show that handling these kinds of disputes in a power politics fashion (in terms of repeating disputes and arms races) increases the probability of war, as was the case in the early period, al-beit at much lower levels. A difference with the 1816–1945 period is that regime disputes are more war prone than policy disputes in the Cold War years, some-thing which makes sense given the highly ideological nature of that era.

Finally, one of the main differences with the earlier period is that in the Cold War era, having no alliances or having only one outside ally are the most war-prone configurations, while both sides with outside alliances is the least likely to go to war. In the 1816–1945 period, the most war-prone alliance con-figurations are both sides with outside alliances and allied to each other plus an outside alliance, with no alliances the least likely to be associated with war. Again, this suggests that it is something about the alliance system of the Cold War era and its relationship to nuclear weapons that is the key for explaining the anomaly, while at the same time suggesting that certain fundamentals re-main constant across the two time periods. Nevertheless, the Cold War period shows that human agency can change structures, in this case alliance struc-tures, to have more benign effects, although how conscious these actions were requires further investigation.[33]

The remaining question we address in this chapter is whether the post–Cold War period and the immediate future will be more like the Cold War pe-riod or the classic international politics period of 1816–1945. Our analyses here

---

[33] Of course, consciously relying on classic realist theory cannot count for producing the be-nign effect, because this was used in the previous period to the opposite effect. More likely, alliances were stripped of their belligerent consequences, because of a system of rules of the game and norms that developed to regulate U.S.-Soviet competition; see George (1983).

must at best be seen as exploratory because of the limited number of years we have available and the absence of alliance data after 2000.

The 1990–2001 Period

The logit findings for the post–Cold War period are reported in table 6.6. The first thing that should be stated about this period is that it is only a little over a decade old and so one must be careful in comparing it to periods approximately twelve and four times longer. Nevertheless, what is noticeable about this period is that the probability of interstate war continues to decline from the Cold War period, now reaching a base probability of .032. Even in this time of the breakout of peace, at the end of the Cold War, territorial disputes continue to be the most war prone, compared to both policy and regime disputes.[34] This makes proposition 6.1 consistently supported across all the periods and the most robust finding in our analyses. Adding the other steps to war in our subsequent models does not alter the significance of territorial disputes for promoting interstate war.

The second major finding deals with the role of politically relevant alliances. The war proneness of outside alliances was the major difference between the pre-1946 and Cold War periods. The findings for the post–Cold War period are far from definitive, but they reflect some theoretically interesting trends. Before beginning, it is important to point out that after 1990 the absence of alliances is a perfect predictor of peace and, therefore, drops out of our statistical models. Since "no alliances" has been our reference category to this point, we are forced to select another grouping category in order to estimate models for this most recent period. Theoretically, since dyads that are only in the same alliance and have no outside alliances are expected to be less war prone than dyads with outside alliances, the former variable seems like a plausible candidate. To probe this possibility we ran a cross tabulation, presented in table 6.7, to compare the statistical profile of the "no alliance" variable with that of the "only in the same alliance" variable. The pattern is very close. The former has seventy-four cases at peace and zero at war, while the latter has seventy-nine at peace and one going to war; so we opt for making dyads that are only in the same alliance the new reference category, to which we will compare the war proneness of the other alliance patterns.

---

[34] In this period, regime disputes are a perfect predictor of peace. However, it should be pointed out that regime concerns are a secondary issue in the U.S.-Afghan War, even though this is coded by the Correlates of War project as primarily a dispute arising over policy disagreement (specifically the Taliban harboring al Qaeda). Likewise, classifying the 2003 War in Iraq would have to take account of regime concerns, but it is not in our temporal domain. The point here is simply a cautionary note that regime disputes should not be seen as intrinsically peaceful in this period.

Table 6.6
Escalation of the Current or Any MID within Five Years to War, 1990–2001

Variables	Model 1	Model 2	Model 3a	Model 3b
Territorial MID[a]	2.16	2.41	2.27	2.26
	(.639)***	(.772)***	(.776)***	(.778)***
Regime MID	Perfect Predictor	Perfect Predictor	Perfect Predictor	Perfect Predictor
Other MID[a]	.79	.75	.60	.60
	(1.16)	(1.26)	(1.26)	(1.26)
No Alliances		Perfect Predictor	Perfect Predictor	Perfect Predictor
One side has outside alliance[b]		.96	.54	.54
		(1.14)	(1.15)	(1.15)
Both sides have outside alliances[b]		1.32	.94	.93
		(1.11)	(1.13)	(1.13)
Allied to each other & outside alliance[b]		2.71	2.20	2.19
		(1.09)**	(1.11)**	(1.11)**
# prior MIDs1990			−.54	−.68
			(.316)*	(.854)
# prior MIDs1990[2]				.02
				(.141)
Arms race				NA
Constant	−4.68	−6.15	−4.73	−4.60
	(.580)***	(1.24)***	(1.38)***	(1.59)***
Chi-square (df)	16.46***	30.72***	35.73***	35.75***
	(2)	(5)	(6)	(7)
Pseudo R^2	.0985	.2006	.2334	.2335
Number of cases	577	475	475	475

Note: Estimations were performed in Stata (logit). Main entries are parameter estimates, with standard errors in parentheses. All tests are two-tailed.
[a]As compared to the reference category of policy MID.
[b]As compared to the reference category of allied and only in the same alliances.
*$p \le .10$; **$p \le .05$; ***$p \le .01$

The distribution in table 6.7 also provides the first hint of the relationship between outside alliances and the likelihood of war. As can be seen, there is a clear progression in the war proneness of alliances as one moves from one side having an outside alliance to both having an outside alliance, with an even further jump if states that are allied to each other have an outside alliance. These findings suggest that the direction of the relationship on outside al-

Table 6.7
Alliance Patterns and Escalation to War within Five Years, 1990–2000

Escalation to War	No Alliances	Allied & Same Alln	One side Outside Alln	Both sides Outside Alln	Allied & Outside Alln	Total
No War	74	79	212	138	53	556
	100%	98.75%	98.15%	96.50%	86.89%	96.86%
War in 5 yr	0	1	4	5	8	18
	0%	1.25%	1.85%	3.5%	13.11%	3.14%
Total	74	80	216	143	61	574

liances and escalation to war within five years is consistent with the steps-to-war explanation. This makes the post–Cold War period more like the classic international politics period (pre-1946) than the Cold War era.

Models 2 and 3 in table 6.6 reflect this conclusion, although it must be emphasized that only one coefficient is statistically significant—allied to each other and having an outside alliance. Nevertheless, the other two outside alliance variables are in the right direction, and while the number of cases with this pattern are not enough to support proposition 6.2, and the standard errors are sometimes high, they do suggest that this period is more like the classic international politics period, where having outside alliances is not benign, but dangerous. This would also suggest that the Cold War system of alliances coupled with nuclear superpowers at the top may have been responsible for stripping alliances of their belligerent effect. Time will tell, but at this point alliances seem to be reverting to their classic pattern.

Models 3a and 3b look at the effect of repeated disputes. This behavior had been positively related to war in all the other samples in the analysis. Here, we see a change. Model 3a shows "# of prior MIDs 1990" with a negative sign and significant at the .086 level. A comparison of models 3a and 3b shows that the impact of repeated disputes is best interpreted as a linear negative effect, since neither prior MID variable is statistically significant in model 3b.

The measure of # of prior MIDs used in table 6.6 restarts the clock at 1990. We also ran the models using the two previous measures we have employed—starting the clock at 1816 and resetting it at 1945—but they did not produce as good a set of results.[35] The fact that starting the clock at 1990 leads to significant results lends empirical support to the notion that after 1989 the so-called new world order is really the start of a new era, where the memory

[35] Starting the clock at 1816 produces insignificant results, but starting it at 1946 approaches significance with prior 1946 having a −1.62 Z score (p = .105) and prior 1946² having a Z score of 1.58 (p = .115), indicating a U-shaped curvilinear relationship.

of previous MIDs back to 1816, which had played a role in the two earlier periods, is now gone. In the post–Cold War period, primarily disputes after 1989 have an effect on the probability of war.

The effect of these disputes is to make for war early on, which is not to say that historical rivals will not go to war. Rather, it may be that a new era may involve new actors who are born feuding, much like India-Pakistan and Israel and its neighbors in 1947 and 1948 were new actors at the beginning of the 1946–89 period. It appears from the aggregate results that such wars are dominating the data for the time being. If war fails to resolve these disputes, however, these new actors are likely to become rivals and the pattern may become positive as in the previous two eras. Given this analysis, we would not expect existing rivals to now suddenly become more peaceful; historical rivalries, unrelated to the Cold War, will continue to fester in the current period.

An examination of the five wars in the data set for this period is not inconsistent with these speculations. Examples of new wars that in due time may give rise to a pattern of rivalry and war are, in part, reflected by the 1998 Eritrean-Ethiopian War, which escalates to war on their first MID, and the 2001 U.S.-Afghan War, which escalates on their second MID. Conversely, wars like the India-Pakistan 1999 Kargil War (with forty-one prior MIDs since 1946 and three since 1990) is a classic war between rivals that clearly supports the steps-to-war explanation.[36]

Lastly, if one looks at the cases with high MIDs (eight and above), none of which go to war in the data set, some interesting results are found. Of the seven dyads involved, three of them include Iraq: U.S.-Iraq (nine), Kuwait-Iraq (eleven), Turkey-Iraq (eight). The other cases are North and South Korea (eight), Honduras-Nicaragua (eight), Greece-Turkey (eight), and the U.S.-Sudan with the highest (sixteen). As of this writing, the United States and Iraq are involved in a war with limited involvement by Kuwait and Turkey. The other dyads all remain hot spots. Far from being a clear negative relationship, this closer examination suggests that ultimately the claims of the steps-to-war about repeated disputes and rivalry may very well be borne out in the current period.

[36] The other two wars are the 1999 Kosovo War and the 1990 Persian Gulf War. Both of these are preceded by multiple MIDs. For instance, several parties in the Persian Gulf War, like the United Kingdom, Kuwait, and the United States have five to nine disputes with Iraq when the Gulf War breaks out, and the United States and United Kingdom have four disputes with Serbia when the Kosovo War breaks out. Both of these cases are similar to Diehl and Goertz's definition of enduring rivals and proto-rivals, respectively (without the twenty-year time limit). If one takes this measure of rivalry, then three of the five wars are wars of rivalry (the Persian Gulf War, Kosovo War, and the India-Pakistan Kargil War). Reviewing this handful of wars, however, reminds us that the small number of cases in this period should make one cautious about overgeneralizing and making too much of the findings from this period.

What can be concluded about proposition 6.3 in light of these findings and discussion? First, the effect in the aggregate is linear and negative, which indicates that this current era, at least at its beginning, is different from the previous two. This lends statistical support to the idea that the post–Cold War period is in fact the start or a transition to a new era. Second, while the evidence does not support the proposition, the period of years on which it is based and the nature of the handful of wars that have been fought leads us to be cautious in placing too much weight on the analysis, so we prefer to wait for more evidence to come in before declaring the effect of recurring disputes to be truly different. Our strong suspicion, based on an examination of the cases with high MIDs that do not go to war, is that as time goes on the evidence will show that the relationship is positive.

Finally, the few arms races after the end of the Cold War make it impossible for us to run any of our models. We have data for arms races only through 1992, and three variables are dropped because they are perfect predictors, so model 4 is reduced to thirty-five cases, and these are too few to make a logistic regression analysis meaningful.

We now turn, in table 6.8, to the predicted probabilities for this period. Again, given the limitations of the data, our purpose here is to really see if the current period is more like the classic international politics period of 1816–1945 or whether the trends indicated during the Cold War are continuing. The probabilities in table 6.8 are based on model 3a in table 6.6. As with the previous periods, territorial disputes are more likely to go to war than either policy or regime disputes. This finding makes territorial disputes the only consistently strong result across all four samples (the full and three subperiods). Their probability of war increases depending on the alliance pattern of the contenders, providing support for the notion that whether territorial disputes go to war depends on how they are handled (ranging from .067 to a high of .313).[37] Also, it is clear from the table that in the post–Cold War period, as in the previous periods, the probability of policy disputes going to war is consistently lower than that of territorial disputes. Only once do policy MIDs get above .05, although they are associated with important wars in this period.

Given the consistent findings on territorial disputes across all the samples, the findings on alliances become the key for determining whether the post–Cold War period is more like the classic international politics period or Cold War period. Here, we do see evidence of a reversion back to the early period, which fits the steps-to-war explanation quite well. Before looking at

---

[37] The confidence intervals for the post–Cold War territorial MIDs are reported in table 6. The war probability of .071 only falls outside the lower confidence level for the .313 and .196. Thus, our interpretation rests primarily on the direction of the predicted probabilities.

Table 6.8
Probabilities for Escalation of the Current or Any MID within Five Years to War, 1990–2000

Conditions	Territorial MID	Policy MID
Allied & only in same alliances	.071	.011
	(.008–.207)	(.001–.040)
Both sides with outside ally	.119	.018
	(.052–.220)	(.003–.048)
Both sides with outside ally & mean MID	.067	.009
	(.024–.138)	(.002–.029)
Allied but also outside alliance	.313	.057
	(.180–.473)	(.010–.142)
Allied but also outside alliances & mean MID	.196	.031
	(.083–.358)	(.006–.090)

Note: Main entries are predicted probabilities derived from model 3a in table 6.6. The base probability of war for this period (including all missing data for arms races, but not dropped MIDs labeled nonapplicable) is .032.

these probabilities in detail, it must be remembered that the only alliance configuration that is significantly different from the reference category in this model (3a) is being allied to a state and simultaneously having an outside alliance. This combination with territorial disputes produces the highest probability of war (.313), up from the probability of war for the reference category (.071) allied only to each other.

For territory, these probabilities are higher than those in the Cold War period. This supports the notion that the peaceful Cold War alliance structure may have been unique to that period. Also providing important evidence that this period is like the earlier period is that the absence of alliances is associated with peace, whereas in the Cold War era, the absence of alliances was associated with war. The more belligerent effect of alliances, however, is strongest with territorial disputes. For policy disputes, the probabilities are much lower and do not reach important levels.

The findings on recurring disputes show that as more disputes occur, the probability of war decreases. Thus, for both territorial and policy disputes, a higher probability of war occurs on the first MID than on the mean number of disputes (2.31), which has very low probabilities (.119 versus .067 and .313 versus .196).[38] If this finding were to persist, it would need to be explained away for the theory to be intact. It would also indicate that there is something different about the post–Cold War period than the previous two periods. We have our doubts about whether this pattern will persist, however.

[38] Keep in mind, however, that the mean # of prior disputes is a low 2.31. A further analysis (not shown in the table) of territorial disputes for dyads that are allied but have outside alliances shows that the probability of war goes down as MIDs increase from 3 to 16 (beginning with a high of .151 for the third MID and going down to .06 and .04 for those with 6 and 15 prior MIDs, respectively). Fifteen prior MIDs is the maximum value during this post–Cold War span.

All in all, we think that the current post–Cold War period is more like the classic international politics era of 1816–1945. At least in terms of the relationship between alliances and war, it appears different from the Cold War era. This implies that the steps-to-war explanation is not simply of use for the past, but very much relevant for the present era. It also suggests that one should be cautious about relying on lessons from the Cold War for avoiding war in the future. The alliance and bipolar structure of the Cold War may be difficult to replicate. The one aspect where our statistical analysis suggests the current period does not clearly fit the steps-to-war explanation deals with the effect of repeated disputes. Here, we think that this will change with time and that rivalry will continue to be associated with war as it has in both previous periods.

Conclusion

This chapter has provided evidence that the steps-to-war explanation can deepen our understanding of the process by which war occurs. First, it has tested and provided evidence consistent with four major propositions derived from the steps-to-war model for the 1816–1945 period. It has been shown that the probability of war breaking out is higher for territorial disputes than for policy or regime disputes (proposition 6.1). More important, having both sides with politically relevant outside allies in territorial disputes greatly increases the probability of war (proposition 6.2). If, in addition, these territorial disputes with outside allies are part of a pattern of recurring disputes, then the probability of war is higher still (proposition 6.3a). Finally, if these MIDs, having all these factors present, also occur in the context of an ongoing arms race (proposition 6.4), then their probability of war approaches such high levels (.90 range) that war is almost certain within five years.

Second, for the Cold War 1946–1989 period, territory and a history of prior disputes still have positive and significant impacts on the probability of war, but having outside alliances generally does not, nor do arms races. These latter two (statistically insignificant) factors do, however, under certain circumstances, for example—territorial disputes with one side having an outside alliance—increase the probability of war in a manner consistent with the predictions of the explanation. Why these two factors do not behave more clearly in ways anticipated by the explanation needs further analysis, but it may well have something to do with the Cold War alliance structure and nuclear weapons.

Third, this chapter has shown that the various foreign policy practices states use in pursuing their territorial disputes help distinguish those territorial disputes that go to war from those that do not. This holds for all three pe-

riods (but not for all practices, especially during the Cold War). States that resort to the threat or use of force to contest territory are on a path to war, but
so long as they avoid recurrent disputes, making politically relevant alliances
with outside parties (in all eras except the Cold War), or arms racing, they can
keep the probability of war fairly low. When dyads dispute territory and engage in even one of these steps, the probability of war goes up. Of these three
steps, the most dangerous in the 1816–1945 period is arms racing, followed by
both sides having an outside ally, followed by a history of recurring disputes.
In the less war-prone nuclear Cold War period, the most dangerous is having
a territorial dispute or any dispute that festers and recurs. However, it is also
clear that states that have very large numbers of MIDs in the Cold War period
learn to manage them so that at a certain point MIDs are less likely to go to
war than those that preceded them. In the post–Cold War period (1989–2001),
territorial disputes are most likely to go to war when states that are in the
same alliance hedge their bets—with at least one of them forming an outside
alliance.

Fourth, our analysis has shown that the Cold War era is fundamentally
different from the earlier 1816–1945 period. This has important implications
for the study of international conflict. Failing to control for historical era can
mask, even distort, important patterns. Similarly, our comparison of periods
shows that generalizing from studies based primarily on the post-1945 period,
as many studies of the democratic peace do, is not legitimate and may lead to
empirically unsound conclusions.

Fifth, the analysis has shown that resorting to the use of power politics to
handle disputes increases the probability of war. The only exception to this is
with some of the alliance configurations during the Cold War, which generally reduce the probability of war. These findings, especially for the earlier period, support the claim that the use of power politics is a separate path to war,
and inherently dangerous even in the absence of territorial disputes.

Overall, the most dangerous condition, as shown in our test of proposition 6.4 (tables 6.3 and 6.5), is when multiple factors are present. While we
have examined only the presence or absence of these conditions, the underlying theoretical rationale of the steps-to-war explanation suggests that these
factors are interrelated and can form a syndrome of behavior where one thing
leads to another. Thus, as steps are added, it may become increasingly difficult
to avoid taking additional steps.

Finally, our probes of the 1989–2001 period suggest that international
politics in the present and the future may look more like the classic international politics of the past than the long peace of the Cold War. In particular,
the effects of outside alliances may be reverting to their association with increasing the likelihood of war.

When we also keep in mind that the classic international politics period (1816–1945) covers 130 years versus the 44 years of the Cold War (about three times longer), there is considerable evidence in support of the steps-to-war explanation. In many ways, these findings constitute a new body of empirical knowledge, at least in terms of identifying the factors that increase the probability that a crisis will escalate to war. Based on this chapter, we now know that for most of post-Napoleonic history crises that occur over territorial disputes and are one in a series of repeated disputes are at a risk of escalating to war within five years. In addition, except for the Cold War era, states that resort to outside alliances to support them in their territorial disputes are at a greater risk of war than those that either do not have alliances or are allied to each other without being a member of any outside alliance.

All of these findings are highly consistent with the findings from the previous chapter. Not only are states whose long-term relations are dominated by territorial disputes and power politics apt to go to war, but so too are individual crises or MIDs that embody these steps to war. The analysis of individual MIDs in this chapter further buttresses the conclusions reached in chapter 5 because the research design of this chapter permits a precise measuring of the timing of steps—clearly identifying that they occur before (or in the case of arms races during the year) the MID arises.

This chapter has brought together a number of factors that have been studied in isolation to see how they combine to affect the probability of war. It has done this by looking at how these risk factors might combine in an additive fashion, and it has shown that there are important additive effects that heretofore have not been widely demonstrated. The next chapter sees if more complicated combinations are operating in the steps to war by testing a series of interaction models.

7

Exploring Interactions in the Steps to War

The world of international politics is complex.
What a surprise!

The world of international politics is complex, and few phenomena within international politics are as complex as war. This is why precise measurement and rigorous analyses will be necessary to elucidate the forces that shape political relationships and that increase the probability that they might turn violent and degenerate into war. In this chapter, we examine the main propositions of the steps-to-war explanation to see if they are better seen as conforming to a multiplicative process than to the additive processes that we examined in the previous chapter.

The steps-to-war explanation has several aspects that imply statistical interaction, but as a verbal theory it can be constructed in terms of the simpler and more parsimonious manner of the last chapter or in terms of a set of more complicated statistical interaction models. The reason for this, as noted at the beginning of the last chapter, is that a verbal theory is always more ambiguous than a mathematical model. By exploring, testing, and falsifying a variety of mathematical models derived from the same verbal theory, our knowledge of underlying processes becomes more precise. We start with the assumption that the steps-to-war are *at least* additive in terms of the logic of the theory, and the evidence in the previous chapter, especially for the 1816–1945 period, provides empirical evidence highly consistent with that claim. Nevertheless, many of the propositions also imply multiplicative processes. Here, we explore the major areas in which multiplicative processes can be expected.

The steps-to-war explanation implies that war arises out of a process where specific actions or steps taken by states to deal with issues are linked, typically by a realist strategy that tells decision makers how to deal with security issues. Although it is difficult *ex ante* to specify which of these linkages are apt to produce multiplicative processes and interaction effects, some factors seem better candidates than others. We would expect that territory would have the most interactions, rivalry or recurring disputes the next, and arms races the least, if any. The reason for this is the temporal ordering by which the steps typically progress. Territorial disputes start the ball rolling. They are in many ways a prerequisite for the process we depict. Their high salience leads to disputes recurring and a sense of rivalry, and to the formation of alliances. These linkages provide many an opportunity for multiplicative processes, and the salience of territorial disputes and the role they play in the domestic arena are likely to bring these opportunities to fruition.

Rivalry and recurring disputes are the engines that keep the process going down a path to war, but as a risk factor for crises escalating to war it comes further down the road. Put another way, it appears further down the decision tree, after other risk factors are already in place. Consequently, there is less room (and opportunity) for it to have an explosive impact, characteristic of multiplicative processes.

Arm races are expected to come very late in the process. By then most risk factors for war are already in place (see Valeriano, 2003). While the explanation expects a significant increase in the probability of war when arms races are ongoing during crises, the presence of other causal factors that have already had an impact limits how much the impact of arms races will be contingent on these previous factors in enhancing the probability of war. Thus, it is expected that this factor will have an additive impact rather than a multiplicative one.

This chapter will test certain key aspects of the above analysis.[1] In doing so, it will focus on whether certain practices that link territorial disputes and the use of power politics have an elevated likelihood of war that follow a multiplicative process and not just an additive one. In locating multiplicative linkages, we can further clarify the exact nature of each step's effect on dispute escalation, particularly whether it is contingent on the presence (or absence) of some other step.

To assess the presence of multiplicative processes among the steps to war, we include statistical interaction terms in our empirical models. These interactions allow us to test for conditional relationships. The inclusion of the multiplicative terms is a crucial component of the analyses because it allows us to estimate the *particular* conditional relationships among territory, rivalry, alliance making, and arms racing and not just the *general* ones explored in our

---

[1] The tests in this chapter are both numerous and complicated. To ease the burden on the reader, we have placed a large amount of technical information in the footnotes for scholars and students doing research in this area. These almost constitute a text within a text. We recommend, for those interested in the details, that they read the chapter through, skipping the footnotes, to get an overview of the big picture and then go through the chapter a second time reading the footnotes.

previous tests using additive models (see Friedrich (1982: 806).[2] For instance, we examine whether the strength of the territory effect is amplified among rivals compared to its effect among those who have little history of conflict with one another. In this way, the results will detail the potentially contingent effects of rivalry based on the presence (or absence) of territorial disputes, as well as those of territory based on the presence (or absence) of rivalry. Such possibilities are inherent within the steps-to-war explanation, as is the potential of conditional relationships involving alliances and arms racing.

Not many studies have been conducted testing for interactions with regard to the steps to war. Senese and Vasquez (2004) examine territorial disputes and outside alliances from 1816 through 1992 and find a statistical interaction between one type of alliance pattern and territorial MIDs that increases the probability of escalation to war either immediately or within five years.[3] Colaresi and Thompson (2005) look at several factors (alliances and repetition of crises; mutual military buildups and repetition of crisis) from 1919 through 1995. Both of these studies provide support for the steps-to-war explanation using the two major data sets in the field—the Correlates of War MID data and the International Crisis Behavior (ICB) data. Both, however, test only a couple of the interactions that can be derived from the explanation.

Research Design

The variables and data we employ in this chapter are the same as in the previous chapter, since we view the two as intimately linked: escalation of a MID to war, type of dispute (territorial, etc.), outside alliances (including a summary variable of any outside alliance), # of prior disputes, and arms races. All models run in this chapter differ from the models run in the previous chapter primarily in that they have an interaction term included in the model.

Our dependent variable is whether the current MID or one between the same parties that arises within five years escalates to war. We look at the three subperiods that we focused on in the previous chapter—1816–1945, 1946–89, 1990–2001. To test the robustness of our findings, in this chapter we have also run the analyses for the two major periods, 1816–1945 and 1946–89, with a second dependent variable—whether the current MID escalates to war; that is, we drop the five-year window. We do not report these findings systematically

---

[2] On the use of interaction models, see also Braumoeller (2004); Brambor, Clark and Golder (2005); Jaccard (2001).

[3] For an in-depth look at the contingent effects of territory and contiguity on both dispute and war onset, see chapter 4 above.

Table 7.1

Main Steps-to-War Interactions

	Terr	One Outside	Both Outside	Allied & Outside	Any Outside	# Prior MID	Arms Race
Terr	—	Terr × One	Terr × Both Outside	Terr × Allied & Outside	Terr × Any Outside	Terr × Prior MID	Terr x Arms Race
# Prior MID	—	Prior MID × One Outside	Prior MID × Both Outside	Prior MID × Allied & Outside	Prior MID × Any Outside	—	Prior MID × Arms Race
Arms Race	—	Arms Race × One Outside	Arms Race × Both Outside	Arms Race × Allied & Outside	Arms Race × Any Outside	—	—

in the chapter since they are essentially the same. On the whole, the findings are slightly more significant without the five-year window. This means that for the 1816–1945 period the findings for the steps-to-war explanation are slightly stronger and for the Cold War period, they are slightly weaker for some of the rivalry interactions because generally the explanation does not fit this period as well as the earlier one. The couple of differences found are reported in the footnotes where appropriate.

Given the findings in the previous chapters, we focus on the variables that are most related to the onset of war, both theoretically and empirically, to determine which interaction terms to derive from the steps-to-war explanation. Specifically, we look only at the interaction of territorial disputes and not policy, regime, or "other" disputes; we also do not form any interactions with the "allied and only in the same alliances" variable, since theoretically and empirically it is not a factor that increases the likelihood of war. Table 7.1 lists the interactions we test.

Our interactions terms are mostly dummy variables, but we do have some integer variables when we use the # of prior disputes. Interaction terms are generated by multiplying the values of the two variables in question. A "one" in a dummy variable indicates that the condition of the interaction has been fulfilled; for example a territorial dispute occurs in the presence of "any outside alliance." The integer variables are the rivalry interactions. These variables are created by multiplying one times the number of prior disputes when the value of the other variable (territorial dispute, alliance pattern, or arms race) is present. A zero indicates the absence of either a prior dispute or the other variable (territorial dispute, alliance pattern, or arms race). The rivalry inter-action terms range from zero to the highest number of prior disputes, which is fifty-six. The rivalry measures that were most successful in chapter 6 are employed here, which means that for the post–Cold War era we utilize a shorter memory measure (disputes since 1990). Also to reduce complexity for the Cold War period, we run our interactions using the linear measure of rivalry, # of prior disputes, and do not attempt interactions using our quadratic specification.

We utilize logistic regression to conduct our tests. Since there are a large number of tests, and they can get complicated, we do not calculate any predicted probabilities. Each interaction term can be tested utilizing several models, depending on how many steps to war are included. We look at three of the four basic models previously used in chapter 6 (all except that with the quadratic specification) to determine multiplicative effects in the steps to war. These produce two different samples because of missing data:

Full Sample: (Territorial, Policy, Regime, other MIDs, and all the out-side alliance patterns, and the # of prior MIDs—reference categories—policy, no alliances) (N = 1,040 for 1816–1945; 1,319 for 1946–89; 559 for 1990–2001).

Military Expenditure Sample: (The same variables as in the full sample plus arms races, which reduced the number of cases because of missing data) (N = 724 for 1816–1945; 1,065 for 1946–89; NA for 1990–2001).

Our preference is for the full sample because it has the most cases and all but one of the variables (i.e., it does not have arms races in the model). Unfortunately, including the arms-races variable produces a loss of over three hundred cases, about one-third of the data for 1816–1945. If both samples produced the same results, this would not be a concern. Unfortunately, we find only a few interaction terms that are significant across both the larger and smaller samples. Because our purpose here is to identify all the multiplicative processes that might be at work, we report the findings for any model that shows a significant interaction term. However, when the smaller military expenditure sample (724 or 1,065 cases) results in findings discrepant from the larger sample (1,040 or 1,319 cases), we also scrutinize the cross tabulations, which we have routinely run for each interaction term and our dependent variable, to make sure that the finding is not just a function of the shift in cases. In instances where there are doubts or where an in-depth case study might be useful for future research, we discuss the cross tabulations and specific cases that are relevant, mostly in the footnotes.

For one model in the 1816–1945 period, we dismiss a significant finding for an interaction term, because we have become convinced that it is an artifact of the sample size and not a reflection of what is actually going on historically. We outline our reasons primarily in the footnotes. Generally, however, we accept all the multiplicative results, but place greater weight on those that are robust, that is, those that are supported in both samples. Substantive differences between the two samples will be discussed when these differences become most pertinent to the specific findings at hand.

Findings

We have run a great number of statistical models; reporting the results of each in any detail would quickly become tedious. Instead, we emphasize and discuss the results where we find multiplicative processes actually at work. The additive processes were extensively examined in the previous chapter. When we state that the findings show an insignificant interaction term, we mean by definition, unless otherwise stated in a footnote, that we have compared it to one of the additive models in chapter 6 and found the latter superior. By that we mean simply that the additive model presented in the previous chapter showed that the relevant (lower-order) variables were significant without the interaction term present and that when the interaction term is present, as in the runs presented in this chapter, it is insignificant. Conversely, when we say a multiplicative process is at work, we mean that when an interaction term is included in the model it is statistically significant. In addition, as in chapter 4, we compare the relevant models with and without the interaction terms to see whether the former provides a significant improvement (see Jaccard, 2001: 15–19). Unless otherwise noted, all the models that have a significant interaction term pass such a hierarchical test of changes in the chi-square values.

We organize our findings according to the three historical periods we have used in the previous chapters, 1816–1945, 1946–89, 1990–2001. Within these periods we first look at the interactions of territory with alliance patterns, rivalry, and arms races. Then, we examine the interactions of rivalry with alliance patterns and arms races. Lastly, we look at the remaining interactions with arms races. In this manner, we cover all the major bivariate possibilities within our propositions. For a variety of reasons, at this point we do not explore more complex combinations of interactions, but leave that for future research. Given time and resources, we have opted to provide a more systematic and in-depth analysis of the major bivariate interactions rather than spread ourselves too thin.

Interactions in the 1816–1945 Period

Territorial Disputes

Our first set of findings examines the interaction of territorial disputes and recurring disputes leading to rivalry. What we find in model 1 in table 7.2 is some evidence, although not terribly robust, supporting the notion that as states develop a history of prior conflict, the probability increases that any subsequent territorial dispute will lead to war. The interaction term (Tx prior) is significant at the .117 level,[4] but a model (not shown) with all nonterritorial disputes (policy, regime, other) as the reference category is significant at the .08 level. These are two-tailed tests, however, and since our hypotheses specify direction, the reported results can be cut in half.

The finding means that the likelihood of war is enhanced when a territorial dispute occurs in the context of recurring disputes. More generally, it means that there appears to be a multiplicative process, and not just an additive one, at work with regard to rivalry and territorial disputes. A caveat is that this interaction process is present only for the sample of states for which military expenditures are available (724 dyadic disputes). When the full sample of (1,040) dyadic disputes is employed, the interaction term is insignificant.[5]

What can be concluded about the role of prior disputes in conjunction with territorial MIDs? There appears to be a statistical interaction between these two variables for certain states, which indicates that the steps to war are generating a multiplicative process. When these states contend over territorial disputes, their probability of going to war in light of repeating disputes is greater than just adding the effects of their probability of going to war due to the mere presence of territorial MIDs or the repeating of disputes. Rivalry, in terms of recurring disputes, interacts with the presence of territorial disputes to enhance the likelihood of war.

Since statistical interaction is found for only one category of dyads (those for which military expenditures are available), it behooves us to examine briefly who these states are compared to those in the full sample. It turns out

---

[4] Likewise, the hierarchical test shows that the difference between the additive model and the multiplicative (with the interaction term) is significant only at the .11 level. Using the dependent variable without the five-year window produces a slightly better result for the individual interaction term with p = .107.

[5] If we drop all the variables in the model except the two lower-order ones (territory and order), the interaction term, and the arms-race variable, then the significance level of the interaction term increases to .06. If we then drop the arms-race variable, the interaction term again becomes insignificant. This suggests that while the other control variables (type of dispute, alliance, and # of prior disputes) are having some impact in reducing the relationship, most of the impact is coming from losing cases.

Table 7.2
Territorial Interactions and Escalation of the Current or Any MID within Five Years to War, 1816–1945

Variables	Model 1	Model 2	Model 3	Model 4	Mode
Territorial MID[a]	.38 (.28)	.40 (.29)	.99 (.17)**	.38 (.25)	.87 (.22
Regime MID[a]	−.31 (.54)	−1.00 (.42)*	−.92 (.43)*	−.45 (.55)	−.36 (.55
Other MID[a]	1.02 (.49)*	.65 (.41)	.93 (.42)*	1.00 (.49)*	1.15 (.50
Allied & only in same alliances[b]	−.77 (.82)	.69 (.46)	.54 (.46)	−.56 (.80)	−.68 (.81
One side has outside alliance[b]	.52 (.23)*		.58 (.20)**	.19 (.28)	.55 (.24
Both sides have outside alliances[b]	1.54 (.28)**		1.76 (.22)**	1.48 (.28)**	1.88 (.32
Allied to each other & outside alliance[b]	1.46 (.35)**		1.07 (.35)**	1.40 (.34)**	1.48 (.35
Any outside alliance		.59 (.24)*			
# of prior MIDs	.04 (.02)+	.03 (.01)*	.03 (.01)*	.06 (.02)**	.06 (.02
Arms race	1.72 (.33)**			1.65 (.33)**	1.67 (.33
Tx prior	.05 (.03)[c]				
Tx any aln		.98 (.34)**			
Tx all-out			1.06 (.50)*		
Tx one out				.75 (.39)++	
Tx both out					−.96 (.50
Constant	−2.19 (.25)**	−1.75 (.23)**	−2.13 (.20)**	−2.16 (.25)**	−2.44 (.25
Chi-square (df)	120.7** (10)	114.1** (7)	154.8** (9)	121.8** (10)	121.8** (10)
Pseudo R^2	.14	.09	.12	.14	.14
Number of cases	724	1040	1040	724	724

Note: Estimations were performed in Stata. Main entries are parameter estimates, with standard errors in parentheses. All tests are two-tailed. [a]As compared to the reference category of Policy MID. [b]As compared to the reference category of no alliances. [c]$p = .117$
$+p ≤ .10$ $++p ≤ .06$ $*p ≤ .05$ $**p ≤ .01$

that most of the missing cases (lacking data on military expenditures) are those centered around World War II, World War I (and its aftermath),[6] and 1866 (Seven Weeks' War). This suggests that the full sample does not have different states (e.g., more bureaucratic states with good record keeping), but dyads in special circumstances (e.g., during a war when military expenditure data are not collected by the Correlates of War project for belligerents and nonbelligerents). It is also the case that some of these states with missing data are joiners in an ongoing war. Since it does not seem that it is the attributes of the states that makes them different, but truly problems related to obtaining data for states in special circumstances (like in 1941), this gives us more confidence that the findings on multiplicative processes are generalizable and not confined to a certain category of actors.[7]

The next set of findings examines the interaction between having a territorial dispute while having an outside alliance. The following types of alliance patterns were examined: one side has an outside alliance, both sides have an outside alliance, allied but at least one side has an additional outside alliance, and a summary category of the last three variables, which looks at the presence of any outside alliance. Three of these variables (all but both sides having outside alliances) show significant statistical interaction between territorial and outside alliances, although there are slight differences in terms of which sample supports the finding. It can be seen in model 2 in table 7.2 that the summary variable of any outside alliance (Tx any aln) has a significant interaction term with territorial MID. This means that as states dispute territorial questions and they have outside allies to which they can turn for support, the likelihood of war is enhanced. This holds, however, only for the full sample. The interaction term becomes insignificant when the sample is confined to states for which military expenditure data are available.

---

[6] This includes the Allied intervention in Russia and the fighting in Turkey. It should also be noted that while the missing cases are dominated by these wars, most of the main cases associated with the origin of these wars are not missing.

[7] An examination of the bivariate cross tabulations for both samples also supports this conclusion. To run the cross tabulation we have a variable equivalent to the interaction term with the absence of a territorial dispute and # of prior MIDs equal to 0 and the rest equal to 1 $\times$ the number of prior disputes. For both the "full" sample (1,040) and the military expenditure data sample (724) the bivariate cross tabulation with the interaction term is positive and significant with respective gammas of .358 and .259. We suspect that the insignificant results in the interaction model is a function of the cases where military expenditure data are missing when the interaction term is 0 and does not go to war. Of the 316 dropped cases, about half are of this ilk and presumably if included would make the relationship positive and significant for the full sample. Examples of the dropped dyads are: Germany with Spain, Norway, Denmark in 1915; United Kingdom with Greece, Netherlands in 1916; France with Greece, Argentina in 1916; United Kingdom with Portugal, Yugoslavia, Soviet Union, Sweden, Norway in 1940; Soviet Union with Bulgaria, China, Iran in 1944.

Dyads that are allied and have an outside alliance also have a significant interaction term with territorial MIDs and follow the same pattern as the summary variable (discussed above); namely, the interaction term is significant for the full sample, but not for states that have military expenditure data (see model 3 in table 7.2). Dyads that have one side with an outside alliance also have a significant interaction term, but for the opposite sample (see model 4 in table 7.2); namely the interaction term is significant for states that have military expenditure data but not for the full sample.

These patterns show that for three of the alliance patterns a multiplicative process is at work. They indicate (albeit for different samples) that the probability of escalation to war is enhanced in the presence of these three alliance patterns when territorial MIDs are the focus of contention. A multiplicative process frequently occurs, but not always, and the findings specify when it does. Whether it is one or the other turns on what cases are in the sample. Overall, however, the extent of statistical interaction here is impressive in that all three models show statistical interaction involving outside alliances. These findings are consistent with the steps-to-war explanation, although they are sensitive to the sample employed.

The findings on territorial disputes while both sides have outside alliances are more complicated. We ultimately conclude that the additive model presented in the previous chapter is the better model, which means that there is no significant interaction going on here, but that the presence of a territorial MID and both sides having outside alliances work in an additive process to increase the likelihood of war. The full sample shows an insignificant interaction term, but we also found a significant negative interaction term for the sample for which military expenditure data are available (see model 5 in table 7.2). Initially (Senese and Vasquez, 2006: table 4), we thought this was a valid finding, but on further investigation we have become convinced that it is primarily a function of the sample and the research design rather than "reality." The relationship becomes significant and negative when many of the war cases are dropped. Of the thirty-five cases that are dropped where the interaction term equals one, twenty-nine go to war and five do not. These dropped war cases are what produces the finding. When these are added, as they are in the full sample, they make the negative interaction term insignificant. An examination of the bivariate cross tabulations further supports this point in that both the full sample and the one for military expenditure data show significant positive relationships.[8] We conclude that the relationship is best seen as

---

[8] The full (1,040) sample has significant gamma of .688 with the cross tabulation showing 45 escalations to war when 20.4 are expected. The military expenditure sample (724) has a significant gamma of .477 with the cross tabulation showing 16 escalations to war when 8.8 are expected. Of

additive and positive (as shown in chapter 6, see Table 6.2) and that the tests of the interaction models are best interpreted as indicating a negative but insignificant interaction between territorial MIDs and both sides having outside alliances, which is what the tests of the full model show.[9]

The next set of findings relate to the interaction of contesting territorial disputes while engaged in an arms race. Three models are run related to this question; none show any significant interaction effects (not shown). As discussed in chapter 6, these two variables have significant additive effects when no interaction term is included in the model. In terms of arms races and territorial disputes, it can be concluded that the steps to war reflect solely an additive process, not a multiplicative one.

Rivalry

We now turn to the findings related to rivalry. We begin with the relationship between rivalry (in terms of recurring disputes) and alliance patterns. Several models are run examining the impact of the interaction between the # of prior MIDs and the following types of alliances: one side has an outside alliance, both sides have an outside alliance, allied but at least one side has an additional outside alliance, and the summary variable of "any outside alliance." The only interaction term having a significant impact (at the .10 level or lower) is both sides having an outside alliance (see model 7 in table 7.3), which in the presence of recurring disputes enhances the likelihood of a MID escalating war within five years.[10]

---

course, these results are without any control variables, which shift the relationship in the negative direction.

[9] An examination of the military expenditure sample shows that there are 31 cases fulfilling the condition of the interaction. The 15 that do not go to war are worth investigating to see precisely what it is that reduces the likelihood of territorial MIDs going to war in the presence of both sides having an outside alliance. Realists will be quick to jump to the conclusion that both sides having an outside alliance indicates a balancing effect, but this might not be the case. Four of the cases that do not go to war within five years are between France and England (1893 [2 MIDs], 1896, 1898), and these may very well have something to do with the democratic peace (Ray, 1995). Three involve Nazi Germany and the dissolution of Czechoslovakia (1938, 1939) and Austria (1938), which are related to the Czech-Polish MID (1938) and the Germany-Lithuania MID (1939). In the cases of Czechoslovakia, rather than the outside allies preventing war through a balancing process, they actually urge appeasement, which results in Czechoslovakia's capitulation and dissolution. These can be considered cases of extreme "deterrence" failure or "deterrence" abandonment. Cases that might better fit realist expectations are the two MIDs between Prussia and Piedmont in 1859 and the MID between Austria-Hungary-Serbia in 1908, although these must be investigated. The remaining three cases of the 15 are Bolivia-Argentina (1866), England-Russia (1885), Iran-Iraq (1934).

[10] Note the interaction term is significant only at the .10 level. The hierarchical test comparing the additive and multiplicative models is only significantly different at the .066 level. Using the dependent variable without the five-year window, the interaction of rivalry with both sides having outside alliances is insignificant, but the interaction with the summary variable (any outside alliance) is positive and significant (p = .067) for the full sample.

The analysis in chapter 6, which does not include the interaction terms, however, reveals significant additive impacts for the other alliance patterns. The previous chapter shows that models including only the lower-order terms (main effects) of rivalry and one side having an outside alliance, allied and one outside alliance, and the summary category of any outside alliance show that each individual variable has a positive impact on the likelihood of war.

These findings reveal the complex nature of international politics. What we see here is that only a specific alliance pattern reflects a multiplicative process, while the others remain additive in nature. In this instance, it is only when contending parties both have an outside alliance that the repetition of disputes produces an enhanced probability of war greater than the additive effect of the separate components. The multiplicative process, however, is present only in states for which military expenditure data are available. In the other situations, the various alliance patterns and repeated disputes increase the probability of war individually, but show no enhanced effect when the two are present simultaneously. Thus, one can conclude that there is a statistical interaction for rivalry only when contenders both have outside allies. The other patterns of outside alliances do not produce this effect, but reflect simpler (additive) processes at work with regard to the probability of MID escalation to war.

The last area we examine is the relationship between repeated disputes and arms races. There is no statistical interaction when these two steps to war are brought together (table not reported). Models without the interaction term show that each step increases the likelihood of war in an additive fashion (see chapter 6 above).

What then can we conclude about the overall relationship between rivalry and the other steps to war? First, a history of prior conflict does interact with a current contention over territory to increase the probability of war through a multiplicative process. The two factors (steps) when present can be seen as having an explosive effect on the likelihood of war. This process, however, fits only states for which there are military expenditure data. A full sample of dyads shows that when rivalry and territorial disputes are both present there is no statistical interaction, which most likely means that states for which military expenditures are not available reflect a more additive process.

Second, repeated disputes and outside alliances generally reflect additive processes. The major exception is when both sides have outside alliances. In the presence of this alliance pattern and rivalry (or repeated disputes), the probability of war is enhanced, reflecting a multiplicative process. As with the previous finding on territorial disputes and rivalry, this finding only holds among states for which military expenditures data are available.

Third, rivalry and arms races have no statistical interaction. Each reflects an additive process for the steps to war. As with arm races and territorial disputes, this means that the separate effects are bringing about an increase in the probability of war, and while this can produce high probabilities of war as shown in the previous two chapters, it does not necessarily mean that a multiplicative process is at work.

Arms Races

The last set of findings deals with the interaction of alliance patterns and arms races. Of the four alliance patterns we have been examining, the only one that results in a significant interaction effect is that between arms races and each side being allied but with at least one side also having an outside alliance. As can be seen in model 8 in table 7.3, this interaction term is negative and significant (at the .087 level). The individual lower-order variables remain positive and significant. The same pattern is found for the full period for which we have data, 1816–1992.[11] This means that while arms races and alliances generally increase the probability of war, this special combination actually reduces it.

This finding on arms races and being allied with at least one side having an outside alliance introduces a level of complexity into the analysis that we have not had up to this point. Both multiplicative and additive processes are at work in the causes of war, depending on the particular alliance pattern and the sample of states. What is more unexpected, however, is that sometimes special combinations, in this case being allied with at least one side having an outside alliance while engaging in an arms race, can go against the tide and actually reduce the probability of war, when the individual effects and similar interaction effects increase it.

This result is unexpected by the steps-to-war explanation and raises the question of why and how this comes about in light of the thrust of the other findings that show positive additive effects.[12] Two obvious explanations would be (1) that the arms race induces a fear factor that restrains contenders (see Richardson, 1960a) and (2) that the outside allies restrain the potential belligerents, perhaps in part because of the arms race. Neither explanation readily gives rise to many examples; only further study, most likely in the form

---

[11] The significance level for the full period is .06. The hierarchical test comparing model 8 with the additive model, however, is only significantly different at the .098 level.

[12] For a theoretical discussion of some factors that might be at work in reducing the likelihood of war in the presence of arms racing and military buildups, see Diehl (1983) and the discussion of the preparedness model in Wallace (1982).

Table 7.3

Recurring MIDs/Arms Race Interactions and Escalation of the Current or Any MID within Five Years to War, 1816–1945

Variables	Model 7	Model 8
Territorial MID[a]	.65 (.20)**	.68 (.20)**
Regime MID[a]	−.34 (.54)	−.42 (.55)
Other MID[a]	1.01 (.49)*	1.07 (.49)*
Allied & only in same alliances[b]	−.58 (.80)	−.62 (.80)
One side has outside alliance[b]	.48 (.23)*	.48 (.23)*
Both sides have outside alliance[b]	1.06 (.39)**	1.54 (.28)**
Allied to each other & outside alliance[b]	1.41 (.35)**	1.64 (.36)**
# of prior MIDs	.05 (.02) **	.06 (.02)**
Arms race	1.69 (.33) **	1.95 (.37)**
Prior × both out	.10 (.06)+	
Arms × alln out		−1.36 (.80)+
Constant	−2.22 (.24)**	2.32 (.24) **
Chi-square (df)	121.6 ** (10)	120.9 ** (10)
Pseudo R²	.14	.14
Number of cases	724	724

Note: Estimations were performed in Stata. Main entries are parameter estimates, with standard errors in parentheses. All tests are two-tailed.
[a]As compared to the reference category of policy MID.   [b]As compared to the reference category of no alliances.
$+p \leq .10$ $++p \leq .06$ $*p \leq .05$ $**p \leq .01$

of case research, will provide an answer. Nevertheless, the finding on arms races and being allied but having outside alliances goes against prevailing patterns and expectations. It shows that special combinations can reverse effects. How stable a finding it is, however, remains an open question.

The remaining interaction terms, arms races with the other three alliance patterns, are not statistically significant (results not shown).[13] The analysis of additive models in the previous chapter shows that for this period arms races

[13] The lower-order variables—arms races and the specific alliance patterns—in question are positive and significant.

Table 7.4

Summary of Findings on Interaction Patterns, 1816–1945

	Terr	# Prior MID	One Outside	Both Outside	Allied & Outside	Any Outside	Arms Race
Terr	—	Multiplicative	Multiplicative	Additive*	Multiplicative	Multiplicative	Additive
# Prior MID	—	—	Additive	Multiplicative	Additive	Additive	Additive
Arms Race	—	—	Additive	Additive	Multiplicative (Negative)	Additive	—

*Some evidence of a negative interaction was found, but not accepted; see text.

and the various alliance patterns always have a positive, significant, and additive effect on the likelihood of war.

Summary

Table 7.4 brings together the findings on the numerous tests that have been conducted in this section. We have labeled cells as multiplicative based on the analysis given above and as additive by comparing the results of the interaction models with the additive models run in the previous chapter. Usually, statistical interaction is found to be significant for one sample than for both (e.g., for dyads for which military expenditures data are available, but not for the full sample). Keeping this caveat in mind, several conclusions can be reached.

First, multiplicative processes are not the typical means by which escalation to war occurs, but they are clustered around a specific set of variables associated with the presence of territorial disputes. Territorial disputes are most apt to experience multiplicative processes. This means that their impact on the probability of war, which is already higher than other issues, can be even stronger depending on whether states have an outside alliance or disputes repeat to create a rivalry. This finding is highly consistent with the tenor of the territorial explanation of war.

Second, rivalry generally reflects an additive process in terms of the steps to war. Only two of six possibilities show any statistical interaction (territorial MIDs with prior disputes, and prior disputes with both sides having outside alliances). Similarly, arms races reflect primarily an additive process. Having an arms race can increase the probability of war, but this probability is not enhanced in the presence of any of the other factors (steps) examined in the analysis.

Third, the steps to war, overall, increase the probability of a MID escalating to war within five years. However, certain unique combinations can produce a reduction in the probability of war. There appears to be a negative in-

Table 7.5

Territorial/Recurring MIDs Interactions and Escalation of the Current or Any MID within Five Years to War, 1946–1989

Variables	Model 1	Model 4	Model 5	Model 6	Model 7
Territorial MID[a]	2.09 (.31)**	1.03 (.45)*	2.32 (.26)**	2.19 (.25)**	1.98 (.270)**
Regime MID[a]	1.41 (.35)**	1.23 (.40)**	1.40 (.34)**	1.42 (.35)**	1.39 (.403)**
Other MID[a]	1.23 (1.10)	perfect predictor	1.31 (1.09)	1.23 (1.09)	perfect predictor
Allied & only in same alliances[b]	−3.50 (1.04)**	perfect predictor	−3.54 (1.04)**	−3.00 (1.05)**	perfect predictor
One side has outside alliance[b]	.09 (.27)	−.55 (.47)	.077 (.27)	−.23 (.30)	.10 (.37)
Both sides have outside alliances[b]	−1.63 (.38)**	−1.55** (.46)	−1.04 (.45)*	−1.22 (.39)**	−.52 (.53)
Allied to each other & outside alliance[b]	−1.84 (.57)**	−1.46 (.61)*	−1.82 (.57)**	−1.69 (.57)**	−1.46 (.62)*
Any outside alln					
# of prior MIDs	.02 (.02)	.04 (.01)**	.03 (.01)**	−.03 (.02)	.05 (.01)**
Arms race		.07 (.59)			−.04 (.59)
Tx prior	.01 (.02)				
Tx one out		1.31 (.52)*			
Tx both out			−1.24 (.62)*		
Prior x one out				.06 (.03)*	
Prior x both out					−.09 (.04)*
Constant	−3.04 (.34)**	−2.84 (.41)**	−3.19 (.33)**	−2.93 (.33)**	−3.42 (.40)**
Chi-square (df)	210.1** (9)	151.2** (8)	214.2** (9)	217.6** (9)	154.5** (8)
Pseudo R²	.23	.22	.23	.23	.22
Number of cases	1319	1065	1319	1319	1065

Note: Estimations were performed in Stata. Main entries are parameter estimates, with standard errors in parentheses. All tests are two-tailed.
[a]As compared to the reference category of policy MID.   [b]As compared to the reference category of no alliances.
$+p \leq .10$ $++p \leq .06$ $*p \leq .05$ $**p \leq .01$

teraction between arms races and being allied but at least one side having an outside alliance. In this instance, the presence of one factor in face of the other reduces the probability of war. Why this occurs, if it found to be a stable result, is an important area for further research. We now turn to the Cold War period.

Interactions in the Cold War Period, 1946–89

As can be recalled from chapter 6, the Cold War period had a number of differences from the classic international politics period of 1816–1945. Again we find differences, but not as many as one would have anticipated given the earlier findings. We begin our discussion with an examination of the interaction of territorial disputes with the other variables, and then move on to an examination of rivalry and of arms races.

Territorial Disputes

The first major difference with the 1816–1945 period in terms of the presence of multiplicative processes is that the interaction between territorial disputes and the # of prior MIDs is not significant, as can be seen in model 1, table 7.5.[14] This means that for the Cold War period that while each of these variables increase the probability that a MID will escalate to war within five years, this is best seen as an additive process and not a multiplicative one.[15]

Territorial disputes do evince some statistical interactions with the outside alliance patterns, but not as many as in the 1816–1945 period. As can be seen in model 4 in table 7.5, the finding most consistent with the earlier period and the steps-to-war explanation is that territorial disputes in the presence of one side having an outside alliance enhances the likelihood that a MID will escalate to war. This multiplicative process, however, holds only for those sample of states for which military expenditure data is available (the same was true for the 1816–1945 period).[16] When comparing this finding with the other

[14] When the dependent variable without the five-year window is used, the interaction term becomes significant and negative at the .044 level. This is the main discrepancy using the alternate dependent variable. The reason the relationship is negative (by definition) is that all prior disputes that do not go to war (that would under the five-year window) are now being counted against the hypothesis. This gives more weight to dyads that go to war with few MIDs thereby giving what we regard as a misleading result.

[15] This was shown in chapter 6. Here an examination of the main effects shows that territorial disputes and #of prior disputes are significant (p < .10) for the sample for which military expenditure data are available, but for the full sample, only territorial disputes are significant.

[16] Our previous analysis of alliances and territorial disputes (Senese and Vasquez [2004: 211–13]) did not find this interaction significant because it did not include the arms-race variable in the model and thus was based on the full sample. The interaction becomes insignificant in the full sam-

Cold War findings, this implies that states that have territorial disputes are most likely to go to war when one side has an outside alliance and the other is without allies.

The other multiplicative process found for territorial disputes during the Cold War is between the presence of territorial disputes and both sides having outside alliances. However, this process is negatively related to war onset. This means that instead of enhancing the likelihood of war, as expected by the steps-to-war explanation, this combination actually reduces it (see model 5 in table 7.5). This holds for both the full sample and the sample for which military expenditure data are available. The finding is consistent with what we know about the restraining effects of Cold War alliances and alignments. Whether it is the alliance structure or the Cold War conflict itself that acts as the key restraint is very much an open question, but the fact that it could restrain territorial disputes is theoretically important.[17]

---

ple largely because there are twenty-two cases with missing arms-race data that do not go to war that "should" (i.e., they fulfill the conditions of the interaction term (txpr2 = 1) and twenty-three cases of war that "should not" (i.e., they do not fulfill the conditions of the interaction txpr2 = 0). An examination of these suggests that the smaller sample is the more accurate finding.

Of the twenty-two missing cases that are coded as fulfilling the conditions of the interaction (i.e., txpr2 = 1), and do not go to war, eleven involve dyads that at other times go to war. These include eight Arab-Israeli dyads (such as Iraq-Israel, Saudi Arabia–Israel) and three North Korea postwar conflicts. Half of the cases that do not go to war, but should be easily explained away. On the other side of the equation, of the twenty-three cases that do go to war but should not (since they do not fulfill the conditions of the interaction term), slightly over half involve diffusion effects. Ten involve joiners in the Korean War, two involve joiners in the Arab-Israeli conflict (United Kingdom and France in 1956), and two involve the United States and Thailand joining the Vietnam "civil" war. Two other cases are also related to the Arab-Israeli wars. Diffusion plays a large role here and reflects a separate path to war; see Vasquez (1996a). Since about half of the most anomalous cases can be explained away, we have accepted the finding of the smaller sample that there is indeed a significant positive interaction between territorial MIDs and one side having an outside alliance.

[17] An examination of the specific cases (without any control variables) shows that there are 78 cases of peace when 73.6 are expected and 5 war-related MIDs when 9.4 are expected. The 5 war-related cases occur late in the Cold War (1974–82): Somalia-Ethiopia (3), Libya-Tanzania, UK-Argentina. Some of the nonwar cases include the fairly rare Cold War territorial disputes where both sides have outside alliances, such as: US-USSR (1954), German Democratic Republic-US (1958), German Democratic Republic-France (1961), USSR-France (1962), USSR-Turkey (1957), USSR-UK (1958), USSR-France (1958), USSR-Taiwan (1958), USSR-Japan (1982). There are also a host of USSR-China MIDs from 1964 through 1968 and 1977 through 1980, 1988. There are a number of United Kingdom MIDs that appear to be a legacy of its imperial era, including several with Latin American states: Colombia, Chile, Argentina, Guatemala, Spain, Yemen Arab Republic. There are several straightforward territorial disputes between minor states: Iran-Iraq, Bulgaria-Yugoslavia, Bulgaria-Greece, Afghanistan-Pakistan, Libya-Chad, Cambodia-Thailand. The extent to which the Cold War kept all these disputes from exploding into war is worth study, especially in comparison to the three that did escalate to war late in the Cold War. This query suggests that Cold War alignments coupled with some sort of norm(s) acted as a restraint. A number of cases, however, consist of those that will eventually go to war (after five years) or are postwar conflicts. These include the already listed Iran-Iraq, UK-Argentina, as well as Pakistan-India, Somalia-Ethiopia, China-India, China-Vietnam.

The remaining alliance patterns show no multiplicative processes at work, contrary to the findings for the earlier period. However, the interaction of territorial disputes and the third alliance pattern—allied but with at least one side having an outside alliance—is a perfect predictor of peace, again providing additional evidence that alliances during the Cold War are playing a pacific role, although in this case they are intra-Arab alliances. Since territorial disputes are so war prone, whatever restrains them is worth a second look, and here we have a perfect predictor.[18]

The analysis also shows that the interaction between territorial disputes and the summary variable (any outside alliance) is statistically insignificant. This is not too surprising since having one side with an outside alliance has a positive effect on the likelihood of war and having both sides with an outside alliance has a negative effect. Looking at the additive models (without the interaction terms) gives us some idea of the overall impact of outside alliances. It seems that outside alliances, have a negative impact on the likelihood of war with one side having an outside alliance being the only exception for the Cold War period. In addition, we can say, albeit somewhat tentatively, that the combination of territorial disputes and the summary variable (any outside alliance) seems to follow an additive, but complex process in that the main effect of territorial disputes is to increase the likelihood of war, but the effect of any outside alliance is to reduce it in this period, although the latter is usually not significant.[19]

Lastly, we find that territorial disputes show no statistical interaction with arms racing. Likewise, the lower-order arms-races term has no significant impact. This is not surprising, however, in light of the analysis in chapter 6, which

---

All of this is to say that a simple balancing-deterrence argument as to why this finding holds may not account for all these cases, although capability may play some role with other variables (cf. Colaresi and Thompson [2005: 359]).

[18] The bivariate cross tabulation reveals that there are thirty cases where territorial MIDs are present when states are allied but at least one side has an outside alliance. Of these, 3.4 could be expected to escalate to war within five years, but none do. These thirty cases are mostly in the Middle East and in North Africa involving the following: Syria, Egypt, Jordan, Iraq, Iran, Sudan, Saudi Arabia, Kuwait, Morocco, Algeria, Libya, Tunisia. These cases suggest some muting role for Arab alliances, norms, and/or identity. With the end of the Cold War and the Persian Gulf War, this pattern comes to an end. The interaction between territorial MIDs and allied with one outside alliance for the post–Cold War period is positive and significant (see below), with all the war cases related to the Persian Gulf War. Whether the perfect predictor pattern is broken solely by Iraqi decision making or because of the ending of the Cold War structure is worthy of investigation. The other cases that more clearly illustrate the ways in which alliances may restrain territorial disputes are the five disputes between Greece and Turkey (1958, 1974–78) and the three between the Soviet Union and China (1947–48).

[19] We did not use the summary variable, any outside alliance in chapter 6, so the additive models without the interaction term were run here. The alliance variable is always negative when the interaction term txpr5 is not included; however, it was only significant ($p = .11$) for the full sample.

showed that arms races during the Cold War have no significant impact, so we cannot even say that an additive process is at work.

Rivalry

The findings on rivalry also reflect some complex processes during the Cold War. The logistic analyses of model 6 in table 7.5 show that the # of prior MIDs, which we use as an indicator of rivalry, in the presence of one side having an outside alliance, embodies a multiplicative process that significantly enhances the likelihood of war. This relationship holds both for the full sample and the sample for which military expenditure data are available.[20] This finding is consistent with the steps-to-war logic in that recurring disputes are expected to increase the likelihood of war. It is also consistent with one side having an outside alliance enhancing war in the presence of territorial disputes (see model 4 in table 7.5). These two findings related to one side having an outside alliance with a positive impact on war are the major findings that reflect steps-to-war multiplicative processes during the Cold War period.

These positive effects, however, are a function solely of the interaction between this type of alliance pattern and the presence either of territorial disputes or the repetition of disputes. Recall in chapter 6, in the absence of an interaction term, that one side having an outside alliance during the Cold War period was statistically insignificant.[21]

Since in this period only one side having an alliance has a positive impact on the likelihood of war, it is of interest to see what cases these are. They are mostly associated with the typical wars of the Cold War—those involving rivalries outside the Cold War (such as the Arab-Israeli wars, India-Pakistan, China-India, Somalia-Ethiopia, Iran-Iraq, Kenya-Tanzania) and those Cold War conflicts where one side did not have an alliance (Korean War, Vietnam War, Sino-Vietnamese War). All of this makes sense historically.

Rivalry also interacts significantly with both sides having outside alliances, but this time instead of increasing the likelihood of war, it reduces it (see model 7 in table 7.5). This relationship holds for both the full sample and the sample for which military expenditure data are available. This is the same pattern found between both sides having an outside alliance and the presence

---

[20] Using the dependent variable without the five-year window, the relationship of rivalry with one side having an outside alliance is also significant but only for the full sample (p = .117).

[21] Further support for this conclusion is provided by the fact that the main effect of the one outside alliance lower-order term is negative (albeit insignificant), while the interaction term is positive. This suggests the hypothesis that as disputes repeat, alliances—which are generally stripped of their belligerent effects during the Cold War—in the instance of only one side having an outside alliance now increase the probability of war, as they do in the classic international politics period of 1816–1945.

of territorial disputes (see model 5 in table 7.5, above). It means, contrary to the expectation of the steps-to-war explanation that in the presence of both sides having outside alliances and disputes repeating, the likelihood of war is significantly reduced. As with the previous finding, the reason for this outcome needs to be investigated further, but it is probable that the Cold War alliance structure and/or the factors associated with it (e.g., nuclear weapons, ideological disagreements as opposed to territorial disputes, or the construction of rules of the game to avoid escalation) play some role.

This finding is fairly consistent with what we know about the Cold War alliance structure—namely, that when NATO and Warsaw Pact countries were involved in a MID they never went to war.[22] This alignment structure also seems to mute war between all the major states in the Cold War with the exception of the early Korean War. It is also consistent with the idea that after Korea a norm emerges between the United States and the Soviet Union that whenever one side is in a war the other will refrain from sending troops (see Mansbach and Vasquez, 1981: 441–46). Whether the rules of the game that were established between the Cold War competitors, including China and the West, the danger of nuclear holocaust and the doctrine of nuclear deterrence, the conventional notion of balancing, or some combination of these factors is driving this finding is something that must be carefully investigated by future research. The point here is that the evidence does not automatically support a realist hypothesis of balancing to the exclusion of competing hypotheses.

This pattern of one outside alliance being more war prone than both sides having outside alliances is similar to a finding of Colaresi and Thompson (2005: 359–60) for the 1919–95 period using ICB data. They interpret this as supporting a balancing/deterrence explanation. We are not sure, for the reasons outlined above, that this is the case, at least for our findings. We have already seen that for territorial disputes in the presence of both sides having outside alliances that some of the cases that do not go to war (Germany-Czechoslovakia and Germany-Austria [1938]) are deterrence failures not deterrence successes. For the Cold War period, it is also important to distinguish between balancing and nuclear deterrence. The latter is the more common explanation given for the absence of major state war in the Cold War, but it is not the only one (see Mueller, 1989; Vasquez 1991).

The remaining two alliance patterns show no multiplicative processes at work. An increasing # of prior MIDs in the presence of two parties that are

[22] Interestingly, this finding disappears when using the dependent variable without the five-year window (p = .810) for the full sample, which adds face validity evidence in light of the historical record that the five-year window provides more accurate findings, especially with regard to the rivalry variable.

allied, but where at least one has a separate outside alliance, does not have a significant interaction effect on the likelihood of war. The effect here, as shown in chapter 6, is complex but additive, repeating disputes having a positive effect on war and the alliance pattern having a negative effect.[23] No significant interaction was found between the summary variable (any outside alliance) and the # of prior MIDs, although it comes close to a positive relationship (p = .12 [not shown]).[24] As with the previous finding on the summary outside alliance variable (with territorial MIDs), the lower-order terms indicate an additive process at work with rivalry having a positive impact on the likelihood of war, and any outside alliance a negative impact (p = .11).[25]

Rivalry also does not interact with arms races to enhance the likelihood of war. In this period, as shown in chapter 6, while repeated disputes increase the probability of war, arms races are insignificant, so the absence of an interaction effect is not unexpected.

Arms Races

Not surprisingly none of the other interactions involving arms races are significant.[26] What is unexpected, however, is that two of the interactions between arms races and outside alliances are perfect predictors of peace—arms races with both sides having outside alliances, and arms races with allied to each other and at least one side having an outside alliance. This finding is contrary to the steps-to-war explanation in that both arms racing and alliance making should increase the likelihood of war. Further investigation with a cross tabulation revealed that in both instances there are ten cases of peace when 9.2 are expected and zero cases of war when 0.8 were expected. These are slight differences that appear to be random, but they deserve mention given the rarity of perfect predictors.[27]

---

[23] An examination of the two lower-order terms in the interaction model shows the same relationship for the full sample, but not the sample with military-expenditure data available. For the latter, the alliance lower-order term is negative, but insignificant.

[24] Without the five-year window, this relationship is significant at the .031 level for the full sample. Nevertheless, given the fact that the interaction term with one outside alliance is positive and the interaction term with both outside alliances is negative not much emphasis should be placed on the summary variable. All it really means is that outside alliances, in general, are more positively than negatively related to war, which supports the steps-to-war explanation, but obscures an important negative finding.

[25] This holds only for the full sample.

[26] The two arms-race models (with one outside alliance and the summary variable, any outside alliance) initially did not run because of collinearity problems. We were able to run them after dropping the arms-race lower-order term, and each turned out to have an insignificant interaction term. For our general procedure for dealing with collinearity, see the beginning of the section on the post–Cold War period.

[27] The list of the cases making up the perfect predictor includes some well-known rivals. For the interaction of arms races and both sides having outside alliances, these include: Iraq-Iran (1974)

Table 7.6

Summary of Findings on Interaction Patterns, 1946–89

	Terr	# Prior MID	One Outside	Both Outside	Allied & Outside	Any Outside	Arms Race
Terr	—	Additive	Multiplicative	Multiplicative (negative)	Perfect predictor	Additive Terr + Alln ns	Terr + Arms ns
Prior MID	—	—	Multiplicative	Multiplicative (negative)	Additive Alln −	Prior + Alln ns	Prior + Arms ns
Arms Race	—	—	Non-significant	Perfect Predictor	Perfect Predictor	Non-significant	—

Summary

Table 7.6 summarizes the findings on the Cold War period. We label a cell as multiplicative if any of its tests show a statistically significant interaction term. What can we learn about the steps to war from this table? First, even though there are fewer multiplicative processes at work than in the classic international politics period of 1816–1945,[28] they occur with the two main variables that one would expect—territorial disputes and rivalry (each respectively interacting with some form of outside alliance). When multiplicative processes are not operating, the main effects of territorial disputes and of recurring disputes are positive and significant. These findings are also consistent with what was found generally about the Cold War in chapter 6; namely, that the only two significant factors promoting war are territorial disputes and rivalry.

Second, what is more supportive of the steps-to-war explanation when we examine interactions than just testing additive models, as in chapter 6, is that now some alliance patterns during the Cold War significantly enhance the likelihood of war; whereas, in chapter 6 outside alliances were either insignificant or negatively related to war. The introduction of the interaction terms makes it clear that when only one side has an outside alliance, war is likely if the parties are either disputing territory or have a recurring number of MIDs (see rows one and two in table 7.6 under the appropriate alliance pattern). Alliances are not always restraining in the Cold War, as one is led to believe from

---

and Ethiopia-Somalia (1978, 1980). For the interaction of arms races between allied states where at least one side has an outside alliance, these include: Iraq-Kuwait (1975), Turkey-Greece (1975, 1976, 1978), and Algeria-Morocco (1975). Of course, some of these eventually go to war, but not while they are arms racing and have these alliance patterns. This might be a relationship worth monitoring in the future, but with so few cases it may very well be a coincidence.

[28] The 1816–1945 period has five positive interaction terms and one negative, and the Cold War period has two positive and two negative.

the analysis in chapter 6, although generally they are less war prone than in the earlier period.

Third, the alliance pattern in the Cold War that most reduces the onset of war is when both sides have outside alliances. This interacts respectively with territorial disputes and with rivalry to reduce greatly escalation to war. In the few cases where it interacts with arms races, it is a perfect predictor of peace. This is theoretically a very interesting finding because we believe that in the previous period, having both sides with outside alliances increases the likelihood of war. The polarized system of alliance blocs simply did not operate in the Cold War the way they did in the past. This is probably not an accident. This suggests that there is something about this alliance pattern during the Cold War that makes for different effects than was typically the case for the previous era. Since in both eras there is a kind of "balancing alignment" (but these produce contradictory effects), this is probably not the factor. Rather this irenic effect seems more likely to come from the raising of the provocation threshold due to nuclear weapons and/or to the bipolar structure of the alignment structure itself. Whatever the reason, the interaction analysis can be credited with more clearly delineating the processes (which are multiplicative) that are reducing the propensity for war.

Fourth, arms races, on the whole, do not evince significant multiplicative processes. They do not significantly interact with territorial disputes, or with rivalry. None of this is unanticipated given that the additive models show that arms races are not significantly related to war onset during the Cold War. What is unexpected (and again underlines the complexity at work in international politics) is that two interaction terms involving arms races are perfect predictors of peace. When arms races are ongoing and either both of the contenders have an outside alliance or the contenders are allied to each other and at least one side has an outside alliance, then the dispute does not escalate to war, during the Cold War period. While these are only around ten cases in each instance, they are similar to what was found in the earlier period with the interaction between arms races and states allied to each other significantly reducing the likelihood of war.

What can we conclude about the adequacy of the steps-to-war explanation based on this period? While the steps-to-war explanation clearly does not fit the Cold War period as nicely as it fits the classic international politics period, parts of it fit well, and on the whole, the explanation fits slightly better than one would conclude on the basis of examining only additive models. Both territorial disputes and rivalry are important factors in bringing about war. In the Cold War period, even though it does not evince as many multiplicative processes at work as in the 1816–1945 period, when it does evince multiplicative processes, it involves territorial disputes and rivalry with each producing interactions (with an alliance pattern of one side having an outside alliance) that greatly enhance escalation to war. When the interactions of the steps are examined its dangers in this period (especially with regard to certain alliance patterns) are more fully appreciated.

A second important conclusion is that under certain circumstances, steps taken that normally help bring about war can actually reduce the likelihood of war. Evidence has been uncovered that when both sides have outside alliances, the war propensity of territorial disputes, rivalry, and arms racing can be attenuated. Such findings may give us hints as to why and how the Cold War was a "long peace." Even though such findings are contrary to the steps-to-war explanation, it should be given credit for at least identifying phenomena that are of theoretical importance for bringing about a wary peace when one would have expected war. We now turn to the post–Cold War period.

Interactions in the 1990–2001 Period

As will be recalled from the analysis in the previous chapter of this period, we can not use "no alliances" as the reference category because it is a perfect predictor of peace, so we use "allied to each other and only in the same alliances" as a reasonable surrogate, since it is negatively associated with escalation to war. In the interaction analyses for the post–Cold War period, however, we encountered some collinearity problems that we did not in the previous subperiods. Testing interaction models with several dummy variables is prone to collinearity, although we have been fortunate in having generally avoided these up to this point. To deal with these problems, we implemented two conventional solutions. One was to exclude certain variables from our models, while retaining them in the data (which thereby puts them in the reference category). We took a strategy of incrementally excluding one variable at a time until the model ran successfully.[29] The other was to examine the effect of one

[29] We would begin by excluding the perfect predictors (of peace), which typically were regime disputes and the absence of alliances. This usually did not work and we were forced to drop one of the lower-order terms. (Although we include lower-order terms in all our analyses, this is not always done by other scholars, who give a reasonable argument for exclusion; see Colaresi and Thompson [2005, table 1].) For example to get the txpr3 (territory interacting with both sides having outside alliances) model to run we needed to drop the pr3 alliance variable. This means that the coefficient looks at the likelihood of war in the interaction compared to (in this instance) the likelihood of war in a reference category consisting of: allied only to each other (the original reference category) no alliances, regime disputes (the excluded perfect predictors), and both sides having outside alliances (the excluded lower-order term). When this sort of model is run, we increase the number of cases from 475 to 559, but in doing so, of course, we make it slightly easier to get a significant relationship, since the reference category contains several perfect predictors. To reduce this "bias," we reintroduce the perfect predictors, which are then dropped from the data as perfect predictors, making the reference category (in this instance) just the original variable (allied only to each other)

variable, X_1 (e.g., territorial MID) on escalation to war in the presence of X_2 (e.g., when one side has an outside alliance) and then run a chi-square test to see if that model was significant. We report the latter results for this "alternate method" in the footnotes, and the models with excluded variables in the tables.

As before, we report the findings for models that show any multiplicative process at work. We begin by looking at the territory interactions and then those on rivalry. The interactions for arms races could not be run because of the arms-race data limitations discussed in the previous chapter. Just as in chapter 6, our primary interest is to see if the post–Cold War period is more like the classic international politics 1816–1945 period or the Cold War period.

The first major finding is that territorial disputes do not significantly interact with # of prior disputes (see model 1b in table 7.7). The additive model, which was reported in chapter 6, is better. This model showed that territorial disputes increase the likelihood of war, but that as disputes repeat, the probably of war decreases. As noted in the previous chapter, what this really means is that most wars occur with one or two disputes.

The findings on outside alliances, which are reported in table 7.7, are the most interesting. Here we find that three interaction terms, between territory and the outside alliance patterns, have significant effects.[30] The likelihood of territorial disputes escalating to war is enhanced in the presence of (a) both sides having outside alliances (model 5),[31] (b) states being allied to each other

---

and the excluded lower-order term. The tables reported in the chapter are the most conservative ones for which the model ran, except in one instance (territory with both sides having outside alliances) which we discuss in a footnote.

[30] The interaction terms of territory with (a) one side having an outside alliance and with (b) both sides having outside alliances had collinearity problems when run initially. The interaction term with territory and the summary variable, any outside alliance, had a collinearity problem with the lower-order territorial MID variable.

[31] The significance of the interaction of territory with both sides having an outside alliance (txpr3) varies depending on the sample size and the model run. With the perfect predictors dropped ($N = 475$) and # of prior disputes not in the model, $p = .113$. When # of prior disputes is added to the model, the interaction becomes insignificant $p = .195$. However, with the perfect predictors excluded but kept in the data, the interaction term is significant ($p = .051$ without # of prior disputes, and $p = .067$ with # of prior disputes in the model). The latter is what is reported in model 5, in table 7.7.

Using the alternate method of including all the variables, the interaction term has a coefficient of 15.05, and the territorial MID a coefficient of 1.84. The effect of a territorial MID on the likelihood of war when both sides have outside alliances is: territory (1.84) + txpr3 (15.05) = 16.89. This tells us that the interaction of territorial MID in the presence of both sides having outside alliances increases the coefficient of the likelihood of escalation to war from 1.84 (in the absence of both sides having outside alliances) to 16.89 (in the presence of this alliance pattern). A chi-square test of the model (territory + txpr3 = 0), shows this to be a significant positive relationship ($p = .000$). Our thanks to Mark Souva for suggesting the use of this "alternate" method. We take sole responsibility for the specific analysis presented here, of course.

Table 7.7

Territorial Interactions and Escalation of the Current or Any MID within Five Years to War, 1990–2001

Variables	Model 1b	Model 2	Model 4	Model 5	Model 3
Territorial MID[a]	3.41 (1.32)**		2.54 (.78)**	2.10 (.80)**	1.78 (.82)*
Regime MID[a]	perfect predictor	perfect predictor			perfect predictor
Other MID[a]	.73 (1.27)	.72 (1.18)	.81 (1.25)	.74 (1.27)	1.05 (1.25)
No alliances	perfect predictor	perfect predictor			perfect predictor
One side has outside alliance[b]	.49 (1.15)			1.44 (1.13)	.71 (1.14)
Both sides have outside alliances[b]	.86 (1.13)		.45 (.70)		1.15 (1.12)
Allied to each other & outside alliance[b]	2.14 (1.11)++		1.69 (.67)*	3.07 (1.09)**	
Any outside alliance		−.43 (1.18)			
# of prior MIDs 1990	−.09 (.42)	−.61 (.32)++	−.54 (.31)+	−.50 (.31)[c]	−.53 (.31)+
Arms race					
Tx prior 90	−.71 (.62)				
Tx any alliance		2.35 (.73)**			
Tx one out			−1.14 (1.15)		
Tx both out				2.07 (1.13)[d]	
Tx all out					2.78 (1.14)*
Constant	−5.49 (1.55)**	−3.09 (1.17)**	−4.50 (.93)**	−5.58 (1.29)**	−4.60 (1.34)*
Chi-square (df)	37.0** (7)	27.0** (4)	39.2** (6)	41.2** (6)	39.0** (6)
Pseudo R²	.24	.18	.25	.26	.25
Number of cases	475	475	559	559	475

Note: Estimations were performed in Stata. Main entries are parameter estimates, with standard errors in parentheses. All tests are two-tailed.
[a]As compared to the reference category of policy MID.   [b]As compared to the reference category of allied and in the same alliances.   [c]$p = .109$ [d]$p = .067$
$+p \leq .10$ $++p \leq .06$ $*p \leq .05$ $**p \leq .01$

with at least one side having an outside alliance (model 3),[32] or (c) the summary variable of any outside alliance (model 2).[33] The only variable not evincing a significant interaction is "one side having an outside alliance" (model 4).[34] Thus, the expectation that territorial disputes would exhibit a greater proclivity to multiplicative processes of war is upheld. These findings are very similar to the findings for the classic international politics period of 1816–1945, in that both periods have several positive interaction terms between territory and the alliance patterns, albeit not always precisely the same terms (cf. tables 7.4 and 7.9). While the pattern is not as consistent as in the 1816–1945 period, it is much stronger than that of the Cold War period, which has only one positive interaction term for territorial disputes.

The findings on rivalry have only one significant positive interaction term—# prior MIDs and allied to each other with one side having an outside alliance (see model 10 in table 7.8).[35] This means that as disputes recur the likelihood of war is enhanced in the presence of this alliance pattern. One or both sides with an outside alliance show neither additive nor multiplicative associations.[36] Rivalry coupled with the summary variable of any outside al-

[32] The alternate method that includes all variables also shows a positive significant relationship with escalation to war. The effect of a territorial MID on the likelihood of war when the two states are allied and at least one side has an outside alliance is: territory (1.73) + txpr4 (17.64) = 19.37 (chi-square, p = .000).

[33] The positive interaction for territorial MID and the summary term that we report is based on excluding territorial MID because of collinearity. If that lower-order term is included, we get a coefficient of 15.5 for territorial MIDs and a significant negative interaction term (coefficient −12.90). The effect of a territorial MID on the likelihood of war in the presence of "any outside alliance" is territory (15.5) + txpr5 (−12.90) = 2.6. This tells us that the interaction of territorial MIDs in the presence of an outside alliance reduces the coefficient of the likelihood of escalation to war from 15.5 (in the absence of an outside alliance) to 2.6 (in the presence of an outside alliance). This is a much smaller coefficient, but the model is still positive and significant (p = .0005). Likewise, the bivariate cross tabulation of the interaction term shows a positive relationship with a significant .854 gamma and 15 war-related MIDs where 4.2 are expected versus 117 cases of peace when 126.8 are expected.

[34] The alternate method also produces a nonsignificant result: The effect of a territorial MID on war when one side has an outside alliance is (19.15) + (−19.03) = 0.12 (chi-square, p = .92).

[35] The allied with one side having an outside alliance was excluded because of collinearity problems. Using the alternate procedure showed that the effect of being allied to each other but with one side also having an outside alliance on the likelihood of war as disputes recur is: allied with outside alliance (20.71) + the interaction term (099xpr4 (−17.40) = 3.31). A chi-square test of (pr4 + 099xpr4 = 0) was significant (p = .0032). This is consistent with the results reported in the table excluding the lower-order term. The hierarchical test shows that the difference between the additive model and model 10 is significant at the .067 level.

[36] There are no collinearity problems using the one outside alliance interaction term. The model using both sides having outside alliances exhibited collinearity problems and the alliance lower-order term had to be excluded. When this was done the interaction term was found to be nonsignificant. Using the alternate method of including all variables and comparing coefficients also found the difference between both sides having outside alliances and the interaction term 099xpr3 to be nonsignificant using a chi-square test, although it was close (p = .068), since with the alternate method we have been using the .05 cutoff.

Table 7.8

Recurring MIDs and Escalation of the Current or Any MID within Five Years to War, 1990–2001

Variables	Model 10	Model 9
Territorial MID[a]	2.43 (.77) **	2.42 (.77) **
Regime MID[a]		perfect predictor
Other MID[a]	.97 (1.24)	.95 (1.24)
One side has outside alliance[b]	−.10 (.69)	
Both sides have outside alliances[b]	.26 (.65)	
Allied to each other & outside alliance[b]		
Any outside alliance		3.52 (1.97)+
# of prior MIDs 1990	−.85 (.37)*	.13 (.39)
Prior 90x all out	.73 (.38)++	
Prior 90x any out		−1.12 (.63) +
Constant Chi-square (df)	−3.82 (.88)** 31.0** (6)	−6.63 (1.99)** 31.5** (5)
Pseudo R^2	.20	.21
Number of cases	559	475

Note: Estimations were performed in Stata. Main entries are parameter estimates, with standard errors in parentheses. All tests are two-tailed.

[a]As compared to the reference category of policy MID.

[b]As compared to the reference category of allied and in the same alliances.

$+p \leq .10$ $++p \leq .06$ $*p \leq .05$ $**p \leq .01$

Table 7.9
Summary of Findings on Interaction Patterns, 1990–2001

	Terr	# Prior MID	One Outside	Both Outside	Allied & Outside	Any Outside	Arms Race
Terr	—	Additive Terr + Prior −	Nonsignificant	Multiplicative	Multiplicative	Multiplicative	NA
# Prior MID	—	—	Nonsignificant	Nonsignificant	Multiplicative	Multiplicative (negative)	NA
Arms Race	—	—	NA	NA	NA	NA	—

liance has a significant negative interaction term, meaning that in the presence of the summary variable and recurring disputes the likelihood of war is reduced (see model 9 in table 7.8).[37]

Table 7.9 provides a summary of the findings for the post–Cold War period. Multiplicative processes are most evident with the interaction of territory and certain outside alliance patterns. Only one interaction term reduces the likelihood of war—# prior MIDs and the summary outside alliance variable. By comparing this table with the summary tables of the previous two periods (tables 7.4 and 7.6), it can be seen that the post–Cold War period is more like the 1816–1945 period than the Cold War period. This is consistent with the findings and conclusion of chapter 6. It implies that the Cold War period may indeed have been unique and that the present era more closely fits the steps-to-war explanation. This conclusion is also consistent with the findings on dyads in chapter 5.

Conclusion

We are now in a better position to understand how the steps to war unfold over the course of history. Dividing the post-Napoleonic era into three distinct periods gives us a better idea of the underlying patterns that have shaped interstate war and how changes within the structure of the global political system can influence those patterns.

What is most clear is that the steps-to-war best fits the long and classic international politics period of 1816–1945. This period, which has seen the most

---

[37] There are no collinearity problems in this model. Since "allied but one side having an outside alliance" is positively related to war, this finding is probably a function of the two other alliance patterns. When the perfect predictors are excluded from the model and added to the reference category, the significance of the interaction term improves to .045. The hierarchical test shows that the difference between the additive model and model 9 is significant only at the .087 level.

devastating wars since the Napoleonic Wars, follows the steps-to-war process outlined in the first chapter. Territorial disputes arise and if handled by repeated militarized confrontations, the making of alliances, and arms races, they increase the likelihood that a crisis will emerge that escalates to war.

Along this road to war, some steps reflect multiplicative processes while others reflect additive processes. At the outset it was stated that territory (because it starts the ball rolling and is a powerful source of conflict) would be the factor most likely, theoretically, to exhibit multiplicative processes that greatly enhance the likelihood of war, and this has turned out to be the case. Contending over territorial disputes interacts with recurring disputes (rivalry) and most outside alliance patterns to enhance greatly the likelihood of war within five years. This means that when these respective combinations of two factors appear simultaneously, the likelihood of war is greater than simply adding the separate effects of each. The only exception to this for alliances is for territorial disputes and both sides having outside alliances, where we believe the effect is additive. The combination of territorial disputes and arms races is also additive, but arms races are not expected to exhibit multiplicative processes, since they usually occur so late on the road to war. Overall, the interaction findings on territory fit the theoretical expectations of the steps-to-war explanation fairly closely.

Rivalry is expected, theoretically, to be the factor to exhibit the next most frequent tendency toward multiplicative processes. It is the only other key factor to evince a positive multiplicative process, but it has only one in addition to the interaction with territory (reported above). This is fewer than were anticipated, but it occurs in the area where one would most likely expect it—rivalry with both sides having outside alliances. When this (interaction) condition is fulfilled, war is more likely than would be predicted by simply adding the effects of rivalry and both sides having outside alliances. The remaining rivalry and alliance patterns are also associated with escalation to war, but in an additive fashion.

The findings on arms races are not expected to have any multiplicative processes that increase the likelihood of war because by the time an arms race develops, as measured in the fairly precise way we employ (i.e., Horn, 1987), it is fairly late in a rivalry and most all of the other risk factors are present. The findings support this in that no positive significant interaction terms are identified and all but one of the alliance patterns show positive additive effects in the presence of an ongoing arms race. The one exception is completely unexpected from the steps-to-war theoretical perspective and will be discussed below.

The second major conclusion that can be made is that at least certain aspects of the steps to war can be manipulated to strip them of their war proneness and even, under certain conditions, turn them into factors promoting peace. We see this mostly in the Cold War, but we also see it in the one exception to the steps-to-war's expectations in the 1816–1945 period. In the latter, we find that arms racing (in the context of being allied to each other while at least one side has an outside alliance) significantly interacts to reduce the likelihood of war. Normally, these factors individually increase the probability of war in an additive fashion (see chapter 6) in the early period, but when they co-occur they form an interaction that instead of producing war greatly enhances the likelihood of peace. This sort of irenic process is rare within the 1816–1945 period and the fact that it occurs illustrates the complexity of world politics in that factors that typically give rise to war can under special circumstances be associated with the reverse.

The Cold War is more prone to these irenic factors and has been called "the long peace" (Gaddis, 1986) for this reason, although it exhibits numerous wars. Nevertheless, a war involving the strongest major states never occurred, the closest being the Korean War. The statistical analyses in the previous three chapters support this historical assessment in that the theoretical expectations of the steps-to-war explanation fit this period the least well of the three we have examined. What we find consistently is that certain alliance configurations generally act as a restraining device to reduce the likelihood of war. Similarly, arms races—which were highly war prone in the previous era—are now insignificant statistically. These two factors are not working they way they did in the past to bring about major state war. Why this is the case undoubtedly has something to do with nuclear weapons.

At the same time, however, there are wars during the Cold War, and important aspects of the steps-to-war explanation hold for this period. In particular, territorial disputes are still a major factor increasing the likelihood of war. One should also point out that the superpower rivalry that dominates this period does not involve a major direct territorial dispute between the United States and the Soviet Union. Conversely, many of the wars that do break out (and repeat) involve territorial rivalries among minor states (Arab-Israeli, India-Pakistan, China-India, China-Vietnam), including Cold War minor state rivals (Korea, Vietnam). Statistically, with two exceptions (see below), territorial MIDs are always positively associated with the onset of war. These generally reflect additive processes, but of the two positive multiplicative processes found for the Cold War, one of them involves territory. The interaction of territorial disputes with one side having an outside alliance greatly enhances the likelihood of war.

The other factor that increases the likelihood of war across all three periods, including the Cold War, is rivalry. With one exception (see below) it is also always positively associated with escalation to war. Of equal importance is that it has the only other positive multiplicative process found in the Cold War—rivalry and the presence of one side having an outside alliance. This is the same alliance pattern found with territory that enhances the likelihood of war. The findings on territory and rivalry, then, support the steps-to-war explanation.

Nevertheless, what is remarkable about the Cold War is that the major rivalry of its era—the nuclear rivalry of the United States and Soviet Union does not end up in a direct war, let alone a world war, as could be reasonably expected given the history of the twentieth century. Many reasons have been given for this outcome in the international relations literature. What this analysis adds are some statistical facts and profiles, which in retrospect are historically plausible, while at the same time providing some theoretical insights.

The most important statistical finding in this regard is that during the Cold War there is a significant negative interaction between the number of prior MIDs (rivalry) and the presence of both sides having outside alliances. This means that as disputes repeat and both sides have outside alliances, the probability of war is greatly reduced. This is contrary to the logic of the steps-to-war explanation, so the question is why this occurs. The answer to that question is beyond the scope of this chapter. Suffice it to say that in terms of the statistical profile, both sides having outside alliances are acting as a restraining device not only on the main contenders within the East-West bloc but, after Korea, on all the major states contending in the Cold War. This has, of course, been known for some time, but now it is confirmed statistically by some of the most rigorously collected data available and by comparing these statistical patterns with those both before and after the Cold War.

Furthermore, the precision of the analysis tells us some things that are not as obvious. The process by which the bipolar alliance structure worked to bring about a long peace was not just additive, but multiplicative. This is a key finding of this chapter. The centrality of that process can be seen by comparing it to what happens when only one side has an outside alliance. In this circumstance war is greatly enhanced (through multiplicative processes) for states that are rivals and/or are contending on a territorial MID. States in the same two conditions (territorial MID or rivalry), but where both sides have outside alliances, are likely to have the opposite experience—they are highly likely to avoid war, even though they are in a MID. Something about the alignment structure of the Cold War or the nature of the issue of the Cold War itself is changing the underlying pattern that has operated from 1816 through 1945. The most likely candidate for this is nuclear weapons; however, it may not be just the weapons, but the effects they have on creating restraining doctrines, like mutual assured destruction, or by spurring arms control and the creation of rules of the game to manage crises.

Another less obvious statistical pattern that has implications about why the Cold War was a long peace is that this period has the fewest positive multiplicative processes producing war. It has only two compared to five for the earlier period and four for the very short post–Cold War period of 1990–2001. In addition, it has as many negative multiplicative processes (those enhancing peace) as it does positive ones. Of course, what is probably equally important is that the negative multiplicative processes are working among the major states in the system.

The patterns on the Cold War suggest that it is different from the thrust of history, at least from the time of Napoleon. The statistical analyses presented here (in the theoretical context of the steps-to-war explanation) provide some hints as to why and how it was different. In doing so, they lay the foundation for future research on why the Cold War was a long peace. We hope the cases we have delineated in some of the footnotes will provide an aid to that research by providing more in-depth and historical answers for some of the statistical profiles we have uncovered here.

Lastly, if the Cold War period provides for some optimism, the analysis of the brief post–Cold War period serves as a warning. The latter period appears to be much more like the classic international politics 1816–1945 period than the Cold War. Territorial disputes, although they generally promote war, do so here through multiplicative processes as in the 1816–1945 period. With one exception alliances are not acting to restrain competition in any significant fashion, which was one of the main differences between the Cold War and the first half of the war-torn twentieth century. The comparison with the post–Cold War period suggests that the presence and absence of the number of multiplicative processes may in itself be an indicator of the prevalence (and even the severity) of interstate war. The analysis of this most recent period provides some evidence that the steps-to-war explanation is very much relevant to the current period and that the current period itself is not on a magic trajectory of peace that takes the irenic trends of the Cold War and builds on them in a progressive fashion that is the end of history. Instead, the limited evidence we have suggests that the fundamental factors that produced interstate war in the distant past are reasserting themselves.

From this analysis, one final thing is clear: International politics can be quite complex. Rather than glossing over such intricacy, sophisticated statistical analyses can uncover some of its complexity and begin, if not to make complete sense of it, to at least map it out. To a certain extent this is one of the main contributions of this chapter.

The final chapter will use the findings presented in the book to map out what we have learned about the probability of war and the possibility of peace.

IV

Conclusion

8

Explaining War, Thinking about Peace

Thinking can lead to knowledge and knowledge can lead to change, but only political will can bring about peace.

This book has been devoted to an analysis of the factors that increase the probability of interstate war. It provides a set of rigorous and systematic tests of an explanation of war that mostly predates the data used to test it. While it is very much an empirical study, like most peace science research, it is not conducted in a normative vacuum. Like Lewis Richardson and many in peace science, we study war in the hope that explaining and understanding the factors that bring it about will aid in reducing its incidence.

Empirical knowledge, however, does not automatically lead to a given set of normative preferences, even if these might be widely shared, which is not always the case with regard to questions of war. Nor does knowledge about why certain behaviors occur mean that such behaviors can be changed. We are not so naive as to think that our work and that of those who work in the same vein will produce, in and of itself, fundamental changes in collective violent behavior. Scientific knowledge (as uncertain and as tentative as it is) is but one step. All it can do is lay out a path(s) by which a desired result might be brought about. Whether that result is truly desired or whether it will become a goal are questions that cannot be answered by empirical study, but only by a normative analysis. Political change can only be brought about by politics. Science plays a role by uncovering underlying patterns and helping us to learn from history. The alternative, as has often been the case, is to base action on trial and error, on immediate self-interest, or worse still theories that purport to be true but are actually based on little scientific evidence. Ultimately, science is an aid, a tool—it is not a substitute for normative thinking nor does it provide political will.

Nonetheless, while we have been studying war, we have all along been thinking about peace—about how scientific knowledge might help make the world less prone to war. With Richardson (1960b), we have assumed that one way of eliminating war is to eliminate its causes, but to do that, we must first uncover them. We hope that explaining the steps to war will someday lead to an understanding of the steps to peace. The intellectual journey along this road is collective and our work and that of other scholars shows that it will be long journey. This book will not end with a set of deductive policy implications that will solve the problem of war once and for all. Unfortunately, no such panacea is available. Our collective knowledge is too limited, and such recommendations would be premature. It must be kept in mind that scientific knowledge, even when it is fairly advanced, as in physics, must still be applied. Physics is not engineering! And we are a long way from being a science like physics. What we will do instead, and what we believe is more responsible, is talk about what we think we have found that may tell us about how the probability of war might be reduced. These, however, are mere suggestions—food for thought.

We will begin by mapping our findings on war and conflict. In doing so, we will report the major underlying processes we have uncovered that lead to war in the modern global system and delineate the factors that most put states at risk for going to war. This understanding of what increases the probability of war will be used as a foundation to discuss in a tentative way how the probability of war might be mitigated. Before doing so, we will discuss what remains to be done in terms of empirical work on the steps to war and where this research program needs to go next to improve and deepen our knowledge about the probability of war.

There are three main areas for future inquiry—the factors that generate militarized confrontations in the first place (the steps to conflict), how the steps to war are interrelated (endogeneity questions), and the factors associated with peace between dyads and within certain systems (historical systems and neighborhoods). The question of peace and its foundation will be discussed, in terms of both the findings and the theory, at the end of the chapter. In this final section, we will give some attention to propositions in the steps-to-war explanation that we have not tested but are relevant to the question of peace.

Explaining War

We have presented many findings in this book, and some, like those in the previous chapter, can get quite complex. What do we empirically know now that we did not know before, and how well does that mesh with our theoretical understanding? By addressing these questions on the basis of our findings, we hope to provide a pure analytic narrative of some of the ways in which war comes about (see Suganami, 2002).[1]

The first thing we have learned is that militarized conflict has two sources—territorial disagreements and contiguity. States that have territorial claims against each other are more apt to have a militarized interstate dispute than those that do not. Also states that are neighbors (i.e., contiguous) are more apt to have a MID. These processes can give rise to any MID and not just territorial disputes. In this sense, examining these processes can be seen as a beginning in the mapping of the steps to conflict.

Our main focus in this book, however, has been to see how these temporally prior processes—those sources of conflict that give rise to an initial resort to the use of force—are related to the escalation of a militarized dispute to war. Since Bremer's classic (1992) study of dangerous dyads, there have been two major questions guiding research: What distinguishes dyads that go to war from those that do not, and what distinguishes the many MIDs that do not escalate to war from the few that do?

Although much still needs to be done, this book provides more definitive answers to these questions based on empirical tests than we as a field have had before. Much of this testing builds on prior work, but it advances knowledge by looking at how individual factors—like rivalry and arms races—combine with heretofore underappreciated factors—like territorial disputes—to form a series of steps to war.

Dyads and MIDs that go to war can be distinguished from those that do not by two factors—(1) the substance and nature of the underlying issue or grievance that gives rise to the use of force and (2) the way the issue is handled. Thus, we would expect, and we find, that one of the major things that distinguishes MIDs that escalate to war is the nature of the disputes—the issue under contention. Theoretically, the unique contribution of the territorial explanation to recent studies in peace science is to point out that human territoriality is a source of conflict that is apt to give rise to war, especially between neighbors.

Empirically, through a series of tests predating this book, we find that classifying MIDs according to whether they involve territory, regime, or policy discriminates which are more apt to go to war (Vasquez, 1993; Senese, 1996; Vasquez and Henehan, 2001; see also Hensel, 1996, 2000). In chapter 6, we reconfirm this finding and, in chapter 5, we show that dyads whose relations are

---

[1] Bates et al. (1998: 3) have popularized this phrase, but what they mean by it—using theory to describe historical cases—is slightly different from the way we use the term. Although analytical narratives have been written on the steps to war according to their usage (see Vasquez [1998b]; Vasquez and Gibler [2001]), what we mean here by the term is a more abstract or pure analytical narrative that presents a stylized or natural history of war without the use of any proper nouns.

dominated by territorial disputes or who simply have recurring territorial disputes (even if these are not dominating their relations) are more apt to go to war than those that are not contending over territory.

One of the main intellectual contributions of chapters 3 and 4 is to demonstrate that territorial disputes are, in fact, more likely to escalate to war than other disputes and that the relationship cannot be explained away by some selection bias in the data. The early studies on territory are subject to the criticism that one does not know whether territorial disputes are more war prone than nonterritorial disputes or whether it is some factor that gives rise to territorial MIDs in the first place that makes for war. In other words, some unknown or unobserved factor may lead states to use force over territory or some other issue, and it is this factor, which produces MIDs in the first place, that really makes MIDs escalate to war, and not whether the MID is over territory. Put more technically, the criticism says that the MID data constitute a biased sample because there are reasons why states have MIDs in the first place and those reasons *could* be the "real causes" of war. Logically, of course, this is a valid point; this *could* be the case in that it is logically possible, but whether it is, must be determined empirically.

Prior to the studies in chapter 3 and 4 the best that could be said was that once states have MIDs, those that are over territory are more apt to escalate to war, but this leaves open the possibility that if one controlled for the factor(s) that gave rise to the MID, the relationship between territorial MIDs and war could be wiped out. Chapters 3 and 4 theoretically identify the main factors that might be operating in this fashion to see whether this is the case by presenting a two-stage analysis where the first stage is MID (or conflict) onset and the second stage is MID escalation to war. These chapters also conduct a more general test of selection bias based on correlation-of-error terms.

Chapter 3 draws upon the territorial approach itself to identify the key variable that might be responsible for selection bias. It tests the proposition that it is the presence of a territorial claim in and of itself and not how it is handled (i.e., by the use of force) that is the "real" factor that increases the likelihood of war. Controlling for the effect of MID onset at the first stage will tell us whether the relationship between territorial MIDs and war is sustained or merely a function of the fact that states have territorial claims. What we find is that the original explanation and finding are sustained. It is not the mere presence of a territorial issue (claim) that makes for war, but how that territorial issue is handled. The presence of a territorial claim increases the likelihood of a MID of some sort, but whether war is likely depends on whether an MID is over territorial questions (as opposed to regime or policy questions).

Chapter 4 draws upon the competing contiguity explanation of why neighbors fight to identify the key variable that might be responsible for selection bias. The contiguity explanation of conflict and war (see Bremer, 1992; see also Vasquez, 1995) maintains that states that are closer to one another (and especially states that are contiguous) have more contact with each other than those farther away. More contact means more of an opportunity for conflict, and more conflict increases the likelihood of severe conflict that will escalate to war. Just as the probability of a car accident increases with the frequency of driving, so most war occurs between neighbors because they interact frequently.

Chapter 4 tests this proposition in a two-stage analysis. It finds that dyads that are contiguous are indeed more apt to have a MID than noncontiguous dyads. However, it also finds that controlling for the effect of contiguity at the MID onset stage does not eliminate the effect of territory at the escalation-to-war stage. This means that while contiguity increases the likelihood of a MID, what makes for war is not that process, but whether the MID is over territory. This finding is consistent with what we found in chapter 3, and the findings for both chapters mean that it is the presence of a territorial dispute that is the primary determinant of whether a MID is likely to escalate to war. On the basis of this finding, we can conclude that the territorial explanation of war and of why neighbors fight war is superior to the contiguity explanation of why neighbors fight. This conclusion is consistent with previous studies (Hensel, 2000; Vasquez, 2001), but the study in chapter 4 is the first that looks at the effect of the onset stage on the escalation-to-war stage, thereby providing a more rigorous test and addressing the question of selection effects.

Both chapters also provide for a general test of selection bias by determining whether the error terms are correlated. It is found that no overall selection bias is present, although sometimes it is necessary to include some standard control variables to get this result. An important lesson here is that logical possibility is not the same as empirical probability. The implication is that the MID data set may be used to test propositions about escalation to war without worrying too much about selection bias issues, especially if data do not exist to conduct a two-stage analysis. On the basis of these two studies, we conclude that in general territorial MIDs have a higher probability of going to war than either disputes over regime questions or general foreign policy questions.

Part III of the book examines whether the adoption of power-politics practices, especially in the handling of territorial disputes, constitutes a series of additional steps to war. While territorial disputes increase the probability of war—and in that sense the first step to war is handling territorial claims by resorting to the threat or use of force—most territorial MIDs do not escalate to war. What distinguishes the ones that do? Chapters 5 through 7 test the idea that following realist prescriptions—to increase power by making alliances or building up arms, and to show resolve by using realpolitik tactics—actually increases the probability of war by leading to a set of reciprocating counter-actions that reflect a security dilemma that draws each side into a conflict spiral.

Our analyses show that for most of the post-Napoleonic era (1816–1945 and to a limited extent 1990–2001) the steps to war conform to the way we outline them in chapter 1. For the Cold War period, there are some anomalies, especially with regard to the role of arms races and certain alliance patterns. Nevertheless, even in this period, territorial disputes and rivalry increase the probability of war the way the steps-to-war explanation anticipates.

The findings in chapters 5 and 6, although based on MID data, have very different units of analysis. The unit of analysis in chapter 5 has one observation for each dyad for its entire history in three given time spans—1816–1945, 1946–89, and 1990–2001. It compares dyads (that have had at least one MID from 1816 on) that never go to war to those that do. The unit of analysis in chapter 6 is the dyadic dispute. It compares individual dyadic disputes that escalate to war within five years with those that do not. The findings for both chapters are highly consistent, and the research designs nicely complement each other with the dyad-history data overcoming problems of atomization and lack of independent observations, and the dyadic-dispute data overcoming problems of timing.

For the 1816–1945 period, we find that the probability of war increases as states contending over territorial disputes get outside allies (especially when both sides succeed in getting outside allies), engage in repeated MIDs (thereby fostering a sense of rivalry), and have arms races. As each of these risk factors becomes present, the probability of going to war progressively increases. A dyad has the highest probability of war when it has a territorial dispute and simultaneously has outside allies, has an enduring rivalry, and has an arms race. Although this pattern is most prominent in the presence of territorial disputes, any dispute (e.g., policy disputes) will have an increased proclivity to going to war if handled in the above manner, although the probability of war is lower than that for territorial disputes.

During the Cold War, 1946–89, this pattern is broken. Outside alliances, and to a certain extent arms races, no longer increase the likelihood of war.[2] Indeed, when both sides have outside alliances, the probability of war decreases. Nevertheless, certain steps still operate as expected. Territorial MIDs still increase the likelihood of war and so does rivalry, although with the lat-

---

[2] For the dyadic dispute sample, arms races during the Cold War are not significantly related to escalation to war (see also Sample [2000]). For the dyad-history sample, however, we do find some evidence (not based on the superpowers, of course) between war onset and dyads that have had an arms race during the Cold War.

ter, we find a definite curvilinear effect operating. Specifically, we find an inverted U-shaped relationship between the # of prior disputes and the probability of war.

These deviations are consistent with what we know historically about the Cold War period and the absence of a direct war between the Soviet Union and the United States, which have led some to refer to the Cold War as a "long peace" (Gaddis, 1986). A common explanation for this phenomenon emphasizes the role of nuclear weapons. We do not necessarily dispute this, but our findings show that alliance configurations play a role, since certain alliance patterns (namely both sides having outside allies), which for most of previous history increase the likelihood of war, in the Cold War reduce the likelihood of war.

One of our major conclusions, therefore, is that the Cold War era is fundamentally different from the earlier 1816–1945 period. This has important implications for the study of international conflict. Failing to control for historical era can mask, even distort, important patterns. Generalizing to all of international history on the basis of studies confined to the post–World War II period, as many do who study the democratic peace and civil war, is equally fraught with risks. On the basis of our analysis, we recommend controlling for the two eras in all analyses of interstate conflict and war/peace. Such controls, we expect, will sometimes reveal different patterns, if not opposite findings.

Of final interest are the findings for the short post–Cold War period 1990–2001. While our findings in this period must be preliminary because of the limited arms-race data and the generally small number of years, what evidence we have is that war in this period seems similar to the patterns revealed in the 1816–1945 period and not those in the Cold War. In particular, we find some evidence to indicate that outside alliances are no longer reducing the likelihood of war as they did in the Cold War. Meanwhile, territorial MIDs are as war prone as they were in both the early period and the Cold War. If these findings should be sustained in future research, that would underline the unusual nature of the Cold War. It would also indicate that the steps-to-war explanation is as relevant today as it is to the classic international-politics period of the past. Put another way, it means that whatever variables (most likely specific alignment configurations) made for the long peace are no longer operating.

While our tests of the steps-to-war explanation are very systematic, the one thing the previously discussed chapters do not test for is interactions. A number of interactions are implied by the verbal theory, and we specify and test some of the more important in chapter 7. We examine whether the steps to war are better seen as following multiplicative processes (as indicated by interaction terms) or additive processes, like the models tested in chapter 6. As with chapters 5 and 6, the findings on statistical interaction also differ by period, although not as starkly, especially for the alliance variables. We actually find that certain alliance interactions during the Cold War are less discrepant with the steps-to-war explanation than the findings in chapter 6 on additive models. As before, we discuss the steps to war by historical period. Across all the periods we find that multiplicative processes are not the typical means by which escalation to war occurs, but that interaction does occur.

For the 1816–1945 period, we find two sorts of interactions, one between territorial MIDs and rivalry and one between territorial MIDs and outside alliances. The first finding indicates that territorial disputes have an enhanced likelihood of escalating to war as disputes repeat (i.e., when states are in a rivalry). In other words, as the number of prior disputes increases in the presence of territorial disputes, there is a higher likelihood of war than simply adding the individual effects of each.

The same is true for the interaction of territorial disputes and having outside alliances for three variables: the summary variable (having any outside alliance), one side having an outside alliance, and being allied to each other but also having an outside alliance. This second finding indicates that as dyads have outside allies they usually (but not always) have a higher likelihood of war in the presence of territorial disputes.

The interaction term—having a territorial MID in the presence of both sides having an outside alliance—produced mixed results that led to further testing after which it was concluded that there is no significant statistical interaction, but simply an additive effect with both sides having an outside alliance increasing the likelihood of war regardless of the presence of territorial MIDs. There are no significant interaction effects between territorial MIDs and arms races. This relationship is best seen as additive and positive for each of the lower-order terms.

Rivalry has two significant positive interactions. One (mentioned above) is the interactions of rivalry and territorial MIDs, and the second is the interaction of rivalry with outside alliances. The latter, however, interacts with only one alliance pattern—when both sides have outside alliances, the one pattern that did not interact with territorial MIDs. The latter means that when states have a history of MIDs, and both sides have outside alliances, there is an enhanced likelihood of war over and above that which exists when each is individually present. Other forms of outside alliances do not exhibit this tendency. A positive additive model best captures the relationship of these other alliance patterns.

There are no positive statistical interactions between arms racing and the other steps to war; rather, with one exception, the relationship is positive and additive. The exception is the combination of arms races in the presence of one alliance pattern. Unexpectedly, being allied but having an outside alliance actually reduces the likelihood of war in a multiplicative fashion. This is one of the few significant negative interactions we uncover.

In sum, for the classic international politics era (1816–1945) we find that multiplicative processes are mostly confined to territorial MIDs and rivalry interacting with each other and with several of the outside alliance variables. Rivalry also interacts with one of the alliance patterns. The only negative (and unexpected) interaction is between arms racing and being allied and having an outside alliance. All the other steps are best seen as following additive processes that increase the likelihood of war.

There are considerably fewer positive interactions between the steps to war in the Cold War, and this may be related to why the Cold War was a long peace. Nevertheless, there are some—both territorial MIDs and rivalry are positively related to one side having an outside alliance. This means that in the presence of this alliance pattern both territorial MIDs and rivalry (# of prior MIDs) enhance the likelihood of war. This finding is more consistent with the steps-to-war explanation than the lower-order findings on alliance patterns, which show no relationship between one outside alliance and the likelihood of war in the Cold War period (and a negative relationship with the two other major outside alliance patterns).

Two significant negative interactions occur when territorial MIDs and rivalry are in the presence of both sides having outside alliances. Instead of enhancing the likelihood of war (as one side having an outside alliance does) this alliance pattern greatly reduces the likelihood of war. We also find that the interaction of both sides having outside alliances and arms races is a perfect predictor of peace. The findings on both sides having outside alliances are consistent with what we know historically about the Cold War, namely, that countries allied in the East-West bloc did not fight each other. The findings on interaction give us a better idea of the specific factors that made the Cold War a long peace and avoided war.

Alliance patterns seem to be a key for explaining why certain MIDs do not escalate to war during the Cold War. If both sides have outside allies or they are allied to each other and one or more has an additional outside alliance, then the likelihood of war is reduced. The finding on the former appears especially robust. If, however, only one side has an outside alliance, then this enhances the likelihood of war in the presence of either territorial MIDs or rivalry, a finding consistent with the steps-to-war explanation. Put another way, the interaction effects identify when the steps-to-war explanation fits and when it has the opposite results.

On the whole, two things are noteworthy about the Cold War. First, there are two negative interactions and three that are perfect predictors of peace, all of these involve certain alliance patterns that reduce the likelihood of war. Second, although there are two positive interactions involving one side having an outside alliance, these are fewer than those found in the 1816–1945 period (which has five). Therefore, we can conclude that the long peace is characterized by fewer multiplicative processes that enhance the likelihood of war and, more importantly, negative interactions that lower the likelihood of war. As far as we know, this is the first study of the long peace that has uncovered this pattern.[3]

Our main interest with the post–Cold War period, 1990–2001, is to see whether some of the irenic factors that reduce the likelihood of war in the Cold War persist or whether this period is more like the classic international politics era of 1816–1945. Our evidence here is limited because we do not have arms race data for the entire period and because we are dealing with little over a decade. What we do find is that the post–Cold War period is more like the 1816–1945 period in terms of the sheer number of positive interactions (four versus five for 1816–1945 versus two for the Cold War). More important, our findings show that the main negative interaction pattern that we thought was operating to make the Cold War a long peace—both sides having an outside alliance—is no longer operating to reduce the likelihood of war. In fact, when both sides have outside alliances and they are contending over territorial disputes, this enhances the likelihood of war. We make the tentative conclusion that the multiplicative processes operating in the post–Cold War period tend to be more consistent with the steps-to-war explanation than those in the Cold War. Generalizing on the basis of ten years is risky, so whether the conclusion will hold, only time will tell. The evidence we do have, however, suggests that the Cold War peace is more of a deviation from the sweep of history than a new trend.

The processes we outline above give an overview of what brings about war. These can be seen as a set of risk factors that place states in danger of having a crisis or MID that will, within five years, escalate to war. The steps-to-war explanation most consistently fits the 1816–1945 period. For the Cold War, two key components of the explanation—territory and rivalry—still account for the process by which wars occur. Alliances and arms races, however, do not always produce the wars that are expected, with the exception of certain interactions with one side having an outside alliance, which increases the likelihood of war. These findings make the steps-to-war explanation less of a fit for the Cold War period. The factors that make the Cold War an anomaly also

---

[3] Further discussion of these findings and their implications for the "long peace" is provided in Vasquez and Senese (2007). Of the negative interactions, the most important are those when both sides have an outside alliance.

seem to account for why it is a long peace. The Cold War, however, was not the start of a new trend. The post–Cold War 1990–2001 period is more like the 1816–1945 period and appears to conform to the steps-to-war explanation, especially with regard to the war proneness of alliances.

The latter suggests that the steps-to-war explanation is not simply of historical interest, but is relevant to the present, as well as to the sweep of modern history. Keeping in mind that the 1816–1945 period covers 130 years and the Cold War only 44, the fit of the explanation is not bad at all. Where it is probably most limited is in the relations of nuclear states, and this limitation is true for a number of theories, for example classical realism. Nuclear weapons have made states more risk averse. What would have provoked a war in the past, in the Cold War no longer does so. The risks posed by the steps to war do not seem to be as risky for nuclear states and their formal allies as they were in the past. But the reason for this may well lie with the conscious management of relations between nuclear adversaries *and* superpower management of their allies.

The data analysis in this book has provided important evidence about the fundamental underlying factors that increase the probability of war. We know things that we did not know before. The territorial explanation of war enunciated fifteen years ago in the absence of any scientific data on territorial disputes (Vasquez, 1993) now has a substantial body of evidence consistent with it for the entire 1816–2001 period. The broader steps-to-war explanation that delineates a realist road to war also has passed a number of tests and fits the classic international politics period of 1816–1945 and parts of the Cold War period. Deviations from the expectations of the steps-to-war explanation in the Cold War suggest which factors may have made the Cold War a long peace. A probing of the post–Cold War period (1990–2001) suggests that the relevance of the steps-to-war will be greater for the future than it was during the Cold War. Nevertheless, many questions remain, and we turn to these now, delineating the most important for future research and for thinking about peace.

Future Research

In science, theories are tested piecemeal. Falsification of parts of a theory can lead to reformulation and further theory construction. Of the tests we have conducted, only one—that dealing with the Cold War—would lead us to want to qualify our theory. Certainly this is one of the pressing questions of future research, and we have already suggested some of the ways in which we might address this question. What we most want to do in this section, however, is to specify the parts of the existing steps-to-war explanation that we have not yet tested, and should be the subject of future research, and to outline some of the new research suggested by this study. In particular, we want to focus on where the testing process has opened up new areas that require us to build theory. The new research areas deal with examining the processes by which MIDs occur in the first place and how the steps are interrelated. The parts of the existing explanation that have not yet been tested deal with a number of propositions on peace and the factors associated with it.

Steps to Conflict

Our work on testing for selection bias led us early on to go beyond just dealing with the methodological question of whether the MID data were a nonrandom sample to the more theoretically interesting question of what makes states resort to the threat or use of force in the first place. This moves analyses from a focus on what causes war to what makes states resort to militarized force. The latter covers a great deal of ground, especially when expressed in this manner. Operationally, however, existing data make the question more manageable by using onset of a MID as the main dependent variable. Some work, particularly that associated with testing for selection effects, has produced fruitful research using MID onset as a dependent variable in a two-stage analysis. Reed (2000), in particular, finds that there is no statistically significant relationship between joint democratic states and war onset, once one controls for MID onset. In other words, the reason democratic states tend to not fight each other is that they tend to not become involved in many MIDs. Reed's (2000) study, however, focuses primarily on selection bias and it is read in this context, rather than as an attempt to explain why states get involved in MIDs.

The sources of conflict will need much more theorizing if we are to get at a unified explanation of the relationship between conflict onset and escalation to war. Reed's study and our own in chapters 3 and 4 seek to form a unified explanation by trying to develop an explanation of conflict and war that looks at MID onset and MID escalation to war as a two-stage process. Treating the steps to conflict in this fashion will prevent the new dependent variable from diverting attention from the main focus of inquiry—the causes of war. Still, conflict (MID) onset is a legitimate inquiry in its own right and there has been some research focusing solely on it. This dependent variable, however, is often conflated with MID involvement, slightly different, but equally relevant.

The earliest study on conflict onset was by Wallensteen (1981) who reviews four conflict literatures (geopolitik, idealpolitik, kapitalpolitik, and realpolitik) to develop and test hypotheses that specify the sufficient and necessary conditions for militarized confrontations. Maoz (1989) develops hypotheses that predict that new states entering the system are apt to generate conflict (involvement in MIDs), especially if they enter the system through a violent process. Bennett and Stam (2004) provide the most systematic analysis of MID onset to date.

Several studies examine the onset of territorial disputes. Vasquez (1993) asks early on: What are the sources of conflict most likely to give rise to war? He focuses on human territoriality and hypothesizes that aggressive displays are used by humans, just as they are by other mammals, to demark borders. He maintains that looking at human territoriality can provide important insights into why collectivities fight over certain things and not others. Huth (1996b) was the first in international relations to collect scientific data on territorial issues between states. His study examined what types of territorial claims are more apt to escalate (into what we would call MIDs) (see also Huth and Allee [2002] who extend the data back to 1919). Hensel (2001) has the most ambitious data collection effort, the Issue Correlates of War project (ICOW), which will collect data going back to 1816 on various issue claims (disagreements) between states before they give rise to MIDs.[4] He is currently collecting data on all interstate territorial claims, maritime claims, and river claims. When completed the project will permit an examination of whether certain types of issues are more prone to MIDs and to war than other types. Preliminary research by Hensel (2006) using these data seems quite promising, particularly his research on what makes MIDs abate between states with a history of disputes.

All of these studies and data projects provide specific hypotheses as to what might bring about militarized confrontations in the first place. They tend to emphasize individual sets of sufficient conditions. What they lack is an overarching theory that explains conflict onset in its entirety and explains how the various sufficient conditions relate to each other.

Our approach to the question is to look at MID onset the way we look at war onset; that is, What are the sequences or stages that lead from the origin of the initial disagreement to resorting to a MID? Thus, we label our approach "steps to conflict." Specification of these steps makes it possible to construct a unified explanation of conflict and war by showing how one step leads to another. Theory and research in this area will lead to a more complete explanation of war by providing an analysis of what produces the kinds of militarized confrontations that lead to war. It is an area where several different strands of

---

[4] For analyses on the role territorial disputes play in internal conflict, see Toth (2003), Walter (2003), and Tir (2006).

research are beginning to converge and where more data are becoming available. Before his untimely death, Senese had hoped to focus part of his subsequent research in this area. It is an area where we anticipate quite a bit of new research in the next ten years and where the steps-to-war research program can provide a theoretical guide.

Endogeneity

Questions about the origins of MIDs lead naturally to questions about the origins of each of the purported steps to war. As with the selection-bias criticism, these questions have been raised in the literature primarily in a nontheoretical fashion from the perspective of research-design criticism rather than from a substantive concern about the origins and consequences of certain behaviors. The criticism is typically posed as one of endogeneity (which is simply a broader form of selection-bias concerns) (see for example, King et al., 1994: 197–98). Rather than just trying to address such questions methodologically by tinkering with research designs (for example, by lagging variables), more progress will be made by specifying how these factors are expected to affect each other from the logic of the steps-to-war theoretical perspective. This will involve additional theory construction within the steps-to-war research program. Dealing with the question of the origins will require even more since each step will require an explanation. We begin by discussing the question of endogeneity and how it can give rise to a fruitful research program.[5] We next briefly discuss how each step might be the focus of its own research without losing sight of the main goal—seeing how the steps fit together to bring about war.

Research on endogeneity in the steps to war can be of two sorts, and both should be encouraged. The first is to specify alternate hypotheses to the steps-to-war explanation in terms of the sequencing of the steps. Of particular interest would be those hypotheses that undercut the logic of the steps-to-war explanation. Generally, criticism stemming from endogeneity concerns has not been very theoretically informed, but rather based on logical possibilities, such as "could not war give rise to territorial disputes, rather than territorial disputes give rise to war?" Such piecemeal questions are best handled historically to see if they are even worth systematic data collection.

Our sense is that in the post-Napoleonic era there are few wars that give rise to territorial disputes that did not have prior claims. For example, after

---

[5] Since we have already addressed aspects of this question in chapter 1 (namely those parts of the steps-to-war explanation subject to criticism based on assumptions of endogeneity), we will not repeat that discussion in this section.

the Franco-Prussian War, Alsace and Lorraine were taken by Germany and this then became a territorial dispute between the two of them, but conflicting claims to that area go way back, and even if they did not, taking by conquest something that has clearly been part of another's territory even when neither side disputed the land in question before the war hardly undercuts the logic of the steps-to-war explanation that territorial disputes lead states to take actions that then increase the probability of war. This is not the sort of endogeneity on which one need spend a great deal of effort, especially since we think that the more typical scenario is that states raise claims first and then fight. Hitler's claims to lebensraum with regard to Poland and later the Ukraine are a clear example of the typical sequence, as are Japanese imperial desires in China.

Similar are all the other steps that might follow a war, such as alliance making, rivalry, and arms races. Whether a war actually brings these about or reinforces existing ties is not easily determined statistically, but best examined historically. Does World War II produce NATO and the Warsaw Pact, or is this a new game? Since the steps to war involve a dynamic, one must look at each state's relations with the other to determine when a new game is starting. We think NATO is a new game.

The more serious questions that grow out of endogeneity concerns relate to the sequencing of the steps to war. A research program that would make headway on these sorts of questions would be to compare an alternate sequencing hypothesis with the standard sequence of the steps to war (territorial disputes, repetition of disputes [eventually producing a rivalry], alliance making, and arms racing). For example, one alternate hypothesis is that rivalry leads to war, alliance making, and arms racing, but that the really causal factor is rivalry, and that states make alliances and engage in arms races because they anticipate war. In other words, these last two variables have no real causal effect on the likelihood of war.[6] A random sample of cases could be selected (or a theoretical sample based on where endogeneity is most suspected) to see what sequence is present and what is endogeneous and what is not. Even if deviations from the typical pattern are found, these might be accommodated in the theory if these anomalies conformed to the logic of the steps to war.

---

[6] A variation on this hypothesis is that rivalry produces alliance making and arms races, but the latter have no impact on war (not even through an anticipation of war). In contrast, the steps-to-war explanation maintains that while rivalry increases the probability of alliance making and arms racing, these two variables increase the probability of war separate from the impact of rivalry. While they are a reaction to threat perception, they also produce a step-level increase in threat perception.

Such deviations might inform our understanding of the dynamics of the steps and how they are interrelated, which is the second type of research we want to encourage. How the steps to war are interrelated among various actors, from our perspective, is frankly a much more interesting question than treating endogeneity as a methodological problem that needs to be solved. For instance, Kennedy (1980: 251) suggests that the German initiation of a naval race at the end of the nineteenth century actually helped bring about an Anglo-German antagonism that we think of as a rivalry. Whether that claim would be sustained by a statistical analysis is an open question,[7] but even if it did not, what it would mean is that arms racing increased the perceived extent of rivalry and had a strong domestic impact. Such a case is important from a steps-to-war perspective because a sense of rivalry is typically expected from a repetition of disputes, with arms racing coming fairly late in the rivalry. A series of theoretically focused cases studies such as these would increase our understanding of how the steps are interrelated and how their sequencing might vary.[8]

Once various sequences are identified empirically, it would be of great interest to determine whether certain sequences have a higher probability of going to war than others. Our current data do not permit us to examine the question of timing; we have simply looked at the number of steps present, not their sequence.[9] Once we have data for each dyad regarding which type of sequence is present, we could see whether what is proposed as the typical sequence of the steps to war is actually the modal sequence and the most war prone.

Other closely related research questions are those that deal with the origins of each of the sets of behaviors we have labeled as steps to war. Why do states fight over territory, and what increases the likelihood of neighbors and others having territorial disputes? As a field, international relations has only begun to ask these questions, and as we have stated before, the best way of investigating these question is to turn to the life sciences for answers about territoriality to see how applicable they might be to interstate relations.

A second set of questions asks why states seek alliances and why and how they become involved in arms races. The steps-to-war explanation focuses on the security dilemma as one of the main factors leading states to seek alliances, build up their military, and take actions that increase the likelihood of war. Nevertheless, some nonrealist theorizing as to why states seek alliances would

---

[7] Our very cursory examination of the MID data show six MIDs by 1899 with five occurring by 1888.

[8] Case studies might also suggest possible measures that could be used in statistical studies across the entire population or at least a considerably larger sample.

[9] For a preliminary probe of various sequences see Vasquez (2004: 20–22).

fill an important gap. A good place to start is Palmer and Morgan (2006), although, as our analysis of steps makes clear, we think that the realist road to war makes substitutability a temporary solution at best. Some fine case studies on alliances exist on which to base some theorizing (see Walt, 1987; Snyder, 1997), and an incorporation of constructivist perspectives is highly compatible with the kind of theory we outline in chapter 1 (see Barnett, 1998, 2003; see also Levy and Barnett, 1992).

There is less work on why and how states become involved in arms racing, but beginning with Richardson (1960a), much of the mathematical modeling provides important insights on which to build (see Zinnes, 1976: chs. 14– 15; Isard, 1989). It would be nice to have more case studies of arms races, like those on alliances, on which to build, but there are only a few, and those are being conducted by historians (see the exemplary study by Stevenson, 1996).[10]

Lastly, of all the steps to war we examine, rivalry has received the most research attention in terms of its origins and unfolding. The pathbreaking work of Goertz and Diehl, Wayman, Hensel, Thompson, and Bennett has been supplemented by the work of younger scholars, like Colaresi, Valeriano, and Di-Cicco. Still, there are important theoretical questions that need to be investigated further. For example, is rivalry the correct concept or should we be focusing on the repetition of disputes (or crises) as Leng (1983, 1993) does? Are there different kinds of rivalry, as Rasler and Thompson argue (2000), and if so, do their origins differ? The entire question of rivalry linkages, which Diehl and Goertz (2000: ch. 12) raise, is still wide open, as is the question of multiple rivalries and war expansion (Thompson, 2003; Valeriano, 2003).

Questions of endogeneity, then, are not so much a criticism of existing findings as an opportunity to both deepen our empirical knowledge and make our theory more precise. These things will only happen, however, if endogeneity is seen as a door that existing findings opens and not a door that closes down research because obstacles exist to empirically addressing logical possibilities whose existence is uncertain.

Steps to Peace

The main area that we have not investigated in this study, and where there are a number of specified propositions, has to do with the conditions of peace. The reason for this is simply time. Data exists for testing some of the key propositions, although more data, especially on norms, would make for better tests. For now, we will simply highlight some key untested propositions.

[10] While not case studies, see the useful collection of theoretical essays in Gleditsch and Njolstad (1990).

The War Puzzle (Vasquez, 1993) lists ten propositions on the factors related to peace. Most of these maintain that the prevalence of peace varies in historical periods depending mainly on the global institutional context. In certain periods the global institutional context provides an alternative to the practices of power politics for dealing with conflict, and in these periods, peace is more likely. Similarly, certain periods and dyads are less likely to have territorial disagreements, and in these, there is also likely to be less war. One of the first areas for further research would be to delineate the correlates of peaceful eras. Some of this has already been done in the project, but only in a preliminary fashion (see Vasquez, 2001; Henehan and Vasquez, 2006). They focus on the absence of territorial disputes during these periods and the absence of certain steps to war (such as arms racing). Nevertheless, a precise identification of peaceful eras using a variety of measures has yet to be done by anyone, an indication that most peace research has been on war and not peace.

If the identification of peaceful eras is one key task, the other is the identification of peaceful dyads. Maoz (2004) has already made important strides in this area by identifying dyads that have never had a war. The next step, as with research on peaceful eras, is to see what factors appear to be correlated with these peaceful dyads. Again the absence of territorial disputes and a resort to the practices of power politics is a starting point, but as we will discuss in the next section, there are other structural factors that are promoting peace in a positive fashion and that need to be explored, such as the number and effectiveness of inter-governmental organizations (IGOs).[11]

The research program that has done the most on identifying factors related to peaceful relations between dyads is that on the democratic peace. There has been a plethora of studies in this area, and they have progressed in a nice fashion adding to our knowledge regarding the extent to which democratic dyads do not fight each other and why they are at peace (see Ray, 2003b; Chernoff, 2004). An interesting connection with the steps-to-war research program is whether one of the reasons democratic states do not fight each other is because they do not have territorial disputes and tend to not use power politics to resolve the disputes they do have. On the former, Mitchell and Prins (1999) find that joint democracies tend to not have territorial disputes but mostly maritime disputes. Gibler (2007) argues that controlling for the presence of territorial disputes can wipe out the effects of the joint democracy on peace (see also the earlier James, Park, and Choi [2006]). In other words, it may be the absence of territorial disputes and not joint democracy that is the most important factor in the democratic peace. This implies that nondemo-

---

[11] See Leskiw (2002) for an analysis of different types of IGOs and their impact on peace.

cratic states that do not have territorial disputes are more likely to be at peace than those that do. In addition, Gibler (2007) and Hutchison and Gibler (2007) go on to explore whether the presence of territorial MIDs also has an internal impact on the centralization of the state, that is, making states less democratic. They find evidence consistent with this claim. Gibler (2007) also shows that the absence of territorial MIDs is related to the rise of democratic dyads.

Of course it is only once we have a better idea of not only the factors that increase the probability of war, but also the conditions under which peace flourishes that we can begin to think about what steps can be taken to bring about peace. This, however, is not a question on which there is no historical evidence. Since many periods and dyads have moved from war to peace (and sometimes back), one area of policy relevant research is to see what steps states took to get from war to peace. Again this is an area in which little quantitative work has been done.

Research on peace gets us closer to our ultimate aim, which is to make the world a more peaceful place. In the last section, we address some of the policy implications of our work and those of other peace scientists and how that work can help us think about future steps to peace.

Thinking about Peace

In this section we discuss two major implications for peace for the analysis on the steps to war. The first deals with implications in the short run, for providing knowledge that might improve decisions about war. Here we seek to provide a clear and usable policy instrument that would provide early-warning indicators to decision makers and their publics that a given crisis might pose a high risk of war. Such indicators would also be useful both to policy influencers within the contending parties and to outside third parties—such as potential mediators, IGOs and NGOs, and regional powers and major states. We believe theory and research on the steps to war can be used to construct a Risk Barometer for War that could predict the probability of war in a specific crisis.

Such an instrument would be an aid to peace mostly by alerting decision makers and followers that they are on a likely path to war. As an instrument for peace, such a barometer would have practical applications as a warning tool, not unlike hurricane warnings. It would alert leaders that conditions are present that pose a danger. It would point out that disputants have structured their relationship in such a way that violence is likely. The main policy advice would be to try to change that structure, but because the history of interactions has built this structure, disputants may be locked into it and either unable or unwilling to change it. This may not always be the case, however, especially in the incipient stages of a rivalry. Nonetheless, even when states are further down the realist road to war, timely warning will provide more options than warnings for some natural disasters.

A more long-term and ultimately more useful strategy for peace is to look at the implications of the findings for identifying the main structure of war in the system and seeing whether there is some alternate structure that would promote peaceful relations even in the context of sharp political disagreement. Our second set of implications draws upon our theory, as well as our research, to develop some policy suggestions along these lines. In particular, we compare some of the patterns we have articulated in this book with peace research findings on zones of peace and historical systems of peace that are consistent with the steps-to-war explanation.

Constructing a Risk Barometer for War

Stuart Bremer in his (1980) study of national capabilities and war proneness ended his analysis with a list of the ten most powerful states in the world, and he predicted (based on his findings that the stronger the state, the more apt it is to be involved in war) that one of these "top ten" states could be expected to be involved in a war in the next decade. Depending on whether one wants to take 1979 or 1980 as the start date, up to four states on the list end up being involved in a war in the next ten years.[12] This is quite a successful prediction. How successful it is can be seen by comparing the ability of quantitative international politics to predict wars with the ability of natural scientists to predict earthquakes. Scientists are pretty good at identifying the conditions that are likely to produce earthquakes and very good at identifying where earthquakes are apt to occur. They are not so good at predicting when they are likely to occur. Instead, they give very broad predictions, like sometime in the next fifty years. As a field, peace science can do better than that. We can predict, in certain circumstances, where wars are apt to occur, when they will occur (say within ten years), and with whom (see also Bremer 2000). The barometer we propose predicts the probability of war within five years.

While we will not present a fully developed barometer, which would entail a separate project of its own, we will show how one could be constructed on the basis of the research we have conducted on the steps to war, and we will

[12] The top ten and their wars are: (1) United States 1990 Persian Gulf, (2) Soviet Union 1979 Invasion of Afghanistan, (3) China 1979 Sino-Vietnamese War, (4) India none during this time, (5) United Kingdom, 1982 Falklands, 1990 Persian Gulf, (6) W. Germany none (7) France 1990 Persian Gulf, (8) Japan none, (9) Italy 1990 Persian Gulf, (10) Indonesia none.

offer some illustrations. We are able to do this, in principle, because our study has identified the factors that put states at risk for having a war within the next five years. In addition to identifying these risk factors, we have, through the calculation of predicted probabilities from our logit analyses, measured the level (i.e., the probability) of that risk. This knowledge enables us to construct barometers that could be used to measure the risk of war.

The two barometers we are in a best position to propose are those that would be based on the occurrence of a MID between two states. Once a MID occurs, it would then be classified in terms of how many and the kinds of steps to war that are embodied in the dispute. For example, is the MID over territory, are outside allies involved, what number dispute is this between the same parties (is it one in a series, are they engaged in a rivalry), is there an ongoing arms race? From this and related information we could construct two barometers—a simple barometer that would indicate the level of risk (in general) and a precise barometer that would give an actual probability range.

A simple barometer would not be unlike many of the diagnostic tools used in medicine that are derived from epidemiological research to assess the risk of patients for getting a heart attack, colon cancer, breast cancer, and so on. The practical use of the barometer would be similar—the information would be used to try to identify cases (disputes and disputants) at risk for war and then to try to reduce this risk either by eliminating existing risk factors or preventing new ones. The assumption, in many instances, is that the more risk factors present, the greater the likelihood of an event happening. For instance, the risk of a heart attack goes up as each of the following risk factors is present: high cholesterol, male over fifty-five, overweight, diabetic, family history of heart disease. Our research shows that a similar situation occurs with the characteristics of MIDs; as each of the risk factors occurs and combines with others there is a progressive increase in the probability of war. In addition, we have tentatively identified certain interaction effects that enhance these probabilities.

The simple barometer would just count these risk factors with perhaps eventually adding a weighted effect for interaction terms. Table 8.1 illustrates a simple unweighted Risk Barometer for War. As the number of risk factors goes from one to four the risk of war increases. Our research shows that when MIDs have four risk factors present the probability of war can reach as high as .90. Fortunately, only a few MIDs ever have four risk factors. Unfortunately, when they do, not only is the probability of war high, but the war is apt to be quite severe.

The simple barometer depicted in table 8.1 can be derived from the four basic steps to war: (1) the presence of territorial disputes, (2) the presence of outside allies, (3) the repetition of MIDs (especially having six or more within

Table 8.1
Simple Risk Barometer for War

Factors Promoting War	Risk Level
Four Steps	4
Three Steps	3
Two Steps	2
One Step	1
No Steps to War (No Territorial MIDs, No Power Politics)	0

twenty years), and (4) an ongoing arms race. The simple barometer counts any combination of these factors as increasing the risk of war. It does not however measure the precise probability of war occurring within five years or give odds ratios for war.

The precise Risk Barometer for War would do that. Instead of just counting each risk factor equally, the predicted probabilities derived from the logit models could be used to measure the extent of the risk. Confidence intervals could be used to give a range of probabilities, or a range could be based on an analysis of different data samples (e.g., different historical samples or samples of different types of states—major-major, Latin American states). The barometer could also be adapted to different data and different theoretical assumptions. Likewise, different variables could be weighted. For example, instead of just counting the number of recurring MIDs they could be weighted by their level of hostility. Until the precise barometer is fully refined and tested, it can be seen as *an applied research tool* that takes existing research and theory on the steps to war to produce an applied product—an open and transparent risk assessment of the probability of war.

An illustrative precise barometer based on the analyses in chapter 6 is presented in table 8.2. It gives what we think are the maximum probabilities for the specific conditions depicted. Predicted probabilities can be derived for a number of combinations and only the key steps to war are presented. Basically, to use the barometer one takes the crisis at hand and identifies its attributes (in terms of how many and which steps to war have been taken). Then one looks up the risk of this combination of attributes in the table. For example, if in the future two states have a MID over a territorial dispute but this is the first such MID and none of the other factors listed in the table are present, we think the maximum probability of war would be .15. If the MID in question is the sixth between them and both sides have outside allies, then we think the maximum probability of war would be .55. If however, this is the fif-

Table 8.2
Precise Risk Barometer for War

Factors Promoting War	Risk Level (illustrative probabilities)
Territorial Disputes, Outside Alliance,* fifteen disputes, arms race	.90
Territorial Disputes, Outside Alliance,* fifteen disputes	.65
Territorial Disputes, Outside Alliance,* six disputes	.55
Territorial Disputes and Outside Alliance*	.45
Territorial Dispute	.15
Policy Dispute	.09

*No actor or ally has nuclear weapons

teenth dispute and the other conditions hold then the maximum probability would be .65. Finally, with all four risk factors present the maximum probability of war would approach .90. All of these probabilities are based on the predicted probabilities that appear in table 6.3 in chapter 6 with some rounding down to a midpoint, and they are used here strictly for illustrative purposes. The table takes predicted probabilities for a specific set of historical data and uses it to predict what the probability of war will be for future MIDs that share these conditions in a different time period.

How accurate these predictions are depends on a number of factors—for example the amount of measurement error in the data and the applicability of the past to the future. To deal with measurement error and other statistical imprecision one could report a probability range based on confidence intervals. We report what we think is the maximum probability based on the historical sample that produces the highest probabilities of war—the 1816–1945 period. Because we think, albeit based on limited evidence, that the future will be more like this period than the Cold War, we use predicted probabilities from it to predict what the probability of war might look like for future MIDs that share these characteristics. An alternative would be to use predicted probabilities from the entire 1816–2001 span. These would be lower given the distribution of the probabilities of war across the three historical samples. Yet another alternative would be to calculate an average between the maximum and what is found for the entire period. Our only point here is that the final algorithm used would be the result of testing, as it is in most applied products.

The accuracy of these predictions could be improved by introducing certain standard control variables, like the ones we used in chapter 3—whether the disputants are major-major, minor-minor, or major-minor; whether they are neighbors; their level of economic development; whether they have a certain regime type. Other questions that need to be addressed in constructing a precise barometer are: Is the dispute multiparty? Are the disputants originators or joiners? Addressing such questions involves setting up an applied research program using the barometer not only as a policy instrument but also as a research tool that moves us as a field away from just making retrodictions to making actual predictions and forecasts as a way of testing explanations. Such a research program is necessary if the policy instrument is to be useful and not prematurely deployed. Only after the precise barometer has passed such testing should it be employed in a policy context and then carefully with data specifically collected around a clear research design aimed to address the specific policy question at hand. Until then, the simple barometer can be used. Despite these caveats the construction of a barometer illustrates the policy utility of the steps-to-war findings.

Our findings already enable us to construct a simple Risk Barometer for War and put us within reach of constructing a precise barometer. Both of these are based on an understanding of what makes war probable once a MID arises. The strategy for peace embodied in these barometers is to look for exits off the realist road to war. Based on the steps-to-war findings our advice is: If territorial disputes arise, avoid making outside alliances. Once territorial disputes emerge, try to avoid further uses of realpolitik tactics that make the disputes recur and escalate. The theoretical component of the explanation tells us to try to control hard-line reactions and to be aware of how hard-line constituencies can make territorial disputes recur. Even if both of these processes are in place, the findings tell us it is still useful to try to avoid arms races, since these often push the probability of war to the highest levels.

An example of specific policy recommendations that can be made from such general advice may be illustrated by the case of NATO enlargement after the Cold War. Since outside allies increase threat perception, the advice would be to not enlarge an alliance, especially in the sphere of influence of the former rival (see Gibler, 1999a). Nor should one after admitting Estonia to NATO, fly NATO planes over Estonia to demonstrate resolve in defending it against Russia. Likewise, proposing placing part of a missile defense system in Poland and the Czech Republic, as was suggested in 2007 by the Bush administration, is not a step toward peace, but increases threat perception and hostility, as evidenced by the Russian reaction.

While our theoretical approach bases its policy prescriptions on avoiding taking steps to war, and the thrust of our findings supports this stance, we also have found that sometimes the world is more complex. Sometimes unusual combinations produce a statistical interaction that theoretically we would expect to increase the probability of war, but in fact actually reduces it. For the classic international politics period, the interaction of arms racing with allied to each other but with one side having an outside alliance is a negative interaction that reduces greatly the likelihood of war, instead of enhancing it (as we would expect) or as the additive models show. Such anomalies will need to be fully understood if a precise barometer is going to avoid alarmist predictions (see Singer, 1982), not to mention overlook useful complicated strategies that might reduce the likelihood of war. Identification of these negative statistical interactions is a first step to making the barometer more accurate. Identifying the underlying causal factors that reduce the probability of war is the next step.[13]

Still, when all is said and done, a barometer based on the nature of MIDs is a tool that is going to be used for disputants that are already a good ways down the road to war. A more forward-looking strategy would be to try to create a barometer based on what makes states at risk for a MID in the first place and especially what makes them at risk for the kinds of MIDs that are known to be more war prone. With this we move from the steps to war back to the steps to conflict. We are only beginning to get sophisticated two-stage analyses that do more than just test for selection effects, and we have only a few studies that treat MID onset as their main dependent variable (see, among others, Hensel 2006). In this area we would want to know not only what makes for MID onset, but also the factors that reduce the likelihood of states having recurring MIDs once they have had one. Because this sort of research is more infrequent, we are very far away from creating this sort of risk barometer for war. We hope, however, that this discussion points out in a very specific manner how the steps-to-war research program can move from a "causes of war" approach to a more "peace research" approach—that is, to an approach that consciously seeks to reduce the risk of war. One of our major recommendations, therefore, is that peace researchers take seriously the idea of constructing a precise Risk Barometer for War and invest the time and resources necessary to make it come to fruition.

Ultimately, however, we believe that such an approach, while very important in the short term because it could help states avoid and prevent specific wars, is really a Band-Aid (but remember sometimes you really need a Band-Aid to prevent infection). A barometer deals with specific disputes and tries to change specific relationships; it does not deal with the problem of war itself. To do the latter, there must be changes at the structural level, including

---

[13] Here there is a wealth of opportunity for conducting comparative case studies on these negative interactions to get at the exact nature of these processes.

the structure of the system and the structure of the relationship between two parties or within a given neighborhood. Because our findings in this study are at the dyadic level and deal with interstate interactions rather than the system that gives rise to those interactions, they cannot really tell us much about such structural factors. However, the steps-to-war explanation is broader than the hypotheses tested here. We have tested only an aspect of the explanation. Much of the structural component of the explanation has not been tested, but it has important policy implications for establishing peace on a more permanent basis.

Examining Structures of War and Comparing them to Structures of Peace

While we have not tested many of the structural propositions in the steps-to-war explanation or specific propositions on the conditions of peace, there have been some tests conducted outside this study as well as other evidence relevant to structures of peace. The steps-to-war explanation has two components most relevant to an analysis of peace—one deals with the international system as a whole, and the other with establishing long-term peaceful relations among neighbors. We will briefly examine the implications of each in turn.

The first component of peace deals with the overall nature of politics within the system. From a systemic perspective the most important implication for peace from this study is that there are basically two different worlds in international relations. One is a world of power politics, often associated with territorial disputes, where the use of force is employed to gain one's way and leads to repeated militarized confrontations, rivalry, and security dilemmas that foster alliance making and arms races. This is a syndrome of behavior that poisons relations and for most of international history has increased the probability of war, typically in a progressive fashion as each of these additional practices has come into play. This world is structured for war.

The major exception has been the Cold War. In this period, a specific alliance system, buttressed by nuclear weapons that raised the provocation threshold for war, managed to keep war from breaking out between states that were in the opposing blocs. The presence of territorial disputes and rivalry, however, still increased the probability of war as did the interaction of these two factors with an alliance pattern where only one side had an outside alliance. Thus, even in the Cold War certain aspects of power politics made for war, although nuclear weapons and most likely alliance management reduced the number of wars that might have occurred if neither had been present.

Alongside this world of power politics and war, there is another world where power politics is generally absent. These states tend to not have territorial disputes, and if they do, they eschew making outside alliances, engaging in repeated confrontations that lead to a sense of rivalry, or building up their military in a fashion that leads to arms races. This is a world where peace is more likely. This world can dominate the relations of some states, even if they have had militarized disputes. Attaining peace involves understanding this other world, why it works without war, and how it came to be that way. We believe, and it is only a belief, that this other world provides alternate mechanisms for making binding decisions in the presence of anarchy and that these mechanisms are employed because the issues under contention are not so salient and sensitive that states are unwilling to absorb some losses that may occur from resorting to these mechanisms. This world is structured for peace.

Evidence in support of this notion of two worlds is provided by Wallace (1972) on which the steps-to-war explanation builds (see Vasquez, 1993: ch. 8). Wallace conducts a series of path analyses in which he uncovers a path to war and a path to peace (looking solely at major states). His path to war consists of status-inconsistent nations engaging in alliance making, which in turn leads to arms racing, which has a high likelihood of escalation to war. The path to peace, in contrast, consists of states that are status consistent, which is positively related to IGOs, which in turn is negatively related to arms racing—the absence of which reduces the likelihood of war. These two paths provide an interesting empirical and theoretical contrast that is worth much further investigation, especially the path to peace. Getting from the steps to war to the steps to peace involves moving from one structure to the other. While we do not know what steps would take us to the structure of peace, we do know that structure exists in certain spaces. We know this from the West European peace that has now persisted for over sixty years and is expanding into Eastern Europe. We also know it from the research on the democratic peace. At the center of both these examples of peace seems to be some set of mechanisms—norms, IGOs—for nonviolently resolving disputes. Creating and implementing such forms of "governance without government" is an important strategy for reducing the incidence of war, according to steps-to-war theory (see Vasquez, 1993: ch. 8).

Such global structures are often built after major wars (Doran, 1971, 1991; Randle, 1987). They consolidate the outcome of the previous war and set up a structure of peace for the major states (see Gilpin, 1981; Modelski and Thompson, 1989). All previous structures of peace in modern history have eventually decayed and ended in war. Although there is less evidence on this question, here too, territory may be a key. World War II grew, in part, out of the territorial ambitions of Hitler's lebensraum and Japan's attempt to create the Greater East Asia Co-prosperity Sphere. After 1945, both Germany and Japan avoided war by becoming trading states (Rosecrance, 1986). Economics provides an important foundation for peace, when trade keeps territorial issues off the agenda. As long as major states can buy what they need and trade benefits all, there is no need to conquer territory to be economically satisfied. When trading systems no longer benefit major states, or collapse, as in the Great Depression, states try to become self-sufficient through territorial conquest. Current trends toward globalization may make for peace not because they eliminate borders, but because in a world of trading states it is easier to accept existing borders. Once this is done, one of the major sources of war is removed from the political agenda. This in turn makes the job of IGOs easier because the issues they must deal with are not as likely to be seen as "life and death" issues.

Some evidence that supports this line of thinking comes from an examination of historical periods of peace. Wallensteen (1984) has identified temporal periods of peace in the post-Napoleonic period where major states do not fight. Henehan and Vasquez (2006) build on this work to show that during these periods of peace there are fewer territorial MIDs on the agenda and sometimes just one or none, as in the early Concert of Europe (1816–48) and the early League of Nations (1919–30), respectively.

Thus, the first component of peace is to build for the international system, as a whole, an overall structure that moves states, especially the major states, out of a world of power politics. In many ways since the end of the Cold War, the current period has seen that transition come about. The probability of war among any of the major states is at the lowest it has ever been since 1871. The likelihood of a war breaking out between the United States, Russia, China, the United Kingdom, France, Germany, or Japan is extremely low. This is what major state peace looks like. Yet there are still wars. These wars, however, are less systemic in nature and more reflective of fundamental problems within specific neighborhoods that then prompt major state involvement.

The second component of peace deals with the role territory plays between neighbors. We maintain that a key to explaining war and understanding peace is understanding the role territorial disagreements play in the history of relations between neighbors. The territorial explanation of war maintains that most borders are established through aggressive displays and often some form of collective violence. Territorial disputes may very well give rise to power-politics behavior and the characteristic struggles for power that are the hallmark of realist analysis. We argue, however, that not all history, and clearly not all relations between neighbors and other pairs of states are like that. Unlike realism, the territorial explanation of war maintains that once borders are accepted (even if that acceptance comes about violently), neighbors can have long periods of peace, even if other salient issues arise. These are territorial zones of peace. Studying them and how they come about can tell us how to replace a structure of war with a structure of peace at the dyadic and neighborhood levels. The main factor seems to be the resolution of territorial disputes and their removal from the agenda.

The steps-to-war explanation maintains, and some limited research demonstrates, that the acceptance of borders is central to establishing peaceful relations. Neighbors do not have to be locked into a long-term struggle for power punctuated periodically by war. Acceptance of borders can, as Simmons (2006) shows, offer mutual benefits, which may with time even make borders more porous (Diez et al., 2006). The implication of this for the establishment of a structure of peace is that peace could be built dyadically between individual neighbors. The acceptance of borders by neighbors provides groundwork for peaceful neighborhoods. Peace is built in parts, neighborhood by neighborhood.[14] These large neighborhood zones of peace—like in Europe and in the Western Hemisphere—can then serve as a foundation for an architecture of peace: by first establishing regional systems of cooperation and then linking these to various global forms of governance and regimes already established by the major states in certain issue areas—for example, in trade (WTO) and economics (G-8), law of sea, environment (Kyoto agreement), and even in inchoate form in security (OSCE [Organization for Security and Cooperation in Europe] and for certain regions a nuclear nonproliferation regime).

Spelling out some of the above implications for peace shows that as a field we still have a long way to go. This does not mean, however, that we have not made some progress. Long ago, Lewis Richardson stated that by a careful examination of statistical evidence, one could begin to identify the factors responsible for war. The analyses in this book have been based on that assumption, and we believe that our results have shown his assumption to be valid. We hope that the research reported in this study will provide a step toward solving the puzzle of interstate war.

---

[14] The major problem since the end of the Cold War has been to build peace in certain neighborhoods, especially the Middle East.

References

Achen, Christopher H. 1986. *The statistical analysis of quasi-experiments*. Berkeley: University of California Press.

Alker, Hayward R., Jr. 1996. "The presumption of anarchy in world politics." In *Rediscoveries and reformulations*, ed. Hayward R. Alker, Jr., 355–93. Cambridge: Cambridge University Press.

Ardrey, Robert. 1966. *The territorial imperative*. New York: Atheneum.

Ashley, Richard K. 1984. The poverty of neorealism. *International Organization* 38 (Spring): 225–86.

Azar, Edward E. 1972. Conflict escalation and conflict reduction in an international crisis: Suez, 1956. *Journal of Conflict Resolution* 16 (June): 183–201.

———. 1980. The conflict and peace data bank (COPDAB) project. *Journal of Conflict Resolution* 24 (March): 143–52.

Barnett, Michael N. 1998. *Dialogues in Arab politics: Negotiations in regional order*. New York: Columbia University Press.

———. 2003. "Alliances, balances of threats, and neorealism: The accidental coup." In *Realism and the balancing of power: A new debate*, eds. John A. Vasquez and Colin Elman, 222–49. Upper Saddle River, NJ: Prentice Hall.

Barnett, Michael N., and Jack S. Levy. 1991. Domestic sources of alliances and alignments: The case of Egypt, 1962–1973. *International Organization* 45 (Summer): 369–95.

Bates, Robert H., Avner Greif, Margaret Levi, Jean-Laurent Rosenthal, and Barry Weingast. 1998. *Analytic narratives*. Princeton: Princeton University Press.

Bateson, Patrick. 1989. "Is aggression instinctive?" In *Aggression and war*, eds. J. Groebel and R. Hinde, 35–47. New York: Cambridge University Press.

Beck, Nathaniel, Jonathan N. Katz, and Richard Tucker. 1998. Taking time seriously: Time-series-cross-section analysis with a binary dependent variable. *American Journal of Political Science* 42 (October): 1260–88.

Bennett, D. Scott. 1996. Security, bargaining, and the end of interstate rivalry. *International Studies Quarterly* 40 (June): 157–83.

Bennett, D. Scott, and Alan Stam. 2000. EUGene: A conceptual manual. *International Interactions* 26 (August): 179–204.

———. 2004. *The behavioral origins of war*. Ann Arbor: University of Michigan Press.

Ben-Yehuda, Hemda. 1997. Territoriality, crisis and war: An examination of theory and twentieth century evidence. Paper Presented to the Annual Meeting of the International Studies Association, Toronto, March 19.

———. 2004. Territoriality and war in international crises: Theory and findings, 1918–2001. *International Studies Review* 5 (December): 85–105.

Berger, Peter L., and Thomas Luckmann. 1966. *The social construction of reality.* New York: Doubleday.

Boulding, Kenneth. 1962. *Conflict and defense.* New York: Harper.

Braithwaite, Alex, and Glenn Palmer. 2003. The escalation and geography of militarized interstate disputes, 1993–2001. Paper Presented to the Annual Meeting of the Peace Science Society, Ann Arbor, November.

Brambor, Thomas, William Roberts Clark, and Matt Golder. 2006. Understanding interaction models: Improving empirical analyses. *Political Analysis* 14 (Winter): 63–82.

Brams, Steven J., and Alan D. Taylor. 1996. *Fair division: From cake-cutting to dispute resolution.* New York: Cambridge University Press.

Braumoeller, Bear. 2004. Hypothesis testing and multiplicative interaction terms. *International Organization* 58 (October): 807–20.

Braumoeller, Bear, and Anne Sartori. 2004. "The promise and perils of statistics in international relations." In *Models, numbers, and cases: Methods for studying international relations*, eds. Detlef Sprinz and Yael Wolinsky-Nahmias, 12–51. Ann Arbor: University of Michigan Press.

Brecher, Michael, and Jonathan Wilkenfeld. 1991. "International crises and global instability: The myth of the 'long peace.'" In *The long postwar peace*, ed. Charles Kegley, Jr., 85–104. New York: Harper Collins.

———. 1997. *A study of crisis.* Ann Arbor: University of Michigan Press.

Bremer, Stuart A. 1980. "National capabilities and war proneness." In *The correlates of war*, vol. II. ed. J. David Singer, 57–82. New York: Free Press.

———. 1992. Dangerous dyads: Conditions affecting the likelihood of interstate war, 1816–1965. *Journal of Conflict Resolution* 36 (June): 309–41.

———. 1995. "Advancing the scientific study of war." In *The process of war: Advancing the scientific study of war.* eds. Stuart A. Bremer and Thomas R. Cusack, 1–34. Amsterdam: Gordon and Breach.

———. 2000. "Who fights whom, when, where, and why? In *What do we know about war?* ed. John Vasquez, 23–36. Lanham, MD: Rowman and Littlefield.

Bremer, Stuart A., and Thomas R. Cusack, eds. 1995. *The process of war: Advancing the scientific study of war.* Amsterdam: Gordon and Breach.

Brodie, Bernard. 1945. The atomic bomb and American security. Memorandum No.18. Yale Institute of International Studies.

Bueno de Mesquita, Bruce. 1981. *The war trap.* New Haven: Yale University Press.

———. 1996. "The benefits of a social-scientific approach to studying international affairs." In *Explaining international relations since 1945*, ed. Ngaire Woods, 49–80. New York: Oxford University Press.

Bueno de Mesquita, Bruce, and David Lalman. 1992. *War and reason.* New Haven: Yale University Press.

Bueno de Mesquita, Bruce, and J. David Singer. 1973. Alliances, capabilities, and war: A review and synthesis. *Political Science Annual,* Vol. IV. Indianapolis: Bobbs-Merrill, 237–80.

Bull, Hedley. 1977. *The anarchical society.* New York: Columbia University Press.

Burton, John. 1990. *Conflict: Resolution and provention.* Houndmills, UK: Macmillan.

Chernoff, Fred. 2004. The study of democratic peace and progress in international relations. *International Studies Review* 6 (March): 49–78.

Choucri, Nazli, and Robert C. North. 1975. *Nations in conflict.* San Francisco: W. H. Freeman.

Cioffi-Revilla, Claudio. 1998. *Politics and uncertainty: Theory, models and applications.* Cambridge: Cambridge University Press.

Cioffi-Revilla, Claudio, and Harvey Starr. 2003. "Opportunity, willingness, and political uncertainty: Theoretical foundations of politics." In *Necessary conditions: Theory, methodology, and applications,* eds. Gary Goertz and Harvey Starr, 225–48. Lanham, MD: Rowman and Littlefield.

Clark, David H., and William Reed. 2005. The strategic sources of foreign policy substitution. *American Journal of Political Science* 49 (July): 609–24.

Clark, David H., and Patrick M. Regan. 2003. Opportunities to fight: A statistical technique for modeling unobservable phenomena. *Journal of Conflict Resolution* 47 (February): 94–115.

Colaresi, Michael P., Karen Rasler, and William R. Thompson. 2008. *Strategic rivalries in world politics: Position, space, and conflict escalation.* Cambridge: Cambridge University Press.

Colaresi, Michael P., and William R. Thompson. 2002. Hot spots or hot hands? Serial crisis behavior, escalating risks, and rivalry. *Journal of Politics* 64 (November): 1175–98.

————. 2005. Alliances, arms buildups and recurrent conflict: Testing a steps-to-war model. *Journal of Politics* 67 (May): 345–64.

Copeland, Dale C. 2000. *The origins of major war.* Ithaca: Cornell University Press.

Coplin, William D., Stephen L. Mills, and Michael K. O'Leary. 1973. "The PRINCE concepts and the study of foreign policy." In *Sage international yearbook of foreign policy studies* Vol. I: 73–103.

Crawford, Neta C. 2000. The passion of world politics: Propositions on emotion and emotional relationships. *International Security* 24 (Spring): 116–56.

Crescenzi, Mark, and Andrew Enterline. 2001. Time remembered: A dynamic model of interstate interaction. *International Studies Quarterly* 45 (September): 409–31.

Damasio, Antonio R. 1995. *Descartes' error: Emotion, reason, and the human brain.* New York: Avon Books.

Deutsch, Karl, Sidney Burrell, Rober Kann, et al. 1957. *Political community and the North Atlantic area.* Princeton: Princeton University Press.

Diehl, Paul. F. 1983. Arms races and escalation: A closer look. *Journal of Peace Research* 20 (3): 205–12.

―――. 1985a. Arms races to war: Testing some empirical linkages. *Sociological Quarterly* 26 (Fall): 331–49.

―――. 1985b. Armaments without war: An analysis of some underlying effects. *Journal of Peace Research* 22 (September): 249–59.

―――. 1985c. Contiguity and military escalation in major power rivalries, 1816–1980. *Journal of Politics* 47 (November): 1203–11.

―――. 1991. Geography and war: A review and assessment of the empirical literature. *International Interactions* 17 (May): 11–27.

―――. 1992. What are they fighting for? The importance of issues in international conflict research. *Journal of Peace Research* 29 (August): 333–44.

Diehl, Paul F., and Mark Crescenzi. 1998. Reconfiguring the arms race-war debate. *Journal of Peace Research* 35 (January): 111–18.

Diehl, Paul F., and Gary Goertz. 2000. *War and peace in international rivalry.* Ann Arbor: University of Michigan Press.

Diez, Thomas, Stephan Stetter, and Mathias Albert. 2006. The European Union and border conflicts: The transformative power of integration. *International Organization* 60 (Summer): 563–93.

Dixon, William J. 1993. Democracy and the management of international conflict. *Journal of Conflict Resolution* 37 (March): 42–68.

Dixon, William J., and Paul D. Senese. 2002. Democracy, disputes, and negotiated settlements. *Journal of Conflict Resolution* 46 (August): 547–71.

Doran, Charles F. (1971) *The politics of assimilation: Hegemony and its aftermath.* Baltimore: Johns Hopkins University Press.

―――. (1991) *Systems in crisis: New imperatives of high politics at century's end.* Cambridge: Cambridge University Press.

Doran, Charles F., and Wes Parsons. 1980. War and the cycle of relative power. *American Political Science Review* 74 (December): 947–65.

Easton, David. 1965. *A framework for political analysis.* Englewood Cliffs, NJ: Prentice-Hall.

Falger, Vincent S. E. 1997. Human nature in modern international relations. *Research in Biopolitics* 5: 155–75

Fearon, James D. 1994. Domestic political audiences and the escalation of international disputes. *American Political Science Review* 88 (September): 577–99.

Foucault, Michel. 1980. *Power/knowledge.* ed. C. Gordon, New York: Pantheon.

Friedrich, Robert. 1982. In defense of multiplicative terms in multiple regression equations. *American Journal of Political Science* 26 (November): 797–833.

Gaddis, John Lewis. 1986. The long peace: Elements of stability in the postwar international system. *International Security* 10 (Spring): 99–142.

Garnham, David. 1976. Dyadic international war, 1816–1965: The role of power parity and geographical proximity. *Western Political Quarterly* 29 (June): 231–42.

Gartner, Scott S., and Randolph M. Siverson 1996. War expansion and war outcome. *Journal of Conflict Resolution* 40 (March): 4–15.

Gartzke, Erik. 2005. Rich neighbors: War, peace, and economic development. Columbia University. Typescript.

Geller, Daniel S. 1992. Capability concentration, power transition, and war. *International Interactions* 17 (February): 269–84.

Geller, Daniel S. 2000. "Explaining war: Empirical patterns and theoretical mechanisms." In *Handbook of War Studies II*, ed. Manus I. Midlarsky, 407–49. Ann Arbor: University of Michigan Press.

Geller, Daniel S., and J. David Singer. 1998. *Nations at war: A scientific study of international conflict.* Cambridge: Cambridge University Press.

George, Alexander L. 1983. *Managing U.S.-Soviet rivalry: Problems of crisis prevention.* Boulder, CO: Westview.

George, Alexander L., Philip J. Farley, and Alexander Dallins, eds. 1988. *U.S.-Soviet security cooperation.* New York: Oxford University Press.

Gerner, Deborah J., Philip A. Schrodt, Ronald Francisco, and Judith Weddle. 1994. Machine coding of event data using regional and international sources. *International Studies Quarterly* 38 (March): 91–119.

Ghosn, Faten, and Glenn Palmer. 2003. Associated document for the militarized interstate dispute data, version 3.0. Correlates of War 2 Project, Pennsylvania State University (http://cow2.la.psu.edu).

Ghosn, Faten, Glenn Palmer, and Stuart A. Bremer. 2004. The MID3 data set, 1993–2001: Procedures, coding rules, and description. *Conflict Management and Peace Science* 21 (Summer): 133–54.

Gibler, Douglas M. 1996. Alliances that never balance: The territorial settlement treaty. *Conflict Management and Peace Science* 15 (Spring): 75–97.

———. 1997a. Control the issues, control the conflict: The effects of alliances that settle territorial issues on interstate rivalries. *International Interactions* 22 (April): 341–68.

———. 1997b. *Reconceptualizing the alliance variable: An empirical typology of alliances.* PhD diss., Vanderbilt University.

———. 1999a. East or further east? *Journal of Peace Research* 36 (November): 627–37.

———. 1999b. An extension of the correlates of war formal alliance data set: 1648–1815. *International Interactions,* 25 (April): 1–28.

———. 2000. "Alliances: Why some cause war and why others cause peace." In *What do we know about war?* ed. John Vasquez, 145–64. Lanham, MD: Rowman and Littlefield.

———. 2007. Bordering on peace: Democracy, territorial issues and conflict. *International Studies Quarterly* 51 (September): 509–32.

Gibler, Douglas M., Toby Rider, and Marc Hutchison. 2005. Taking arms against a sea of troubles: Interdependent racing and the likelihood of conflict in rival states. *Journal of Peace Research* 42 (March): 131–47.

Gibler, Douglas M., and Meredith Sarkees. 2004. Measuring alliances: The correlates of war formal interstate alliance dataset, 1816–2000. *Journal of Peace Research* 41 (March): 211–22.

Gibler, Douglas M., and John A. Vasquez. 1998. Uncovering the dangerous alliances, 1495–1980. *International Studies Quarterly* 42 (December): 785–807.

Gilpin, Robert. 1981. *War and change in world politics.* Cambridge: Cambridge University Press.

Gleditsch, Kristian S. 2004. A revised list of wars within and between states. *International Interactions* 30 (July–September): 231–62.

Gleditsch, Kristian S., and Michael D. Ward. 1999. Interstate system membership: A revised list of independent states since 1816. *International Interactions* 25 (December): 393–413.

Gleditsch, Nils Petter, and Olav Njolstad, eds. 1990. *Arms races: Technological and political dynamics.* London: Sage.

Gleditsch, Nils Petter, and J. David Singer. 1975. "Distance and international war, 1816–1965." In *Proceedings of the international peace research association fifth general conference,* ed. M. Rafiq Khan, 481–506. Oslo: International Peace Research Association.

Gochman, Charles S. 1980. "Status, capabilities, and major power conflict." In *The correlates of war,* Vol. II, ed. J. David Singer, 83–123. New York: Free Press.

———. 1990. The geography of conflict: Militarized interstate disputes since 1816. Presented at the annual meeting of the International Studies Association, Washington, D.C.

Gochman, Charles S, and Russell J. Leng. 1983. Realpolitik and the road to war. *International Studies Quarterly* 27 (March): 97–120.

Gochman, Charles S., and Zeev Maoz. 1984. Militarized interstate disputes, 1816–1976: Procedures, patterns, and insights. *Journal of Conflict Resolution* 28 (December): 585–615.

Goertz, Gary, and Paul F. Diehl. 1992a. The empirical importance of enduring rivalries. *International Interactions* 18 (December): 151–63.

———. 1992b. *Territorial changes and international conflict.* London: Routledge.

Goertz, Gary, and Harvey Starr, eds. 2003. *Necessary conditions: Theory, methodology, and applications.* Lanham, MD: Rowman and Littlefield.

Goodall, Jane. 1990. *Through a window.* Boston: Houghton Mifflin.

Greene, William H. 2000. *Econometric analysis.* 4th ed. Upper Saddle River, NJ: Prentice Hall.

Guetzkow, Harold. 1950. Long-range research in international relations. *American Perspective* 4 (Fall): 421–40.

———. 1968. "Some correspondences between simulations and realities in international relations." In *New approaches to international relations,* ed. Morton Kaplan, 202–69. New York: St. Martin's.

Guetzkow, Harold, and Joseph J. Valdez. eds. 1981. *Simulated international processes.* Beverly Hills: Sage.

Hagan, Joe D. 2003. Oppositions, ruling strategies, and the domestic road to war: Political explanations of foreign policy and the great powers since 1815. Paper presented to the CEEISA/ISA International Convention, Budapest, June 26–28.

Heckman, James J. 1979. Sample selection bias as a specification error. *Econometrica* 47 (January): 153–61.

Heldt, Birger. 1999. Domestic politics, absolute deprivation, and the use of armed force in interstate territorial disputes, 1950–1990. *Journal of Conflict Resolution* 43 (August): 451–78.

Hempel, Carl G. 1966. *Philosophy of natural science.* Englewood Cliffs, NJ: Prentice-Hall.

Henehan, Marie T. 2001. The effect of territory on dispute escalation among initiators, 1816–1992: A research note. Paper presented to the ISA–Hong Kong Meeting of International Studies, July 26–28.

Henehan, Marie T., and John A. Vasquez. 2006. "The changing probability of interstate war, 1816–1992." In *The waning of major war: Theories and debates,* ed. Raimo Vayrynen, 289–99. London: Routledge.

Hensel, Paul R. 1994. One thing leads to another: Recurrent militarized disputes in Latin America, 1816–1986. *Journal of Peace Research* 31 (August): 281–98.

———. 1996. Charting a course to conflict: Territorial issues and interstate conflict, 1816–1992. *Conflict Management and Peace Science* 15 (Spring): 43–73.

———. 1998. "Interstate rivalry and the study of militarized conflict." In *Conflict in world politics: Advances in the study of crisis, war and peace,* eds. Frank P. Harvey and Ben D. Mor, 162–204. London: Macmillan.

———. 1999. An evolutionary approach to the study of interstate rivalry. *Conflict Management and Peace Science* 17 (Fall): 179–206.

———. 2000. "Territory: Theory and evidence on geography and conflict." In *What Do We Know about War?* ed. John A. Vasquez, 57–84. Lanham, MD: Rowman and Littlefield.

———. 2001. Contentious issues and world politics: The management of territorial claims in the Americas, 1816–1992. *International Studies Quarterly* 45 (March): 81–109.

———. 2006. Territorial claims and armed conflict between neighbors. Paper presented to the Lineae Terrarum International Borders Conference at the University of Texas–El Paso, New Mexico State University, Colegio de la Frontera Norte, and Universidad Autonoma de Ciudad Juarez, March.

Hermann, Charles F. 1969. "International crisis as a situational variable." In *International politics and foreign policy,* 2nd edition, ed. James N. Rosenau, 409–21. New York: Free Press.

Herz, John. 1950. Idealist internationalism and the security dilemma. *World Politics* 2 (January): 157–80.

Hewitt, J. Joseph. 2003. Dyadic processes and international crises. *Journal of Conflict Resolution* 47 (October): 669–92.

Hewitt, J. Joseph, and Gary Goertz. 2005. Fighting chances: Choosing populations in conflict research." University of Missouri, Columbia. Typescript.

Hobbes, Thomas. 1651. *Leviathan* (1950 ed.). New York: E. P. Dutton.

Holsti, Kalevi J. 1991. *Peace and war: Armed conflicts and international order.* Cambridge: Cambridge University Press.

Holsti, Ole, Robert North, and Richard Brody. 1968. "Perception and action in the 1914 crisis." In *Quantitative international politics,* ed. J. David Singer, 123–58. New York: Free Press.

Horn, Michael Dean. 1987. *Arms races and the international system.* PhD diss. University of Rochester.

Huntingford, Felicity Ann. 1989. "Animals fight, but do not make war." In *Aggression and war*, edited by J. Groebel and R. Hinde, 25–34. Cambridge: Cambridge University Press.

Hutchison, Marc, and Douglas M. Gibler. 2007. Political tolerance and territorial threat: A cross-national study. *Journal of Politics* 69 (February): 128–42.

Huth, Paul K. 1996a. Enduring rivalries and territorial disputes, 1950–1990. *Conflict Management and Peace Science* 15 (Spring): 7–41.

———. 1996b. *Standing your ground: Territorial disputes and international conflict.* Ann Arbor: University of Michigan Press.

Huth, Paul K., and Todd L. Allee. 2002. *The democratic peace and territorial conflict in the twentieth century.* New York: Cambridge University Press.

Isard, Walter. 1989. *Arms races, arms control, and conflict analysis: Contributions from peace science and peace economics.* New York: Cambridge University Press.

Jaccard, James. 2001. *Interaction effects in logistic regression.* Thousand Oaks, CA: Sage.

Jaggers, Keith., and Ted R. Gurr. 1995. Tracking democracy's third wave with the polity III data. *Journal of Peace Research* 32 (November): 469–82.

James, Patrick. 2002. *International relations and scientific progress: Structural realism reconsidered.* Columbus: Ohio State University Press.

James, Patrick, Johann Park, and Whan Choi. 2006. Democracy and conflict management: Territorial claims in the western hemisphere revisited. *International Studies Quarterly* 50 (December): 803–18.

James, Patrick, Eric Solberg, and Murray Wolfson. 1999. An identified systemic analysis of the democracy-peace nexus. *Defence and Peace Economics* 10 (February): 1–37.

———. 2000. Democracy and peace: Reply to Oneal and Russett. *Defence and Peace Economics* 11 (March): 215–29.

Jervis, Robert. 1976. *Perception and misperception in international politics.* Princeton: Princeton University Press.

———. 1978. Cooperation under the security dilemma. *World Politics* 30 (January): 167–214.

———. 1989. *The meaning of the nuclear revolution.* Ithaca: Cornell University Press.

Johnston, Alastair Iain. 1996. "Cultural realism and strategy in Maoist China." In *The culture of national security: Norms and identity in world politics*, ed. Peter J. Katzenstein, 216–68. New York: Columbia University Press.

Jones, Daniel. 1993. *Preliminary user's manual: Militarized interstate disputes*, version IX. Ann Arbor: Correlates of War Project.

Jones, Daniel, Stuart A. Bremer, and J. David Singer. 1996. Militarized interstate disputes, 1816–1992: Rationale, coding rules, and empirical patterns. *Conflict Management and Peace Science* 15 (Fall): 163–213.

Kahneman, Daniel, and Jonathan Renshon. 2007. Why hawks win. *Foreign Policy* 158 (January/February): 34–38.

Kegley, Charles W., Jr., and Gregory A. Raymond.1990. *When trust breaks down: Alliance norms and world politics.* Columbia, SC: University of South Carolina Press.

Kelly, Raymond C. 2000. *Warless societies and the origin of war.* Ann Arbor: University of Michigan Press.

Kennedy, Paul M. 1980. *The rise of the Anglo-American antagonism, 1860–1914*. London: Allen and Unwin.

Khong, Yuen Foong. 1992. *Analogies at war: Korea, Munich, Dien Bien Phu, and the Vietnam decisions of 1965*. Princeton: Princeton University Press.

King, Gary, Robert D. Keohane, and Sidney Verba. 1994. *Designing social inquiry: Scientific inference in qualitative research*. Princeton: Princeton University Press.

King, Gary, Michael Tomz, and Jason Wittenberg. 2000. Making the most of statistical analyses: Improving interpretation and presentation. *American Journal of Political Science* 44 (April): 347–61.

Kinsella, David, and Bruce Russett. 2002. Conflict emergence and escalation in interactive international dyads. *Journal of Politics* 64 (November): 1045–68.

Kocs. Stephen. 1995. Territorial disputes and interstate war, 1945–1987. *Journal of Politics* 57 (February): 159–75.

Kriesberg, Louis, Terrell A. Northrup, et al. 1989. *Intractable conflicts and their transformation*. Syracuse, NY: Syracuse University Press.

Kuhn, Thomas S. 1970. *The structure of scientific revolutions* 2nd ed. enlarged. Chicago: University of Chicago Press.

Lakatos, Imre. 1970. "Falsification and the methodology of scientific research programmes." In *Criticism and the Growth of Knowledge*, eds. Imre Lakatos and Alan Musgrave, 91–196. Cambridge: Cambridge University Press.

Lebow, Richard Ned. 1981. *Between peace and war*. Baltimore: Johns Hopkins University Press.

Leeds, Brett Ashley. 2003a. Alliance reliability in times of war: Explaining state decisions to violate treaties. *International Organization* 57 (Autumn): 801–27.

———. 2003b. Do alliances deter aggression? The influence of military alliances on the initiation of militarized interstate disputes. *American Journal of Political Science*, 47 (July): 427–39.

Leeds, Brett Ashley, Andrew G. Long, and Sara McLaughlin Mitchell. 2000. Reevaluating alliance reliability: Specific threats, specific promises. *Journal of Conflict Resolution* 44 (October): 686–99.

Legro, Jeffrey W. 2005. *Rethinking the world: Great power strategies and international order*. Ithaca, New York: Cornell University Press.

Lemke, Douglas 2002. *Regions of war and peace*. Cambridge: Cambridge University Press.

———. 2003. African lessons for international relations research. *World Politics* 56 (October): 114–38.

Lemke, Douglas, and William Reed. 2001a. The relevance of politically relevant dyads. *Journal of Conflict Resolution* 45 (February): 126–44.

———. 2001b. War and rivalry among great powers. *American Journal of Political Science* 45 (April): 457–69.

Leng, Russell J. 1983. When will they ever learn? Coercive bargaining in recurrent crises. *Journal of Conflict Resolution* 27 (September): 379–419.

———. 1993. *Interstate crisis behavior, 1816–1980: Realism vs. reciprocity*. Cambridge: Cambridge University Press.

Leskiw, Christopher S. 2001. The weight of issues: Revisionist claims and international conflict. Paper presented to the Peace Science Society (International), Atlanta, Georgia, October 26–28.

———. 2002. *Sown for peace? International organizations and interstate conflict*, PhD diss., Vanderbilt University.

Levy, Jack S. 1981. Alliance formation and war behavior: An analysis of the great powers, 1495–1975. *Journal of Conflict Resolution* 25 (December): 581–613.

———. 1989a. "The causes of war: A review of theories and evidence." In *Behavior, society, and nuclear war* Vol. I, eds. Philip Tetlock et al., 209–333. New York: Oxford University Press.

———. 1989b. "Quantitative studies of deterrence success and failure." In *Perspectives on deterrence*, eds. Paul Stern, Robert Axelrod, Robert Jervis, and Roy Radner, 98–133. Oxford: Oxford University Press.

———. 1992. Prospect theory and international relations: Theoretical applications and analytical problems. *Political Psychology* 13 (June): 283–310.

———. 1994. Learning and foreign policy: Sweeping a conceptual minefield. *International Organization* 48 (Spring): 279–312.

———. 1996. Loss aversion, framing, and bargaining: The implications of prospect theory for international conflict. *International Political Science Review* 17 (April): 179–95.

———. 1997. Prospect theory, rational choice, and international relations. *International Studies Quarterly* 41 (March): 87–112.

Levy, Jack S., and Michael N. Barnett. 1992. Alliance formation, domestic political economy, and third world security. *Jerusalem Journal of International Relations* 14 (December): 19–40.

Liao, Tim Futing. 1994. *Interpreting probability models: Logit, probit, and other generalized linear models.* Thousand Oaks, CA: Sage.

Liska, George. 1962. *Nations in alliance.* Baltimore: Johns Hopkins University Press.

Luard, Evan. 1986. *War in international society.* New Haven: Yale University Press.

Mansbach, Richard W., and John A. Vasquez. 1981. *In search of theory: A new paradigm for global politics.* New York: Columbia University Press.

Maoz, Zeev. 1982. *Paths to conflict: International dispute initiation, 1816–1976.* Boulder, CO: Westview.

———. 1989. Joining the club of nations: Political development and international conflict. *International Studies Quarterly* 33 (June): 199–231.

———. 1996. *Domestic sources of global change.* Ann Arbor: University of Michigan Press.

———. 2004. Pacifism, and fightaholism in international politics: A structural history of national and dyadic conflict history, 1816–1992. *International Studies Review* 6 (December): 107–33.

———. 2005. Dyadic MID dataset (version 2.0): http://psfaculty.ucdavis.edu/zmaoz/dyadmid.html.

Maoz, Zeev, and Bruce Russett. 1993. Normative and structural causes of democratic peace, 1946–1986. *American Political Science Review* 87 (3): 624–38.

Marcus, George E., W. Russell Neuman, and Michael Mackuen 2000. *Affective intelligence and political judgment*. Chicago: University of Chicago Press.

Masters, Roger D. 1989. *The nature of politics*. New Haven: Yale University Press.

Mead, Margaret. 1940. Warfare is only an invention—not a biological necessity. *Asia* 40/8: 402–405.

Mearsheimer, John J. 2001. *The tragedy of great power politics*. New York: W. W. Norton.

Midlarsky, Manus I. 1975. *On War: Political violence in the international system*. New York: Free Press.

———. 1986. *The disintegration of political systems*. Columbia: University of South Carolina Press.

———. 1988. The onset of world war. Boston: Allen and Unwin.

———. ed. 1989. *Handbook of war studies*. Boston: Unwin Hyman.

Mitchell, Sara McLaughlin, and Brandon D. Prins. 1999. Beyond territorial contiguity: Issues at stake in democratic militarized interstate disputes. *International Studies Quarterly* 43 (March): 169–83.

Modelski, George, and William R. Thompson. 1989. "Long cycles and global war." In *Handbook of war studies*, 23–54. Boston: Unwin Hyman.

Morgenthau, Hans J. 1948. 1960. 1978. *Politics among nations: The struggle for power and peace*. 1st, 3rd, and 5th ed. revised. New York: Alfred A. Knopf.

———. 1952. Another great debate: The national interest of the United States. *American Political Science Review* 46 (December): 961–88.

Morrow, James D. 1989. Capabilities, uncertainty, and resolve: A limited information model of crisis bargaining. *American Journal of Political Science* 33 (November): 941–72.

———. 1993. Arms versus allies: Trade-offs in the search for security. *International Organization* 47 (Spring): 207–33.

Most, Benjamin A., and Randolph M. Siverson. 1987. "Substituting arms and alliances, 1870–1914: An exploration in comparative foreign policy." In *New directions in the study of foreign policy*, eds. Charles F. Hermann, Charles W. Kegley, Jr., and James N. Rosenau, 131–57. Boston: Allen and Unwin.

Most, Benjamin A., and Harvey Star. 1980. "Diffusion, reinforcement, geopolitics, and the spread of war. *American Political Science Review* 74 (December): 932–46.

———. 1984. International relations theory, foreign policy substitutability and "nice" laws. *World Politics* 36 (April): 383–406.

———. 1989. *Inquiry, logic and international politics*. Columbia: University of South Carolina Press.

Mousseau, Michael. 2000. Market prosperity, democratic consolidation, and democratic peace. *Journal of Conflict Resolution* 44 (August): 472–507.

Mousseau, Michael, and Yuhang Shi 1999. A test for reverse causality in the democratic peace relationship. *Journal of Peace Research* 36 (November): 639–63.

Mueller, John. 1989. *Retreat from doomsday: The obsolescence of major war*. New York: Basic Books, 1989.

Nagel, Ernest. 1961. *The structure of science*. New York: Harcourt, Brace, and World.

Nevin, John. 1996. War initiation and selection by consequences. *Journal of Peace Research* 33 (February): 99–108.

Newman, David. 2006. "The resilience of territorial conflict in an era of globalization." In *Territoriality and conflict in an era of globalization*, eds. Miles Kahler and Barbara F. Walter, 85–110. Cambridge: Cambridge University Press.

Oneal, John R., and Bruce Russett. (2000) Why "an identified systemic model of the democracy-peace nexus" does not persuade. *Peace and Defense Economics* 11 (March): 197–214.

Organski, A.F.K., and Jacek Kugler. 1980. *The war ledger.* Chicago: University of Chicago Press.

Ostrom, Charles W., Jr., and Francis W. Hoole. 1978. Alliances and wars revisited: A research note. *International Studies Quarterly* 22 (June): 215–36.

Palmer, Glenn, and T. Clifton Morgan. 2006. *A theory of foreign policy.* Princeton: Princeton University Press.

Palmer, Glenn, Scott C. Wohlander, and T. Clifton Morgan. 2002. Give or take: Foreign aid and foreign policy substitutability. *Journal of Peace Research* 39 (January): 5–26.

Petersen, Karen, John Vasquez, and Yijia Wang. 2004. Multiparty disputes and the probability of war, 1816–1992. *Conflict Management and Peace Science* 21 (Summer): 1–16.

Popper, Karl. 1959. *The logic of scientific discovery.* London: Hutchinson.

———. 1963. *Conjectures and refutations.* New York: Routledge.

Pruitt, Dean G., and Jeffrey Z. Rubin. 1986. *Social conflict: Escalation, stalemate, and settlement.* New York: Random House.

Randle, Robert F. 1987. *Issues in the history of international relations.* New York: Praeger.

Rasler, Karen, and William R. Thompson. 2000. Explaining rivalry escalation to war: Space, position, and contiguity in the major power system. *International Studies Quarterly* 44 (September): 503–30.

———. 2006. Contested territory, strategic rivalries, and conflict escalation. *International Studies Quarterly* 50 (March): 145–67.

Ray, James Lee. 1990. "Friends as foes: International conflict and wars between formal allies." In *Prisoners of war? Nation-states in the modern era*, eds. Charles S. Gochman and Alan Ned Sabrosky, 73–91. Lexington, MA: Lexington Books.

———. 1995. *Democracy and international conflict.* Columbia: University of South Carolina Press.

———. 1998. *Global Politics.* 7th ed. Boston: Houghton Mifflin Company.

———. 2003a. Explaining interstate conflict and war: What should be controlled for? *Conflict Management and Peace Science* 20 (Fall): 1–31.

———. 2003b. "A Lakatosian view of the democratic peace research program. In *Progress in international relations theory: Appraising the field*, ed. Colin Elman and Miriam Fendius Elman, 205–43. Cambridge, MA: MIT Press.

Raymond, Gregory A. 1994. Democracies, disputes, and third-party intermediaries. *Journal of Conflict Resolution* 38 (March): 24–42.

———. 2000. "International norms: Normative Orders and Peace." In *What do we know about war?* ed. John Vasquez, 281–97. Lanham, MD: Rowman and Littlefield.

Reed, William. 2000. A unified statistical model of conflict onset and escalation. *American Journal of Political Science* 44 (January): 84–93.

Richardson, Lewis F. 1960a. *Arms and insecurity.* Pacific Grove, CA: Boxwood Press.

———. 1960b. *Statistics of deadly quarrels.* Pittsburgh: Boxwood Press.

Rosecrance, Richard N. 1986. *The rise of the trading state: Commerce and conquest in the modern world.* New York: Basic Books.

Rosen, Stephen P. 2005. *War and human nature.* Princeton: Princeton University Press.

Rosenau, James N. 1966. "Pre-theories and theories of foreign policy." In *Approaches to comparative and international politics,* ed. R. Barry Farrell, 27–93. Evanston: Northwestern University Press.

Roy, A. Bikash. 1997. Intervention across bisecting borders. *Journal of Peace Research* 34 (August): 303–14.

Ruggie, John Gerard. 1993. Territoriality and beyond: Problematizing modernity in international relations. *International Organization* 47 (Winter): 139–74.

Rummel, Rudolph J. 1979. *Understanding conflict and war: Vol. 4: War, power, peace.* Beverly Hills: Sage Publications.

Russett, Bruce, and John R. Oneal. 2001. *Triangulating peace: Democracy, interdependence and international organizations.* New York: W. W. Norton.

Sack, Robert David 1986. *Human territoriality: Its theory and history.* Cambridge: Cambridge University Press.

Sample, Susan G. 1996. Arms races and the escalation of disputes to war. PhD diss., Vanderbilt University, May.

———. 1997. Arms races and dispute escalation: Resolving the debate. *Journal of Peace Research* 34 (February): 7–22.

———. 1998a. Furthering the investigation into the effects of arms buildups. *Journal of Peace Research* 35 (January): 122–26.

———. 1998b. Military buildups, war, and realpolitik: A multivariate model. *Journal of Conflict Resolution* 42 (April): 156–75.

———. 2000. "Military buildups: Arming and war." In *What do we know about war?* ed. John Vasquez, 165–95. Lanham, MD: Rowman and Littlefield.

———. 2002. The outcomes of military buildups: Minor states vs. major powers. *Journal of Peace Research* 39 (November): 669–92.

Sarkees, Meredith Reid 2000. The correlates of war data on war: An update to 1997. *Conflict Management and Peace Science,* 18 (Spring): 123–44.

Sarkees, Meredith, Frank Wayman, and J. David Singer. 2003. Inter-state, intra-state, and extra-state wars: A comprehensive look at their distribution over time, 1816–1997. *International Studies Quarterly* 77 (March): 49–70.

Schrodt, Philip A., and Deborah J. Gerner. 1994. Validity assessment of a machine-coded event data set for the Middle East, 1982–92. *American Journal of Political Science* 38 (August): 825–54.

Schroeder, Paul W. 1976. "Alliances, 1815–1945: Weapons of power and tools of management." In *Historical Dimensions of National Security Problems*, ed. K. Knorr, 227–62. Lawrence: University Press of Kansas.

———. 1994. *The transformation of European politics, 1763–1848*. Oxford: Clarendon Press.

Schultz, Kenneth A. 1999. Do democratic institutions constrain or inform?: Contrasting two institutional perspectives on democracy and war. *International Organization* 53 (Spring): 233–66.

———. 2001. *Democracy and coercive diplomacy*. Cambridge: Cambridge University Press.

Senese, Paul D. 1996. Geographic proximity and issue salience: Their effects on the escalation of militarized interstate conflict. *Conflict Management and Peace Science* 15 (Fall): 133–61.

———. 1997. Between dispute and war: The effect of joint democracy on interstate conflict escalation. *Journal of Politics* 59 (February): 1–27.

———. 1999. Democracy and maturity: Deciphering conditional effects on levels of dispute intensity. *International Studies Quarterly* 43 (September): 483–502.

———. 2001. Dyad-years and data management. *The conflict processes newsletter*, June. American Political Science Association. http://www.apsanet.org/~conflict/.

———. 2002. Two forms of contingency: Linking the roles of territorial revision attempts and geographic proximity. Presented at the annual meeting of the American Political Science Association, Boston.

———. 2005. Territory, contiguity, and international conflict: Assessing a new joint explanation. *American Journal of Political Science* 49 (October): 769–79.

Senese, Paul D., and Stephen L. Quackenbush. 2003. Sowing the seeds of conflict: The effect of dispute settlements on durations of peace. *Journal of Politics* 65 (August): 696–717.

Senese, Paul D., and John A. Vasquez. 2000. From territorial issues to territorial disputes and war: An examination of potential selection effects. Presented at the annual meeting of the International Studies Association, Los Angeles.

———. 2003. A unified explanation of territorial conflict: Testing the impact of sampling bias, 1919–1992. *International Studies Quarterly* 47 (June): 275–98.

———. 2004. "Alliances, territorial disputes and the probability of war: Testing for interactions." In *The scourge of war: New extensions on an old problem*, ed. Paul. F. Diehl, 189–221. Ann Arbor: University of Michigan Press.

———. 2005. Assessing the steps to war. *British Journal of Political Science* 35 (October): 607–33.

———. 2006. Rivalry, territorial disputes, and the probability of war: Testing for interactions, 1816–1945. Paper presented at the annual meeting of the International Studies Association, San Diego, March 25.

Shaw R. Paul, and Yuwa Wong. 1989. *Genetic seeds of warfare: Evolution, nationalism, and patriotism*. Boston: Unwin Hyman.

Signorino, Curtis S. 1999. "Strategic interaction and the statistical analysis of international conflict." *American Political Science Review* 93 (June): 279–98.

———. 2002. Strategy and selection in international relations. *International Interactions* 28 (1): 93–115.

Simmons, Beth A. 1998. Compliance with international agreements. *Annual Review of Political Science* 1: 75–93.

———. 1999. "See you in "court"? The appeal to quasi-judicial legal processes in the settlement of territorial disputes." In *A road map to war: Territorial dimensions of international conflict*, ed. Paul. F. Diehl, 205–37. Nashville: Vanderbilt University Press.

———. 2006. "Trade and territorial conflict in Latin America: International borders as institutions." In *Territoriality and conflict in an era of globalization*, eds. Miles Kahler and Barbara Walter, 251–87. Cambridge, Cambridge University Press.

Simmons, Beth A., and Daniel J. Hopkins. 2005. The constraining power of international treaties. *American Political Science Review* 99 (November): 623–31.

Singer, J. David. 1958. Threat-perception and the armament-tension dilemma. *Journal of Conflict Resolution*, 2 (March): 90–123.

———. 1961. "The level of analysis problem in international relations." In *The International System*, eds. Klaus Knorr and Sidney Verba, 72–92. Princeton: Princeton University Press.

———. ed. 1979. *The correlates of war*, vol I. New York: Free Press.

———. ed. 1980. *The correlates of war*, vol II. New York: Free Press.

———. 1982. Confrontational behavior and escalation to war 1816–1980: A research plan. *Journal of Peace Research* 19 (1): 37–48.

———. 1987. Reconstructing the correlates of war dataset on material capabilities of states, 1816–1985. *International Interactions* 14 (May): 115–32.

———. 1991. "Peace in the global system: Displacement, interregnum, or transformation?" In *The long postwar peace*, ed. Charles Kegley, Jr., 56–84. New York: Harper Collins.

Singer, J. David, Stuart Bremer, and John Stuckey. 1972. "Capability distribution, uncertainty, and major power war, 1820–1965." In *Peace, war, and numbers*, ed. Bruce M. Russett, 19–48. Beverly Hills: Sage Publications.

Singer, J. David, and Melvin Small. 1966. National alliance commitments and war involvement, 1815–1945. *Peace Research Society (International) Papers* 5: 109–140.

———. 1968. "Alliance aggregation and the onset of war, 1815–1945." In *Quantitative international politics*, ed. J. David Singer, 247–86. New York: Free Press.

———. 1972. *The wages of war, 1816–1965*. New York: John Wiley.

———. 1974. Foreign policy indicators: Predictors of war in history and in the state of the world message. *Policy Sciences* 5 (September): 271–96.

Siverson, Randolph M. 1996. Thinking about puzzles in the study of international war. *Conflict Management and Peace Science* 15 (Fall): 113–32.

Siverson, Randolph, and Harvey Starr. 1991. *The diffusion of War: A study of opportunity and willingness*. Ann Arbor: University of Michigan Press.

Small, Melvin, and J. David Singer. 1969. Formal alliances, 1816–1965: An extension of the basic data. *Journal of Peace Research* 6 (3): 257–82.

————. 1982. *Resort to arms: International and civil wars, 1816–1980.* Beverly Hills: Sage Publications.

Smith, Alastair. 1995. Alliance formation and war. *International Studies Quarterly* 39 (December): 405–25.

————. 1996. To intervene or not to intervene: A biased decision. *Journal of Conflict Resolution* 40 (March): 16–40.

————. 1999. Testing theories of strategic choice: The example of crisis escalation. *American Journal of Political Science* 43: 1254–88.

Snyder, Glenn H. 1997. *Alliance politics.* Ithaca, NY: Cornell University Press.

Snyder, Glenn H., and Paul Diesing. 1977. *Conflict among nations: Bargaining, decision making, and system structure in international crises.* Princeton: Princeton University Press.

Somit, Albert. 1990. Humans, chimps, and bonobos: The biological bases of aggression, war, and peacemaking. *Journal of Conflict Resolution* 34 (September): 253–82.

Sprout, Harold, and Margaret Sprout. 1965. *The ecological perspective on human affairs.* Princeton: Princeton University Press.

Starr, Harvey. 1978. "Opportunity" and "willingness" as ordering concepts in the study of war. *International Interactions* 4 (4): 363–87.

————. 2005. Territory, proximity, and spatiality: The geography of international conflict. *International Studies Review* 7 (October): 387–406.

StataCorp. 2001. Stata statistical software: Release 7.0. College Station, TX: Stata Corporation.

————. 2005. Stata statistical software: Release 9.0. College Station, TX: StataCorp LP.

Stevenson, David. 1996. *Armaments and the coming of war: Europe 1904–1914.* Oxford: Clarendon Press.

Stinnett, Douglas, Jaroslav Tir, Philip Schafer, Paul Diehl, and Charles Gochman. 2002. The correlates of war project direct contiguity data, version 3. *Conflict Management and Peace Science* 19 (Fall): 59–66.

Suganami, Hidemi. 2002. Explaining war: Some critical observations. *International Relations* 16 (December): 307–26.

Thompson, William R. 1988. *On global war: Historical-structural approaches to world politics.* Columbia: University of South Carolina Press.

————. 1995. Principal rivalries. *Journal of Conflict Resolution* 39 (June):195–223.

————. 1996. Democracy and peace: Putting the cart before the horse? *International Organization* 50 (Winter): 141–74.

————. 2001. Identifying rivalries in world politics. *International Studies Quarterly* 45 (December): 557–86.

————. 2003. A streetcar named Sarajevo: Catalysts, multiple causation chains, and rivalry structures. *International Studies Quarterly* 47 (September): 453–74.

Tir, Jaroslav. 2006. *Redrawing the map to promote peace.* Lanham, MD: Lexington.

Tir, Jaroslav, and Paul F. Diehl. 2002. Geographic dimensions of enduring rivalries. *Political Geography* 21 (February): 263–86.

Toft, Monica. 2003. *The geography of ethnic violence: Identity, interests, and the indivisibility of territory.* Princeton: Princeton University Press.

Tomz, Michael, Jason Wittenberg, and Gary King. 1999 (2001, 2003). CLARIFY: Software for interpreting and presenting statistical results. Cambridge, MA: Harvard University, Dept. of Government. June 1. http://gking.harvard.edu/.

Valeriano, Brandon. 2003. *The steps to rivalry: Power politics and rivalry formation,* PhD diss., Vanderbilt University.

Valeriano, Brandon, and John A. Vasquez. 2005. Mapping the spread of war: Classifying complex wars. Paper presented to the Peace Science Society (International), Iowa City, November 5.

Valzelli, Lugi. 1981. *Psychobiology of aggression and violence.* New York: Raven Press.

Van Evera, Stephen. 1999. *Causes of war: Power and the roots of conflict.* Ithaca: Cornell University Press.

Vasquez, John A. 1983. The tangibility of issues and global conflict. *Journal of Peace Research* 20 (2): 179–92.

———. 1985. Domestic contention on critical foreign-policy issues: The case of the U.S. *International Organization,* 37 (Fall): 643–66.

———. 1987. The steps to war: Toward a scientific explanation of correlates of war findings. *World Politics* 40 (October): 108–45.

———. 1991. "The deterrence myth: Nuclear weapons and the prevention of nuclear war. In *The Long Postwar Peace,* ed. Charles Kegley, Jr., 205–223. New York: Harper Collins.

———. 1993. *The war puzzle.* Cambridge: Cambridge University Press.

———. 1995. Why do neighbors fight? Proximity, interaction, or territoriality. *Journal of Peace Research* 32 (August): 277–93.

———. 1996a. Distinguishing rivals that go to war from those that do not. *International Studies Quarterly* 40 (December): 531–58.

———. 1996b. Territorial issues and the probability of war: A data-based analysis. Paper presented at the Annual Meeting of the Peace Science Society (International), Rice University, Houston, Texas, October 26.

———. 1997. The realist paradigm and degenerative versus progressive research programs: An appraisal of neotraditional research on Waltz's balancing proposition. *American Political Science Review* 91 (December): 899–912.

———. 1998a. *The power of power politics: From classical realism to neotraditionalism.* Cambridge: Cambridge University Press.

———. 1998b. "The steps to war in Europe, 1933–1941." In *Conflict in world politics: Advances in the study of crisis, war, and peace.* eds. Frank P. Harvey and Ben D. Mor, 207–40. London: Macmillan.

———. 2000. "Reexamining the steps to war: New evidence and theoretical insights." In *Handbook of war studies II,* ed. Manus I. Midlarsky, 371–406. Ann Arbor: University of Michigan Press.

———. 2001. Mapping the probability of war and analyzing the possibility of peace: The role of territorial disputes. Presidential Address to the Peace Science Society (International). *Conflict Management and Peace Science* 18 (Fall): 145–74.

———. 2004. The probability of war, 1816–1992. *International Studies Quarterly* 48 (March): 1–28.

Vasquez, John A., and Colin Elman eds. 2003. *Realism and the balancing of power: A new debate.* Upper Saddle River, NJ: Prentice-Hall.

Vasquez, John A., and Douglas M. Gibler. 2001. The steps to war in Asia, 1931–1945. *Security Studies* 10 (Spring): 1–45.

Vasquez, John A., and Marie T. Henehan. eds. 1992. Editors' commentary. *The scientific study of peace and war: A text reader.* New York: Lexington Books.

———. 2001. Territorial disputes and the probability of war, 1816–1992. *Journal of Peace Research* 38 (March): 123–38.

Vasquez, John A., and Christopher S. Leskiw. 2001. The origins and war proneness of interstate rivalries. *Annual Review of Political Science* 4: 295–316.

Vasquez, John A., and Paul D. Senese. 2007. How and why the cold war became a long peace: Some statistical insights. Paper presented to the annual meeting of the Midwest Political Science Association, Chicago, April 14.

Vayrynen, Raimo, ed. 2006. *The waning of major war: Theories and debates.* London: Routledge.

Waal, Frans de. 1989. *Peacemaking among primates.* Cambridge, MA: Harvard University Press.

Walker, Thomas. 2000. *Peace, rivalry, and war: A theoretical and empirical study of international conflict.* PhD diss., Rutgers University.

Wallace, Michael D. 1972. "Status, formal organization, and arms levels as factors leading to the onset of war." In *Peace, war, and numbers,* ed. Bruce M. Russett, 49–69. Beverly Hills: Sage.

———. 1979. Arms races and escalation: Some new evidence. *Journal of Conflict Resolution* 23 (March): 3–16.

———. 1982. Armaments and escalation: Two competing hypotheses. *International Studies Quarterly* 26 (March): 37–56.

———. 1990. "Racing redeux: The arms race-escalation debate revisited." In *Prisoners of war,* eds. Charles Gochman and Alan Sabrosky, 115–22. Lexington, MA: Lexington Books.

Wallensteen, Peter. 1981. Incompatibility, confrontation, and war: Four models and three historical systems, 1816–1976. *Journal of Peace Research* 18: 57–90.

———. 1984. Universalism vs. particularism: On the limits of major power order. *Journal of Peace Research* 21 (September): 243–57.

Walt, Stephen M. 1987. *The origins of alliances.* Ithaca, New York: Cornell University Press.

Walter, Barbara. 2003. Explaining the intractability of territorial conflict. *International Studies Review* 5 (December): 137–53.

Waltz, Kenneth N. 1959. *Man, the state, and war.* New York: Columbia University Press.

———. 1979. *Theory of international politics.* Reading, MA: Addison-Wesley.

———. 1981. *The spread of nuclear weapons: More may be better.* Adelphi Paper 171. London: International Institute for Strategic Studies.

Ward, Michael D. 1982. *Research gaps in alliance dynamics.* Denver Monograph Series in World Affairs 19 Denver: University of Denver.

Wayman, Frank W. 1990. "Alliances and war: A time-series analysis." In *Prisoners of war?* eds. Charles Gochman and Alan Sabrosky, 93–113. Lexington, MA: Lexington Books.

———. 1996. "Power shifts and the onset of war." In *Parity and war*, eds. Jacek Kugler and Douglas Lemke, 145–62. Ann Arbor: University of Michigan Press.

———. 2000. "Rivalries: Recurrent disputes and explaining war." In *What do we know about war?* ed. John Vasquez, 219–34. Lanham, MD: Rowman and Littlefield.

Wayman, Frank W., and Daniel Jones. 1991. Evolution of conflict in enduring rivalries. Paper Presented at the Annual Meeting of the International Studies Association, Vancouver.

Wayman, Frank W., Meredith Reid Sarkees, and J. David Singer. 2005. Inter-state, intra-state, extra-state, and non-state wars, 1816–2004. Paper Presented at the Annual Meeting of the International Studies Association, Honolulu, Hawaii, March 1–5.

Weede, Erich. 1976. Overwhelming preponderance as a pacifying condition among contiguous Asian dyads, 1950–1969. *Journal of Conflict Resolution* 20 (September): 395–411.

Wendt, Alex. 1992. Anarchy is what states make of it: The social construction of power politics. *International Organization* 46 (Spring): 391–425.

———. 1999. *Social theory of international politics.* Cambridge: Cambridge University Press.

Werner, Suzanne. 1999. The precarious nature of peace: Resolving the issues, enforcing the settlement, and renegotiating the terms. *American Journal of Political Science* 43 (July): 912–34.

White, George W. 2000. *Nationalism and territory: Constructing group identity in southeastern Europe.* Lanham, MD: Rowman and Littlefield.

Wilkenfeld, Jonathan, Gerald Hopple, Paul Rossa, and Stephen Andriole. 1980. *Foreign policy behavior: The interstate behavior analysis model.* Beverly Hills: Sage.

Wilson, Edward O. 1975. *Sociobiology: The new synthesis.* Cambridge, MA: Harvard University Press.

Winch, Peter 1965. *The idea of a social science.* New York: Humanities Press.

Wrangham, Richard. 2006. "Why apes and humans kill." In *Conflict*, eds. Martin Jones and A. C. Fabian, 43–62. Cambridge: Cambridge University Press.

Wright, Quincy. 1942. 1965. *The study of war*, 1st ed., 2nd ed. Chicago: University of Chicago Press.

Zacher, Mark. 2001. The territorial integrity norm: International boundaries and the use of force. *International Organization* 55 (Spring): 215–50.

Zinnes, Dina. 1996. *Contemporary research in international relations.* New York: Free Press.

Zinnes, Dina, Joseph L. Zinnes, and Robert D. McClure. 1972. "Hostility in diplomatic communication: A study of the 1914 case." In *International crises: Insights from behavioral research*, ed. Charles Hermann, 139–162. New York: Free Press.

Name Index

This index includes all names of persons mentioned in the text or cited in parenthetical author-date citations or in the footnotes. Corporate names are included in the subject index. Page numbers in italics refer to tables or figures in the text.

Subject Index

Page numbers in italics refer to tables or figures in the text.